Profiles of

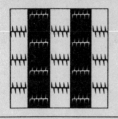

Great

African

Americans

CONTRIBUTING WRITERS
DAVID SMALLWOOD
STAN WEST
ALLISON KEYES

CONSULTANTS
CHARLES R. BRANHAM, PH.D.
JEAN CURRIE CHURCH
JOYCE ANN JOYCE, PH.D

PUBLICATIONS INTERNATIONAL, LTD.

David Smallwood is associate editor of *N'Digo*, a bimonthly Chicago magazine for African Americans. He is the former entertainment editor for *Jet* magazine and was a journalism writing instructor at Columbia College. He is a freelance writer for both print and television and a speechwriter.

Stan West is a writer, former associate editor of the *Chicago Daily Defender*, and producer and talk show host on Chicago's WNUA-FM. He is the author of *Prism: An African-American Reporter's Multi-Cultural View of the New South Africa* and coauthor of *Why L.A. Happened: Implications of the '92 Rebellion*. He was nominated for an Emmy for his 90-minute WTTW-TV show *Combating Racism: Where To Begin?*

Allison Keyes is a line producer for New York 1 News, the Time-Warner 24-hour cable news station. She is a former newswriter and producer for ABC affiliate WLS-TV Chicago reporter and columnist for *N'Digo* magazine, and political editor and anchor for National Public Radio's WBEZ-FM. She is a member of the National Association of Black Journalists and the former vice president of the Chicago Association of Black Journalists.

Charles R. Branham, Ph.D., is senior historian for the DuSable Museum of African American History in Chicago and adjunct professor of Minority Studies at Indiana University Northwest. He was the writer and coproducer of *The Black Experience*, a series of 60 half-hour programs for Chicago's WTTW-TV. He is the author of *The Transformation of Black Political Leadership* and coauthor of *Black Chicago Accommodationist Politics Before the Great Migration*.

Jean Currie Church is the chief librarian for the Moorland-Spingarn Research Center at Howard University, a major repository of materials for the study of Black history and culture. She is a member of the American Library Association, the Black Caucus of the ALA, and the Academy of Certified Archivists.

Joyce Ann Joyce, Ph.D., is professor of English and associate director of the Gwendolyn Brooks Center at Chicago State University. She is the author of *Warriors, Conjurers, and Priests: Defining African-Centered Literary Criticism* and *Native Son: Richard Wright's Art of Tragedy*. She has coauthored several books, including *Langston Hughes: The Man, His Art, and His Influence*.

Editorial Assistant: Rosa L. Anthony

Special thanks to Donna Wells and Joseph Hill, Moorland-Spingarn Research Center, Howard University.

CONTENTS

INTRODUCTION

The African-American historical experience was forged in the crucible of struggle but it is more, much more, than merely the recorded history of that struggle. It is also the story of the transcendence and triumph of the human spirit, of remarkable men and women who challenged myths and misconceptions, hurdled barriers, blazed trails, invented, created, transformed, and reinvigorated our common culture and, in the process, refashioned our common American heritage. These extraordinary weavers of dreams and rewriters of record books are monuments to the pride and persistence that has always permeated the African-American past, and these men and women are but a small sample of the rich reservoir of ambition and energy that marks the diverse and still unfolding story of the African-American past.

Here are their stories: an unlettered slave who read her poetry to our first President; a brilliant man of letters, one of the most catholic thinkers of the 20th century, who forsook the cloistered halls of academe to pursue a lifelong struggle for human rights; a boy, once traded for a horse, who discovered hundreds of uses for the peanut and sweet potato; an apostle of nonviolence who was cut down by an assassin's bullet.

There is an irony here: "Moses" was a woman who led 300 slaves "out of the House of Bondage"; a brash young army officer who challenged racial segregation in the army would later demonstrate remarkable patience and forbearance in the face of catcalls and death threats as he shattered the color line of professional sports; a great composer would die unheralded and unknown, and a half century later his music would provide the score for an Academy-Award-winning movie and revive public appreciation of a forgotten musical genre.

Here Sojourner Truth asks plaintively, "Aren't I a Woman?" Marcus Garvey commands, "Up you Mighty Race! You can accomplish what you will!" Here DuSable explores, Ellington composes, and Michael Jordan soars high above the rim. Here Malcolm X undergoes a spiritual conversion in a dank prison cell, Ralph Bunche brokers peace in the Middle East, and Paul Robeson sacrifices a career for the cause of social justice. They are all here, the famous and the little known, the men and women whose lives have touched our lives, subtly, sometimes imperceptibly reshaping our world.

Of course, no selection of the "Greatest" is without controversy. It was not an easy task to select the names and, unquestionably, the debate will continue over their relative merits and notables who just missed making the list. Any list is at best an approximation, a starting point for discussion and debate.

But these profiles represent a beginning point, a serious attempt to briefly summarize the lives and contributions of African Americans in all of the rich and varied aspects of the American experience. If we stand taller and see farther, it is because we stand on the shoulders of these titans of the African-American past. We are indebted to them, their courage, their sacrifice; we are inspired by their example, and emboldened to create a future worthy of their legacy.

Charles Branham, Senior Historian
DuSable Museum of African American History

HANK AARON

Hank Aaron hit his 649th home run
on June 10, 1972, to pass second-place
Willie Mays in pursuit of Babe Ruth's
career mark of 714 dingers. Despite
being heaped with racial abuse,
derogatory letters, and death threats,
Aaron kept hitting home runs to
finally break Ruth's record on
April 8, 1974.

It was a record that most baseball fans thought would never be broken—Babe Ruth's 714 career home runs. But on April 8, 1974, in front of 53,775 fans in Fulton County Stadium, 40-year-old Henry Louis "Hammerin' Hank" Aaron blasted a fastball from pitcher Al Downing 385 feet to surpass Ruth's formidable achievement.

Aaron went on to set the new record for home runs at 755 before he retired.

Aaron is arguably the most prolific baseball player of all time. In addition to holding the home run record, he has the most runs batted in with 2,297, is second in runs scored with 2,174, and third in hits with 3,771.

During his career, Aaron appeared in 24 All-Star Games. He's the only National League player to hit 40 or more homers in eight seasons and was the first player to collect 500 home runs and 3,000 hits. No slouch defensively, Aaron won Gold Gloves as the top right fielder from 1958 to 1960. As soon as he was eligible, in 1982, Aaron was voted into the Baseball Hall of Fame—quite an accomplishment for a kid who originally didn't know how to bat correctly.

Aaron was born on February 5, 1934, in segregated Mobile, Alabama, where his high school didn't have a baseball team. In honing his skills playing sandlot ball, Aaron originally batted with the wrong hand on top, but he had exceptionally quick wrists.

Nonetheless, he was impressive enough that the Indianapolis Clowns of the Negro leagues scouted him and offered the skinny 17-year-old a $200-a-month contract in 1951. But his Negro league career would not last long. When Jackie Robinson joined the Brooklyn Dodgers in 1947 (he signed with the organization in 1945), breaking baseball's racial barrier, it was the beginning of the end of the Negro leagues. By 1952, the financially strapped Clowns sold Aaron's contract to the Milwaukee (now Atlanta) Braves.

In his first year in the minors, Aaron batted .336 and was named the Rookie of the Year. The next year, after moving up a level, he was named the league's Most Valuable Player (MVP).

In 1954, Aaron was called to the majors after the Braves' second baseman broke his ankle. In his first game, Aaron had three hits, including a mammoth home run. In 1955, he had an All-Star year statistically. In 1956, he led the National League in hitting with a .328 average and was considered one of the foremost players in the game.

Then in 1957, he hit the home run that helped the Braves win the pennant and hit three more home runs to help them capture the World Series. Aaron was also named league MVP that year, but 1957 was the only time he would win that award or a World Series championship.

Aaron retired after a 23-year major-league career, rewriting baseball's batting record books along the way. He holds more major-league batting records than any other player in history. He currently serves as senior vice president of the Atlanta Braves. He also sits on the National Board of the NAACP and the Sterling Committee of Morehouse College.

ROBERT S. ABBOTT

Robert S. Abbott founded the
Chicago Defender in 1905. It would
later become the most successful,
influential, and widely circulated Black
weekly newspaper in the country.
Abbott started the paper with just
25 cents and no staff, but the paper's
success made him one of Chicago's
first Black millionaires.

A legendary figure in the annals of American journalism, Robert Sengstacke Abbott founded the *Chicago Defender* in 1905. In its heyday, it was the most successful and influential Black newspaper in the country.

Abbott was born on November 24, 1870, to former slaves in St. Simon's Island, Georgia. But it was his stepfather, John Sengstacke, who aroused young Robert's passion to secure equal rights for African Americans. Abbott was so impressed with his stepfather that he later took Sengstacke as his middle name.

Abbott earned his law degree in 1898 from Chicago Kent College of Law and for a few years practiced in Gary, Indiana, and Topeka, Kansas. But he returned to Chicago with the dream of publishing what he called "The World's Greatest Weekly, the *Chicago Defender.*"

Even though Abbott reportedly had only a total of 25 cents to undertake this great endeavor, he was not deterred. Financial support and articles written by friends kept him going. Working out of his small apartment, Abbot peddled the *Defender* from door to door and through barber shops, churches, bars, and poolrooms in Chicago's African-American community.

Although the city had a number of Black papers at the time, none matched the strong political and social stance Abbott had the *Defender* take. From the beginning, he intended the paper to be an important voice against racial oppression and injustice. That voice spurred a circulation growth that reached 230,000 only ten years after the paper started.

The *Defender* was distributed throughout the South by Pullman porters on the railway cars. So intense were Abbott's angry articles against lynching and oppression in the South, many historians credit him with being a primary cause of the great migration of Blacks from the South to the North during the 1920s and 1930s.

Abbott wanted the paper to speak for and provide advice to the Black community. As such, the *Defender* voiced the concerns and outrage Blacks felt—these opinions would never have seen print elsewhere.

The bloody Chicago Race Riot of July 1919 started when a group of Whites stoned and drowned a young Black man who swam beyond an imaginary point in Lake Michigan that Blacks were not allowed to cross. There was much loss of life. Two years earlier, the *Defender* had pointed out that pent-up anger of Blacks over jobs, housing, and politics would eventually lead to just such an explosive situation. The *Defender* gave exhaustive coverage to the five days of rioting. Afterward, Abbott was named a member of the Chicago Commission on Race Relations, which in 1922 published the frequently cited report "The Negro in Chicago." This report examined the causes of the 1919 riots and the great migration of Blacks to Chicago.

One of Abbott's important legacies was started in 1929, when he created the Bud Billiken "Back-to-School" Parade to promote education among Black children.

Abbott died of Bright's disease on February 29, 1940. At the time, the *Chicago Defender* was the most widely circulated Black weekly in the country.

MUHAMMAD ALI

Muhammad Ali was arguably the
greatest heavyweight boxer of all time,
and he was certainly the most flashy
and charismatic. In his 21-year pro
boxing career, Ali won 56 fights with
only five defeats before retiring as the
first boxer to win the heavyweight
championship three times.

The colorful phrase "Float like a butterfly, sting like a
bee," created by his cornerman Drew Bundini Brown, per-
fectly sums up the boxing style of Muhammad Ali, the
self-proclaimed and widely acknowledged "greatest fighter
of all time!"

He was the first man to win the heavyweight championship three times. Ali's astonishing speed, punishing

punching power, brilliant footwork, awesome defensive skills, and lethal left jab contributed to his boxing legend. To watch him was to see a dancing Ali, circling, carving up an opponent with a jab too fast for his opponent to react to, while inviting punches that he gracefully slipped.

It was his prowess in the ring, boisterous personality, flashy showmanship, and strongly held religious and moral convictions that first made Ali a figure of deep controversy. These traits later made him a folk hero.

Born Cassius Marcellus Clay on January 17, 1942, in Louisville, Kentucky, Ali began boxing at age 12, training in a community recreation center. Instead of taking the bus to school, he ran to build his endurance and dodged rocks thrown by his brother to improve his ability to slip punches.

Ali won 100 of 105 amateur fights, capturing six Kentucky Golden Gloves and two national Golden Gloves championships before winning the Olympic light heavyweight title in 1960. Turning pro the same year, he beat 19 opponents before taking his first heavyweight title from Charles "Sonny" Liston in 1964.

Ali was a seven-to-one underdog against Liston, but that fight brought him international fame, which was bol-

stered by his self-promotion. Ali spouted poetry and frequently predicted, with accuracy, the round in which he would vanquish his opponents.

After the Liston fight, Ali acknowledged his religious conversion to Islam and proclaimed his name change, which helped make the Black Muslims a major religious force in America. Ali then defended his title nine times until 1967, when he refused, as a conscientious objector, to enter the draft and go to Vietnam. He was stripped of his title for three and a half years, but during this time, Ali became a worldwide symbol of moral consciousness.

After the Supreme Court reversed his draft-dodging conviction in 1971, Ali returned to the ring for a series of legendary fights. He suffered his first professional loss to "Smokin'" Joe Frazier in March 1971, in an attempt to regain his title. Later he would go on to defeat Frazier twice. In the famous "Rumble in the Jungle" fight in Kinshasa, Zaire, in October 1974, Ali recaptured the heavyweight title in a surprising eighth-round knockout of George Foreman.

After losing the title to Leon Spinks and then regaining it from him—both fights came in 1978—Ali retired from boxing in 1979. He came out of retirement for financial

reasons twice, in 1980 to lose to Larry Holmes and in 1981 to lose to Trevor Berbick. Finally, a month before he turned 40, Ali hung up his boxing gloves for good.

Ali continues to make personal appearances and speeches around the country, usually speaking of his deeply held spiritual beliefs.

RICHARD ALLEN

Hearing his call to the ministry at age 17, Richard Allen became America's first Black licensed preacher and ordained deacon. In 1816, after a series of successful court battles, he founded the African Methodist Episcopal Church as an independent religious denomination.

Richard Allen was a slave who had a religious conversion experience at the age of 17, which made him pursue the ministry as his life's work. In so doing, he became the first African American licensed to preach (1782) and the first ordained as a deacon (1799) in this country.

Allen was born on February 14, 1760, in Philadelphia, where his family was owned by Quaker lawyer Benjamin Chew. When Chew's law practice failed, he sold the Allen family to a Dover, Delaware, plantation owner.

Methodist preachers were active in the area. Allen heard the teachings and in 1777 converted. With his master's permission, he joined the Methodist Society, taught himself to read and write, and soon began leading the meetings. In 1781, Allen's master allowed him to purchase his freedom and he returned to Philadelphia.

During the Revolutionary War, Allen used his job as wagon driver to preach at regular stops. In 1786, he joined the mostly White St. George's Methodist Episcopal Church in Philadelphia, where he was allowed to hold separate prayer meetings for Blacks.

But one Sunday morning, Allen and some Black friends were met at the church door and directed to the upstairs gallery. When they entered the main floor anyway, they were not allowed to kneel in prayer. Allen and his group walked out. Such difficulties were becoming a growing problem for Black Methodist worshipers everywhere.

The next year, Allen and Absalom Jones organized the independent Free African Society, a beneficial and mutual aid organization. By 1794, the Society had saved enough money to build the Bethel Church, which Allen established as an independent African Methodist Episcopal (AME) congregation.

However, a legal struggle ensued between the church and the Methodist Society over control of Bethel Church. But in 1816, the Pennsylvania Supreme Court ruled that Bethel could become an independent denomination.

Along with other AME congregations that had sprung up in Baltimore, Wilmington, and elsewhere, Bethel's congregation established the African Methodist Episcopal Church in April 1816. The newly formed denomination consecrated Allen as its first Bishop.

Afterward, Allen opened day schools for Black students, supported moderate antislavery activities, and encouraged moral reform. He used the basement of Bethel Church to give safe haven to fugitives as they traveled the Underground Railroad. Allen also led the call for the first national Black convention to protest the assault on free Blacks launched by the American Colonization Society.

Allen and his wife, Sara, were entombed long after their deaths in that same church basement in 1901. In 1876, a monument to Allen was erected in Philadelphia's Fairmont Park—it is considered to be the first statue erected for a Black man by other Black Americans.

MARIAN ANDERSON

Marian Anderson was one of
America's most celebrated singers of
the 20th century, with a nearly three-
octave voice that ranged from low D
to high C. She was the first African
American to solo with New York's
Metropolitan Opera.

Known as the "baby contralto" when she sang in Philadelphia churches as a child, Marian Anderson became one of the 20th century's most celebrated singers and broke several racial barriers in American music along the way.

Anderson made history twice. In February 1939, the by-then-famous contralto was refused permission by the Daughters of the American Revolution to sing in Constitution Hall in Washington, D.C., because of her color.

A resulting nationwide protest caused First Lady Eleanor Roosevelt to resign from the group and arrange for Anderson to give a free Easter morning concert that April on the steps of the Lincoln Memorial. A crowd estimated at 75,000 people, including government officials, Supreme Court judges, and everyday citizens, attended. She eventually sang at Constitution Hall, but not until 1953.

She made history again, however, in 1955, when she was invited to become the first African-American soloist to perform at the Metropolitan Opera House in New York. Langston Hughes called Anderson's performance as Ulrica in the Verdi opera *Un Ballo in Maschera*, "a precedent-shattering moment in American musical history." *The New York Times* deemed the breakthrough so important to the issue of race relations in America that it ran a front-page story on Anderson's debut the next morning.

Anderson was born in Philadelphia on February 27, 1902, with what she called a compulsion to make music. She ran errands for neighbors to earn enough money to buy a violin from a pawn shop, and she later persuaded her father to buy a piano, on which she and her sisters taught themselves to play.

But what she did most was sing. In fact, she often missed her classwork because she was singing at nearby schools and at churches. In 1919, Anderson began studying with the famous music teacher Giuseppe Boghetti. Her church paid for the first year of instruction, but after, Boghetti was so enamored that he tutored her for free for years.

In 1925, Anderson bested 300 other young singers in a competition to win a contract for concert tours. This led to her appearance with the New York Philharmonic Orchestra. From 1933 to 1935, she toured Europe on fellowships and sang for royalty in England, Sweden, Norway, and Denmark. It was during this extended excursion that the famous Arturo Toscanini called one of Anderson's concerts something you hear only once every 100 years.

Three years after her return to America, Anderson was considered one of America's leading contraltos. Her recordings were national hits and her concerts sellouts. By 1941, she was one of America's highest paid concert artists, and in 1978, she received the John F. Kennedy Center for the Performing Arts Award for her "lifetime achievements in the arts." Anderson died in 1993.

LOUIS ARMSTRONG

Louis Armstrong was an
internationally known jazz singer and
trumpet player considered by many to
be an improvisational genius. His
innovations and technical mastery
changed the course of jazz music and
influenced the performances of many
other artists.

Louis Armstrong was the father of the jazz swing movement that was popular in the early 1920s. His talent for improvisation, technical prowess, and feel for the music made him the principal model for jazz musicians of his time and for many artists who remain popular today.

Armstrong was born in 1900, in the impoverished Storyville neighborhood in New Orleans. Raised partly by

his grandmother, and later by his mother, Armstrong grew up listening to blues and ragtime played at popular neighborhood hangouts. He started singing tenor with a barbershop quartet as a teenager, then learned the bugle while sentenced to a reform school for delinquency. Eventually, he moved up to the cornet, then became bandleader at the Home for Colored Waifs. Armstrong had never touched a horn before the music teacher at the reform school handed him an alto horn in practice one day.

When Armstrong was released, he began sitting in with local bands, and later replaced legendary New Orleans cornet player King Oliver as leader of the city's most popular jazz band. From age 18 to 22, he performed in clubs and on riverboats before moving to Chicago in 1922. There he played as second cornet in Oliver's Creole Jazz Band, a group that heavily influenced the Windy City's jazz musicians. In 1924, he moved to New York and joined Fletcher Henderson and His Black Swan Troubadours. By this time, musicians were beginning to recognize and to imitate Armstrong's innovative style.

Armstrong returned to Chicago in 1925 and began a series of recordings known as the Hot Five and Hot Seven, which revolutionized the way jazz music was performed.

During this time, he switched from the cornet to the trumpet because of its brighter tone. One of the songs in that series, "Heebie Jeebies," became his first recording as a scat singer, allegedly because he dropped the music. He also perfected the so-called "swing" style of jazz, where notes are placed a fraction before or behind the beat. He also created the stop-time solo break, where the music stops for the featured player then picks up again. His gravelly singing voice became a trademark that is still imitated today.

Armstrong then went back to New York in 1929 and became a prolific performer on stage and on screen. He was one of the first African Americans to have a sponsored radio show, and he appeared often in feature films. But some critics feel his commercial success robbed his music of the flair it once had, and most experts consider Armstrong a pop singer after the mid-1930s.

Later, the government sponsored numerous international tours for Armstrong, who became a goodwill ambassador for American music. He suffered a heart attack in 1959, and increasing health problems caused him to curtail his performances. He died July 6, 1971, in New York City.

CRISPUS ATTUCKS

Crispus Attucks carried the torch for freedom as the first man to die in the historic Boston Massacre. A runaway slave who became a sailor and taught himself to read and write, Attucks was the ultimate symbol of the American battle for independence.

Crispus Attucks epitomized all that was best in colonial America. Born a slave in Massachusetts, he escaped and became an educated man. He eventually helped begin America's armed resistance against British rule. Attucks was the first to die in the Boston Massacre, and he became a beacon for the American struggle for independence.

Attucks was born a slave about 1723 (he has no known birth date), in Framingham, Massachusetts. He was the son of an African father and a Native American mother.

As a child, he was repeatedly sold from one master to another, until he escaped in 1750. Attucks became a sailor and whaler; following the sea became his destiny.

The muscular mulatto learned to read and write, and he joined the American struggle for freedom from the British. Attucks attended meetings with other patriots to discuss ways to fight the burdensome taxes levied by England. He then wrote a letter of protest to Governor Thomas Hutchinson, who was the top Tory politician of the province.

According to most accounts, on March 5, 1770, Attucks spearheaded a noisy crowd of protesters who confronted a company of British soldiers stationed at the Custom House on Boston's King Street. Witnesses said Attucks and the demonstrators, who were armed with banners and clubs, began throwing snow and ice at the soldiers. Attucks then grabbed one British soldier's bayonet and knocked him down. The frightened soldiers fired into the crowd, leaving Attucks dead on the ground. Four others also died. The Boston *Gazette and Country Journal* for March 12, 1770, reported that Attucks was killed instantly. His death became a symbol of the Revolutionaries' struggle.

According to testimony at the later trial of the British soldiers, prosecutors said Attucks had been "assaulted with force and arms, feloniously, willfully, and of malice aforethought." But defense lawyers for the soldiers accused Attucks of not only having formed the patriots' attack party, but said "it was Attucks to whose mad behavior, in all probability, the dreadful carnage of that night is chiefly ascribed."

After the Revolutionary War, Attucks continued to be a symbol for the fight for freedom. African-American military companies called themselves the Attucks Guards. And from 1858 to 1870, African Americans in Boston held a Crispus Attucks Day every year. By 1888, Blacks convinced city and state officials that Attucks's contributions were important enough to warrant a monument on the Boston Common. The statue bears the name of all five men who died for the cause.

The five heroes are buried in historic Granary Burying Ground, along with other famous Revolutionary War figures, including John Hancock, John Adams, and Governor William Bradford of Plymouth County.

JAMES BALDWIN

James Baldwin is one of the most
popular, widely read African-
American writers of the 20th century.
His major works include the novel *Go
Tell It on the Mountain*, the plays
The Amen Corner and *Blues for
Mister Charlie*, and the essay
collections *Notes of a Native Son*
and *The Fire Next Time*.

James Baldwin is perhaps the most widely read and best
known African-American author of the middle 20th century. He was a prolific writer popular with both Black and
White audiences worldwide.

He sensitively and honestly examined issues of race,
gender, and class. And while he argued against racial in-

justice, Baldwin was more apt to stress the positive, life-affirming values of Black culture than to simply blast a White racist hierarchy.

Through six novels, four plays, and seven collections of essays, among his other works, Baldwin examined America's soul.

His first novel, *Go Tell It on the Mountain,* was released in 1953 to vast critical acclaim. It tells the story of a young Black boy's battles with his minister father over the issue of worship. Baldwin took up the same autobiographical theme in *The Amen Corner,* his play about a female evangelist, which was published in 1965.

Baldwin was born August 2, 1924, in Harlem, the oldest of nine children. Raised by a zealously religious minister stepfather, Baldwin preached from the revivalist pulpit from the ages of 14 to 17. But his real passion was writing. Editor of his high school newspaper, he eventually earned enough writing awards and accompanying cash prizes to move to Paris after graduation, where he lived for eight years, beginning in 1948.

While there, he had his first novel published. He then wrote a collection of well-received essays, which he compiled as *Notes of a Native Son* in 1955. In 1956, he wrote

Giovanni's Room, the first of two novels dealing with bisexuality; the other was *Another Country* in 1962.

Baldwin returned to the States in 1957 to work in the growing Civil Rights Movement. He made the cover of *Time* magazine in 1963 as an eloquent spokesman for Black rights. His *New Yorker* magazine article on the Black Muslims and parts of the civil rights struggle was published as the book *The Fire Next Time* in 1963. The next year, his important play about racial oppression, *Blues for Mister Charlie*, opened on Broadway.

In 1968, Baldwin's popular novel *Tell Me How Long the Train's Been Gone* was released. Then in 1971, *A Rap on Race* was published, detailing a conversation with anthropologist Margaret Mead about world racism. In 1974, Baldwin enjoyed another best-seller with *If Beale Street Could Talk*, the tale of a pregnant, unmarried 19-year-old.

In 1982, after releasing more essay collections interpreting Black and White relations in the United States, Baldwin became a professor of writing and African-American history at the University of Massachusetts at Amherst. In 1987, he received the French Legion of Honor Award. Baldwin died in France later that year from cancer.

BENJAMIN BANNEKER

Benjamin Banneker was considered the
first Black man of science in the
United States. The math whiz built
the country's first clock, published
almanacs based on his astronomical
calculations, and helped lay out the
design of Washington, D.C. He did
it all with little formal education.

Benjamin Banneker was a walking contradiction to the
proposed theory of his day that Blacks were mentally inferior to Whites. Considered the first Black American man
of science, Banneker was a math wizard, astronomer, and
inventor.

Despite having little formal education, the self-taught,
voracious reader is credited with building a wooden time-

piece—the first clock entirely made in America—which kept accurate time until he died. Banneker's study of astronomy and natural phenomena enabled him to write and publish a popular annual almanac from 1791 to 1802.

In his forties, after reading math books lent to him by neighbors, Banneker became proficient enough in math to solve any problems submitted to him. He even found and corrected miscalculations that the books' authors had made. He also wrote a treatise on bees, conducted a mathematical study on the cycle of the 17-year locust, and correctly predicted a solar eclipse in 1789.

Banneker was born outside Baltimore as a freeman on November 9, 1731. His grandmother had been a White dairymaid who came to America as an indentured servant. His grandfather was an African prince who had been her slave until she freed him. They then married.

His grandmother, Molly, began a small farm after fulfilling her service. His father, a freed slave from Guinea who married Molly's daughter, expanded the farm to 100 acres. It was on this farm that Banneker was raised and where he spent most of his life pursuing his scientific studies.

When he was young, his grandmother and mother taught him to read the Bible, primarily so he could read it to them as they relaxed in the evening. Later, he bought what few books he could afford and borrowed many others. He taught himself literature, history, and math in his spare hours.

In his early twenties, Banneker built his clock, which was a testament to his mathematical wizardry. He had never seen a wooden, striking clock before, but he had seen a pocketwatch. Banneker used math ratios to determine the relationship of the gears and wheels and carved them from wood with a pocketknife. The clock operated accurately until his death more than 50 years later. It only stopped running because Banneker's house caught fire and the clock burned.

Eventually, Banneker took over the family farm, raising tobacco, wheat, and corn as cash crops. He also kept a large vegetable garden for his personal use, and he collected beehives for honey, which he sold. He even learned to play flute and violin to entertain himself. After his parents' deaths, Banneker sold portions of the farm for the money that would allow him to continue his scientific studies.

A few years earlier, Banneker had befriended his neighbors, the Ellicotts, a Quaker family of surveyors and industrialists. They had lent him books on astronomy and instruments to work out calculations. After they saw his abilities, they enlisted Banneker's assistance.

When President George Washington assigned the Ellicotts to survey a 10-square-mile area that would become the new national capital of Washington, D.C., in 1790, Banneker helped them. He made calculations and used astronomical instruments for marking base points. Though 60 years old, he worked on the project for several months until they had established the baselines and initial boundaries for the new territory.

When Banneker returned to his farm, he became even more interested in astronomy. During this period and for the next ten years, Banneker made startlingly accurate studies of the stars. He published his results nationally and internationally in his popular almanacs. More than 29 editions of the almanacs were issued.

Thomas Jefferson himself was a fan of Banneker's almanacs—particularly because they displayed the mental aptitude African Americans were capable of. Jefferson sent many almanacs overseas to European scientists and leaders, who learned of, studied, and consequently praised Banneker's work.

In the later part of his life, Banneker lived alone on his farm. He often entertained friends and visitors who were aware of his great repute. Banneker graciously engaged them in deep, philosophical conversations. He also became involved with the abolitionist movement, especially after the invention of the cotton gin entrenched the institution of slavery in the South in 1793.

Banneker died quietly at his home on October 9, 1806, after taking a final walk in his garden. He was 74 years old.

JAMES P. BECKWOURTH

An explorer, trader, and scout, James P. Beckwourth was a mountain man in the legendary tradition of pioneers who conquered the West. He discovered a pass between California and Reno that became part of a major emigrant route.

James P. Beckwourth was a tireless pioneer who helped tame the Wild West. The curmudgeonly but talkative frontiersman led several expeditions, including the one that opened up a barren patch of land in the Sierra Nevada Mountains. Beckwourth epitomizes the myth of an American hero.

Born in Fredericksburg, Virginia, the son of a White Revolutionary War veteran and an African-American mother with Native American blood, Beckwourth was the third of 13 children. As a child, he lived on the banks of the Missouri River. Beckwourth endured only four years of education before running away to New Orleans. But racism kept the young, ambitious man from getting a job, so in 1823, he became a scout for the Rocky Mountain Fur Company.

From there, the hardy man known for his strong legs and his ability to travel quickly became almost a legend, working for the next 13 years as a miner, guide, trapper, army scout, soldier, and hunter. Beckwourth was accepted as an equal by Native American nations, including the Blackfoot and Crow, who respected his outdoor skills. By 1842, he was fighting in the Second Seminole War as well as on the side of other Native Americans in battles among various groups.

Beckwourth was also an entrepreneur, building and operating three trading posts nestled in the headwaters of the Arkansas and South Platte rivers. By 1840, he had established his own trading posts, first in what is now Taos, New Mexico, then later in present-day Los Angeles. But Beckwourth was caught up in the bloody battle for western land, fighting first in the California revolution against Mexico, then in the War with Mexico, where he served as a guide and dispatch carrier.

After these wars ended, Beckwourth made his final trip to California. In 1848, Beckwourth made a historic discovery while working as chief scout for the exploring expedition of General Charles Fremont. The canny frontiersman found a pass winding through the Sierra Nevada Mountains that led to the Sacramento Valley. The route, named Beckwourth Pass, later became a popular way to emigrate to California.

In 1866, the U.S. government needed a liaison with the Crows, and Beckwourth was the logical choice. Beckwourth had even married into several nations, including the Crows. But some accounts say Beckwourth's devotion to his Native American friends led to his murder by those who were once enamored of his courage and strength. Reportedly, the Crows wanted Beckwourth to stay with them and restore them to their preeminence among the Native Americans. When he refused, it is said that they poisoned Beckwourth in 1886, even as they honored him with a grandiose farewell feast usually reserved for great chiefs.

MARY McLEOD BETHUNE

Mary McLeod Bethune spent
60 years fighting to uplift African
Americans and women from the
political, economic, and social
black hole to which they were
relegated by racism and sexism. Founder
of several schools and the National
Council of Negro Women, she
championed humanitarian values
throughout her life.

Mary McLeod Bethune was a beacon of hope to generations of Black youths and a tireless crusader for the African-American cause. She helped shape what would become the Civil Rights Movement, was a friend and advisor to the Roosevelt Administration, and facilitated the

distribution of federal dollars into Black education and vocational training. Bethune founded scores of schools and organizations, most notably Bethune-Cookman College and the National Council of Negro Women. She was also one of the top social activists of the New Deal years.

Bethune was born in 1875, near Mayesville, South Carolina, the fifteenth of 17 children. Bethune attended Scotia Seminary in North Carolina and what became the Moody Bible Institute in Chicago. By 1895, after failing to get a job as a missionary in Africa, she moved first to Georgia then to Florida to teach.

Believing that education was the primary route to equality for Blacks, Bethune founded the Daytona Educational and Industrial Institute for young Black women with just five students and $1.50. By using her charisma and strong belief in the project to raise money, she molded the facility into what is now Bethune-Cookman College.

But the big, dark-skinned woman with the implacable will didn't stop there. In 1924, she became president of the National Association of Colored Women. Bethune had a brilliant vision of Black women taking an active role in public affairs at a national level. By 1935, she had established the National Council of Negro Women (NCNW),

an umbrella organization that grew to include 22 national groups with a strong lobbying presence in Washington.

The next year, Bethune took the helm of the Division of Negro Affairs for the National Youth Administration (NYA), which was an agency geared to helping young people get jobs during the Great Depression and the war effort. Bethune worked to achieve equal benefits for Blacks and Whites, lobbying for money for Black college students, and fighting to get African-American people decision-making positions in NYA and other social organizations. Her efforts finally made it possible for Blacks to get pilot training and defense department jobs.

In 1936, the strong-minded pioneer formed the Federal Council of Negro Affairs, more popularly known as the Black Cabinet, which facilitated two precedent-setting national Black conferences.

Ill health forced Bethune to cut back her activities in the 1940s, and she began writing newspaper columns for both the *Chicago Defender* and the *Pittsburgh Courier*. She died of a heart attack at home in 1955. In 1974, a statue was built in her honor in Washington, D.C., the first in the capital to portray either a woman or an African American.

GWENDOLYN BROOKS

Gwendolyn Brooks was the first
African American to win a Pulitzer
Prize of any kind, which she did in
1950 for her book of poetry titled
Annie Allen. Brooks's esteemed
lifetime body of work and superb
language skills led to her appointment
as poet laureate for the state of Illinois.

Gwendolyn Brooks is a Pulitzer Prize-winning poet who uses her unique vision of the African-American community to focus on the rigourous conditions of urban existence, empowerment, and the flavor of street life. A muse to the Black experience and the former poet laureate of Illinois, she has been awarded more than 60 honorary degrees.

Gwendolyn Brooks started writing when she was only seven years old. Strongly influenced by writers ranging from e. e. cummings to Langston Hughes, her poetry has provided a voice for, and given a portrait of, the African-American struggle.

Her writings include award-winning poetry for both adults and children, an autobiographical novel, and short stories. A humanitarian, Brooks remains a symbol of achievement in the arts.

Brooks's poetry is praised for its technical brilliance and craftsmanship, and includes the influences of colloquial speech, spirituals and blues, in addition to traditional rhyme and sonnet forms. Writing often in free verse, Brooks has such skill with language that her work is appreciated by the most highbrow of literary critics, yet is still accessible and enjoyable for the most ordinary of readers.

Brooks was born June 7, 1917, in Topeka, Kansas, the daughter of a teacher and a janitor who had once studied medicine. During her happy childhood on the streets of a south side Chicago neighborhood known as Bronzeville, Brooks learned early to appreciate education, literature, and music.

She attended predominantly White high schools and discovered that it was difficult for a quiet Black girl to fit in. A shy and somewhat lonely child, Brooks displayed a penchant for concocting rhymes as early as age seven.

By age 11, Brooks was already keeping her poems in a notebook. She studied the poetry of T. S. Eliot, Shakespeare, Ezra Pound, Paul Laurence Dunbar, and Countee Cullen. She developed a love for alliteration and the music of language. At a very early age, she decided that her life's work would be as a poet. By the age of 13, she had already been published in local newspapers and a national magazine. While in high school, Brooks sent poems to legendary Black poets James Weldon Johnson and Langston Hughes. Hughes's enthusiasm over the writings of a 16-year-old sustained Brooks in her desire to succeed as a writer. In 1941, a modern poetry class at the South Side Community Art Center in Chicago helped hone Brooks's talent in serious poetic technique. A 1943 award from the Midwestern Writer's Conference validated her efforts.

By 1945, Brooks published her first book of poetry, *A Street in Bronzeville*, which depicted the lives of poor and working-class Blacks. The same year, she was chosen as one of America's Top Ten Women by *Mademoiselle* magazine. A review in *Poetry* at the time said her writing showed "a capacity to marry the special quality of her race with the best attainments of our contemporary poetry tradition."

Brooks received Guggenheim fellowships in 1946 and 1947, plus grants from the American Academy of Arts and Letters and the National Institute of Arts and Letters. Brooks became the first African American in the country to win a Pulitzer Prize, for her 1950 book *Annie Allen*. Some Black critics accused her of writing it for White approval. Several other books followed, including the 1953 novel *Maud Martha*, a semiautobiography of a Black woman growing up in Chicago. The book describes Black-White relations between the period of the Depression and World War II.

Brooks changed the direction of her writing when the Black empowerment movement began in the 1960s. Her 1960 collection of poems, *The Bean Eaters*, marked the transition and revealed her growing consciousness about the oppression of African Americans. Her 1968 book, *In the Mecca*, examines life in Black tenements and includes odes to Malcolm X and Medgar Evers. *In the Mecca* was nominated for a National Book Award.

With *Riot*, in 1969, Brooks began publishing exclusively with Black presses. Her previous works had been published primarily by Harper's. In the early 1970s, *Aloneness, A Brookside Treasury, Jump Bad, Beckonings,* and her autobiography, *Report From Part One,* were all published by Broadside Press, the Detroit-based company owned by Detroit Poet Laureate Dudley Randall. In 1987, Brooks herself published *Blacks,* an anthology of her published works from the beginning of her career.

Brooks was chosen poetry consultant to the Library of Congress for 1985 and 1986, and she received a Lifetime Achievement Award from the National Endowment for the Arts in 1989. In 1990, she became the first scholar to hold the new Gwendolyn Brooks Distinguished Chair in the English department at Chicago State University.

Brooks continues to write and give readings of her works. She also funds promising young writers out of her own pocket and through an annual poetry contest she hosts. She lives on Chicago's South Side.

JAMES BROWN

One of the most popular and
influential performers in the history of
American music, James Brown is also
an astute businessman who has owned
fast-food franchises, record and
publishing companies, radio stations, a
booking agency, and a private jet. The
two-time Grammy winner has also
been inducted into the Rock and Roll
Hall of Fame.

Just as a dam harnesses the raging currents of water to make electricity, James Brown captured the power of raw energy, pure feeling, and infectious rhythms to become one of the most influential performers of American popular music.

It's unclear whether this dynamo was born in 1928, 1933, or 1934. But it is known that he grew up in Augusta, Georgia, in abject poverty. He did whatever he could to earn extra money. But when he took to crime in 1949, Brown was sentenced to reform school, where he served three and a half years. After his release, he joined the Gospel Starlighters in 1952. The group soon became known as James Brown and the Famous Flames and they switched to rhythm-and-blues (R&B) music.

One story about how Brown got discovered was that before a Little Richard show in Toccoa, Georgia, the Flames took the stage and gave an impromptu performance. Richard's manager caught it and signed the group. However it happened, Brown's career began in 1956 with a contract with King Records.

The Flames released their first single, "Please, Please, Please," in 1956, which soon became one of Brown's signature hits. The group then began a grueling string of one-night stands across the country, where they honed their sound into razor-sharp precision.

Brown's rugged concert schedule, his insistence on rehearsing his band (which eventually grew to 40 members) until they reached his standard of excellence, and the enormous energy he expended dancing and singing earned him the title "The Hardest-Working Man in Show Business."

Brown hit the top in 1963 with his *James Brown Live at the Apollo.* It rose to number 2 on the *Billboard* charts, and along with his 1965 single "Papa's Got a Brand New Bag," catapulted him into international superstardom in the 1960s and 1970s.

Brown was the leading proponent of "soul" music, and his songs reflected growing racial pride among African Americans. His hit "Say It Loud, I'm Black and I'm Proud" became a new Black national anthem.

His rhythmic arrangements featured tight, repetitious, almost hypnotic grooves, accented by a heavy bass line and flashy horns, with an unusual emphasis on the first beat, not the normal second and fourth. These arrangements created the foundations of funk music, which crested in the 1970s and 1980s.

Brown won a Grammy Award in 1965 for best R&B recording with "Papa's Got a Brand New Bag" and another for best R&B performance for "Living in America" in 1987. In 1986, he was inducted into the Rock and Roll Hall of Fame.

WILLIAM WELLS BROWN

William Wells Brown was an escaped
slave who became an impassioned
abolitionist, lecturer, and Underground
Railroad conductor. In 1853, he
became the first African-American
author to have a novel published. The
book, *Clotel,* was the story of a slave
child considered to have been fathered
by President Thomas Jefferson.

William Wells Brown was a light-skinned man who apparently could have easily passed for White. He chose not to in order to fight the institution of slavery. Brown had been a slave for almost 20 years before escaping to freedom and becoming an impassioned abolitionist and precedent-setting author.

Brown wrote the first Black novel, play, travel litany, and military study of Black America. In his written work, he was detached, calm, and objective. He gave an astonishingly detailed life of a slave who held a variety of positions in his autobiography, *Narrative of William W. Brown, a Fugitive Slave,* published in 1847. That book reportedly sold more than 10,000 copies in only two years.

He was born simply as William in 1815 in Lexington, Kentucky. His father, according to his attractive mulatto mother, was the cousin of their slave owner, physician John Young. Through this bloodline, Brown claimed to be related to Daniel Boone. In 1816, Young moved to Missouri and William spent his next 19 years near St. Louis. He worked the gamut of slave positions after being hired out to more than 10 different owners.

He escaped in January 1834, over eight harrowing days before he happened upon and was befriended by Quaker Wells Brown, who housed the youth for two weeks while he recuperated.

Grateful for Brown's assistance, William adopted his name and departed, settling in Cleveland. He stayed there for two years, where he married and began raising a family. He then moved to Buffalo, New York.

As a steamboat worker, Brown safeguarded and spirited scores of slaves to freedom in Canada by way of the Underground Railroad. In just seven months in 1842, he's credited with safely shepherding 69 passengers along the route.

A pleasant, highly intelligent man with an engaging sense of humor, Brown became a welcome lecturer dedicated to speaking against slavery. He taught himself to read and write, and he pursued studies in English, math, history, and literature.

In 1843, Brown gave up his life as a boat steward to work full-time as an antislavery lecturer. He worked in close association with abolitionists Wendell Phillips and William Lloyd Garrison.

Brown soon gained some national renown. In 1849, he was sent to represent the American Peace Society at a Paris conference and on an extended tour to win British support against slavery.

However, while Brown was abroad, America passed the Fugitive Slave Act of 1850. This meant that he could be captured and sent back to slavery upon his return to America. Brown remained in England until 1854. He wrote and lectured until friends there raised enough

money to purchase his freedom so that he could return home.

During this period, Brown reportedly traveled more than 25,000 miles, addressed more than 1,000 meetings, and learned French, German, and Latin in the process. He wrote a book on his tours of Europe, *Three Years in Europe; Or, Places I Have Seen and People I Have Met* (1852), which made him the first Black American travel writer.

In 1853 he wrote *Clotel; Or, The President's Daughter: A Narrative of Slave Life in the United States.* Although published in England, the book is the first novel written by a Black American.

Clotel focused on the sexual exploitation of female slaves. Even though a novel, it was no doubt based on the experiences of his mother. The president in question in the book was Thomas Jefferson, who allegedly had a number of children by his Black slave concubine, Sally Hemings. Well-received in Europe, *Clotel* caused so much public uproar in America that it wasn't published in its original form until 1969. It was, though, revised and republished under different titles for 14 years after Brown returned to America.

After his return to the States, Brown sensed that the country was moving toward war, and he endorsed slave uprisings. He wrote the first play published by an African American, called *The Escape; Or, a Leap for Freedom*, printed in 1858.

After the Civil War, Brown devoted himself to medicine, which he had learned from his former master John Young. He also continued writing, especially about Black life. He wrote *The Black Man: His Antecedents, His Genius, and His Achievements* in 1863, and *The Negro in the American Rebellion: His Heroism and His Fidelity* in 1867.

Brown's last book was *My Southern Home: Or, The South and Its People*, written in 1880, which was about the increasingly devastating conditions under which African Americans were finding themselves living. It was also a prelude to W.E.B. DuBois's legendary work *The Soul of Black Folks*. Brown died in Boston on November 6, 1884.

RALPH BUNCHE

Diplomat and scholar Ralph Bunche
achieved a number of firsts as an
African American: he received a
Ph.D. from Harvard University in
Political Science; he held an important
position in the State Department; he
mediated a major global conflict (the
1948 Arab-Israeli War); and he won a
Nobel Peace Prize. He was also
instrumental in developing the charter
of the United Nations.

After spending his youth in abject poverty, Ralph Bunche
rose to become one of this country's greatest diplomats.
His primary mission was to secure and maintain peace
throughout the world. In the process, he helped establish

the United Nations, mediated an Arab-Israeli peace accord, and was the first African American to win the Nobel Peace Prize.

Bunche was born August 7, 1904; his father was a barber in a Detroit ghetto. His parents' poor lot in life worsened after his birth. The dismal conditions they lived in contributed to the deaths of his father and his mother from tuberculosis and rheumatic fever, respectively, when he was only 12.

Bunche had shown early scholarly promise in elementary school. After moving to Los Angeles with his grandmother, he graduated from high school as class valedictorian in 1922. In 1927, he graduated from the University of California at Los Angeles summa cum laude and as a member of Phi Beta Kappa, with a degree in international relations.

His studies earned Bunche a graduate spot at Harvard University, where he received his master's degree in government in 1928 and his Ph.D. in political science in 1934. He was the first African American to earn that doctorate at Harvard.

Bunche went on to study at Northwestern University, the London School of Economics, Capetown University, and throughout Africa. He also established the Political Science Department at Howard University in Washington, D.C. Between 1938 and 1940, he collaborated with Swedish sociologist Gunnar Myrdal on *An American Dilemma*. This book was a landmark study of race relations in the United States.

During World War II, Bunche became a specialist on African affairs with the State Department, making him the first African American to hold an important position with that government branch. Afterward, he helped draw up the charter for the United Nations and developed the framework for governing the defeated countries.

Bunche earned his stripes during the 1948 Arab-Israeli War, when he became the key mediator of the conflict after the original United Nations negotiator was assassinated. Bunche secured a truce in 1949 and won the Nobel Peace Prize for that effort the next year. He dedicated the rest of his life to the United Nations, calling it the greatest peace effort in history.

A key United Nations member for two decades, Bunche rose to the post of undersecretary for special political affairs. The chief troubleshooter for resolving global unrest, his most important accomplishments involved resolving

MARGARET BURROUGHS

Margaret Burroughs is founder and
director emeritus of the DuSable
Museum of African American
History in Chicago, the nation's first
and foremost Black museum. With
more than 50,000 artifacts, it
contains Joe Louis's boxing gloves and
W. E. B. DuBois's graduation robe.

Margaret Burroughs's lifelong work has been in the creation, administration, and preservation of art and Black history in all their varied forms.

Although this multitalented artist is renowned for her painting, poetry, and sculpture, her greatest contribution to her African-American heritage is the DuSable Museum of African American History in Chicago, which she founded in 1961 as the nation's first major, and still foremost, Black museum.

Becoming keeper of the culture and heritage of a people was something Burroughs aspired to since childhood. She was born Margaret Taylor on November 1, 1917, in Saint Rose Parish, Louisiana. Her family moved north to Chicago in 1920. By the time she graduated high school in 1933, Burroughs was participating in local art fairs.

In 1937, she earned her teaching certificate for elementary grades, and in 1939, she earned her teaching certificate for upper grades but elected to pursue her art instead. It wasn't until Burroughs received her bachelor's degree in art education from the Art Institute of Chicago in 1946 that she combined her vocation and avocation as an art instructor at DuSable High School in Chicago, a position she held for 22 years.

In 1940, she had already become a charter member of Chicago's famed South Side Community Arts Center, which was created as part of the Works Progress Administration and dedicated by First Lady Eleanor Roosevelt. The Center was an important location for African Americans to take classes and display their art; Burroughs would remain there for 20 years as an officer and trustee.

The Arts Center was the centerpiece of what Yale English Professor Robert Bone dubbed "The Chicago Renaissance," between 1945 and 1960.

Meanwhile, she exhibited her own works throughout the country, including the annual national showcase of Black art at Atlanta University. In 1947 and 1955, Burroughs won awards at the showcase for her print and watercolor works, respectively. In 1949, she married Charles Burroughs, a writer who had lived for 17 years in the Soviet Union. In the 1950s, she enjoyed international success in Mexico and Europe for her oils and acrylics.

In the late 1960s, after producing a series of works portraying great African Americans including Harriet Tubman, Crispus Attucks, and Frederick Douglass, Burroughs wrote a poem to her grandson, Eric Toller, explaining her responsibility in producing the series. Another poem, *What Shall I Tell My Children Who Are Black?*, became nationally famous, and it refers to a collection of African-American folk expressions she had published in 1955.

In 1961, in order to "preserve, interpret and display our heritage," as Burroughs says, she opened the Ebony Museum of Negro History in her own home. Soon, she renamed the museum the DuSable Museum in honor of

Chicago's first settler, a Black man. An overwhelming grassroots response caused the city to donate an old park building, which in 1968 became the permanent site of the museum.

In 1979 Burroughs retired as a humanities professor at Chicago's Kennedy-King College and has been director emeritus of her museum since 1985, when Mayor Harold Washington appointed her to the Chicago Park District Board.

GEORGE WASHINGTON CARVER

George Washington Carver was a
famous Black scientist who
revolutionized farming in the South
with his crop combinations and new
uses for peanuts and sweet potatoes.

Who would have guessed that a little African-American
boy kidnapped from his owner's plantation and ransomed
by his master in exchange for a racehorse would later rev-
olutionize agriculture? But those were the humble be-
ginnings for Dr. George Washington Carver. The famous
African-American scientist looked at the damage America's one-crop system was doing and revolutionized farming. He developed an agriculture made for the problems
of the South. This saved the South's dying farming system by introducing the right crop combinations and finding and promoting markets for them.

71

Carver pressed for the introduction of vegetables that did not rob soil of nitrates as cotton does. Since fertilizer was scarce, his idea of planting peanuts made sense.

Carver was born a slave, possibly in 1860 or 1861. At 13, he ventured off by himself to make his way in a troubled world. He had no money, support, or education. All he had was a dream—education at all costs. He courageously worked for his high school diploma. That whetted his appetite for higher education.

After several rejections, Carver became the first Black student at Simpson College in Iowa and at Iowa State University. He paid his tuition by opening a laundry business. In 1894, he received a bachelor's degree in agricultural science, and a few years later, he received a master's degree. This was the same year the Supreme Court embraced segregation with its ruling supporting the *Plessy* v. *Ferguson* decision, which declared "separate was equal" constitutionally. That same year, Carver became the first Black faculty member at his alma mater. Simpson would later award him a science doctorate.

Carver went on to make a big name for himself with his teaching and research activities. In 1896, Booker T. Washington, head of Tuskegee Institute in Alabama, offered Carver the top position in the school's agriculture department. He accepted. Carver stayed at Tuskegee, turning down royalties for his inventions and publicity, except when he could talk about Tuskegee, the school he loved. He received several lucrative job offers, including some from Henry Ford and Thomas Edison, but he preferred to stay at Tuskegee.

By 1921, when Carver appeared before the House Ways and Means Committee to discuss the many uses of the peanut, he was on the verge of becoming a nationally known scientist. He became known as the "Wizard of Tuskegee." Carver first experimented with peanuts in 1903. In a decade and a half, he developed more than 300 products, including foods, beverages, dyes, and cosmetics from the peanut. Because of Carver's testimony, the U.S. government imposed a tariff on imported peanuts, which delighted Southern peanut farmers who were producing 40 million bushels annually by 1920. Another thing that came out of Carver's appearance before the House Committee was his emergence as a folk hero. He became the subject of several biographies and a movie, and for years, he was one of a handful of African Americans ever mentioned in textbooks.

Books about Carver note his discoveries of several uses of the sweet potato, and also how he made his scientific crop knowledge accessible to the average person. Farmers needed to understand the information about new crops in order to use it effectively. To achieve this, at the suggestion of Tuskegee founder Booker T. Washington, Carver took his science show on the road in a wagon outfitted for agricultural demonstrations and exhibitions called the "Jesup Wagon."

Carver died in 1943, and he left his estate to the George Washington Carver Foundation as his unselfish way of giving back all the love, knowledge, and attention he had received.

SHIRLEY CHISHOLM

Shirley Chisholm, an activist,
educator, and former presidential
candidate, may be best remembered as
America's first Black congresswoman.
She was also the first woman and first
African American to make a serious
bid for the White House.

Like most immigrants who came to America in the
1920s, Shirley Anita St. Hill's parents left Shirley's birth-
place of Barbados to better themselves. And though life
for Blacks was not easy in the United States, her parents
insisted that their children would succeed despite the obstacles. They did decide, though, to send the children back
to Barbados to live with their grandmother in 1928.

Chisholm and her sisters returned to live with their
parents in 1934. Shirley, the oldest, always seemed to

stand out. She expressed herself forcefully and clearly even when her parents did not want her to. Meanwhile, this outspoken little girl excelled in her Brooklyn school just as she had in the demanding one back in Barbados. She was offered scholarships to Vassar and Oberlin colleges but instead stayed in more affordable Brooklyn.

With an education degree from Brooklyn College, Chisholm taught nursery school while she took courses at Columbia University toward her master's degree in early childhood development. She never lost sight of her aspirations; Chisholm continued to work to prove to men and to White America that women and African Americans were as capable as anyone. She fought against racism and sexism her whole life.

She married Jamaican private investigator Conrad Chisholm in 1949. Their life together was good, but Shirley continued to show her concern for her friends and neighbors in her Brooklyn community. She started daycare centers for working mothers. Her biographer, Toyomi Igus, pointed out in the 1991 book *Great Women in the Struggle*, "The centers were so successful that Brooklyn residents chose her to represent them in the New York State legislature in 1964." Four years later, Chisholm was

chosen to represent them in Congress, becoming the first African-American congresswoman. She served seven terms, from 1968 to 1982, and was elected using the slogan "Unbought and Unbossed," which later would be the title of her first autobiography. (*The Good Fight*, published in 1973, was her second autobiography).

Chisholm was always an advocate for the dispossessed, the disenchanted, and always a champion for the poor. She wanted poor people to have the same opportunities other Americans had. So in 1972, Chisholm looked at the political landscape and did not see anyone representing the interests that she held so dear. She decided the only person powerful enough to become president was herself, so she threw her hat into the ring. She campaigned to win the Democratic nomination. She lost. However, Chisholm became a role model to many women, African Americans, and poor people by winning their hearts and earning their respect.

BILL COSBY

Bill Cosby, comedian and television personality, is one of the funniest, highest-paid entertainers in America. An award-winning humorist, Cosby has recorded more than 27 albums and was the first African American to star in a network television drama series.

Bill Cosby started trying out comedy routines while bartending to make ends meet in college. He's now one of the top earners in the business, earning $95 million in 1989 according to *Forbes* magazine. Cosby is well known to television audiences, both through award-winning sitcoms and his neighborly mugging with children in commercials. His life is a success story that has become a beacon for many African-American comedians trying to follow in his footsteps.

William Henry Cosby was born July 12, 1937, in Germantown, Pennsylvania. He dropped out of high school to become a Navy medic. Cosby later enrolled at Temple University, where he played football and tended bar at night. Pleased with his success at entertaining customers, the tall, distinguished-looking man with the expressive face left Temple in 1962 to try his hand in local clubs.

Cosby quickly moved up to shows in New York's legendary Greenwich Village. Audiences were thrilled, and within two years Cosby was performing at some of the nation's top comedy clubs. He also became a fixture on television variety shows and guest hosted for Johnny Carson on *The Tonight Show.* In 1965, Cosby made history as the first African American to get a network television drama show, *I Spy* with Robert Culp. *The Bill Cosby Show* followed in 1969, as well as appearances on the top-rated children's show *The Electric Company.*

Cosby appeared in several hit movies, including *Uptown Saturday Night*, in the 1970s, and he returned to the silver screen in the 1980s and 1990s with features such as *Ghost Dad*. The charming, expressive comedian also became popular at ritzy clubs in Reno, Las Vegas, and Lake Tahoe. However, some of Cosby's best work has been in television commercials, particularly the ongoing series of vignettes with children produced for Jell-O.

Cosby's earnings skyrocketed after five years as star and producer of *The Cosby Show*, a television sitcom focused on the antics of an upper middle-class African-American family. The positive values and the message that Blacks can attain wealth and social status while retaining their cultural identity was a powerful one in the African-American community.

Cosby also shows a strong commitment to education with memberships in various civil rights groups, including Operation PUSH and the NAACP, plus his activities with the United Negro College Fund. In 1977 at age 39, Cosby went back to school, earning a master's degree then a doctorate in education from the University of Massachusetts. In the late 1980s, he donated $20 million to Spelman College, a Black women's facility in Atlanta.

Cosby continues performing across the country and lives in rural New England with his wife, Camille.

MARTIN R. DELANY

A tireless firebrand, Martin R. Delany
was an editor, doctor, army officer,
and Black nationalist who spent his
life fighting for African-American
self-reliance and a dynamic
vision of Black power.

Martin Robinson Delany spent his life championing the cause of African-American empowerment, freedom, and self-elevation. Delany was an editor, author, physician, doctor, colonizationist, and Black nationalist. He attempted to create a self-governing African-American state in Africa, believing that emigration was the only way to keep Blacks away from the scourge of racism.

Delany was born in May of 1812 in Charlestown, West Virginia, the son of a slave and a free Black woman. Early on, his African grandfathers, one a Mandingo prince and the other a Golah village chieftain, regaled the young Delany with grand tales of his homeland. Delany and his four siblings learned to read from a Yankee peddler, causing such consternation among their White neighbors that the family fled to Pennsylvania.

At 19, Delany moved to Pittsburgh, studying medicine briefly and getting involved with the Anti-Slavery Society and the Underground Railroad. He married Catherine Richards and they named their seven children after prominent African Americans. Delany was an advocate for Black self-reliance through education, labor, and property ownership, but he needed a venue to sow his views among the people, so he published a weekly called *The Mystery*. In 1847, he and Black abolitionist Frederick Douglass cofounded and coedited *The North Star* in Rochester, New York.

In 1850, Delany was accepted at Harvard Medical School, but left after just one term when White students protested his admission. Despite limited training, he returned to Pittsburgh a practicing physician and helped the city through a deadly cholera epidemic in 1854.

The enactment of the Fugitive Slave Act, which Delany saw as a threat to the security of African Americans across the country, made him decide that perhaps Blacks would be safest elsewhere. Delany then published *The Condition, Elevation, Emigration and Destiny of the Colored People of the United States, Politically Considered (1852)*, which listed Black achievements, blasted abolitionists for not fighting harder for Blacks' rights, and advocated emigration as a solution to discrimination. "We are a nation within a nation. We must go from our oppressors," Delany wrote. He continued fighting for a Black independent nation for the rest of his life.

Delany moved to Canada, and in 1859 led an investigation into the Niger River Valley in West Africa as a possible place for a Black state. He returned to the United States in 1861. After the Emancipation Proclamation in 1863, he enlisted as a medical officer in the Civil War and became the first Black Army field major, recruiting ex-slaves for regiments in South Carolina.

Delany wrote *Principals of Ethnology* in 1879, tracing Black history from biblical times. Unable to realize his dream of a free Black American state in Africa, Delany died in 1885 in Ohio, still advocating his beliefs in pride of self and the race.

THOMAS DORSEY

Thomas Andrew Dorsey started
playing blues piano in Atlanta saloons
and beer halls at the age of 11, but went
on to become the most prolific
composer in gospel music. He wrote
more than 1,000 songs——the most
famous of which is the standard "Take
My Hand, Precious Lord"——and
elevated gospel music into a nationally
recognized art form.

Born July 1, 1899, in Villa Rica, Georgia, Thomas was the eldest child in the Dorsey family. Raised in a religious household, he began his music career playing piano during the revival services of his father, a traveling Baptist preacher.

But as a youth, he was strongly influenced by blues pianists around Atlanta. To help support his family, Thomas began playing blues piano in area saloons at the tender age of 11 under the stage name "Georgia Tom." In 1916, he moved to Chicago to study at the Chicago College of Composition and Arranging and earned a reputation in the city's blues and jazz club circuit.

In the early 1920s, Dorsey performed with several jazz groups, including the Whispering Serenaders. His own Wildcats Jazz Band toured with popular blues singer Ma Rainey until 1928. Dorsey had several of his blues compositions, notably "Riverside Blues," recorded by major jazz musicians such as Joseph "King" Oliver. He also toured with legendary blues guitarist Tampa Red, with whom he composed and recorded several classic songs, including "Tight Like That" and "Terrible Operation Blues."

Sticking to his upbringing in sacred music, Dorsey continued to write religious compositions. In 1921, his song "Someday, Somewhere" was included in the National Baptist Convention's *Gospel Pearls* Collection.

In the late 1920s, Dorsey turned his focus exclusively toward gospel, combining the spirituality of his lyrics with

blues melodies and rhythms, which were not initially accepted in area churches because of their secular sound.

In 1931, Dorsey experienced a personal tragedy when he lost his wife and daughter in childbirth, an experience that caused him to write "Take My Hand, Precious Lord," which has become a gospel standard and Dorsey's most famous work.

In the same year, Dorsey formed the world's first gospel choir at Ebenezer Church in Chicago and opened the first publishing company dedicated exclusively to the sale of gospel music. In 1932, he became the lifelong choir director of Chicago's Pilgrim Baptist Church and, along with gospel legend Sallie Martin, founded the National Convention of Gospel Choirs and Choruses to train gospel vocal groups and soloists.

Dorsey presided over that organization for 40 years, and for the same period, toured the country extensively with gospel caravans, both performing and lecturing. He remained active in promoting gospel music around the country until his death in Chicago on January 23, 1993, at the age of 93.

FREDERICK DOUGLASS

Militant abolitionist Frederick Douglass was the most famous of all antislavery orators, and the most effective. He challenged liberals and conservatives to accept the rights of Blacks to defend themselves with or without anyone else's help.

The fight against slavery is best exemplified by the words and deeds of one man—Frederick Douglass. In the years that spanned the abolitionist movement, Civil War, Reconstruction, and the post-Reconstruction period, Douglass championed the cause of all oppressed people. The rocklike Douglass's preeminence as race leader was to persist until his death in 1895, the very year Booker T. Washington was thrust into the role of the nation's most famous Negro by his celebrated Atlanta Compromise address, "signaling a strategic retreat with a changed national attitude," wrote Richard Bardolph in his 1959 *The Negro Vanguard.*

Douglass was born in one of the darkest periods of slavery on a plantation owned by Colonel Lloyd of Talbot County, Maryland, the White man who raped his mother. When Douglass was an infant, he was snatched from his mother and put under his grandmother's care. According to Douglass, hunger was his constant companion. "He used to run races against the cat and the dog to reach the bones that were tossed out of the window, or to snap up the crumbs that fell under the table," said his biographer, J. A. Rogers in his 1947 *World's Great Men of Color.* Douglass would later be beaten for sneaking away to get meat.

At age eight, two years after his mother died at a neighboring estate, young Douglass was sent to live with the Auld family, where his life's ambition to learn how to read was fulfilled. Not knowing it was against the law, Mrs. Auld gave him reading lessons. Her husband scolded her when he found out, causing her to stop her literacy crusade. Douglass continued his lessons on his own, grabbing scraps of newspapers, bank notes, or any piece of paper with writing on it to teach himself.

After a series of severe thrashings for fighting and organizing slave revolts, 21-year-old Douglass plotted his 1838 escape. He somehow got hold of a sailor's uniform and a passport and climbed on a ship and sailed. The next day, he arrived in New York where he found work shoveling coal. He took on the last name of Douglass after the hero in Walter Scott's *Marmion*, married a freed woman, Anna Murray, and increased his desire to help those still in bondage by reading *The Liberator*, published by famous abolitionist William Lloyd Garrison. Three years later, he found himself in front of a crowd speaking forcefully against slavery in an antislavery meeting in Nantucket. He had the uncanny ability to transport his audiences to Slave Row. Historian Lerone Bennett said, "He could make people *laugh* at a slave owner preaching the duties of Christian obedience; could make them *see* the humiliation of a Black maiden ravished by a brutal slave owner; could make them *hear* the sobs of a mother separated from her child. Through him, people could cry, curse and *feel*; through him they could *live* slavery."

In 1845, he published his first autobiography, *Narratives of the Life of Frederick Douglass, An American Slave*, which put slavers on his track after the book had huge sales and subsequent controversy. Douglass prepared to flee to England. On his getaway boat, he made a speech so fiery that Southerners nearly killed him by throwing him overboard. His life was saved by crew members. This event garnered huge publicity in England. Lords, ladies, and earls welcomed him to their suburban estates. The now famous baritone orator, with his impressive mane of hair, addressed the Parliament. After 19 months in Great Britain, English friends gave him $2,175, of which he used $750 to buy his freedom.

His liberty now purchased, Douglass went to Rochester, New York, and started his antislavery paper, *The North Star*, and later *Frederick Douglass' Paper*. He wrote his second autobiography, *My Bondage and My Freedom*, in 1855. He returned to this form 26 years later and wrote *The Life and Times of Frederick Douglass*. The most important aspect of his writing is that it crystallized the abolition movement and mobilized both Blacks and Whites to fight slavery. It also created an audience for slave narratives and Black literary and historical works.

In his words and deeds, Douglass challenged liberals who felt he should merely "stick to the facts" in his oratory and "leave the philosophy to them." He challenged

conservatives who thought they were empowered by God to enslave Black people. And he fought both Whites and Blacks who thought his terse verse did not fit into the commonly held notions of what a Black man should be and say. In essence, Douglass challenged himself and his people to be all they could be and not let any obstacle stand in their way. He taught everyone that freedom is never free—it comes with struggle.

CHARLES RICHARD DREW

Charles Richard Drew was a brilliant
doctor who pioneered the use of blood
plasma and created the world's first
blood bank. Drew also fought to
increase the medical establishment's
respect for African-American
physicians, and to make it easier
for them to work at White
medical facilities.

Dr. Charles Richard Drew not only revolutionized the
medical profession by developing a way to store blood
and plasma, he also created the world's first blood bank.
But Drew had another priority—crusading to change the
way African Americans, especially as physicians, were
viewed and treated by Whites.

Born the eldest of five children on June 3, 1904, Drew lived in the racially mixed Foggy Bottom neighborhood of Washington, D.C. The area was an enclave where Blacks rarely had to deal with the federally sanctioned Jim Crow laws. Drew was an exceptional student and athlete at Dunbar High School. He decided to become a doctor after his sister died of tuberculosis in 1920. After graduating from Amherst College in Massachusetts, Drew taught for two years, then went to McGill University in Montreal, Canada, for medical school.

While Drew served his medical internship at the Royal Victoria Hospital in Montreal, he saved an elderly man who needed a blood transfusion in order to have his leg amputated. During that time, many people died because doctors had to match the blood type before a transfusion could take place. Drew's research changed all that.

In 1935, Drew taught and practiced at Freedmen's Hospital at Howard University, where he invented a way to separate plasma from whole blood, making it possible to store blood for a week instead of just two days. More research turned up a bigger revelation: Transfusions could be performed with plasma alone, negating the need for blood typing since plasma contains no red blood cells. In

1938, Drew got a fellowship in blood research at New York City's Columbia Presbyterian Hospital and ran its first blood bank.

In 1940, Drew became the first African American to earn an advanced doctor of science degree, and he invented a technique for long-term plasma storage. He set up the world's first blood bank in Britain that same year, as part of the country's World War II effort. As America prepared to enter the war, Drew was appointed medical director of the American Red Cross's National Blood Bank program. But the U.S. War Department issued an edict forbidding the armed forces to mix Black and White blood, even while admitting in a memorandom that their decision was based on "reasons not biologically convincing, but which are commonly recognized as psychologically important in America." A furious Drew called a press conference, asking, "How have we, in this age and hour, allowed once again to creep into our hearts the dark myths and wretched superstitions of the past? . . . Will we ever share a common brotherhood?" Drew resigned his post.

In April of 1941, Drew was certified as a surgeon by the American Board of Surgery. He then returned to Howard University as a full professor. Two of his students

became the first Howard graduates to qualify for the American Board of Surgery, and Drew continued pushing his students to seek internships and residencies in White establishments. His efforts greatly increased the number of Blacks getting jobs outside the African-American medical community.

Drew was appointed chief of staff at Freedmen's Hospital in 1944, and was awarded the Spingarn Medal by the NAACP. In 1947, Drew began an unsuccessful crusade against the American Medical Association for a policy that effectively kept Blacks from joining. The AMA didn't change its policy until 1968. (In 1996, the AMA elected its first African-American president, Dr. Lonnie R. Bristow.) Drew was later named consultant to the surgeon general of the U.S. Army.

By 1950, despite an international reputation, Drew remained poor, since Black medical researchers made far less money than private practitioners of any race. He died the morning of April 1, 1950, when he fell asleep while driving to a medical conference at Tuskegee. Drew, despite a blood transfusion at the hospital, died of internal injuries. He was 45.

W.E.B. DuBois

W.E.B. DuBois may well have been
this century's greatest Black
intellectual. His words and deeds,
including helping to found the
NAACP and editing its journal, *The
Crisis*, have stood the test of time. He
was a pioneer in sociology, history, and
anthropology, and a major contributor
to the Harlem Renaissance.

William Edward Burghardt DuBois was born poor in
1868 in Great Barrington, Massachusetts, but rose from
his meager roots to become one of the brightest Black
minds in the 20th century.

Showing remarkable brilliance even as a youth, W.E.B.
DuBois won scholarships that took him through Fisk and

Harvard universities. He earned his master's and doctorate degrees from Harvard, and later studied at the University of Berlin.

His first works of importance included *The Suppression of the Slave-Trade of the United States of America, 1638–1870*, published in 1896, and *The Philadelphia Negro; A Social Study*, published in 1899. The latter is a classic about the social conditions of turn-of-the-century Blacks in that city. He wrote several reports about Atlanta a few years later, from 1899 to 1913, with Atlanta University. These social studies were published for the university's Conferences for the Study of Negro Problems. During this same stormy period when Whites' hostility against Blacks reached a fever pitch, DuBois also wrote the oft-quoted classic *The Souls of Black Folk*, which identified the principal problem of the 20th century as the color line.

His uncompromising opposition to injustice and Jim Crow impelled him to write scathing reports about the Atlanta Riots of 1906 and found the Niagara Movement. He later cofounded the National Association for the Advancement of Colored People, which demanded full citizenship for Blacks. DuBois became the NAACP's chief spokesman through the editorship of *The Crisis* magazine. During his stint as editor, DuBois greatly advanced African-American literature by editing many of the important voices of the Black arts revival known as the Harlem Renaissance.

Through his moving editorials, he was to stir the emotions and awaken the sense of outrage in both Blacks and Whites—an act that would draw the ire of Booker T. Washington, the more accommodationist Black leader at the time. Washington said DuBois was an agitator who was always stirring up trouble. DuBois said Washington's strategy would perpetuate oppression. Their debate was legendary and to this day represents the fight between accommodationist versus the integrationist schools of thought within the African-American community. DuBois was also critical of Black nationalist Marcus Garvey. Their conflict symbolized the differences between integrationist and Black nationalist schools of thought.

Throughout DuBois's life, including periods when he embraced Pan-Africanism, socialism, and communism, he believed in three basic goals for Blacks: the right to vote, civic equality, and education of the youth. One of DuBois's most often quoted philosophies was the "talented tenth." It said that Blacks' salvation will come through the accomplishments of its elite.

Hardly modest about his own achievement in defining and transcending caste and class in this country, DuBois boasted in his autobiography, *Dusk of Dawn*: "I was the main factor in revolutionizing the attitude of the American Negro toward caste."

DuBois had a universal outlook. He was concerned, as was Garvey, with the treatment of the darker people of other lands. In 1909, he began thinking of creating an "Encyclopedia Africana." He finally did work on it in his later years in self-imposed exile in Ghana. He was also an organizer of the Pan-African Congress, which brought together for the first time influential Blacks from Europe, Africa, and America. The first conference was held in Paris in 1919.

DuBois traveled to the Soviet Union in the 1930s, praising the communist nation as being virtually free of racial discrimination. Ironically, he left the Communist Party in America, which he joined much later in 1961, because he felt they discounted Blacks with the Party's insistence that class and not race was the problem. Nevertheless, like other Blacks such as Paul Robeson and

Langston Hughes, DuBois would be harassed by the United States government for his views on the Soviet Union. Many were shocked in 1950, therefore, when he ran for the United States Senate on the American Labor Party ticket.

DuBois's universal outlook led to him being one of the few influential African Americans associated with the founding of the United Nations. Like his colleagues Ralph Bunche and Mary McLeod Bethune, who were also U.N. cofounders, DuBois linked the struggle of Africans with that of African Americans—another reason why many Whites and some Blacks criticized him. This resentment and harassment made him increasingly isolated. In 1963, he became a citizen of Ghana, and when he died, on August 27, 1963, he was buried in Accra, Ghana.

In addition to being one of this century's most important thinkers, DuBois was also an important writer. Two of his works include *Black Reconstruction* (1935), which submitted the Civil War to Marxist analysis and argued the heroic role Blacks played in the conflict; and his autobiography, *Dusk of Dawn* (1940), in which he used his life as a metaphor for the race's continuing struggle.

PAUL LAURENCE DUNBAR

Paul Laurence Dunbar was the first
African-American poet to gain
national stature. Though he only wrote
professionally for 14 years before his
untimely death from tuberculosis at age
33, the popular artist turned out four
novels, four collections of short stories,
and six volumes of poetry.

Paul Laurence Dunbar was a brilliant, popular poet, beloved by the Black community, whose experiences he put
into lyrical language. He was one of the first Black poets
to become nationally recognized by White America.

Even early on, Dunbar was seen as a Black prodigy in
a White world. He was the only African American in his
Dayton, Ohio, high school class, but immensely popular.

In his senior year, he was elected president of the literary society and served as editor of the school newspaper.

Dunbar wanted to go to college, but did not have the resources. He was born in Dayton on June 27, 1872, to ex-slave parents. His father died when Dunbar was only 12 and there were other children to support.

So Dunbar took one of the few jobs available to a young Black man at the time, operating an elevator. He continued writing poems and sending them off to publications.

In 1893, he paid to have 56 poems published in a slim volume called *Oak and Ivy*, which he sold to his captive audience of elevator passengers. Thinking there would be opportunities at the World's Fair of 1893, Dunbar moved to Chicago, where he became Frederick Douglass's clerical assistant.

In 1895, Dunbar was able to pay to publish a second collection of his verses, *Majors and Minors*, which presented poems he had written in standard English and in Black dialect. The book became his major breakthrough after being favorably reviewed by William Dean Howells, reigning literary critic of the day for *Harper's Weekly*.

Howells encouraged Dunbar to take the best poems from his two books and reissue them in 1896 under the

title *Lyrics of Lowly Life*, for which Howells wrote the preface. The book made Dunbar a star in White literary circles and gave him the financial security to write full-time.

Offers streamed in from prestigious magazines and publishers for anything that came from his pen, and Dunbar didn't disappoint, turning out a great volume of work including four novels, four volumes of short stories, and three more books of poetry.

But because of the necessity of surviving financially in the literary world, Dunbar compromised his art. He wrote uninspired prose and poems in Black dialect, which his readers seemed to prefer, instead of his preference for verse in standard English. So, despite his success, Dunbar was riddled with disappointment that his greatest talent had gone unappreciated.

However, when Dunbar died from tuberculosis on February 9, 1906, at the age of 33, the American public still considered him the dean of Black poets.

KATHERINE DUNHAM

Katherine Dunham popularized Afro-Caribbean dance and elevated Black dance into a serious, accepted art form. After studying native dance in Africa and the West Indies, Dunham developed a new technique called "dance-isolation," which involved moving one part of the body while other parts remained motionless.

Katherine Dunham, the choreographer who introduced and popularized Afro-Caribbean dance, was also the cultural pioneer who propelled Black dance into a serious art form accepted by mainstream America.

Dunham was so serious about learning and establishing this medium as "art" that she majored in anthropol-

ogy in college—all the way through the doctoral level—
to study the original African and West Indian dance forms
in their native environments.

Dunham was born June 22, 1909, in Chicago, Illinois,
and exhibited an early interest in athletics and music,
which merged into her natural talent for dance. At the age
of 15, Dunham organized a cabaret party to raise funds
for her church. At the age of 21, she had started a dance
school, which folded from lack of funding. But she soon
joined the Negro Dance Group, where she learned ballet
and mime and was allowed to teach her own pupils what
she knew of African tribal dance.

After Dunham trained 150 young dancers for a program at the 1934 Chicago Century of Progress Exhibition, she received a Rosenwald Foundation grant through
Northwestern University to visit Jamaica, Martinique,
Trinidad, and Haiti to study the origins of the people and
their dances. She later received a Guggenheim Fellowship
to continue her studies and eventually received a B.A. and
M.A. from the University of Chicago and a Ph.D. from
Northwestern University in anthropology.

Dunham's first ballet, *L'Ag'Ya*, based on a fighting
dance from Martinique, was accepted by the Federal The-

ater Project of the Works Progress Administration. It was performed with success in Chicago in 1939. A year later, Dunham established her first ensemble, the Katherine Dunham Dance Company, which opened at New York's Windsor Theater with Dunham's own work, *Tropics and Le Jazz Hot*. The piece was a huge success.

Shortly thereafter, the Dunham Dance Company was asked to take part in the all-Black musical *Cabin in the Sky*, with Dunham playing the role of Georgia Brown. The production had a long run, after which Dunham appeared in *Stormy Weather* and choreographed *Pardon My Sarong* and *Windy City*.

In 1943, she was guest artist for the San Francisco Symphony Orchestra, and in 1945, she was guest artist for the Los Angeles Symphony Orchestra. Over the next 20 years, Dunham and her dance troupe visited almost every country in the world.

Dunham gave her last dance performance at the Apollo Theater in 1965. Afterward, she established the Performing Arts Training Center, now called the Katherine Dunham Center for the Performing Arts, at Southern Illinois University located in Carbondale, Illinois. She is now retired.

JEAN BAPTISTE POINTE DuSABLE

The first permanent settler of Chicago, Jean Baptiste Pointe DuSable was a legendary explorer, trader, and entrepreneur. DuSable's legacy helped create one of the most popular trading centers in the area and made him one of the most important African Americans in history.

Jean Baptiste Pointe DuSable founded the settlement of Chicago in 1772 by establishing its first trading post. This handsome frontiersman epitomized the forbearance and spirit of early African Americans, whose accomplishments represent the incredible diversity of the African-American experience.

The details of DuSable's early life are based on much conjecture, but he is believed to have been born in St. Marc, Haiti, in 1745. He was a free Black of African heritage. Since many free Blacks in Haiti were educated in France it is possible that DuSable, too, was educated there. He became a strong patriot for his country. DuSable then moved to New Orleans and ran his father's business there. The Spanish occupied Louisiana in 1764, and DuSable fled with an associate for French-controlled areas along the upper Mississippi River.

During this time, DuSable created what became a lifelong connection with several Native American nations, most notably the Potawatomie. He spent four years (1765–1769) trading furs with the Indians in St. Louis, then moved farther north into their territory, on land controlled by the English and Spanish. He lived at that time with a boyhood friend, Jacques Clemorgan, another Haitian who had received large land grants in return for doing favors for the Spanish government.

DuSable, who remained faithful to the French, left to live among the Potawatomies. His fur trapping expeditions took him across North America, to the sites of what are now Chicago, Detroit, and Ontario, Canada.

DuSable was described in the "Recollections" of Augustin Grignon, of Butte des Morts, Wisconsin, as "a large man. . . . He was a trader, pretty wealthy, and drank freely." Others who knew him described him as "venerable, about six feet in height, with a well-formed figure and very pleasant countenance." DuSable was described by many as a respectable man.

In 1772, DuSable established a historic fur trading post on the Chicago River near Lake Michigan, the first permanent settlement in the area. He bought land and built his house on the north bank of the Chicago River, just where the waterway turned south, on a head of sand that extended between the river and Lake Michigan. The ambitious businessman lived a prosperous life with his Native American wife, Catherine, and their daughter, Suzanne.

The first child born in Chicago was born on his property, which also hosted the city's first marriage and housed its first court and post office. He traded heavily with the Native Americans in the area and became known for acting as peacemaker between various warring tribes.

During the Revolutionary War, DuSable seems to have tried to play a role as peacemaker, but his intentions were questioned by both sides. DuSable was jailed on suspicion of treason by British Colonel Arent de Peyster, who described DuSable as "a handsome Negro, well-educated and settled at Eschikagou." His captor, a Lieutenant Bennett, reported that DuSable had many friends who gave him good character references. DuSable was freed after proving that he was a citizen of the United States.

DuSable later served as liaison officer between White officials and the Indian nations in the Port Huron area on the St. Clair River. He was appointed by the government at the Native Americans' request.

After acquiring and developing an 800-acre property in Peoria, DuSable returned to Chicago in the early 1780s, creating a trading post and home that became legendary for its elaborate furnishings and modern conveniences. DuSable's business was so prosperous that it included two barns, a mill, a bake house, a poultry house, and large livestock holdings.

By 1800, DuSable sold his post to a French trader and moved to Missouri with his old friend Clemorgan. He later moved to St. Charles, Missouri, with his granddaughter and her husband. He was possibly disappointed over his defeat in an election to become chief of the Native American nations in the Mackinac area. DuSable spent most of his time hunting and fishing. Even though his holdings brought the then-unheard-of sum of $1,200, DuSable died a pauper in 1818, apparently forsaken by his relatives. Still, his life and perseverance stand as a symbol of African-American ingenuity and self-reliance.

EDWARD "DUKE" ELLINGTON

Edward "Duke" Ellington was a
common man who rose to royalty.
His legacy of composing more than
1,000 songs spanning several musical
forms has earned him a place
in history as one of America's
greatest composers.

No one played like him. No one arranged music like him. No one loved life like him. And no one, absolutely no one, wrote songs like him. He was one of a kind. While he was born to common parents at the turn of the century, Edward Kennedy Ellington enriched millions worldwide, earning him an eternal place among royalty. Long live the Duke!

His dad, James Edward, was a well-heeled butler and caterer who lived like a king despite his meager means.

His mother, Daisy, had the confidence of a queen, despite living in segregated Washington, D.C., where separate was never equal.

After hearing a terrific pianist named Harvey Brooks in Philadelphia during a summer trip with his parents, Edward decided the musician's life was for him. It was around this time that this well-mannered, fancy-dressing, popular piano-playing boy got his royal nickname—Duke.

By the time he was 22, Duke was already a successful pianist and bandleader. He married Edna Thompson, a pianist who schooled Duke on piano and music theory when they were both still in high school. They had a son, Mercer, in 1919, who followed in his dad's footsteps.

Duke's big break came in the 1920s when he auditioned for Harlem's Cotton Club. During the Cotton Club era, the flamboyant Duke Ellington Orchestra made nationwide radio broadcasts from the club and recorded "Black and Tan Fantasy."

The Duke Ellington Orchestra soon became the first Black musicians featured at Carnegie Hall and among the first prominently featured in major motion pictures. Duke's band became a magnet for the most talented mu-

sicians in this country. Chicago bassist Ernest Outlaw said: "There was no one like him. He always sought to do something different, something unique with his music. He blended sounds like no one else could. He was beyond category."

Historian Dempsey Travis agreed: "Duke's creative abilities reached into classical, gospel, and even African areas of music, in addition to the jazz that he popularized." Travis was interviewed on jazz station WNUA in Chicago, where he discussed his new book, *The Duke Ellington Primer.* "No other American composer had the depth and the production of Duke, which is why he is without question America's greatest composer."

Inspired by his fellow musicians and the high life he lived off the bandstand, Duke wrote more than 1,000 compositions. These include "It Don't Mean a Thing if It Ain't Got That Swing," "Satin Doll," "Sophisticated Lady," and his trademark tune written in collaboration with Billy Strayhorn, "Take the A Train."

Duke, as a person and as a composer, responded to the times. The Civil Rights Movement did not escape his perceptive eye. His contribution, while less vocal than that of others, was nevertheless very significant. In 1963, he

wrote an ambitious show called *My People*. He dedicated it to the immense contributions of many African Americans. The show received rave reviews when it played in Chicago that same year.

Two years later, the Pulitzer committee recommended that Ellington receive its famous prize. The selection board made the unusual decision to ignore the committee's recommendation. Many felt racial bias was the motivation behind the board's decision. Ellington was hurt that he didn't receive the Pulitzer. He mused, "Fate is being very kind to me. Fate doesn't want me to be too famous, too young." He was 66.

That same year, Ellington opened San Francisco's Grace Cathedral with the first of three sets of religious music that he called the Sacred Concerts. They consisted of both vocal and instrumental music composed for performance in large churches, synagogues, cathedrals, and mosques.

In 1967, Billy Strayhorn, friend and collaborator for almost three decades, died. The death of his best friend moved Ellington in ways few could predict. Later that year, he recorded *And His Mother Called Him Bill*, which featured all Strayhorn tunes. "Sweet Pea" Strayhorn's death inspired him in other ways, too.

MEDGAR EVERS

Medgar Evers was the most
prominent civil rights leader in the
state of Mississippi before being
assassinated June 12, 1963 by Byron de
la Beckwith. The murder intensified
the civil rights struggle and was a
factor in President John Kennedy
asking Congress to enact major
civil rights legislation.

One of the most prominent Black leaders of the 1960s
Civil Rights Movement in the state of Mississippi, Medgar
Evers also became one of the Civil Rights Movement's
most important martyrs.

Not that the death of any one human being during that
turbulent struggle was worth more or less than others

who were killed, but the first murder of a nationally known civil rights leader showed the world the degree to which racial violence was practiced in the South.

Evers's death led to increased participation in the movement by outraged Americans, which led to more demonstrations and violence, and was a motivating factor in President John Kennedy's decision a week later to ask Congress to enact comprehensive civil rights legislation.

Medgar Evers was born July 2, 1925, in Decatur, Mississippi, to strongly religious parents—his father was a farmer and sawmill operator, his mother a domestic worker who took in ironing. Evers attended a one-room elementary school in Decatur, then later he walked 12 miles to high school in nearby Newton.

After serving in Normandy during World War II, Evers returned home in 1946 and enrolled in Alcorn A&M College, where he was a popular student—a business administration major and school newspaper editor. Evers met his wife, Myrlie, there; they had three children.

Following college, he sold life insurance, but left that to join the NAACP—and the growing Civil Rights Movement—in 1952. Evers became the group's Mississippi field secretary in 1954. After the Supreme Court outlawed public school segregation that year, he actively sought enforcement of the ruling in his state, which had one of the most rigid systems of segregation.

In 1962, Evers played a key role in enrolling James Meredith as the first Black student at the University of Mississippi, a major victory in the early stages of the Civil Rights Movement.

He went on to spearhead a number of economic boycotts in downtown Jackson, Mississippi, of businesses that practiced segregation. He also helped form the "Jackson Movement," an umbrella of Black organizations that sponsored mass demonstrations throughout the segregated state. The group demanded integration of all public facilities and institutions and increased job opportunities for Blacks on city payrolls. But at the time, opposition to the Civil Rights Movement was perhaps at its most entrenched and violent, especially in Mississippi.

On June 12, 1963, as he returned home, Evers was shot in the back by Byron de la Beckwith, a fertilizer salesman and member of an old Mississippi family. It took three trials and 30 years before Beckwith was convicted.

Medgar Evers, 38, was buried in Arlington National Cemetery with full military honors.

LOUIS FARRAKHAN

Louis Farrakhan is the leader of the
Nation of Islam and a spellbinding
orator who preaches Black self-reliance,
independence, and economic self-
sufficiency. Farrakhan, considered a
racist by some, initiated and co-
organized the historic 1995 Million
Man March on Washington, D.C.

Louis Farrakhan is the Honorable Minister of the Nation of Islam, based in Chicago, with mosques in more
than 120 cities. An intense speaker with a strong belief
in Black independence, Farrakhan has been a thorn in the
side of White America since converting to Islam in 1955.
He tells his followers to buy Black, live clean, and take
care of their own. But Farrakhan's penchant for making

anti-Jewish remarks have made him a pariah in some quarters, and many consider him a racist.

African-American leaders are often asked to disavow Farrakhan. But Farrakhan says, "whenever any Black person . . . rises to speak against the norm that we have accepted as truth, it creates what you call controversy."

The eloquent, magnetic Farrakhan was born in the Bronx, New York, May 11, 1933, to parents who supported Black nationalist Marcus Garvey. Farrakhan attended Winston-Salem Teachers College in North Carolina. He married in 1953 and has nine children.

Farrakhan, an accomplished musician, was performing in Chicago in 1955 when he first heard Nation of Islam leader Elijah Muhammad speak. After sampling the fiery oratory of Malcolm X, Farrakhan joined the Nation that same year. He ran the Boston temple, then took over in Harlem after Malcolm X was murdered. There have been questions as to whether Farrakhan was involved in the assassination, which he vehemently denies.

In 1975, Farrakhan took over the Nation's leadership. He has worked to restore many of the Nation's businesses, he reopened the Chicago mosque, and he opened a school that taught Muslim traditions.

But Farrakhan's speeches exhorting Blacks to defend themselves against White racism and economic repression, stressing the importance of the Black male and family structure, and raging against Whites (especially Jews) for their crimes against African Americans, have made him a controversial figure. He says he wants Jews to "let my people go" and to stop threatening to cut off funds to Black groups who "take a path not desired by outsiders."

Farrakhan initiated and co-organized the Million Man March on Washington, D.C., in October 1995, with the Rev. Benjamin Chavis, Jr. Black men were asked to atone for the mistakes of the past.

In 1996, he took his message of reconciliation to 23 Arab and African countries, including Libya and Nigeria, saying money and support from the nations would help him revitalize Black urban communities. The U.S. government has threatened an investigation, saying he may have compromised national security. Farrakhan, calling himself an "agent of God," says he was trying to link the interests of Blacks and Muslims worldwide.

He continues to lead the Nation of Islam. He currently lives in Chicago.

T. THOMAS FORTUNE

T. Thomas Fortune was a journalist
and civil rights leader who used his
clarion voice to wage war on
discrimination and racial repression.
Fortune founded the *New York Age,*
a militant publication that demanded
full equality for Blacks.

Timothy Thomas Fortune spent his life fighting to free African Americans from racial discrimination. He also worked diligently to keep infighting among Blacks from costing them hard-won gains, both politically and economically. Editor and founder of several African-American newspapers, including the militant *New York Age,* Fortune attempted to convince Black power brokers to consolidate their forces and work to achieve true equality for African Americans.

Fortune was born to slave parents in Marianna, Florida, in October of 1856, with the blood of Blacks, Native Americans, and Irish Whites flowing through his veins. His family's political activities forced them to flee to Jacksonville, Florida, where Fortune had a limited education through the Freedmen's Bureau. Fortune learned the printer's trade and became an expert at composition.

He briefly attended Howard University in Washington, D.C., in 1876, and began his love affair with journalism while working on the *People's Advocate*. While working for this Black newspaper, Fortune met and married Carrie C. Smiley. They later returned to his native Florida.

In the late 1870s, Fortune moved to New York, first as a printer, then almost immediately as part-owner of the weekly tabloid *Rumor*. Fortune became editor of the newspaper, changing its name to the *Globe*. The trailblazing writer then became sole owner of his first newspaper, *The New York Freeman*, which later became *New York Age*. He believed the paper's purpose was to counter negative coverage of Blacks by the White press.

"The great newspapers, which should plead the cause of the oppressed and the downtrodden, which should be the palladiums of the people's rights, are all on the side of the oppressor, or by silence preserve a dignified but ignominious neutrality," wrote Fortune. "Day after day they weave a false picture of facts—facts which must measurably influence the future historian of the times in the composition of impartial history. The wrongs of the masses are referred to sneeringly or apologetically."

Fortune's editorial policies advocated Black self-reliance, demanded full equality for African Americans, and condemned all forms of discrimination. In an 1883 editorial, Fortune blasted the U.S. Supreme Court for its decisions in several cases, noting that "We are declared to be created equal, and entitled to certain rights, . . . but there is no law to protect us in the enjoyment of them."

Two general circulation papers, the *Boston Transcript* and the *New York Sun*, hired Fortune as a reporter and editor, which was unusual for a Black man in the 1880s. Fortune traveled the South, reporting on the conditions. Fortune was an early advocate of the term Afro-American. He considered Negro to be a term of contempt.

Fortune also wrote three books. *Black and White: Land and Politics in the South* (1884), a historical essay on land, labor, and politics in the South, called for the unification of workers of both races. He also wrote *The Negro in Politics*, which was published in 1885, and then *Dreams of Life*, published in 1905.

Fortune later founded the National Afro-American League, an organization that pioneered many programs and methods used by many modern-day civil rights groups. He told the delegates at the Chicago event that "before the rights conferred upon us by the war amendments are fully conceded, a full century will have passed away. We have undertaken no child's play. We have undertaken a serious work which will tax and exhaust the best intelligence and energy of the race for the next century."

The League was short-lived. However, in 1898, Fortune's National Afro-American Council held a conference emphasizing civil rights, women's suffrage, and concern over the fate of Latin Americans after the United States defeated Spain. Political infighting over Fortune's support of Black leader Booker T. Washington severely weakened the organization. The legacies of Fortune's groups helped set the platform for the NAACP, formally organized in 1910, and that group's ongoing fight for an end to discrimination in all forms.

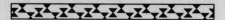

Fortune suffered a bout of mental illness in the early 1900s, possibly related to alcoholism. He was virtually a derelict for several years. When his health returned, Fortune returned to writing fiery editorials for Black nationalist Marcus Garvey's *Negro World.*

Fortune died in Philadelphia in 1928. Kelly Miller of Howard University eulogized him as "the best developed journalist that the Negro race has produced in the Western World."

JOHN HOPE FRANKLIN

John Hope Franklin, historian,
educator, and prolific author, has spent
his life teaching people about the
contributions African Americans have
made to history. Franklin's legacy
makes it possible for Blacks to
understand their importance in building
and maintaining the American dream.

John Hope Franklin is living proof that African Americans play an invaluable role in interpreting the importance of Blacks in history. Franklin, who has been awarded more than 30 honorary degrees and has been a professor at many universities, uses his vast knowledge and clarion voice to trumpet the accomplishments of Blacks in helping to build this country.

Franklin was born January 2, 1915, in Rentiesville, Ohio, the son of Mollie and Buck Franklin. An advocate of education, Franklin graduated magna cum laude from Fisk University in Nashville, a legendary haven for scores of America's best and brightest Blacks. Franklin then enrolled in Harvard University, receiving his master's degree in 1936. The dark-skinned, slim man returned to Fisk to teach for a year, but went back to Harvard for his Ph.D. in 1941.

Believing that education is a path to freedom and equality for Blacks, Franklin launched a journey that included passing his knowledge to students at several colleges and universities. In North Carolina, Franklin taught at St. Augustine's College while writing a dissertation on free Blacks in that state. He moved on to North Carolina College in Durham, North Carolina, in 1943, then to Howard University in Washington, D.C., four years later. In the meantime, Franklin earned prestigious Rosenwald and Guggenheim fellowships for research.

Brooklyn College invited the brilliant young scholar to join its faculty in 1956. Eight years later, Franklin became a professor of history at the University of Chicago, the first major White university to tenure an African-

John Hope Franklin

American scholar. Franklin chaired the history department there and was named the first John Matthews Manly Distinguished Service Professor of History. In 1982, Franklin held the post of James B. Duke Professor of History at Duke University in North Carolina. He retired from that position in 1985 and accepted the appointment as professor of legal history at Duke University Law School. He currently teaches constitutional law at Duke University.

Franklin's achievements haven't been limited to teaching. In 1949, he was the first Black to read a paper before the prestigious Southern Historical Association, of which he later became president. Franklin was also the first African-American president of the American Historical Association, Phi Beta Kappa, and the Organization of American Historians. He was one of the social scientists who drew up the historic brief for the NAACP's legal argument for the plaintiff's cause in the landmark *Brown* v. *Board of Education* case.

A prolific author, Franklin's many books include *The Free Negro in North Carolina, 1790–1860* (1943); *From Slavery to Freedom* (1947, seventh edition 1994), an outstanding college reference and textbook; and *A Southern*

Odyssey: Travelers in the Antebellum North (1976). He also wrote the award-winning *George Washington Williams: A Biography,* which was published in 1985. Franklin's other honors are too numerous to list, including other professional offices, fellowships, and honorary doctorates.

A lifelong champion of civil rights, Franklin spoke against Judge Robert Bork's confirmation as a U.S. Supreme Court Justice before a Senate committee in 1987. Franklin is married and has one son.

MARCUS GARVEY

Marcus Garvey worked to instill
Black pride in many African
Americans in the 1920s. He began
the first mass Black movement of this
century, using the twin themes of
Black nationalism and economic
independence. He also played a
major role in creating the
Harlem Renaissance.

Marcus Garvey not only rocked the boat, but opted to transport Blacks back to Africa by boat. This message would be both his calling card and his swan song.

Marcus Moziah Garvey was born in 1887, in St. Anns Bay, Jamaica. His father, Marcus, was a stonemason by trade and a descendant of the Maroon tribesmen who

200 years earlier had organized slave revolts and created autonomous societies.

By age 20, Garvey led a printers' strike. Although he was fired, he earned a reputation as a social worker, a preacher for the poor, and a speaker for the dispossessed and working classes.

In 1910, Garvey left Jamaica for Costa Rica. After settling in an area where West Indians lived, he started a newspaper, *La Nación/The Nation*, which organized immigrants. After harassment from local authorities, he packed and traveled to other Latin American nations. Two years later, he visited Europe and worked on the docks of England. Then he traveled to France, Germany, Italy, and Austria, writing in many newspapers.

But it was not until 1914, when he returned to Jamaica, that Garvey's role in history would materialize. That is when he founded, on Jamaican Independence Day, the Universal Negro Improvement Association (UNIA). It soon became one of the largest independent Black mass organizations the world had ever seen. Its simple message of race pride and self-reliance struck a chord among Blacks worldwide. UNIA was modeled after Booker T. Washington's Tuskegee Institute.

Inspired by Washington's *Up From Slavery*, Garvey left Jamaica in 1916 for the United States. He began a lecture tour that would organize chapters of the UNIA in America. In 1918, he started the *Negro World*, a newspaper that first published many major writers of the Harlem Renaissance and reached at least 50,000 readers.

Garvey was very successful, acquiring a bevy of businesses, including grocery stores, laundries, restaurants, hotels, and his prized Black Star Line—the steamship company he acquired in 1919 to link people of African descent all over the world. He ultimately bought three ships, naming them after Black leaders such as Booker T. Washington.

In 1920, Garvey campaigned for $2 million and collected $137,000 in the first few months to organize the first International Convention of the UNIA. It attracted tens of thousands of followers who marched through Harlem in colorful uniforms honoring their famous soon-to-be-notorious philosopher-prophet. He sold stock to his followers and admirers under an arrangement that barred White purchasers, according to historian Lerone Bennett, Jr. Garvey created the red, black, and green UNIA flag, which would later represent Black liberation in this century. During this same period, he unsuccessfully appealed to the League of Nations, the precursor to the United Nations, to turn over German-held African nations to independent Black rule.

Garvey had enemies, the most famous of whom was W.E.B. DuBois. Cofounder of the NAACP, DuBois was an integrationist opposed to a Black separate state and the repatriation efforts of Garvey. DuBois was also critical of Garvey's public association with the Klu Klux Klan, his criticism of "mulatto" Black leadership, and his belief in Black racial purity.

In 1923, when his steamship company went bankrupt, Garvey was convicted of mail fraud. He went to jail in 1925 for two years. His sentence was commuted by President Coolidge before he was deported to Jamaica. Garvey died in London of a stroke at age 53 without ever setting foot in Africa.

ALTHEA GIBSON

A restless, troubled youth, Althea
Gibson found solace, success, and
herself in tennis. She became the first
Black player to compete and win at
both Forest Hills (U.S. Open)
and Wimbledon——a feat she
accomplished in 1957 and
repeated in 1958.

Althea Gibson's life has been one of struggle, perse-
verance, and redemption. Overcoming an early pattern of
erratic behavior, inconsistency, and being easily frustrated,
she became the first Black player to win tennis championships at Wimbledon and the U.S. Open.

Gibson was born August 25, 1927, in Silver, South
Carolina. She and her sharecropper parents relocated to

Harlem while she was still a child. In New York, the pretty, gangly girl was frequently truant in school—prone to playing hooky and spending days at the movies.

Eventually placed in a foster home, Gibson was an embittered, restless malcontent who couldn't hold a job. But she showed remarkable prowess in street basketball, stickball, and table tennis. A New York City recreation department worker noticed her talents and introduced her to his friend Fred Johnson, a tennis pro at Harlem's elite Cosmopolitan Club.

Shortly after Gibson won her first tournament, the New York Open Championship in 1942, Cosmopolitan Club members pooled their resources to send her to more tournaments, where she did well. Gibson caught the eye of two Black doctors who were leaders in the American Tennis Association and they became her sponsors. Beginning in 1947, she won the first of ten ATA National Championships.

Her tennis success made Gibson a better student. In 1949, she graduated from high school ranked 10th in her class and went on to Florida A&M College.

Gibson's tennis ability was not to be denied. She received invitations to play in eastern and national indoor

championships and then, in 1950, became the first Black woman asked to play in the U.S. National Championship Tournament at Forest Hills, now known as the U.S. Open.

Though eliminated in the second round at Forest Hills, Gibson later traveled to Europe, Mexico, and Southeast Asia, winning 16 of 18 tournaments. That secured her a bid to Wimbledon.

But Gibson was defeated in that tournament and then again that year at Forest Hills. It wasn't until 1957 that she won the U.S. National and her first Wimbledon title. In 1958, she won both tournaments again.

Then, surprisingly, at the age of 30, Gibson gave up tennis to pursue other activities and make the money that tennis, at that point, didn't provide. She recorded albums, acted briefly, toured with the Harlem Globetrotters, and became a celebrity endorser.

Gibson played pro golf from 1963 to 1967 as the first Black member of the Ladies Professional Golf Association. Later she worked for the New Jersey State Athletic Control Board and has served as special consultant to the New Jersey Governor's Council on Physical Fitness and Sports since 1988.

BERRY GORDY, JR.

Berry Gordy's Motown Records
produced the most popular sound in
music in the 1960s and 1970s with
such stars as Stevie Wonder, Michael
Jackson, Marvin Gaye, Diana Ross,
Smokey Robinson, and The
Temptations. Gordy founded the
company at the age of 30 with an
$800 loan from his family.

Berry Gordy, Jr., parlayed a spare time hobby of writing
songs into the most successful African-American owned
record company in history, and changed the sound of pop
music along the way.

His Motown Records, started in 1959, became the
world's largest independent record company, the first

major Black-owned company in the entertainment industry, and America's largest Black business in 1973, with sales of more than $50 million.

Through Motown, which became a virtual music factory and produced hits as though they came off the assembly line, Gordy engineered superstardom for such diverse performers as Stevie Wonder, Michael Jackson, Diana Ross, Marvin Gaye, Smokey Robinson, The Temptations, and Martha and the Vandellas. These artists would all contribute their talent in altering the sometimes ragged sound of rhythm and blues and convert it into an appealing mix of layered instrumentation and vocal harmonies—appropriately titled the "Motown Sound."

Born November 28, 1929, in Detroit, one of eight children, Gordy dropped out of high school in the 11th grade to pursue a boxing career. That path ended when he was drafted into the army, where he earned his high school equivalency diploma while serving in Korea from 1951 to 1953.

Back in Detroit after the war, Gordy worked at the Ford Motor Company while writing songs when he had the chance. His breakthrough came when a young singer named Jackie Wilson recorded Gordy's song "Reet Petite," which became Wilson's first hit in 1957. In the next two years, Gordy wrote four more hits for Wilson, including "Lonely Teardrops" in 1958.

By then, Gordy had befriended another young singer named Smokey Robinson, who talked him into opening his own recording studio. With the aid of an $800 loan from his family, Berry opened his company.

The hits began immediately. The "Motown Sound," consisting of sophisticated rhythm-and-blues augmented by slick symphonic orchestrations, not only appealed to African Americans but crossed over to White America as well.

Motown's first number one pop hit came that year with "Please Mr. Postman." In 1962, when the company had 11 R&B Top 10 hits, it had four singles in the pop Top 10. The next year it had six, with Stevie Wonder's "Fingertips, Part 2" reaching number one. In 1964, five Motown hits were number one on the pop charts. The legend of Motown was born.

In 1972, Gordy moved the company to Los Angeles and branched off into films, making the successful *Lady Sings the Blues,* for which star Diana Ross received an Academy Award nomination, and *The Bingo Long Travel-*

ing All-Stars and Motor Kings. Gordy's TV special *Motown 25—Yesterday, Today, and Forever,* in 1983, was the most watched variety special in television history, and 1985's *Motown Returns to the Apollo* won an Emmy award.

Gordy sold Motown Records to MCA Inc. in 1984 for $61 million, but retained Motown's publishing company Jobete Music.

FANNIE LOU HAMER

A tireless drum major for African-
American political empowerment,
Fannie Lou Hamer was a bright light
in the firmament of the 1960s civil
rights struggle. "Sick and tired of being
sick and tired," Hamer spent her life
fighting for equality.

A farmer and educator who became a beacon of hope
for the nation's poor and politically disenfranchised, Fannie Lou Hamer became a powerful voice in the fight for
Black equality and self-reliance. Hamer's actions helped
change some of the National Democratic Party's racist
policies, and she increased Black political power by reg-
istering voters in the South.

Hamer said one of the things that made her so committed to helping poor people was watching her share-

cropping parents struggle to raise their 20 children in rural Mississippi. She was born there, in Montgomery County, October 6, 1917, and was working in the cotton fields by the time she was six years old. When she was 13, Hamer could pick 300 to 400 pounds of cotton per day and was troubled by the economic disparity between the Black workers and the White plantation owners. She married Perry Hamer in 1942, and for 18 years she worked as a sharecropper.

But in 1962, Hamer burst upon the civil rights scene after attending a stirring rally for the Southern Christian Leadership Conference (SCLC) and the Student Nonviolent Coordinating Committee (SNCC). She volunteered to challenge voting laws, but had to flee her plantation for trying to register to vote. Hamer was threatened and survived a gun attack. In 1963, she passed the literacy test many southern states used to keep Blacks from voting, and she registered.

Hamer's commitment to the movement caught fire. She became a field-worker for the SNCC. Hamer believed there was a link between Black lack of access to the political process and widespread Black poverty. She helped start Delta Ministry, a community development program.

Hamer continued to register voters and as a result was injured in a brutal beating at a rural Mississippi jail.

Since the state's Democratic party wouldn't allow Black participation, Hamer helped found the Mississippi Freedom Democratic Party (MFDP) in 1964. That group made national headlines by challenging the seating of the all-White Mississippi delegation to the Democratic National Convention in Atlantic City. Hamer spoke to the group in a televised hearing, telling the nation about the plight of Blacks trying to exercise their right to vote. She was a delegate to the 1968 convention.

Later, Hamer worked with day-care centers and developers building homes for the poor and spoke nationwide on behalf of Black self-reliance. She spoke for many oppressed African Americans when she told America, "I'm sick and tired of being sick and tired."

A lifelong force of strength for her people, Hamer died of cancer March 14, 1977.

W. C. HANDY

W.C. Handy, known as "Father of the Blues," was the first to put southern Black folk songs, which previously had been handed down orally, into written form. He reworked them in a blues format and his publishing company helped popularize them across America and the world.

William Christopher Handy's father was a former slave and Methodist minister who discouraged his son's interest in music but allowed him to pursue it only if he did not get involved in what his parents called "that low-down" music—ragtime and blues. But Handy was a teenager; he wanted to do what teens of any era want to do—swing with the rhythms of the day.

Handy was born November 16, 1873, in Florence, Alabama. In high school, he studied organ and trained in formal music theory to satisfy his parents, but on the side he played cornet in a local brass band and sang with church groups and minstrel troupes.

By age 18, he was an outstanding trumpet player. Two years later, his quartet enjoyed acclaim after appearing at the Chicago Columbian Exposition of 1893. Buoyed by that success, Handy's band toured the United States, Mexico, and Cuba, playing ragtime and minstrel music, including the marches of John Philip Sousa and the songs of Stephen Foster.

Traveling through the South, Handy became enamored of the rich musical heritage perpetuated by Black itinerant blues singers playing their folk music on homemade guitars.

In Memphis in 1909, a political jingle he wrote in a bluesy fashion for a mayoral candidate (the infamous "Boss" Crump) enjoyed widespread popularity. Stimulated by that success, Handy started composing blues songs and collecting Black folk music, which he published in blues form. The most famous of these pieces is "St. Louis Blues," which Handy had published in 1914.

He moved to New York to make his first recordings in 1918. Soon, his highly successful publishing company led the field in introducing the music of African-American songwriters to the general public. This led to the "race records" marketing craze of the 1920s. Handy's songs became national hits and moneymakers.

Because of his formal training, Handy was able to capture in written form what was basically orally handed-down folk music of Blacks in the South. His success in the commercial marketplace then allowed him to promote this music nationally and, eventually, worldwide. If not for Handy, the blues may have remained virtually unknown or stayed in regional obscurity.

Handy lost his sight following World War I, then partially regained it. Then in 1943, he fell from a subway platform and became totally blind. He suffered a stroke in 1955, which left him wheelchair-bound, and died March 28, 1958, from pneumonia.

Handy was survived by his second wife, Louise, whom he had married at the age of 80, the same year that Handy was portrayed in the movie *St. Louis Blues* by Nat "King" Cole.

LORRAINE HANSBERRY

Lorraine Hansberry is credited with
beginning the modern era of Black
American theater because of the
success of her Broadway play *A Raisin
in the Sun*, which in 1959 became the
first Black production to win the
prestigious New York Drama Critics
Circle Award.

A bright star who blazed brilliantly but whose light died
out too soon, Lorraine Hansberry wrote the play that is
credited with giving birth to the modern Black American
theater.

A Raisin in the Sun opened on Broadway in 1959. It
won the distinguished New York Drama Critics Circle
Award that year over such heavy competition as plays by

Tennessee Williams, Eugene O'Neill, and Archibald MacLeish.

Her brilliant work, about the experiences and aspirations of a poor Black family living in a Chicago ghetto, was Hansberry's first play. She began writing it at the age of 26, and when she received the Drama Critics Circle Award at age 29, she was the youngest playwright, the fifth woman, and the first Black to receive the honor.

The Broadway production, which ran for 19 months, starred such notable actors as Sidney Poitier, Diana Sands, Claudia McNeil, and Ruby Dee. This original cast also starred in the movie version of the work, which won the Best Picture Award, along with other awards, at the Cannes Film Festival in 1961.

Unfortunately, *A Raisin in the Sun* was the height of Hansberry's short career—she died of cancer six years after its debut on January 12, 1965, at the age of 34.

Hansberry was born May 19, 1930, in Chicago to a well-to-do family. Her parents opened a successful real estate firm and one of the first Black banks in Chicago. The home of her youth was frequented by such luminaries as Walter White, Jesse Owens, Langston Hughes, Duke Ellington, and Paul Robeson.

Hansberry studied art, English, and stage design for two years at the University of Wisconsin, then moved to New York in 1950. There she joined Paul Robeson's Harlem-based *Freedom* magazine. As associate editor from 1952 to 1953, she wrote articles dealing with Africa, women's issues, and social issues. She also wrote several reviews of plays, which provided the impetus for her to write her own plays.

After *A Raisin in the Sun*, Hansberry worked on a number of projects, most of which remained uncompleted, including a novel and collection of essays. Her last completed stage work was *The Sign in Sidney Brustein's Window*, about a Greenwich Village intellectual and his role in a local election. The play made it to Broadway in 1964 for 101 performances and was still running when Hansberry died.

After her death, her unpublished papers were assembled into the play *To Be Young, Gifted and Black*, which toured nationally from 1970 to 1971 and was later expanded into Hansberry's biography.

DOROTHY IRENE HEIGHT

Social activist Dorothy Height has
spent decades trumpeting the fight for
African-American civil rights,
women's issues, and economic
well-being for people worldwide.
Height's work with many private
and government social service agencies
has helped millions.

Dorothy Irene Height is a social worker focused on improving conditions for Blacks, women, and the poor. Her clarion oratory, plus her work with groups ranging from the Young Women's Christian Association (YWCA) and the Delta Sigma Theta Sorority, Inc. (DST) to the National Council of Negro Women (NCNW) have made her a leader in the battle for equality and human rights. Height's cur-

rent project centers on revitalizing African-American family values.

Height was born March 24, 1912, in Richmond, Virginia. Her family moved to the small town of Rankin, Pennsylvania, where Height was a tall, straight-A student who excelled in athletics. She was active in the YWCA as a teenager and has stayed involved most of her life. Height went to New York University for college, earning both her bachelor's and master's degrees in four years. She also studied at Columbia University and the New York School of Social Work.

Height's youth club activities took her to several Christian youth conferences in the United States, Holland, and England. She also helped Eleanor Roosevelt plan a 1938 World Youth Congress in New York. At the same time, while working for New York's Welfare Department, Height was asked to examine the unrest following the 1935 riots in Harlem. During this period, Height met NCNW founder and magnetic civil rights activist Mary McLeod Bethune. Height began volunteering in the group's quest for women's rights.

Height began her long career with the YWCA in 1938, running a lodging home for Black women in Harlem, then

later in Washington, D.C. The powerful speaker ran training programs for YWCA volunteers and developed programs for interracial education. Height eventually helped desegregate the YWCA and later directed its Center for Racial Justice.

In 1939, Height began her tenure with DST, guiding the national Black sorority toward a greater commitment to activism. She was national president from 1947 to 1956, during which time she established the group's first international chapter in Haiti, and she organized bookmobiles for African-American communities in the South.

Height then took on one of her most powerful positions: president of NCNW, an umbrella group for women's rights organizations. The council's goals include uniting Black women of all classes and stressing interrace cooperation. During Height's tenure, NCNW has helped women open businesses, sponsored job training, and run voter registration programs. Height continues to guide its fight for equal rights for women of color worldwide. Since 1986, the council has sponsored annual celebrations nationwide called Black Family Reunions. These reunions are an attempt to renew the concept of the extended Black family and thereby to improve social conditions.

Height, the recipient of numerous awards and honorary degrees, continues to be a firebrand in the struggle to improve the lives of Blacks and women.

CHARLES HOUSTON

Charles Houston was the legal architect retained by the NAACP as special counsel to help dismantle discrimination in public education and transportation. His successful arguments before the Supreme Court and other bodies laid the groundwork for the *Brown* v. *Board of Education* case, which eventually ended all legally sanctioned segregation in America.

Charles Hamilton Houston was a brilliant lawyer. His successful appearances before the U.S. Supreme Court on matters of racial discrimination laid the groundwork for the landmark *Brown* v. *Topeka, Kansas Board of Education* case. This case ended racial segregation in public schools.

Because the *Brown* case led to further court decisions out-lawing various other forms of discrimination and to legislation enacting civil rights laws, it can be said that Houston had a major impact on dismantling legally sanctioned racism in America.

Born September 3, 1895, in Washington, D.C., Houston showed his brilliance early when he graduated from high school at the age of 15. He then graduated from Amherst College four years later as a Phi Beta Kappa and one of six class valedictorians.

Houston earned his law degree from Harvard University in 1922, graduating cum laude and in the top five percent of his class. He became the first Black student selected as an editor of the *Harvard Law Review*, and in 1923, the first African American awarded a doctor of judicial science degree from Harvard.

That same year, he received a one-year fellowship to study civil law at the University of Madrid. Houston was admitted to the D.C. bar in 1924. From 1924 to 1950, Houston had a private practice with his father, William, who was a graduate of Howard University's law school. During those years, however, there were various interruptions in Houston's practice.

Houston also taught at Howard. As vice dean, appointed in 1929, he was in charge of the university's three-year day program and the law school library. His most notable accomplishments there were helping the law school receive accreditation from legal sanctioning bodies and significantly improving the curriculum.

In 1934, Houston took a leave of absence from Howard. The NAACP retained him as special counsel to direct a campaign against discrimination in public education and transportation. This work would establish the strategy of the NAACP to end all legal segregation. His assistant special counsel was Thurgood Marshall, who would go on successfully to argue the *Brown* case in 1954.

In two of Houston's early Supreme Court cases, in 1935 and 1938, the court overturned death sentences of Black defendants who had been convicted by juries from which Blacks had been excluded because of race. In 1938, Houston also won his argument in *Missouri ex rel. Gaines* v. *Canada*. The Supreme Court ruled that the state of Missouri could not bar Blacks from entering the state university law school without providing a separate but equal law school for Blacks.

The *Missouri* case was a major victory for Houston and for the NAACP. It forced the Supreme Court to take a hard look at the good-faith efforts of states to provide equal accommodations under the "separate but equal" policy. In this case, Missouri had been willing to provide scholarships for African Americans willing to go to other states to study law. However, the Supreme Court saw that as a way for Missouri to duck the expense of maintaining its own state law school for Black students.

In the 1940s, as a member of the NAACP's National Legal Committee and as general counsel of the Association of Colored Railway Trainmen and Locomotive Firemen and of the International Association of Railroad Employees, Houston argued two successful cases before the Court that outlawed racial discrimination in union bargaining representation.

When Houston passed away in April 1950, from a heart ailment at the age of 54, five Supreme Court justices attended his funeral. He was respected in legal circles for his ability as a constitutional lawyer and for the brilliance of his attacks on discrimination.

LANGSTON HUGHES

Langston Hughes was a poet with
the genius to set his mellifluous voice
to music——both literally and
figuratively. A prolific novelist and
playwright as well, Hughes used verse
to illustrate Black urban life and
attack social injustice.

Langston Hughes wrote poetry from the time he was
a child. His devastatingly observant yet sorrowful exam-
inations of African-American life in Harlem, and the Black
experience in general, are considered to be some of the
most powerful writings of the 20th century. One of
Hughes's most famous poems, "I, Too, Sing America," is
a powerful plea to the country to recognize and accept
Blacks on the basis of their myriad contributions. He was
mentor to a generation of writers. Hughes was one of the

most important voices of the Harlem Renaissance of the 1920s, and of the Civil Rights Movement of the 1960s.

> Happiness lives nowhere,
> Some old folk said,
> If not within oneself.

That line, from Hughes's poem "I Thought It Was Tangiers I Wanted," speaks volumes about the life of a man whose travels took him to some of the world's most exotic places, including Mexico, Spain, and Africa. Born in February of 1902, Hughes had already lived in seven cities in the U.S. and Mexico by the time he was 12. The handsome writer had been class poet in grammar school, and he didn't lay down his pen throughout his life. For several years after school he traveled, teaching and working as a servant. Then in 1924, writer and critic Vachel Lindsay "discovered" Hughes. He dubbed him the "bus boy poet."

In 1926, Hughes published his first book of poetry, *The Weary Blues*, followed by several volumes remarkable for the musical nature of the language. In later works, Hughes sometimes gave directions for musical accompaniment to his verses, making him one of the earliest writers to combine the two forms. One of Hughes's plays, *Mulatto* (1935), had a successful run on Broadway in New York. In the 1940s, Hughes created Jesse B. Simple, a fictional character in Hughes's *Chicago Defender* column, who represented the lives and racial consciousness of the Black working class.

In all, Hughes published more than ten volumes of poetry, a little over 60 dramas, and scores of operas, anthologies of other Black writers, and two autobiographies. During the 1930s, Hughes took aim at civil rights and economic issues. Ten years later, Hughes took his genius for observation and his talent for relating to the working class to several universities. He taught at Atlanta University, then he was poet-in-residence at the University of Chicago's Laboratory School. In the 1960s, Hughes turned out an incredible volume of material, including *Ask Your Mama: 12 Moods for Jazz* (1961), and his last volume of poetry, *The Panther and the Lash* (1967).

Hughes, considered by many to be the "poet laureate of Harlem," died of congestive heart failure in New York in March 1967.

ZORA NEALE HURSTON

Zora Neale Hurston was a major contributor to the Harlem Renaissance. She was also an anthropologist, playwright, novelist, and feminist who never achieved true fame in her lifetime because she was an outspoken, proud Black woman.

Critics and readers alike marvel at the woman we've come to know as Zora Neale Hurston. A writer, anthropologist, and eccentric personality who reigned during the 1920s and 1930s, Hurston created a stir just about every time she appeared in public.

Always outspoken, flamboyant, and colorful, Hurston never backed down from anyone—friend or foe. She spoke her mind and she wrote with the same ferocious clarity. In doing so, she created a legion of fans who have spanned generations. But during her own lifetime, Hurston stepped on many toes, and those people exacted sweet revenge on her. She proudly said that being misunderstood was the price she paid for daring to be great. And great she was.

Hurston created a prolific body of writing—plays, essays, novels, short stories, and anthropological studies—that both titillated and taunted the working and upper classes of Blacks and Whites. Her sterling masterpiece, *Their Eyes Were Watching God*, thrust her into literary dominance as a major player of the Harlem Renaissance. Ironically, after a few decades of being a celebrity, she died unnoticed in Florida from a long illness and was buried in a pauper's grave.

Hurston was born January 7, 1891, in the all-Black town of Eatonville, Florida. She lived a joyful young life. Her parents and her neighbors gave her the kind of support that was not always available to African Americans, while groping with survival under racial discrimination and a lack of economic opportunities. The world she knew broke apart, however, when her mother died in 1904. Her father then sent her to a boarding school, and her family scattered.

Hurston wandered from job to job until she found a position as a maid and wardrobe assistant in a traveling Gilbert and Sullivan theater company. Although she was bitten by the showbiz bug during this period, she finished high school at Morgan Academy in Baltimore. She received her college education at Howard University, and then earned a graduate degree in anthropology from Barnard College, where she studied under Franz Boas.

With the help of literary lions Charles S. Johnson and Alain Locke, she began her illustrious career by publishing short stories in *Opportunity* magazine. Collaborating with Langston Hughes and Wallace Thurman, Hurston edited *Fire!* magazine.

Four years later, Hurston cowrote *Mule Bone* with Hughes. It is a comedy about African-American life that was never performed during her lifetime because Hurston and Hughes later had a falling out over personal and professional reasons.

Meanwhile, after developing her skills as an anthropologist, she wrote her second volume of folklore, *Tell My Horse*, published in 1938. It was largely ignored at the time because of taboos associated with the subject, but it is the most comprehensive look at voodoo in Jamaica and

Haiti. During the 1940s and 1950s, Hurston suffered a quiet period because the naturalism of Richard Wright's novels and Ann Petry's feminist-naturalism supplanted her popular folk voice. Even in this "quiet" period she published her autobiography, *Dust Tracks on a Road* (1942); another novel, *Seraph on the Suwanee* (1948); and several articles.

Modern audiences might have ignored Hurston's work, especially *Their Eyes Were Watching God*, had it not been for writer Alice Walker's revival of her material in the 1970s. Walker drew attention to Hurston's literary genius and feminism.

Much of the controversy over Hurston's fictional work centered on her rejection of the prevailing notion that Black culture was inferior and immoral. Additionally, Hurston rejected notions that women are subservient to men. These controversies caused her career to plummet, and she died poor and alone in 1960.

JESSE JACKSON

One of the nation's most important
Black leaders, the Rev. Jesse Jackson is
an eloquent, charismatic spokesman for
economic justice and human rights in
America and abroad. In 1984 and
1988, he made serious bids to become
president of the United States,
finishing second in 1988's Democratic
primary. Jackson currently directs
Operation PUSH and the National
Rainbow Coalition.

Rev. Jesse Jackson has spent the last 35 years of public
service in pursuit of economic justice and human rights
for dispossessed Americans from all walks of life. He also
has been instrumental in working for peace in various re-

gions of the world. Jackson's activities have made him one of America's most important African-American leaders and an international statesman.

He is so firmly entrenched as a force for political and social change that in 1984 and again in 1988 he was able to make the most successful bid by a Black candidate in American history to become president of the United States. In 1984, Jackson captured over 3.5 million votes, 21 percent of the popular vote.

In 1988, Jackson, for a time, was the front-runner for the Democratic nomination after winning six southern states, the state of Michigan with 55 percent of the vote, and finishing second in Illinois. Though he eventually came in a strong second behind nominee Michael Dukakis, Jackson's bid attracted almost seven million voters—a "rainbow coalition" from all across America. This allowed him to exert considerable influence on the issues in the Democratic platform.

Being taken seriously as a presidential candidate was quite a rise from Jackson's humble origins. He was born October 8, 1941, in Greenville, South Carolina, to a 17-year-old unwed high school mother. They, along with his stepfather, lived in a three-room cottage with no indoor plumbing until he was in sixth grade. This environment may have produced in Jackson a strong need to prove himself and to succeed.

Jackson won a college athletic scholarship to the University of Illinois, but racism there led him to return to North Carolina A&T College, where he became class president. He attended Chicago Theological Seminary and was ordained as a Baptist minister in 1968.

Jackson joined the Civil Rights Movement while at North Carolina A&T, and during demonstrations in Selma, Alabama, in 1965, he became an aide to Dr. Martin Luther King, Jr. King appointed Jackson head of Operation Breadbasket in Chicago in 1966. As the economic arm of King's Southern Christian Leadership Conference, Breadbasket used boycotts and selective buying strategies to induce White-owned businesses to carry Black-produced products and to hire Black workers.

In 1971, Jackson left the organization to found Operation PUSH (People United to Save Humanity), which expanded the economic mission of Breadbasket into the social and political arenas as well.

In 1984, Jackson also founded the National Rainbow Coalition to address the problems of the disenfranchised.

In July 1990, he was elected "shadow senator" to try to attain statehood for the District of Columbia. He was sworn into office in January 1991.

As he continues these activities, Jackson also mentors his son Jesse Jackson, Jr., who in 1995 was elected Representative from Illinois's Second Congressional District.

JACK JOHNSON

Jack Johnson became the first African-American boxing champion of the world in 1908, holding his title until 1915, when he lost it in a 26th-round knockout by Jess Willard. In total, Johnson's ring career lasted 48 years. He is considered one of the greatest boxers in the history of the sport.

In the early 20th century, when race relations were at one of the lowest points in history and lynchings and race riots occurred with regularity, John Arthur "Jack" Johnson became boxing's first Black heavyweight champion of the world.

In 1908, Johnson won the title with a vicious beating of Canadian Tommy Burns. For 13 rounds, Johnson kept

up a running conversation with Burns, even as he was dismantling him. Although bloodied, Burns would not quit. Finally, police entered the ring in the 14th round to stop the fight.

The new champion became an instant hero to most of Black America and a despised foe for much of White America, whose boasts of superiority over Blacks in all areas were shattered.

Fanning the flames of hatred for Johnson was the fact that he was an arrogant figure in the ring and out—he swaggered, wore flashy clothes and jewelry, had six cars and a large entourage, and displayed a penchant for openly romancing White women.

As a result, the boxing community came up with a succession of "Great White Hopes" to try and dethrone this "uppity" Black fighter. Although controversial, Johnson was also one of the greatest boxers in history. He fought professionally from 1897 to 1928 and boxed in exhibitions as late as 1945. In those 48 years in the ring, he fought 114 bouts and was KOed only three times.

Born on March 31, 1878, in Galveston, Texas, Johnson quit school after fifth grade and worked a variety of odd jobs, including longshoring on the city's docks, which

helped build his muscle strength. Despite his parents' objections, he began training as a boxer. After several amateur events, Johnson turned professional in 1897 at the age of 19, when he stood over six feet in height and weighed 180 pounds.

By 1901, Johnson was the best Black boxer in Texas and began successfully boxing across the country. After winning the "Negro" heavyweight championship in 1903, he demanded to fight Jim Jeffries, the reigning White champion. Jeffries decided to retire rather than demean himself by fighting a Black man.

Tommy Burns won the vacated title, and financial considerations led him to fight Johnson. When Johnson humiliated Burns, Jeffries was lured out of retirement as the major "White hope" to defeat him. Johnson's 15th-round knockout of Jeffries in 1910 led to several deadly race riots around the country.

Johnson was convicted in 1913 of violating the Mann Act for transporting his girlfriend, later his wife, across state lines for unlawful purposes. He was sentenced to a year in jail. He and his wife fled to Canada, then to France.

Johnson defended his title until 1915, when he lost it in a 26th-round knockout by Jess Willard in Cuba. Con-

troversy still reigns about the outcome; there is specula-
tion that Johnson "threw" the fight hoping the government
would drop charges against him. He continued to fight
exhibitions around the world and revel in his flamboyant
lifestyle until June 10, 1946, when he died in a car crash.

JAMES WELDON JOHNSON

An accomplished man of letters,
James Weldon Johnson helped
advance the cause of African
Americans through his literary and
musical contributions, and with a 10-
year stint as head of the NAACP.
He also wrote the Black national
anthem "Lift Every Voice and Sing."

James Weldon Johnson was a true Renaissance man—
historian, novelist, poet, educator. During his storied and
varied life, he elevated the advancement of Blacks in
America through his literary, musical, and educational
contributions, his organizational accomplishments with
the NAACP, and his service as diplomat and U.S. consul
to foreign nations.

Johnson was a conservative man who believed in racial assimilation. Like his friend Booker T. Washington, he considered it the major responsibility of Blacks to lift themselves up by their own bootstraps. He believed that to remove the label of "inferior," Blacks needed to prove their intellectual and physical equality.

Johnson excelled in all his endeavors. His accomplishments made him the most popular leader in the African-American community in his day behind Washington himself.

He is best known for writing the lyrics to "Lift Every Voice and Sing," which is considered the Black national anthem. Also, his 10-year stint as head of the NAACP was during a period when the organization experienced tremendous growth.

Johnson was born on June 17, 1871, in Jacksonville, Florida. His mother encouraged him and his brother, John, to study music, art, and literature. But there was no high school for Blacks in Jacksonville, so James moved to Atlanta to complete his education through college.

After college, Johnson returned to Jacksonville and established courses that would lead to a high school degree for Blacks. He then became principal of that high school.

He also studied law and became the first Black lawyer to pass the Florida bar in 1898.

The racial climate at the time led Johnson and his brother to move to New York in 1902, where they were successful in writing musical comedies. They also penned a string of 200 songs for the Broadway stage.

While in New York, Johnson studied literature at Columbia University. He also began a growing interest in politics. In 1904, he became treasurer of New York City's Colored Republican Club and developed an association with Booker T. Washington.

At the urging of Booker T. Washington, President Teddy Roosevelt appointed Johnson U.S. consul to Venezuela in 1906 and to Nicaragua in 1908. His consular positions gave Johnson enough free time to pursue writing. In 1912, he published *The Autobiography of an Ex-Colored Man*, one of the first accounts of a Black passing for White. He also became an editor and a popular columnist for the *New York Age* in 1914.

Johnson believed success in the literary and arts fields, as well as politics, by African Americans would help break down racial barriers. He became an advocate and literary critic of Black artistic works and compiled such pioneering anthologies as *The Book of American Negro Poetry* and *The Book of American Negro Spirituals.* In *Black Manhattan,* Johnson promoted Harlem as the center of Black culture during the famed Harlem Renaissance.

His works of poetry included two collections—*Fifty Years & Other Poems* and the book for which he is most remembered, *God's Trombones.* The last book is a group of sermons written in verse using Black vernacular.

In 1916, W.E.B. DuBois urged Johnson to accept an offer to become a national organizer for the NAACP. Johnson was particularly successful in opening new branches in the South.

In 1920, he became executive secretary of the NAACP, the first African American to hold that post. For the next decade, Johnson was one of the most prominent Black leaders of his time.

In recognition of his large body of literary work, Johnson was appointed to the Adam K. Spence Chair of Creative Literature and Writing at Fisk University in October 1930. He resigned from the NAACP in December of that year. Working at the university allowed him to write, travel, lecture, and mentor other promising African Americans.

Johnson died an untimely death on June 26, 1938, when a train struck his car during a blinding rainstorm at an unguarded railroad crossing.

JOHN H. JOHNSON

John H. Johnson has been a publishing
magnate for more than 50 years with
his *Ebony* and *Jet* magazines, which
have made him one of the richest Black
men in America. Admitted to
numerous halls of fame, he also sits on
the boards of major American
corporations and institutions.

By sheer strength of will and determination, John Harold
Johnson rose from the poverty he experienced as a child
growing up in rural Arkansas to become one of the richest African-American men in the nation. He founded and
runs the Johnson Publishing Company empire, which for
decades was by far the largest Black business in American history.

Since 1945, Johnson has published *Ebony* magazine, a lifestyle and general interest publication for Black America, which has a circulation of almost two million copies a month and is the crown jewel of his business. Johnson's second gold mine is *Jet*, a pocket-sized weekly magazine that has provided news to the Black community since 1951.

Other facets of his business conglomerate include *EM: Ebony Man* magazine, Fashion Fair Cosmetics, and the Ebony Fashion Fair. Johnson has also owned radio stations, an insurance company, extensive real estate, a mail-order firm, and a nationally syndicated TV show. He has published several other magazines, which have had lives of varying lengths. His combined businesses have given Johnson a net worth of $150 million (as of 1989).

Johnson was born January 19, 1918, in Arkansas City, Arkansas, which had no public high school for Blacks. After taking eighth grade twice, he was brought to Chicago in 1933 by his mother to continue his education.

The ridicule he suffered at school because of his tattered clothes intensified Johnson's efforts to succeed. He pushed himself to become student council president, editor of the school newspaper, and an honor student.

In 1933, Harry Pace, president of Supreme Life Insurance Company, then the largest Black business in America, met young John at an Urban League dinner. He gave Johnson a job so that he could afford college. Johnson attended Northwestern and the University of Chicago, but dropped out to work full-time as Pace's personal assistant. (He eventually bought Pace's company.)

Part of his job was to give Pace a weekly briefing on news events of interest to Blacks, which gave Johnson the idea of developing a magazine to deliver such news to the Black community at large.

When no one would back his idea, he borrowed $500, using his mother's furniture as collateral. With the money, he paid for a mailing to Supreme Insurance's client list seeking prepaid subscriptions to his newly proposed magazine.

The mailing produced enough subscriptions for Johnson to publish his first issue of *Negro Digest* in November 1942. By the end of 1943, the magazine had a circulation of 50,000; circulation had doubled after an October column written by First Lady Eleanor Roosevelt that same year. In November 1945, Johnson was able to launch *Ebony*, which provides positive role models and stories of Black success. The magazine immediately sold out its initial 25,000-copy press run.

Johnson still runs his empire as chairman of the board. Day-to-day operations are now handled by his daughter, Linda Johnson Rice, whom "The Publisher" (as he is called by his friends and associates) named president and chief operating officer of Johnson Publishing Company in 1989.

SCOTT JOPLIN

Known as the King of Ragtime,
Scott Joplin had no equal as the
preeminent composer of the popular
dance music form of his day. His
"Maple Leaf Rag" was the big hit
that caused ragtime to be the moving
force in popular music the world
over for nearly 17 years.

The raucous, intoxicating music form that was the world-wide rage from the turn of the century until about 1917 was largely the result of the work of Scott Joplin. Others may have called ragtime "jig piano," but Joplin preferred the term "syncopated piano music."

Joplin was born November 24, 1868, in Texarkana, Texas. His father was an ex-slave who played the fiddle

and deserted the family early in Joplin's life. His mother was freeborn and she played the banjo. While growing up in a musical household, Joplin showed improvisational talent on the keyboard at an early age. Once his father left, Joplin's mother gave him the music lessons that he needed. She did this despite raising six children by herself. His mother took him along to houses where she did domestic work, so that Joplin could hone his skills practicing on pianos in those family parlors.

Joplin's talent, especially in improvisation, soon led him to become the talk of the area among Blacks and even several Whites. Capable volunteers instructed him in formal piano and harmony. They also instilled in the young man a lifelong interest in music education.

In the mid-1880s, in part to ease the burden on his mother, Joplin left Texarkana. He wandered as an itinerant piano player, becoming a "professa" (a pianist who plays by memory) in the world of honky-tonks and bordellos. It was here that he learned to rag. But he also played in churches, at respected "socials," and in vaudeville with a group called the Texas Medley Quartette (which originally had five members and then reorganized with eight members).

In 1894, Joplin settled in Sedalia, Missouri, attending the George R. Smith College for Negroes. Here he took courses in music composition and harmony. He also resumed his professa-ship at Sedalia's Maple Leaf Club.

Once his major compositions began to be published, in 1899, the richness, originality, and painstaking craftsmanship that marked Joplin's music garnered great appreciation. It also established him as more than a ragtime hack.

His "Maple Leaf Rag" sold more than one million copies of sheet music at the time of publication and fueled the ragtime explosion in popular music. The song earned Joplin the title King of Ragtime and brought him the financial security to break away from the honky-tonk circuit.

He continued to produce great rag piano works, such as "The Entertainer," which was immortalized in the popular 1973 film *The Sting.* Joplin began turning to different forms of music composition that brought him less success and more depression.

He produced a folk ballet called *The Ragtime Dance* in 1899 and then a ragtime opera in 1903 called *A Guest of Honor,* which received lukewarm public reaction at best.

In fact, he went broke trying to stage *A Guest of Honor* on an unsuccessful tour. This forced Joplin to return to creating rags, which were always a source of commercial and financial success for him.

He tried another attempt at serious music with the opera *Treemonisha*, an ode to his mother, which he published in 1911. Repeated unsuccessful attempts to mount a full-scale production of the opera caused Joplin increasingly severe bouts of depression. Over the next five years, his mental deterioration progressed rapidly until the autumn of 1916, when he was committed to the Manhattan State Hospital. He died there on April 1, 1917.

Ironically, because of the interest in Joplin and ragtime in the 1970s, he has attained the status of a serious classical composer. In 1970, a classical label released a collection of his rags performed by classical musician Joshua Rifkin. After the New York City Library published a two-volume set in 1971 called *The Collected Works of Scott Joplin*, classical artists began regularly including his compositions in their concert performances. The movie *The Sting* also popularized several of his rags.

Even his beloved *Treemonisha* was revived, first in concert form by the Atlanta Symphony and then in a full-

MICHAEL JORDAN

Michael Jordan was cut from his high school basketball team as a sophomore, but came back as an upperclassman to become All-American. He helped North Carolina win the NCAA championship in 1982, was named College Player of the Year in 1983 and 1984, and was selected as the third player in the 1984 draft.

No one ever played the game of basketball as fluently as Michael Jordan, nicknamed "Air" because of his extraordinary ability to float off the ground longer than seemingly possible in order to perform his scoring magic. The Chicago Bulls' acrobatic shooting guard led the team to

five National Basketball Association (NBA) championships from 1991 to 1993, 1996, and 1997.

The strength of his game is his completeness as a player. With no weakness, Jordan is equally adept at scoring, defending, passing, and rebounding. Coupled with his limitless physical talents are an intense focus, fierce determination, inspired leadership, and biting sense of competition.

The records, awards, and achievements collected by "His Airness" are a testament to his greatness: Most Valuable Player for four seasons (1988, 1991, 1992, 1996), in five NBA Finals (1991 to 1993, 1996, 1997), and two All-Star Games (1988, 1996); Defensive Player of the Year in 1988; and Rookie of the Year in 1985. He also helped the United States win two Olympic gold medals (1984, 1992).

Attesting to his all-around game, Jordan was named to the All-NBA first team for seven straight years (1987 to 1993) and the All-Defensive first team six straight years (1988 to 1993). He was the second player in league history (along with Wilt Chamberlain) to win seven straight scoring titles (1987 to 1993). He also won that title in 1996, making him the record holder for the title.

Jordan's a virtual scoring machine. He is the Bulls' all-time leader, with more than 24,000 points so far. Jordan's personal highs include 69 points against Cleveland in 1990 and a playoff-record 63 points against Boston in 1986. He's scored 50 or more points 35 times and set an NBA record for consecutive points with 23 scored against Atlanta in 1987.

Jordan holds the career record for scoring in All-Star Games at 21.9 points (he's played in nine of them) and the career scoring average in the playoffs at 34.4 points.

In the 1993 NBA Finals against Phoenix, Jordan set records for highest scoring average at 41 points, most total points at 246, and most baskets made at 101. In the 1992 Finals against Portland, Jordan scored 35 points in the first half of Game 1, setting a finals record; his six three-point baskets in that half tied another record.

Born February 17, 1963, in Brooklyn, New York, Jordan grew up in Wilmington, North Carolina. In 1993, after the Bulls' third championship and the murder of his father, James Jordan, Michael retired from the sport for a year and a half to rest and play professional baseball.

But after batting only .202 as a minor leaguer, Jordan returned to basketball late in the 1994–95 season. In

1996, he led the Bulls to an NBA-record 72-game winning season.

Jordan's efforts are not all on the basketball court, though. In an era where sports stars are no longer heroes, he has remained an example to children. Through a self-named foundation run by his mother, he has worked to help underprivileged kids. Though he is disbanding the foundation, he plans to continue his work with inner-city children and donating to other charities.

MAULANA KARENGA

"Maulana" Ron Karenga created the Kwanzaa cultural holiday for people of African descent in 1966. The seven principles celebrated during the festival are unity, self-determination, collective work and responsibility, cooperative economics, purpose, creativity, and faith. Karenga is chairman of the Black Studies Department at California State University at Long Beach.

For the past 30 years, in the last week of December, African Americans have celebrated the increasingly popular cultural holiday known as Kwanzaa. The ritual, a combination of ancient African traditions fused with the newer traditions of Black Americans, was created in

1966 by Dr. Ron Karenga, chairman of the Black Studies Department at California State University at Long Beach. Karenga is known by the title of "Maulana," a Swahili word meaning master-teacher.

Kwanzaa celebrates seven principles—one each day of the holiday—that are rooted in African history and which were selected by Karenga as keys to building the Black family, community, and culture.

The principles, called *Nguzo Saba*, include *umoja* (unity), *kujichagulia* (self-determination), *ujima* (collective work and responsibility), *ujamaa* (cooperative economics), *nia* (purpose), *kuumba* (creativity), and *imani* (faith). The holiday begins on December 26 and concludes on January 1, as *kwanzaa* itself means first. (Africans have historically held celebrations at the occasion of the first harvests of the year.) In the spirit of *umoja* (unity), Karenga deliberately selected the terms for the principles from the common Swahili language, which represents all of Africa instead of any particular group or tribe. He wanted the Kwanzaa festival to be celebrated by all people of African descent in America and throughout the world, regardless of their individual religious and political beliefs and practices.

Karenga also created the popular red, black, and green flag as a symbol of the Kwanzaa celebration: red for the struggle, black for the people, green for their hope. The idea of the holiday caught on during the Black Power days of the Civil Rights Movement, as African Americans gained a heightened awareness of their heritage and their culture. Kwanzaa has become ingrained in American culture ever since.

Born in Maryland in 1941, Karenga holds two Ph.D.s from the University of California at Los Angeles, one in social ethics, the other in political science. As a doctoral candidate in 1965, Karenga founded the United Slaves (US) Cultural Organization following the riots in Watts in Los Angeles.

Karenga believed that the key to helping Black Americans was rescuing and reconstructing their original African culture and using it as a foundation to learn about and help understand who they are. While he was with US, Karenga created Kwanzaa, after researching African cultures throughout history.

US disbanded in 1974, while Karenga was serving a four-year sentence on a controversial charge of assaulting one of the group's members. He used the time to begin a

MARTIN LUTHER KING, JR.

Dr. Martin Luther King, Jr., was a
prominent civil rights leader who
remains the most outstanding symbol
of that movement, which led to voting
rights for African Americans and an
end to legal employment discrimination
and segregation of public facilities.
King won the Nobel Peace Prize in
1964, and his birthday is now a
national holiday.

The Reverend Dr. Martin Luther King, Jr., was the leading organizer of the Civil Rights Movement of the 1950s
and 1960s, which led to the abolition of legal discrimination against African Americans in employment, desegregation of public places, and voting rights for Blacks.

King's success came from elevating the issue of equality into a moral crusade. He appealed to the conscience of the nation and brought pressure on the federal government to pass legislation that remedied many of society's inequities.

The strategy employed by the self-described "drum major" for peace and justice was nonviolent direct action protests—including demonstrations, sit-ins, pray-ins, marches, and boycotts. These drew attention to discrimination.

This eloquent, stirring orator was able to convince people of goodwill that justice is inherent in the civil rights cause. He galvanized Blacks into actions that were fraught with danger; indeed, actions that cost King his own life when he was assassinated in 1968 at the age of 39.

But his courageous vision and dedication earned him the nation's highest accolades, including the NAACP's Spingarn Medal in 1957; the Nobel Peace Prize in 1964—the youngest recipient and only the second Black so honored; and the Presidential Medal of Freedom in 1977. King became the first Black American to be named *Time* magazine's "Man of the Year" in 1964, and in 1986, Congress designated his birthday a national holiday.

King was born on January 15, 1929, in Atlanta, Georgia, into a family of Black ministers. At age 15, he was accepted into Morehouse College under a program for gifted students and he received his bachelor's degree in sociology at age 19.

Admitted into Crozer Theological Seminary in Chester, Pennsylvania, King graduated first in his class and was the first Black student body president. On a fellowship to Boston University, he received his Ph.D. in systematic theology in 1955. While there, he met and married Coretta Scott.

After college, King accepted the pastorship at Dexter Avenue Baptist Church in Montgomery, Alabama. In December 1955, a Black seamstress named Rosa Parks was arrested for refusing to give her seat to a White man on a Montgomery bus.

Black citizens of the town decided to challenge the city's law requiring segregated bus seating: They formed the Montgomery Improvement Association, with King as head, to take action.

Lawsuits were filed and for more than a year Blacks refused to ride the buses. They walked, carpooled, took taxis, and found other transportation. Though King's home was bombed, the boycott forced the bus company to desegregate, and in late 1956, the Supreme Court declared the bus segregation law unconstitutional.

Afterward, King traveled extensively and lectured about civil rights for Blacks. In India in 1959, he studied Mahatma Gandhi's ideas of nonviolent resistance. He used those ideas when he assumed the presidency of the Southern Christian Leadership Conference in 1960. For the next five years, King's use of nonviolent direct action campaigns throughout the South captured the country's sympathy because of the brutality directed at protesters.

In the spring of 1963, as demonstrators sought to end segregation in downtown Birmingham stores, city officials used attack dogs and fire hoses against unarmed men, women, and children. Hundreds of marchers were jailed, including King, who was placed in solitary confinement. While there, he wrote his famous "Letter from a Birmingham Jail," which explained why he believed in nonviolent direct action. The letter is considered one of the greatest essays in American history. TV coverage of the Birmingham atrocity stunned the nation. The resulting negative reaction forced White business owners to agree to Movement demands.

In August 1963, King and other Movement leaders staged the March on Washington, D.C., where more than 200,000 people gathered to support passage of civil rights legislation. King gave his "I Have a Dream" speech and met with President Kennedy. The Civil Rights Act was passed the next year.

Another bloody confrontation occurred in Selma, Alabama, in 1965, on a march to Montgomery in support of Black voting rights. When protesters were turned back by law enforcement using tear gas and nightsticks, national outrage caused religious leaders of all denominations to join a second attempted march. Afterward, President Lyndon Johnson maneuvered the Voting Rights Act of 1965 through Congress.

After these successes, King's efforts turned toward organizing a multiracial Poor People's Campaign to march on Washington, D.C., to secure basic economic rights. The demonstration was planned for the spring of 1968, but in April, while in Memphis, King was killed by sniper James Earl Ray.

SPIKE LEE

Spike Lee's success as a filmmaker has
opened the doors of the movie industry
for a new group of young African-
American directors. Lee's movies
attempt to portray the richness of
Black life and culture accurately and
without stereotypes. He is best known
for *Do the Right Thing, Jungle Fever,*
and *Malcolm X.*

In 1986, Spike Lee enjoyed huge commercial success
with his first major film, *She's Gotta Have It.* Lee proved
that well-told stories from the Black experience could be
profitable and attract diverse audiences.

Born Shelton Jackson Lee on March 20, 1957, in Atlanta, and nicknamed "Spike" by his mother, Lee grew up

in the Brooklyn section of New York City with an early interest in the arts. His father is noted jazz musician Bill Lee; his late mother, Jacquelyn, took the youngster to plays, museums, and galleries.

As a student at Morehouse College, Lee took an interest in filmmaking, which led to a summer internship at Columbia Pictures in 1979 following his graduation. He entered New York University's film school and for his master's thesis, made the hour-long comedy, *Joe's Bed-Stuy Barbershop: We Cut Heads*, about a Brooklyn barbershop fronting for the local numbers racket.

The film won a student Academy Award from the Academy of Motion Picture Arts and Sciences in 1982 and was received with critical acclaim at film festivals from San Francisco to Switzerland. However, with no offers from the Hollywood film industry to continue his career, Lee decided to produce his movies independently.

Four years later, in 1986, he was able to complete *She's Gotta Have It*, which was shot in 12 days in a small Brooklyn apartment and nearby park. Financing was a major problem. Lee started with only $18,000 and throughout production kept asking everyone he could for any money they could spare.

The film, about the hectic love life of an independent young African-American woman, was completed for a relatively paltry $175,000, but went on to gross over $7 million. For his efforts, Lee won the prize for the best new film at the Cannes International Film Festival and received the Los Angeles Film Critics Award for best new director in 1986. The film was also named on many critics' top ten lists for 1986.

Columbia Pictures picked up Lee's second major film release, *School Daze*, a musical about life at a Black college, for $6 million. The movie made *Variety*'s weekly list of the top ten moneymaking films in March 1988. His third release, *Do the Right Thing*, about racial tensions between Italian Americans and African Americans one hot summer day, became a mainstream hit and cemented Lee's reputation as a bona fide major American filmmaker. Lee was nominated for an Academy Award for his original screenplay.

Lee's movies, though controversial, continue to be box office magic. He has gone on to make *Mo' Better Blues*, *Jungle Fever*, *Malcolm X*, *Crooklyn*, *Clockers*, *Girl 6*, and *Get on the Bus!*, the story of a group of men going to 1995's Million Man March on Washington, D.C.

Lee continues to be involved in many film projects of his own as well as making contributions to others. In 1996, he provided commentary for the Academy Award-winning documentary *When We Were Kings,* which chronicles the famous "Rumble in the Jungle" heavyweight championship fight between Muhammad Ali and George Foreman. Lee recently completed *Four Young Girls,* a documentary about the racially motivated bombing of a Birminghmam church that resulted in the deaths of four girls who were attending Sunday school.

ALAIN LOCKE

Dr. Alain Locke came from a family where education was a tradition. He became the first African-American Rhodes scholar and the only Black recipient of the scholarship for the duration of his lifetime. Head of Howard University's philosophy department, Locke was also the leading intellectual spokesman for the Harlem Renaissance.

In 1907, Dr. Alain Locke had the distinction of becoming the first African-American Rhodes scholar, earning the academic world's highest honor. He remained the only Black recipient of this much coveted scholarship during his lifetime.

It's not difficult to imagine Locke's achievement, considering the intellectual genes coursing through his veins, in addition to his environmental conditioning. In Locke's family, education was somewhat of a tradition. With teachers throughout his family tree, it is not surprising that he became a widely respected educator and intellectual.

Born September 13, 1885, in Philadelphia, Locke contracted rheumatic fever as a child, which left him with permanent heart damage. He adjusted to the limitations by burying himself in books and the arts.

Locke graduated second in his high school class, then studied at the Philadelphia School of Pedagogy. He finished first in his class there. After entering Harvard University, he completed the four-year program in only three years. He graduated Phi Beta Kappa and magna cum laude in 1907.

As a Rhodes scholar, Locke spent three years studying philosophy at Oxford, where he founded the African Union Society. After attending the University of Berlin from 1910 to 1911, he returned to the United States and received his Ph.D. in philosophy from Harvard in 1918.

Locke began teaching at Howard University in 1912, and he taught for almost 40 years until his retirement in

1953 as head of Howard's philosophy department. During his tenure, he reformed Howard's liberal arts program, and Locke's stature as an education reformer became respected nationwide. He also advocated the creation of an African Studies Program, but that was not implemented until 1954.

In 1925, Locke edited an anthology called *The New Negro.* It contained social essays, fiction, poetry, and dramatic and music criticism of the day. This period became known as the Harlem Renaissance, which was characterized by pride in Black culture.

His reputation brought him to the attention of White cultural institutions and patrons, and through them, Locke was able to boost the careers of such literary luminaries as Langston Hughes and Zora Neale Hurston.

Between 1936 and 1942, Locke edited the "Bronze Booklets" series, which detailed cultural and scholarly achievements and progressive views of Black life. For two decades, he reviewed and wrote about Black literature and art. He encouraged high artistic standards for Black authors and urged Black painters, sculptors, and musicians to seek out African subjects and traditions. His numerous essays on Black culture and its dramatic upsurge dur-

ing the Harlem Renaissance led to Locke's recognition as the foremost authority in the field.

Throughout his life, Locke stressed the importance of determining values to guide human behavior and interrelationships. Locke died on June 9, 1954, in New York, from his recurring heart problems.

JOE LOUIS

Joe Louis, a heavyweight boxing
champion during the Depression and
World War II, emerged when all
Americans needed a hero. The fact he
was Black made him that much more
lovable to many. The fact he opened
up professional sports to other African
Americans makes him immortal.

Joe Louis Barrow, the son of Alabama sharecroppers, was
born in 1914 at the beginning of World War I. By World
War II, he would become known as the Brown Bomber
and remembered as perhaps the greatest prizefighter this
country has ever known.

After his family moved from the Deep South to Detroit, Louis's mother had visions of 12-year-old Joe be-

coming a great violinist. But after only a few lessons, he left music. Then a friend who was a 1932 Golden Gloves champion invited him to the gym to work out as his sparring partner. Louis accepted and landed a right punch that almost knocked his friend out of the ring. From then on, as his friend stated, Louis's violin days were gone.

In 1935, after a sensational string of early victories, Louis finally faced a major opponent—former world heavyweight champion Primo Carnera, an Italian. To many, Carnera represented the Fascist ambitions of Italian dictator Benito Mussolini, who was on the verge of invading Ethiopia, the world's oldest Black independent nation. Louis was an African American who symbolized the free world and also the pride of the African people. Holding a record crowd the night of the fight, Yankee Stadium was filled with mostly Blacks and Italians. By the sixth round, the gigantic Italian stallion was soundly defeated, and Louis was the new champion.

In June 1936, Louis faced another opponent who was seen as a symbol of Aryan supremacy—Max Schmeling, the German former heavyweight champion. It was a great fight. In the 12th round, Schmeling knocked out the Brown Bomber.

Louis came back in 1937 to recapture the title from James J. Braddock with an eighth-round knockout. In 1938, he faced Schmeling for a rematch that would take on international attention. In what some have described as the most anticipated fight of this century, Louis avenged himself and his race with a stunning first-round knock-out in two minutes and four seconds. It delighted millions of Black radio listeners and raised the morale of other Americans who needed a lift during the bleakest of the Depression years. In Harlem alone, tens of thousands had a riotous celebration in the streets, chanting, "Joe Louis is the first American to KO a Nazi." Malcolm X described Louis's prominence this way: "Every Negro boy old enough to walk wanted to be the next Brown Bomber."

Louis went on to defend his title a record 25 times. By doing so, he became America's first African-American hero, destroying the myth of racial inferiority as soundly as he defeated his opponents in the ring. He died April 12, 1981, in Las Vegas.

THURGOOD MARSHALL

Thurgood Marshall, America's
first African-American Supreme
Court justice, was also the most
successful lawyer arguing cases
before the high court.

The man who would ultimately grow up to become
America's first African-American Supreme Court justice
was born in Baltimore in 1908. His father was a country
club steward and Pullman car porter and his mother was
a teacher. The judge's name was Thurgood Marshall.

For 25 years prior to joining the high court, Marshall
was "the most important advocate for America," said his
colleague Justice William J. Brennan, referring to Marshall's
29 winning arguments before the Supreme Court—a
record that remains unmatched by any lawyer, Black or
White.

Marshall's mother, who had considerable influence over him, traced her African roots to a 17th-century Congolese slave who caused so much trouble that his slave master finally set him free. Freedom would eventually become Thurgood Marshall's driving force, too.

Marshall's paternal grandfather was a freeman who enlisted in the Union Army during the Civil War. He took the first name "Thoroughgood" in order to satisfy Army regulations that every soldier must have a first and a last name.

During the Depression, Marshall attended Lincoln University in Pennsylvania and Howard University Law School, two of the best historically Black universities. He was a protégé of legal scholar Charles Houston, an NAACP attorney. Eventually, the NAACP would bring ten education cases before the Supreme Court and would be successful at ending segregation in all public schools.

In 1938, after Houston resigned from the NAACP as special counsel, Marshall succeeded him in the legal fight against Jim Crow segregation. Marshall argued the subtleties of the Fourteenth Amendment, winning a number of cases after he was appointed as special counsel to the NAACP's Legal Defense and Education Fund. Marshall's success rate would also win him the coveted NAACP Spingarn Medal in December 1946, for his distinguished service as a lawyer before the Supreme Court.

For the decade or so after Marshall took the helm, case after case dealing with segregation moved him closer to his goal of having the U.S. Supreme Court overturn a previous ruling, *Plessy* v. *Ferguson*, which declared that separate but equal was constitutional.

Finally, on May 17, 1954, after Marshall presented his side, the Supreme Court handed down its landmark decision in *Brown* v. *Board of Education*. The ruling said that segregation in public schools was unconstitutional and that separate but equal had no place in American society. Jim Crow segregation was dead.

But Marshall didn't just work for justice in the United States. During 1960, Marshall worked three months to draft the constitution for the soon-to-be-independent republic of Kenya.

In September 1961, President John F. Kennedy named Thurgood Marshall to the U.S. Second Circuit Court of Appeals. Kennedy did this despite his brother Robert's opposition, who feared that the appointment would upset southern politicos. At that time there was no other Black person working in the courthouse, not even as a clerk or a janitor.

Six years later, President Lyndon Johnson selected Marshall to sit on the Supreme Court, making him the first African American to hold a high court seat. During his tenure on the bench, Marshall wrote the majority opinion on many cases upholding civil rights and constitutional democracy.

Marshall served with great distinction until his retirement June 27, 1991. He was replaced on the bench by neoconservative African-American judge Clarence Thomas. This choice did not sit well with Marshall. Shortly before he died, in 1993, he warned against "picking the wrong Negro," adding "there's no difference between a white snake and a black snake. They'll both bite…."

OSCAR MICHEAUX

Oscar Micheaux was one of the first
and foremost African-American
filmmakers. Between 1918 and 1948,
he made 48 movies, which he
personally distributed throughout
southern and western Black
communities. Micheaux released the
first African-American film to premiere
on Broadway and the first all-sound
motion picture made by an African-
American company.

Oscar Micheaux may not have been the most gifted filmmaker in history, but he was as good a huckster as any
Hollywood producer. Micheaux, one of the first and certainly most determined of African-American filmmakers,

independently wrote, produced, directed, and distributed some 48 silent and sound feature films in the 30-year period between 1918 and 1948.

The films were mostly melodramas, Westerns, and crime films, but these all-Black productions were far more advanced than Hollywood movies in portraying African Americans in anything other than subservient or demeaning roles.

Despite his affinity for genre movies, Micheaux attempted to address serious issues in a few of his films. *Within Our Gates* contains a sequence in which a character is lynched. *God's Stepchildren* concerns a light-skinned Black who tries to pass for White. Whenever he attempted this type of controversial material, he experienced problems with local censors.

Whether following the conventions of familiar genres or dealing with serious issues, Micheaux's movies did what movies are supposed to do—entertain. Millions of Blacks patronized his films in the segregated movie theaters of the day. White audiences even saw his movies at midnight showings.

Micheaux was born January 2, 1884, in rural Cairo, Illinois, one of 13 children of former slave parents. He

left home at 17 to become a Pullman porter, and after working the Chicago to Portland route, he became enchanted with life out West. In 1904, Micheaux purchased a homestead in South Dakota and by all accounts became a successful farmer.

To spread the word to city-dwelling Blacks back East about the opportunities waiting in the West, Micheaux began writing novels based on his own experiences. To sell his books, he took to barnstorming through Black communities in the South and West on promotional tours. He held meetings in churches, schools, and homes and sold directly to that clientele.

In 1918, a Black independent film company sought to buy the film rights to his novel *The Homesteader,* but Micheaux insisted that he be allowed to direct. When they refused, he refused. He raised funds from the same people he sold his books to in order to make the film himself. A moviemaking career was born.

Micheaux's filmmaking style was resourceful, to say the least. Always operating on a shoestring budget, he shot scenes only once, leaving in whatever miscues happened to be caught on camera, using mirrors to enhance whatever natural lighting happened to be available, and

using existing buildings instead of constructing sets. These quickie features were generally finished in six weeks. Then Micheaux, a hefty six-footer, would storm from town to town, stirring demand to see his current movie and raising funds to make the next.

In 1931, Micheaux released *The Exile*, the first all-sound film produced by a Black company, and in 1948, his movie *The Betrayal* became the first African-American-made film to premiere on Broadway. *Body and Soul* (1925) is considered by some critics to be his best picture, and it offered Paul Robeson his movie debut.

Micheaux died April 1, 1951, while, appropriately enough, on a promotional tour.

TONI MORRISON

In 1989, writer Toni Morrison, who
won a Pulitzer Prize for her 1987 novel,
Beloved, joined Princeton University as
the Robert F. Goheen Professor in the
Council of the Humanities. This
made her the first Black woman
writer in American history to hold a
named chair at an Ivy League
university. In 1993, she became the
first African American to win the
Nobel Prize in Literature.

Toni Morrison is one of the most important Black female
writers in the nation's history and certainly one of the
most significant novelists living today. Her primary focus
has been on conveying the realities of life for Black women

and the physical and economic violence that affects them, along with the culture of the larger Black community. Morrison's works have won the Pulitzer Prize and National Book Critics Circle Award, and she won the Nobel Prize in Literature in 1993.

Morrison has had a three-pronged career as writer, editor, and educator. Born Chloe Anthony Wofford on February 18, 1931, in Lorain, Ohio, she was an extremely intelligent child. Morrison was the only Black student in her first-grade class, and she learned to read before her classmates.

After graduating from high school with honors, she attended Howard University as an English major and began using the first name "Toni." Following her graduation in 1953, Morrison earned a master's degree in English from Cornell University in 1955 and began teaching in 1957 at Howard, where she had a short-lived marriage to architect Harold Morrison. Her students at Howard included activist Stokely Carmichael and Claude Brown, author of *Manchild in the Promised Land.*

In the mid-1960s, Morrison left Howard to work as an editor with Random House Books, and a few years later, was promoted to senior editor to work on Black fiction.

She helped develop the writing careers of luminaries such as Angela Davis, Toni Cade Bambara, and Gayl Jones.

Morrison began writing more herself. In 1970, she turned an old short story into her first novel, *The Bluest Eye*, about a little Black girl who wants blue eyes. *Sula*, her second novel, published in 1973, is about an intensely individualistic Black woman and her relationships.

Morrison's third novel, *Song of Solomon*, about a middle-class Black man searching through slavery for his ancestral roots, won her the National Book Critics Circle Award when it debuted in 1977. A fourth novel, *Tar Baby*, stayed on best-seller lists for over three months and caused Morrison to be the first Black American woman to be featured on the cover of *Newsweek* magazine.

The author left Random House in the mid-1980s, after 20 years, to become the Albert Schweitzer Professor of Humanities at the State University of New York at Albany. While there, she wrote her finest work, *Beloved*, in 1987, which won the Pulitzer Prize for fiction.

Beloved is a monument to the millions of Black Americans who endured slavery. Morrison was inspired to create the work after reading the true story of Margaret Garner, who escaped to freedom in Ohio from slavery in

Kentucky, along with her four children. Facing recapture, Garner killed one child and unsuccessfully attempted the same with two others rather than have them returned to lives as slaves.

Morrison recently published her sixth novel, *Jazz*, about a Harlem couple in the 1920s. She also released a scholarly volume of literary criticism titled *Playing in the Dark*. She continues to teach and write.

ROBERT MOSES

During Robert Moses's brief civil
rights career, he spent four dangerous
years as field secretary for the
Mississippi Student Nonviolent
Coordinating Committee, fighting to
register Blacks to vote. He opened
"freedom schools" to teach voter
registration and community action
strategies, held mock elections, and
challenged the state's segregated slate
of Democratic Convention delegates.

Robert Moses played a brief but crucial role in the Civil
Rights Movement. His efforts at voter registration for
Blacks in Mississippi as a representative of the Student
Nonviolent Coordinating Committee (SNCC) was an im-

portant contribution that helped lead to the Voting Rights Act of 1965.

Born January 23, 1935, in Harlem, Moses earned his master's degree in philosophy from Harvard University and taught math in an elite private New York high school.

Stirred by the student sit-in movement of 1960, Moses went to Atlanta and joined SNCC, which was spearheading the protests. He became the first full-time SNCC worker in the Deep South and was subsequently assigned to register Black voters in Mississippi. His job was extremely dangerous and Moses was harassed, beaten, jailed, and almost killed.

In August 1961, he opened voter registration schools in two counties in southwest Mississippi. These schools taught Blacks how to register, the power of community action to combat injustices, and current events. In October, Moses was jailed for leading a protest march. When he was released in December, nearly all the Blacks he worked with had been intimidated into backing out of his registration efforts.

In the spring of 1962, SNCC joined with other Mississippi groups to create the Council of Federated Organizations (COFO), with Moses as head, to unify registration efforts in the state. In 1963, COFO staged the Freedom Election, a mock election open to all Black adults, to show the country how strongly the right to vote was desired by Blacks in Mississippi. More than 80,000 Blacks cast votes on the Freedom Ballot.

The success of that effort led Moses to create the 1964 Freedom Summer Project, in which 1,000 volunteers entered the state to set up "freedom" schools and centers to work on voter registration. The summer was violent—there were a reported 35 shootings, 80 beatings, 60 bombings, and well over 1,000 arrests. Under such conditions, very few Blacks were registered, but the project gained national attention.

During the same summer, Moses helped create the Mississippi Freedom Democratic Party (MFDP) to challenge the segregated Mississippi Democratic Party for seats at the 1964 Democratic National Convention. More than 60,000 people registered as members.

At the Atlantic City Convention in August, a compromise was offered: Only two MFDP members would be seated as at-large delegates. Moses's group rejected the compromise and staged a sit-in on the convention floor before walking out.

Moses was gaining a following that he did not want. He had no wish to be a leader, he just wanted to organize. He began going by the name Robert Parris and soon after, in 1966, he left SNCC and the movement for private life. He taught in Africa for a while, then returned to the United States in 1976 and won a MacArthur Fellowship in 1980.

ELIJAH MUHAMMAD

The Honorable Elijah Muhammad
led the Nation of Islam, also known
as the Black Muslims, in a separatist
movement that stressed the ability
of African Americans to control
and determine their own destiny
through self-reliance. Muhammad and
his one-time spokesman Malcolm X
exposed millions of African Americans
to the Islamic faith.

For 41 years, Elijah Muhammad, the controversial head
of the Nation of Islam, was the leading proponent in
spreading the teachings of the Islamic religion throughout Black America. He was instrumental in developing a
self-help movement through which many African Amer-

icans could now determine and control their own destinies.

Born Elijah Poole in Sandersville, Georgia, on October 10, 1897, Muhammad was one of 13 children of former slaves. A major turning point in his life came when Poole, as a child, secretly witnessed the lynching of a Black man by three Whites.

This traumatic event may have led to Muhammad's ultimate belief that Blacks and Whites should live apart, independently. He spurred the Nation of Islam movement into the direction of a separatist entity.

Poole moved to Detroit in 1923. In the 1930s, he became a follower of Wallace Fard, who preached that by practicing their "original" religion, Islam, Blacks could overcome their conditions of degradation in America.

Fard encouraged Poole to reject his "slave" name and adopt an Islamic one; Poole became Elijah Muhammad. Fard then appointed Muhammad as supreme minister of the Nation of Islam, also known as the Black Muslims. When Fard disappeared in 1934, Muhammad preached that Fard had actually been Allah in disguise, and he shared secrets and teachings with Muhammad. This made Muhammad "The Messenger of Allah." Muhammad began

traveling the country, spreading the teachings of the Muslim movement.

Arrested in 1934 for not sending his children to a public school (they attended a Nation of Islam school), Muhammad lived as a fugitive from 1934 to 1942. In 1942, he was jailed for three years for resisting the draft. After his release in 1946, he continued his influential reign as head of the Nation of Islam. About four years later, Muhammad recruited Malcolm X to be the national spokesman for the Muslims. The 13 years Malcolm X spent in that position were the organization's most fruitful (prior to Minister Louis Farrakhan's rise to power).

Muhammad and the Black Muslims earned growing respect because of their comportment. They were self-respecting, highly moral individuals who did not smoke, drink, gamble, or take drugs. Self-disciplined and courteous, they maintained intact family units.

Muhammad used his followers to show that every Black person had the potential to reach the same level of dignity, with no assistance from White America. To support his ideology of separatism, Muhammad had his organization create and develop their own alternative institutions, such as schools and businesses.

By the time of his death on February 25, 1975, from congestive heart failure brought on by lifelong bronchial problems, Muhammad's Nation of Islam controlled a vast empire estimated at $80 to $100 million. The group's holdings included schools, a university, numerous farms and small businesses, a publishing company, an airplane, an import business, orchards, dairies, refrigerator trucks, apartment complexes, several mansions, and hundreds of houses of worship.

ISAAC MURPHY

Isaac Murphy, one of the greatest jockeys of all time, was the first to win three Kentucky Derbies, a feat unsurpassed for 57 years. He won 44 percent of all his races and at one point had a streak of 49 wins out of 51 races. In 1955, he became the first rider voted to the Jockey Hall of Fame.

Little Isaac Murphy was the closest thing to perfection that any jockey has ever been—he set amazing records that in most respects have not been topped.

Named Isaac Burns, he was a slave born in Lexington, Kentucky, possibly on January 1 (the birth date given for all Thoroughbred horses), in 1866. His father died in the Civil War as a Union soldier. After the Emancipation

Proclamation, his family moved to the Lexington farm of his mother's father, Green Murphy. Isaac took his grandfather's surname.

The story goes that when he was 12, Murphy's family added two years to his age so that he could get an apprentice jockey's license. Murphy ran his first race in Louisville in May 1875, but didn't win a meet until 16 months later. That win began an unparalleled string of successes.

Murphy became the first jockey to win the Kentucky Derby three times—1884, 1890, 1891—and the first to win back-to-back Derbys. He also won four of the first five runnings of the American Derby at Washington Park in Chicago (1884 to 1886, and 1888). In 1882, at Saratoga Downs in New York, he ran an incredible string of 49 victories in 51 starts.

Murphy's three Kentucky Derby wins went unmatched for 39 years, when Earl Sande tied the mark in 1930. The record also went unsurpassed for 57 years, until Eddie Arcaro won his fourth of five Derbys in 1948.

For his career, Murphy won 628 races out of a total 1,412 mounts—an astonishing 44 percent clip. After all of these accomplishments, it's little wonder he was the first rider inducted into the Jockey Hall of Fame, in 1955.

Track aficionados suggest that Murphy knew how to pace a horse better than anyone the sport of racing had ever seen. It was said that he rode only with his hands and heels and only used the whip to satisfy the crowd. Like most of the young riders of his day, Murphy virtually lived and slept at the track. He became proficient at the art of hand-riding, which made the rider more in tune with his mount. Legend had it that a horse could jump straight up and down, but Murphy would never rise off the horse's back. He seemed to be part of the horse. Newspapers and trainers of the day called him the greatest jockey.

Murphy was also noted for his integrity, honesty, honor, and character. He was the undisputed king of his profession, which had the largest spectator attendance of any sport in America at the time.

By 1882, his salary was $10,000 a year. It is estimated that Murphy earned more than $250,000 in his career—an amazing sum of money in those days.

Murphy was the head-to-head winner of one of the most publicized races of the late 19th century. To settle a debate whether he could beat the best White jockey of the day, Snapper Garrison, Murphy emerged from the race victorious.

Ironically, Murphy almost didn't participate in his first Kentucky Derby victory. The horse he was supposed to ride, Buchanan, had almost thrown him in a race only a few weeks before and Murphy wanted nothing more to do with the animal. The horse's owner threatened to suspend him, so Murphy reluctantly rode Buchanan in the Derby, and won.

Unfortunately, Murphy's career virtually ended following his third Derby victory in 1891. He was prone to putting on weight during the off-season and would balloon up to 140 pounds or more over the winter. Then he would diet before the spring races.

This unhealthy practice eventually weakened his body and made him prone to infection. He caught pneumonia and died on February 12, 1896.

Murphy was considered the best of the Black jockeys. In the first Kentucky Derby in 1875, 14 of the 15 riders were Black.

In fact, from 1875 to 1911, 11 Black jockeys won 15 Kentucky Derbies and many other major races throughout the South. The Black jockeys rode so well, however, that their White peers arranged for their ejection from the sport. They created a governing body that refused to reli-

cense the Black jockeys. There has been almost no participation in the sport of horse racing by Black riders since, despite the acclaim Murphy received throughout America in his heyday.

JESSE OWENS

Jesse Owens won four gold medals for
America in the 1936 Olympic
Games in Berlin, Germany, which
embarrassed Adolf Hitler worldwide.
His long jump record stood for 25 years,
and for a time Owens held or shared
the world record for every sprint event
recognized by the International
Amateur Athletic Federation.

Track-and-field specialist James Cleveland "Jesse" Owens
ran like the wind—legend had it that he'd be across the
finish line before you could see him take off. His speed
led to one of America's proudest moments.

Born September 12, 1913, young Jesse had a gift that
came to light early when he consistently outran the local

boys, although the frail lad suffered from malnutrition. An amazed and sympathetic coach, Charles Riley, took Owens under his wing. Riley worked him out for 45 minutes a day before school, while Owens worked several jobs after classes. Riley's efforts paid off: As a high school senior, Owens tied the world record in the 100-yard dash and won three events in the 1933 National Interscholastic Championships in Chicago. It was only the first of several astonishing track meets that would put Owens in the record books.

The next came on May 25, 1935, when, as an Ohio State University student, Owens participated in a Big Ten Conference track meet at the University of Michigan. The 21-year-old tied the world record for the 100-yard dash and set new world records for the 220-yard dash, the 220-yard low hurdles, and the long jump.

His crowning moment on the world stage was yet to come. At the 1936 Olympic Games in Berlin, Germany, Owens won four gold medals and, before the eyes of the world, dashed Adolf Hitler's boasts of Aryan superiority. Not only did Owens win the gold, but he tied the Olympic record for the 100-meter dash and set new Olympic records for the 200-meter run and the long jump.

The coup de grâce came when Owens ran the final leg of the 400-meter relay race, in which the American team broke a world record. Hitler was so disgusted that he refused to shake Owens's hand, though he had personally congratulated other earlier Olympic winners.

Unfortunately, though Owens was celebrated on his return to America, he was not embraced. Promised endorsements never materialized. Penniless, he hired himself out to race against horses and motorcycles. He couldn't afford to finish college and finally landed a job as a city playground worker.

It wasn't until 1955 that America began to recognize Owens's accomplishments. The government sent him abroad as an Ambassador of Sports and he gave speeches on patriotism and fair play. He was also named secretary of the Illinois State Athletic Commission.

Following his death on March 31, 1980, in Arizona, Jesse Owens was posthumously awarded the Congressional Medal of Honor in 1990 and also appeared on a commemorative postage stamp.

ROSA PARKS

Rosa Parks's refusal to submit to White privilege kicked off a liberation struggle that named her the "Mother of the Civil Rights Movement."

She was born Rosa Louise McCauley in Tuskegee, Alabama, in 1913. For the next 42 years, she would live her life in obscurity until one fateful day in Montgomery, Alabama. Then everything would change.

Three weeks before Christmas in 1955, in Montgomery, 42-year-old seamstress Rosa Parks joined the tired workers at the bus stop after a hard day at her tailoring job. It seemed like the bus would never come. When it finally arrived, all the seats in the back, where Blacks were allowed to sit, were quickly taken. Parks sat down in the White section. The bus driver told her and several other African Americans to give up their seats to Whites.

Parks refused to move. The bus driver called the police and Parks was arrested. She and her husband later lost their jobs.

Her refusal to give up her seat sparked a movement against segregation in Montgomery, which started with a 381-day bus boycott by African Americans. The leader of that boycott was a young Black minister named Dr. Martin Luther King, Jr. He used his church to organize the boycott. So successful was the boycott that Dr. King was arrested and his life was threatened. Subsequently, King and his father, Martin Luther King, Sr., and other ministers, including the reverends Ralph Abernathy and Wyatt T. Walker, founded the Southern Christian Leadership Conference (SCLC). These events, kicked off by Parks's nonviolent passive resistance, officially launched the Civil Rights Movement. On December 21, 1956, the boycott ended, with the U.S. Supreme Court declaring bus segregation unconstitutional.

This was not Parks's first attempt to fight discrimination. In the 1930s, Parks and her husband, Raymond, had worked courageously in a futile attempt to free the Scottsboro Boys, nine Black men who were falsely accused of raping two White women. "To do anything open for this cause, could be death," she said. In 1944, Parks had also refused to go to the back of the bus and had been forced to get off. During the 1950s, Parks was the secretary of the Montgomery branch of the NAACP.

These incidents changed Parks's life. Later, she and her husband moved to Detroit, where she still lives. For more than 23 years, she served as a staff assistant to Representative John Conyers of Michigan. In 1994, Parks, then 81 years old, was attacked by a robber. After community help, the robber was caught, convicted, and he apologized.

In the mid-1990s, Parks wrote her first autobiography, *Rosa Parks: My Story*, then authored *Quiet Strength*, an autobiography with Gregory Reed, which focuses on the faith, hope, and heart of a woman who changed a nation by starting the Civil Rights Movement. In her book, Parks recalls her outrage as a Black woman at being asked to stand up so a White man could sit down.

"After so many years of oppression and being a victim of mistreatment that my people had suffered, not giving up my seat—and whatever I had to face after not giving it up—was not important."

SIDNEY POITIER

Sidney Poitier received a Lifetime
Achievement Award from the
American Film Institute in 1992 and
was the first African American to win
a Best Actor Oscar, for his 1963 film
Lilies of the Field. A breakthrough
dramatic actor, Poitier is also proficient
at comedic roles (*Uptown Saturday
Night* and *Let's Do It Again*) and is
an accomplished director.

At one brief point in his life, Sidney Poitier was a homeless teenager sleeping on Harlem rooftops. But he became
a significant film star and the first Black actor to make it
big in dramatic movies. He often had the leading role in
these serious nonstereotypical movies.

Despite a formal education of less than two years, Poitier polished himself to the point that he won the Best Actor Oscar in 1963 for his touching performance as a handyman who helped a group of nuns build a chapel in *Lilies of the Field*. He was the first African-American actor to win the award in that category and helped change the stereotype of Blacks presented in movies.

Poitier was born February 20, 1927, in Miami, the seventh child of West Indian parents, who raised him in the Bahamas. Because of their poverty, Poitier returned to Miami to live with an older brother. He drifted to New York with only a small amount of money and the clothes on his back. He survived by working various jobs, mostly dishwashing, until he lied about his age in order to join the Army.

After being discharged in 1945, Poitier returned to New York and auditioned for the American Negro Theater (ANT), which rejected him because of his thick Caribbean accent and poor reading skills. Undaunted, Poitier listened to the radio for six months to learn how to speak without an accent and had a friend tutor him in reading. When he applied to the ANT again in 1946, he was accepted and began to work.

Poitier played in the Black Broadway production of *Lysistrata* and the Broadway and touring productions of *Anna Lucasta* in 1948. He made an Army training film in 1949. In 1950, he received his first Hollywood role in *No Way Out*. In the mid-1950s, roles in *Blackboard Jungle, Edge of the City,* and *The Defiant Ones* (for which he received his first Best Actor nomination) established Poitier as a box office draw.

Those roles also created a character that would become a Poitier trademark throughout his career—a sincere, sometimes angry, but generally good-hearted, highly moral, intelligent Black man of great dignity. This was typified by his roles in 1967's charming *To Sir With Love* and *Guess Who's Coming to Dinner,* a story of interracial romance.

The biggest exception to that image was Poitier's brilliant portrayal of Walter Lee Younger in the play and movie versions of *A Raisin in the Sun* as a profoundly flawed Black man distraught by the limitations placed on his life because of his race.

Poitier found additional success in the 1970s directing and starring in the Black western *Buck and the Preacher* and several comedies with Bill Cosby and other African-

American stars. He also directed Richard Pryor and Gene Wilder in *Stir Crazy* in 1980, which grossed $58 million.

In 1992, the American Film Institute awarded Poitier the Lifetime Achievement Award, the Institute's highest honor.

ADAM CLAYTON POWELL, JR.

New York Congressman Adam
Clayton Powell, Jr., was one of the first
and loudest voices in what was to
become the Civil Rights Movement.
Only the fourth Black representative
elected in the 20th century, the
flamboyant, immensely popular Powell
fought to end hiring discrimination and
segregation in public facilities.

Ten years before the Civil Rights Movement became full-fledged, New York Congressman Adam Clayton Powell, Jr., was a lone strong voice in government advocating the abolition of segregation and employment discrimination.

When Powell went to the House of Representatives in 1945, he became the first Black congressman from the

northeastern United States and only the fourth Black representative in the 20th century. Powell agitated for immediate, total equality of the races. More conservative Black leaders of his day were arguing for more gradual change.

From the beginning, Powell pushed legislation to desegregate the military and public transportation, make lynching a federal crime, recruit Black nurses into the armed forces, establish a permanent Fair Employment Practices Commission, and deny federal funds to public schools practicing discrimination.

Powell also took his congressional colleagues to task for their racist attitudes, confronting them when they used the word "nigger" on the House floor, and deriding segregationist members—one even punched him during a session.

His brand of uncompromising, defiant agitation endeared Powell to his Harlem constituency, which by large margins reelected him to Congress for 25 years.

Powell was born on November 29, 1908, in New Haven, Connecticut, but came to New York when his father was offered the pastorship of the Abyssinian Baptist Church in Harlem. Although Powell became a notorious

socializer, a trait that compromised his political effectiveness, he promised his parents he would enter the ministry.

Powell graduated from Colgate University in 1930, then received his master's degree in religion from Columbia University in 1932. He took over Abyssinian when his father retired in 1937. Powell used his pulpit to address a variety of political and social issues, particularly employment discrimination. He also wrote political pieces for the *New York Post* and was a popular columnist in Harlem's *Amsterdam* newspaper.

In 1941, Powell was elected to New York's City Council, then in 1944, decided to take his fight national by running for Congress and winning. By 1961, his seniority put Powell in line to chair the powerful House Committee on Education and Labor. In five years, he passed 49 major laws from the committee.

However, Powell's brash nature, flamboyant lifestyle, and controversy about his finances caused his colleagues to strip Powell of his chairmanship and expel him from his congressional seat in 1967. Ironically, he won a special election to fill his own vacancy and the Supreme Court declared Congress's actions against him unconstitutional.

But Powell only occasionally showed up in Congress afterward.

He went into seclusion on the Caribbean island of Bimini and died in Miami on April 4, 1972.

COLIN POWELL

This Yiddish-speaking, Harlem-born
son of Jamaican immigrants rose above
almost insurmountable obstacles to
become the first African-American
Chairman of the Joint Chiefs of Staff
and a best-selling author.

It has only been about 50 years between the segregation of World War II and the present since an African American has risen to one of the highest military posts possible—Chairman of the Joint Chiefs of Staff.

Colin Powell was born April 5, 1937, near the end of the Depression in Harlem. His father was foreman in the shipping department for a garment district firm and his mother was a seamstress. Powell first went to P.S. 39 elementary school and then to Morris High School in the Bronx, like most of the other neighborhood teens. From there he went to City College where he grew to like the discipline of ROTC, the Reserve Officers Training Corps, where young men trained for the military. Powell also worked six years part-time at a neighborhood baby furniture store called Sicksers, owned by Lou Kirschner's father-in-law. It was at this store where Powell picked up Yiddish from Kirschner—a linguistic facility that would later earn him the moniker of "Black Jew" during his early Pentagon years.

In ROTC's "Pershing Rifles" fraternity at City College, Powell adapted well to the structure and discipline in school. After graduating from college as a newly commissioned second lieutenant, he went for military training in the South. After a few years there, he married the Birmingham beauty Alma Johnson, then he went off to fight in Vietnam.

Biographer Howard Means said in *Colin Powell* that Powell was leading a combat unit near the North Vietnamese border when his son was born. A few weeks later, on a patrol near the Laotian border, he was wounded when he stepped into a booby trap rigged with a sharpened punji stick that drove all the way through his left foot. He received a Purple Heart.

Powell's career began to take off in the late 1960s after he enrolled in the prestigious U.S. Army's Command and General Staff College. A decade later, he was a brigadier general. He took several high echelon military courses as well as receiving a master's degree from George Washington University. After that, a succession of Pentagon jobs started coming his way.

He came to the attention of America when he became the first Black National Security Advisor under President Reagan in 1987. Powell moved up to become the Chairman of the Joint Chiefs of Staff under President Bush, just in time for Operation Desert Storm in Kuwait. Powell emerged from Desert Storm as a real American hero.

In 1995, with the release of his best-selling autobiography, Powell flirted with the possibility of running for president. He ultimately decided the time was not right for him and his family, though polls said he was a strong candidate.

A. PHILIP RANDOLPH

Labor organizer A. Philip Randolph
established the first successful Black
trade union and was responsible for the
desegregation of the armed forces and
defense industries. He was also the
predominant Black leader between the
eras of Booker T. Washington and
Martin Luther King, Jr.

Asa Philip Randolph fought a lifelong battle to provide
fair employment opportunities for African Americans.
His work as a trade unionist and organizer directly resulted in the establishment of the first successful Black
labor union, desegregation of the armed forces, and the
end of employment discrimination by companies and government bureaus involved in the defense industry.

Randolph pioneered the use of mass, nonviolent, direct action protests to win gains from the federal government that benefited African Americans. His methods were replicated in the Civil Rights Movement, of which Randolph served as senior statesman.

He was born April 15, 1889, in Crescent City, Florida, to modest middle-class parents. Randolph moved to New York City in 1911 after he was unable to find decent work in his native Florida. That experience had an indelible effect on him—the beginning of his struggle to secure the rights of the Black working class.

Almost immediately, Randolph became involved in union efforts and Socialist politics in New York and he attempted to organize Black workers. He also attended the City College of New York, taking classes in political science, economics, philosophy, and history.

In 1917, following the entry of America into World War I, Randolph and friend Chandler Owen founded *The Messenger* magazine (later called *The Black Worker*), which called for increased hiring in the war industry and armed forces for African Americans. He also helped organize the Socialist Party's first all-Black political club in New York City. Eventually, Randolph relinquished his formal ties to the party, but he continued to consider himself a Democratic socialist.

His growing reputation as a labor organizer brought Randolph to the attention of the Black porters, who took care of passengers on Pullman sleeping car trains. Although being a Pullman porter was a plum job for Blacks, the porters were still besieged with poor working conditions, including low pay and long hours.

In 1925, Randolph was hired as an organizer and founded the Brotherhood of Sleeping Car Porters. The Pullman Company had crushed earlier efforts by the porters to organize. Randolph fought the Pullman Company for 12 years, and in 1937, the company signed a major labor contract with the Brotherhood. Randolph had forged the first successful Black trade union, which he took into the American Federation of Labor (AFL), despite the discrimination in its own ranks.

Randolph's success with Pullman launched his ascension as a national Black leader. Following the certification of the Brotherhood as a bargaining agent, Randolph returned to his fight for Black inclusion in the military and the defense industry. He threatened to lead a massive march on Washington, D.C., in 1941.

Seeing that Randolph was successfully mobilizing the forces needed to make the march a reality, President Franklin Roosevelt issued an executive order banning discrimination by companies with defense contracts. This was the federal government's first commitment to fair employment practices.

The success of that effort gave Randolph leverage to lay down another threat. He proposed that Blacks boycott the draft. The potential of this confrontation may have influenced President Harry Truman to issue an executive order in 1948 to ban segregation in the military. Although Randolph didn't follow through with either threat, the results revealed the power of mass demonstrations.

Randolph spent the 1950s pursuing civil rights activities, particularly in the field of labor. After the AFL merged with the Congress of Industrial Organizations (CIO) in 1955, Randolph became the only Black member of the Executive Council. He used that platform to establish the Negro American Labor Council to attack segregation within the AFL–CIO.

The culmination of his career came when Randolph, at the age of 74, served as director and chairman of the 1963 March on Washington, D.C., for Jobs and Freedom.

The next year, President Lyndon Johnson presented him with the Presidential Medal of Freedom, the nation's highest civilian honor.

He remained involved in his activities as a vice president of the AFL–CIO until 1968, focusing on ending discrimination in unions. His criticism of the union, however, often landed him in hot water with union brass. By the end of his labor career, Randolph's agitation had made the AFL–CIO one of the most integrated public institutions in America.

Randolph died May 16, 1979, in New York City at the age of 90.

PAUL ROBESON

Paul Robeson was a physically imposing
man blessed with a booming, lyrical
voice, incredible athletic skills, and a
brilliant mind. Regarded as one of
Black America's premier actors and
singers, his explosive career was cut
short in the 1950s because of his
human rights activism.

Athlete, actor, activist, academician, orator, singer, lawyer, linguist, Paul Robeson was a true "Renaissance man," whose natural talents were celebrated throughout the world. He also was an outspoken advocate of equality for Blacks.

Robeson was born April 9, 1898, in Princeton, New Jersey, the son of a former slave minister father and school

teacher mother, who died when Paul was six. After graduating high school with honors in 1915, he won an academic scholarship to prestigious Rutgers University. Although he was the only Black student there, Robeson was extremely popular.

He received national attention for his athletic abilities at Rutgers. As an all-around athlete, he earned 12 varsity letters in football, track, baseball, and basketball; he was twice named football All-American.

He excelled just as well in his studies. Robeson won Rutgers' major oratorical contests four years in a row, and he earned Phi Beta Kappa (the nation's highest scholastic honor) in his junior year. In 1919, Robeson graduated as valedictorian of his class.

Deciding not to become a full-time professional athlete, Robeson entered Columbia University to obtain his law degree, which he did in 1923. He played pro football on weekends to support himself and his wife, Eslanda. She was a fellow Columbia student and chemist who was the first African American to work at New York's Presbyterian Hospital.

After graduation, Robeson briefly worked at a prestigious law firm. He soon quit because of the lack of op-

portunity for Blacks in the legal profession at the time and because of discriminatory practices.

Robeson drifted into stage acting, having appeared in amateur productions in college. He met dramatist Eugene O'Neill in 1924 and quickly signed as lead in O'Neill's *All God's Chillun Got Wings* and *The Emperor Jones*. Robeson's booming baritone and acting skills garnered instant acclaim.

Beginning in 1925, he sang immensely successful concerts of gospel spirituals and folk songs across the country. In 1927, the musical *Show Boat* opened in London with Robeson singing "Ol' Man River," a song forever associated with Robeson's deep tones.

With his star steadily rising, Robeson continued giving concerts to capacity crowds and starring in plays such as *John Henry* and *The Hairy Ape*. In 1943, when he starred as Othello with an all-White cast, the production set a record for the longest Broadway run of a Shakespearean play. Some consider it one of the most memorable events in the history of the theater. He also performed the play in London to acclaim.

By 1945, Robeson had become the most famous Black man in America. He appeared in a dozen movies, includ-

ing *King Solomon's Mines, Proud Valley, Sanders of the River, The Song of Freedom,* and the film versions of *Show Boat* and *The Emperor Jones.* In most of these movies, Robeson played Black characters with dignity, in contrast to the stereotypical African-American roles of Hollywood films of that day.

Robeson was a staunch opponent of racism and spent much of his time and energy fighting for equality for Blacks in America. His frequent international concert tours colored his worldview. He learned more than 20 languages, including Russian, and began to study his African heritage and its culture. Robeson and his family visited the Soviet Union in 1934. After being received warmly, they decided to remain for several years.

Robeson became a supporter of progressive causes around the globe, including the rights of oppressed Jews, of anti-Fascist forces in Spain, and of African nations against European colonial powers. The more he studied ideas of universal fellowship and world peace, the more he spoke out here and abroad on the plight of Blacks in America.

Robeson met with President Harry Truman to urge him to do something about the lynchings of Blacks in the

South. His increasingly vocal opposition drew the ire of some people, who labeled him "un-American."

In 1950, as the Cold War with the Soviet Union heated up, the State Department withdrew Robeson's passport because of alleged communist affiliations. Robeson stated that he had never been a member of the Communist Party, but would not sign an oath disavowing communism. This brought the great entertainer's singing and acting career to an end. Both Blacks and Whites in America turned their backs on him. He was not allowed to travel abroad for eight years. The Supreme Court, however, restored his passport in 1958 after declaring the oath he was asked to sign unconstitutional.

With his passport restored, Robeson left the country and toured until 1963. Ill health forced him back to America and retirement. Robeson, 77, died January 23, 1976.

JACKIE ROBINSON

Jackie Robinson will long be
remembered as the first Black major-
league baseball player and the first
African American elected to the
Baseball Hall of Fame.

Jack Roosevelt Robinson was born in Cairo, Georgia, in 1919, when many cities were erupting in race riots. World War I Black soldiers were returning from segregated quarters in the military to increased discrimination at home.

Two decades later, Robinson, a top UCLA athlete, became the school's first four-letter man. He excelled in basketball, football, track, and baseball.

A year later, World War II was starting and Robinson, swept up in the fervor, entered the army as a draftee applying for Officer Candidate School (OCS). He was turned down because he was Black. Robinson, not one to take no for an answer, consulted with his friend and fellow draftee, World Heavyweight Champion Joe Louis. Louis used his clout to get Robinson accepted in OCS. Robinson became a second lieutenant who spent the rest of the war fighting segregation at bases in Kansas and Texas instead of fighting enemies in Germany and Japan.

It was during this tumultuous time that Robinson became friends with Branch Rickey, president of the Brooklyn Dodgers. Rickey encouraged the young athlete to use his talents and energies integrating major-league baseball. According to Rickey, Robinson could help him take a losing team to the winner's circle while breaking the "color line."

Rickey hated segregation as much as Robinson. Rickey had once seen a Black college player turned away from a hotel. He got the player a cot in his room. Rickey never forgot seeing this player crying because he was denied a place to lay his weary head just because of the color of his skin. Rickey wanted to change things. He saw a way to do just that with the talented, poised Jackie Robinson.

Robinson played shortstop with the Negro League Kansas City Monarchs, never losing sight of his ultimate dream—playing with Rickey's Brooklyn Dodgers. Finally, Rickey's scouts caught up with Robinson and invited him to come to New York. Told of the immense difficulties he would have if he played with an all-White team, the ever-confident Robinson agreed anyway. He gave his word there would never be an incident and he kept it despite a lifetime of standing up to bigotry. Robinson had to endure fans calling him ugly names. Players, even sports-writers, defamed him with comments about being the first Black to play on an all-White team. But Robinson didn't fight back. He knew his actions could ruin the chances of other African-American players. Besides, he had given Branch Rickey his word.

While playing for the Dodgers' top farm team, the Montreal Royals, Robinson displayed his amazing skill, winning the hearts of many who saw this Black wizard play ball. In his very first game, he hit a three-run homer. That same year, the team won the Little World Series. At Robinson's last game in Montreal, the crowd stormed the field, chanted Robinson's name repeatedly, hoisted him on their shoulders, and paraded him around the field.

By 1947, after officially joining the Dodgers, Robinson was named Rookie of the Year by *Sporting News* magazine. He helped the Dodgers win a National League pennant. Ford Frick, who was president of the National League, gave Robinson a Silver Bat Award for winning the National League batting title. Robinson also led the league in stolen bases and hit .297. This was the beginning of a series of accolades he would garner in his brilliant 10-year career with the team.

In 1949, the same year he captured the National League Most Valuable Player Award, two former teammates from the Negro leagues joined him on the All-Star Team—Roy Campanella and Don Newcombe. Robinson was still receiving threats on his life for playing a "White man's game," despite his great success. Robinson responded to a hate letter by hitting a home run in the next game he played.

In 1955, the Dodgers won the World Series—a feat that Robinson called "one of the greatest thrills in my life." In 1957, at age 39, he retired with a lifetime batting average of .311. And by 1962, Robinson became the first African American elected to Baseball's Hall of Fame.

Robinson went on to become both a civil rights activist and businessman. On the business end, he became vice president of a company called Chock Full O'Nuts. Now that other Blacks had joined him in integrating baseball, he was free to actively fight discrimination. His activism caught the attention of Martin Luther King, Jr., and Jesse Jackson, both of whom consulted with him on a variety of social justice issues. Additionally, Robinson continued to be a staunch supporter of the NAACP. Robinson's quest for economic justice for African-American entrepreneurs inspired him to reestablish the Freedom National Bank in Harlem in 1964, which was owned and operated by Blacks.

Early in 1972, the Dodgers retired Robinson's number 42. Robinson died of a heart attack on October 24, 1972, in his Stamford, Connecticut, home just a few days after he threw out the first pitch at the 1972 World Series. The Reverend Jesse Jackson eulogized the trailblazing athlete at the funeral.

Robinson's ideas and values are kept alive today through the Jackie Robinson Foundation, a nonprofit organization launched in 1973 by Rachel Robinson, his widow. It provides leadership development and education for underprivileged youths.

JOHN RUSSWURM

To some, he was the cofounder of the
Black Press. To others, critical of his
emigration to Liberia, he was a traitor.
Whatever the view, supporters and
critics alike acknowledge that John
Brown Russwurm was America's first
African-American newspaper editor.

The premiere edition of the first Black newspaper *Freedom's Journal*, under the editorship of writer John Brown Russwurm and minister Samuel E. Cornish, hit the streets March 16, 1827. The place was New York City. Russwurm and Cornish became the fathers of the Black press and among the first champions of a free press, which then was a constitutional guarantee only for Whites.

"It is our earnest wish," they said in their maiden issue, "to make our *Freedom Journal* a medium of intercourse between our brethren in the different states of this great confederacy; that through its columns an expression of our sentiments, on many interesting subjects which concern us, may be offered to the public; that plans which are apparently beneficial may be candidly discussed and properly weighed. We wish to plead our cause. Too long have others spoken for us!"

Their controversial column took issue with the ambivalence of White liberals who said one thing and did another. It was because of the disenchantment Russwurm noticed in liberals and conservatives alike that he decided to pack his bags, turn his back on his White father, and go back to Africa where his West Indian mother's family was once kidnapped from.

Russwurm, who was also one of this country's first Black college graduates (Bowdoin), gave up his editorship and moved to Liberia. While living there, he edited the *Liberia Herald* and served as governor of the colony of Maryland, according to historian Lerone Bennett, Jr. He also worked for some time as the first superintendent for the schools. Russwurm moved to Liberia under the auspices of the American Colonization Society, a proslavery organization. Later, Russwurm and others distanced themselves from it, especially when abolitionists of both races were calling him a "Black traitor." Russwurm's critics contended that a mass exodus would strengthen the bonds of slavery by depriving slaves of support.

Disenchanted with the White male privilege in America, he said: "We consider it a waste of words to talk of ever enjoying citizenship in this country." Referring to the newly founded African republic of Liberia that he helped settle, Russwurm proudly said: "This is our home and this is our country. Beneath its sod lies the bones of our fathers; for it some of them fought, bled, and died. Here we were born; and here we will die."

Like most of the back-to-Africa enthusiasts at the time, such as Paul Cuffee and Richard Allen, Russwurm was an artisan, an entrepreneur, and a pioneer of modest means. He sought to use his resources and talents to better the lot of the millions of American Blacks who were suffering under slavery.

Russwurm and his colleagues were also very much influenced by the example of Touissant L'Ouverture and the Haitian revolutionaries. The equal rights philosophy, prudence, thrift, and sobriety maxims of Benjamin Franklin also motivated them. Russwurm's legacy continues to live on with the Black Press, which in 1997 celebrated its 170th year.

The National Newspaper Publisher's Association (NNPA), a national Black newspaper syndicate reaching 10 million African-Amercan readers, gives the John Russwurm Trophy and Merit Award every year. They award the Merit Award, along with the John Russwurm Trophy, to a newspaper that "represents excellence in journalism," according to Bill Reed, managing director of the Washington-based NNPA.

DRED SCOTT

Slave Dred Scott sued his master
for freedom because he had been
taken into free territories several times.
He believed that this made him a free
man. He lost in a landmark Supreme
Court case that entrenched slavery
even more deeply and ultimately
led to the Civil War.

Dred Scott, a little man scarcely five feet tall, was the principle in a case that many historians believe was one of the most significant events in American legal history.

Most schoolchildren know him as a man who sued his master for his freedom and took his case all the way to the Supreme Court. In 1857, Judge Roger Brook Taney gave the majority decision that Scott's removal to a free state did not make him free; that the state of Missouri determined Scott's status, which ruled that he was not free; and that Scott was not a citizen of Missouri, so could not sue in federal court against a citizen of another state. In essence, he ruled that constitutionally a Black man had "no rights that a White man was bound to respect."

During the 1830s and 1840s, Sam (he was later renamed Dred Scott) accompanied his master, a surgeon in the U.S. Army, on many trips to military posts around the country. These trips included visits to the free state of Illinois and the territory of Wisconsin. In 1846, Scott sued his master for his freedom, asserting that his trips in slave-free areas made him free. A St. Louis paper described him as "illiterate but not ignorant" with "strong common sense."

Many northern states followed the doctrine of a famous English precedent, *Somerset* v. *Stewart*, which established the rule that a slave became free after setting foot in a free jurisdiction. After many delays, trials, and retrials, Scott's case reached the Supreme Court in 1856.

The court responded with nine separate opinions, and Chief Justice Taney delivered the majority opinion. Taney's ruling was consistent with one of his earlier rulings as Andrew Jackson's attorney general, which said that Black sailors on English vessels could be imprisoned in America when their ships docked. In other words, even foreign Blacks had no rights in this country.

Handed down by the Supreme Court in 1857, the Dred Scott ruling permitted slavery in the territories. Abraham Lincoln was dismayed. To him, the Dred Scott decision meant that slavery was again on the march and would possibly be forced upon the free states.

The decision outraged Black abolitionists and made them increasingly radical. It was also a spur to Black immigration attempts.

The ruling was both complex and controversial in that it unfolded against the background of several ominous developments—all of which underlined how Black people had lost ground in America. The first was that the Supreme Court overruled the Missouri Compromise of 1850 on the grounds that Congress did not have the authority to limit the expansion of slavery; slavery was found to be legal in the territories until the citizens voted for or against it. The second was that Africans and their descendants were found to be ineligible for citizenship in the United States as the framers of the Constitution had not viewed Africans as citizens at that time and they had not become citizens since.

Then there followed a second "final" settlement, the Kansas-Nebraska Act, which opened northern territory to settlement by slaveholders unless its settlers adopted an approved state constitution that prohibited it. The net effect of all this was the de facto nationalization of the slave system. The Dred Scott decision was the first instance in which major federal law was declared unconstitutional, and it was a landmark in the growth of judicial power.

Civil rights attorney Standish Willis described the legal impact of the Dred Scott decision this way: "Justice Taney based his harsh conclusion upon the proslavery clauses of the United States Constitution. He argued that under the Constitution slaves were property, just like other property, and consequently, the Constitution permitted no distinction between types of property. In essence, slavery could not be abolished anywhere without first changing the U.S. Constitution."

Dred Scott fought his court battle for 12 years until Taney's Supreme Court decision went against him. He was 51 when the litigation was started on his behalf and

63 when he lost the case. Scott died from tuberculosis 18 months later on September 17, 1858.

For a few years before the Civil War, Dred Scott was the best known Black man in America. The Emancipation Proclamation of January 1, 1863, and the Thirteenth Amendment of the Constitution, adopted January 31, 1865, finally abolished slavery.

BESSIE SMITH

Bessie Smith was an incredible
interpreter of the music of the working
class and of women. Her powerful and
emotional improvisations earned her
the title, "Empress of the Blues."

The turn of the century was a turning point for American culture; it marked the birth of two musicians who would create jazz and blues—Louis Armstrong and Bessie Smith. Two decades later, Armstrong would play on her hit recordings.

At the height of Smith's brilliant recording and performing career, the Harlem Renaissance was the rage. White critics began labeling blues and jazz recordings "race records," a not-so-subtle way to simultaneously disparage and market Black culture. Smith was then earning about $2,000 a week—a phenomenal sum at that time.

Before spellbound audiences, the Empress of the Blues often groaned this song:

> I woke up this mornin'
> Can't even get out of my door
> I woke up this morning
> Can't even get out of my door
> That's enough trouble to make
> A poor girl wonder
> Where she wants to go

Musicians say Bessie Smith, a tall, heavyset woman, became a professional singer in her teens by being discovered by older blues singer Gertrude "Ma" Rainey. Rainey was so impressed with Smith that she hired her to be part of her Rabbit Foot Minstrel Troupe. Some say it was to teach her. Others say it was to prevent a younger and very talented Smith from rising up on Rainey's musical throne and taking over.

A record company scout spotted Smith during a minstrel performance in Philadelphia and immediately signed her to a recording contract. This led to Smith cutting 159 songs in the 1920s and early 1930s, including "Downhearted

Blues." Smith's extraordinary music was enhanced by her legendary producer, John Hammond, who would also discover her successor—Billie Holiday.

In tents, theaters, dance halls, cabarets, juke joints, and on records, Smith sang her blues. Writer Langston Hughes said that Smith's blues were the essence of "sadness . . . not softened with tears, but hardened with laughter." Other fans and critics were enchanted with the power and passion of her delivery. Her words were wellsprings of solace and hope. Like a spiritualist, she helped her patients cope with grief and disappointment. And like many healers, she internalized a lot of the pain.

Onstage, she was invincible, improbable, impregnable. Offstage, she tried to remain humble. This of course was her vulnerable side—a side with whom lovers and booze often found a familiar friend. Blues queens, like other African-American women in the 1920s, quested for independence. This search often manifested itself in the appearance of promiscuity, violence, and arrogance, partly because of the racial and sexual constraints society placed on women like Smith. She did not just sing the blues, she lived it. And by the time of her last appearance, at Harlem's

Apollo Theater, the fee for the Empress of the Blues had dropped significantly.

One could say it was racism and sexism that inspired Smith to fight for her life. One myth about her life says that racism took her life. The official records report she died shortly after a huge truck pushed her off the road somewhere between Memphis and Huntsville, but Smith was possibly refused admittance to three all-White Mississippi hospitals. Whatever the truth may be, in 1937, singer Bessie Smith, the Empress of the Blues, hit that last note.

MABEL STAUPERS

Despite the fact that almost one
million Blacks served in the military in
World War II, America had a
Whites-only policy for nurses. That
policy did not change until seven
months before the Japanese
surrendered. An African-American
activist named Mabel Staupers is
credited with changing that
Jim Crow policy.

Often, little is said about Black women's struggle for
equality. It was a long, hard fight before African-American women were allowed to participate in the military as
nurses. In this campaign, one woman did make a difference: Mabel Staupers.

Staupers was born in 1890 in Barbados, British West Indies. She came to the United States with her family in 1903. She received her R.N. from Freedmen's Hospital in Washington, D.C., in 1917. Staupers became the superintendent of the Booker T. Washington Sanitorium, which was located in New York City, in 1920. She also served as a consultant on nursing to U.S. Surgeon General James C. Magee in 1941, before she was elected president of the National Association of Colored Graduate Nurses (NACGN) in 1949.

The NACGN, led by Mabel Staupers, encouraged its members to enroll in the American Red Cross. At that time, the Red Cross was acting as a medical-staff procurement agency for the military, finding doctors and nurses to serve in the military. While the Red Cross said yes to Black women, the military said no.

In 1941, even after the attack on Pearl Harbor, both the Army and Navy Nurse Corps declared they would not accept Black nurses. The Army Nurse Corps later reluctantly reversed their Jim Crow policy after it was leaked to the press in 1941 that the Army Nurse Corps would accept 56 African-American nurses. These nurses were only to serve in segregated hospitals or wards, tending to

only African-American soldiers, according to Staupers's biographer, Dr. Darlene Clark Hine, an expert on the plight of Black nurses.

Staupers's group was so outraged that they kicked off a huge media campaign to stop the American-style apartheid among military nurses. While their campaign publicly embarrassed a military that was being challenged on seg-regation on other fronts, two things occurred that helped the plight of Black nurses. First, White nurses went off to war, opening incredible opportunities at home. Also, the Cadet Nurse Corps was created to provide education grants to nurses, so many Black women were finally able to afford nursing school. By 1943, the army raised its quota of African-American nurses to 160.

Meanwhile, the handful of Black nurses who were al-lowed in the military were often subjected to harsh treat-ment. Black army nurses stationed in England, for example, were forced to attend to German prisoners of war. Only the White nurses were allowed to treat the U.S. soldiers.

Staupers met with Eleanor Roosevelt in 1944 to protest the humiliation of Black army nurses. This is what she told the First Lady: "It is with high hopes that they [African-American nurses] will be used to nurse sick and

wounded soldiers who are fighting our country's enemies and not primarily to care for these enemies." Her sharp words struck a chord with Mrs. Roosevelt. The restriction was eventually lifted.

Staupers published her autobiography in 1951 titled *No Time for Prejudice*. Because of her work, Staupers was awarded the prestigious NAACP Spingarn Medal in 1951 for her courageous efforts to integrate nurses into the military.

Staupers died of pneumonia October 1, 1989, at her home in Washington, D.C. She was 99 years old.

WILLIAM GRANT STILL

Called the Dean of Black Classical
Composers, William Grant Still was
perhaps the least known of the
important artists in the Harlem
Renaissance. He was the first African-
American classical composer to have
his symphonic work performed by a
major American orchestra.

While much has been written about African-American musical contributions to jazz, blues, and rock, little has been penned about Black classical composers. The first African-American composer to have a symphonic work performed by a major American orchestra was Dr. William Grant Still. Called *Afro-American Symphony*, Still's stellar work premiered in 1931 with the Rochester Philharmonic

under Dr. Howard Hanson. To this day, it remains a classic in its repertoire. *Afro-American Symphony* has since been performed by other major orchestras throughout the world.

Additionally, Still's opera *Troubled Island*, based on a libretto by Langston Hughes, was the first African-American opera to be performed by a major company, the New York City Opera in 1949 under Laszlo Halasz in honor of the company's fifth anniversary. *Troubled Island* is based on the life of Haitian leader Jean-Jacques Dessalines, who ruled the world's first Black independent nation from 1804 to 1806. The libretto deals with the subject of Black liberation and is above the usual operatic standard, in part because of Still's technical prowess and the passion of noted poet Hughes, who fashioned the work from a successful play. Reviewers for the New York *Herald Tribune* praised Still for having a flair for opera music, but punished him for not fully developing his ideas.

Still's work could be divided into three creative periods. The first was his experimental period (1920–1929), which some say was perhaps his most exciting period.

The second period (1930–1939), perhaps his most popular and prolific, was his African-American period

when many of his works carried a Black theme. During this time he wrote "And They Lynched Him on a Tree," the *Sahdji* ballet, *Troubled Island*, and *Afro-American Symphony*.

The third period (1940–1978) was a combination of the first two, with some interesting twists. Here he composed his opera *Highway No. 1 U.S.A.* and his "Poem for Orchestra," which was commissioned by the Cleveland Orchestra.

Still was born in Woodville, Mississippi, on May 11, 1895. Both of his parents were musicians and his father was the town's bandmaster. Still received his early musical training at home, and later he attended the Oberlin College Conservatory of Music. In 1955, Still became the first African American to conduct a major orchestra in the Deep South when he led the New Orleans Symphony Orchestra. He was also the first Black to conduct a major American orchestra, performing his original work with the Los Angeles Philharmonic. He died in 1978.

With today's rising pride in African-American music, interest in Black classical composers such as Still is skyrocketing. In the 1970s, Sister Elise, of the Catholic Order of the Sisters of the Blessed Sacrament, cofounded two

Black opera companies: Opera/South and Opera Ebony. Opera/South featured Still's *Highway No. 1 U.S.A.* and "A Bayou Legend." In 1971, classical singer Natalie Hinderas recorded *Natalie Hinderas Plays Music by Black Composers*, which featured Still's compositions.

Dubbed the Dean of Black Classical Composers, Still's work remains not only a reference point for some of the more contemporary African Americans in this genre, but also a body of work that accurately reflected the times and Still's unique vision of the world.

HENRY OSSAWA TANNER

Like so many talented African-American artists, world-class painter Henry Ossawa Tanner had to leave the United States to get widespread acceptance. His award-winning spiritual art is compared with the religious paintings of Rembrandt and Rubens.

A religious painter who swept the French off their feet at the turn of the century, Henry Ossawa Tanner was an African American who overcame incredible personal and racial obstacles to create beautiful art, which today is still proudly exhibited.

Tanner was born in Pittsburgh, Pennsylvania, in 1859. His father was an African Methodist Episcopal bishop. By his early teens, Tanner had already made up his mind that his life's work would be that of a great painter. His voca-

tional inspiration came from an artist he once saw working in the field. But it seems that his spiritual inspiration came from his minister father, who played a pivotal role.

When his career finally started to get off the ground, he was bothered, like many other artists, with financial and health problems. He was forced to stop and restart his career several times.

Tanner decided his natural talent needed formal instruction if he were ever going to get past selling his paintings for $15 and watching them bring in $250 days later. He became a student at the Pennsylvania Academy for Fine Arts in Philadelphia, where from 1879 to 1885 he endured harassment from White students. Before the Academy for Fine Arts reluctantly accepted Tanner, other Philadelphia art teachers had rejected his work merely because he was Black.

Forced to take a job in the flour business, the overworked, underpaid artist seldom painted. In an attempt to jump-start his career, Tanner sent his artwork to New York publishers. He always received rejection letters, until one day a $40 check arrived. Soon he received an $80 check for his work; then came a job as an art instructor at Atlanta's Clark College.

With hope of succeeding in Europe, Tanner put on an exhibition to raise money. It was a failure. With a borrowed $75 in his pocket, Black themes in his work, dreams in his head, and paintbrushes under his arm, he boarded a boat to Italy. But he made a stop in Paris and decided not to leave. It took him five years to finally get a painting—"Daniel in the Lions' Den"—sold to the Salon. But in 1906, even his beloved Salon awarded Tanner only the second-class gold medal for "The Disciples at Emmaus," "since the first-class gold medal was reserved only for French artists," said Tanner's biographers in a 1992 book published by the Philadelphia Museum of Art, *Henry Ossawa Tanner.*

Tanner's next expedition took the biblical painter to the Holy Land. He used the ancient backdrop for his artwork, including "Christ and Nicodemus" and "The Repentance of St. Peter."

France became his new home. And why not? He was insulted when he returned to America. When Tanner arrived in Chicago to exhibit his work, the Art Institute's prestigious Cliff Dweller's Club, which made him a member, would not let him in the dining room when White ladies were present.

SUSAN L. TAYLOR

Susan L. Taylor went from being a
single mother with a small cosmetics
company to becoming an author,
editor-in-chief of *Essence* magazine,
and an inspirational speaker whose
message of spirituality and personal
growth is an ongoing theme.

Susan L. Taylor began her public career in the 1960s as
an actress with the Negro Ensemble Company. The birth
of her daughter in 1969 caused her to give up acting so
she could spend more time with her child. Taylor went
into business, first becoming a licensed beautician and
then creating her own cosmetics line, Nequai Cosmetics
(named after her daughter).

Her expertise in cosmetology and the success of her
business, along with her stunning beauty, caught the eye

a year later of the editors of *Essence,* a magazine marketed to African-American women. That year, she worked as a freelance writer for the magazine. A year later, she was the beauty editor. From 1971 to 1980, she supervised both the fashion and beauty departments.

Since 1980, Taylor has served as the magazine's editor-in-chief. During her stewardship, circulation has grown. One of her chief responsibilities has been writing the monthly editorial, "In the Spirit." In this column, she shares her intimate thoughts on values and morals she feels are important. She talks about spirituality, and in doing so touches readers in all walks of life. It is that positive message, along with her truly impressive track record, that has made her famous. *In the Spirit* also became the title of her first book.

Her newest book, *Lessons in Living,* is an exploration of intimate themes and issues. It's a celebration of her successes, failures, fears, and triumphs. But most of all, the book is a testament to her faith and commitment.

In the early part of the book, Taylor confesses: "For years, I'd been racing through each day, not living my life, not owning it. I was driven, trying to cover all the bases at home and work while wrestling inwardly with insecu-

rity. For some time, I'd been going round and round in tighter and tighter circles, arriving again and again at the same wordless pain. The people, places and predicaments changed, but the emotional landscape was always the same—stress, doubt and fear."

Later on in the book, Taylor reveals how she found peace in her life and how other people—famous and obscure—have also come to terms with calamity and triumphed.

She has received many awards, including the Women in Communications Matrix Award and an honorary doctorate of Humane Letters from Lincoln University. Since 1986, Taylor has served as vice president of Essence Communications, Inc. She launched a nationally syndicated television magazine show, which received rave reviews during its short time on the air. She has also added a personal touch in managing her magazine's editorial content, insisting that Blacks worldwide get coverage.

Taylor's personal life and her career have intersected on one theme: nurturing the spirit for personal and community growth. A passage in the last chapter of her book, *Lessons in Living,* captures her inspirational message: "More love is our only hope for the future. It is all we

need. Without more love, we will keep shifting from one thing to another in a restless search for satisfaction and peace. But contentment can only be found through self-nurturance balanced with service to others. That is when our joy is full."

MARY CHURCH TERRELL

A supporter of the women's and civil
rights movements, Mary Church
Terrell fought to organize minority
women against the double hardship of
racism and sexism. She was active well
into her old age in successfully
overturning Jim Crow laws.

Mary Church Terrell waged a lifelong struggle against
injustice in any form. She remained active in the struggle for civil and women's rights for 70 years, although
born into a life of relative privilege. Active in many as-
sociations, Terrell also led the fight to desegregate the nation's capital, Washington, D.C., in the 1950s.

Mary Church was born in 1863 in Memphis. Her parents were former slaves. Her father, Robert R. Church,
had a successful saloon business, along with some real es-

tate holdings. Her mother, Louisa, ran a successful beauty salon. The Churches were prosperous enough to send her north to Ohio for a proper education.

Terrell earned her bachelor's degree in 1884 and her master's degree in 1888 from Oberlin College. This made her one of the first Black women in America to earn a graduate degree. After finishing college, she toured and studied languages in Europe for two years before returning to America. She then married future judge Robert H. Terrell in 1891.

Oberlin offered Terrell a job that would have made her the first Black registrar at a White college. She turned it down to marry. However, she did accept an appointment to the Board of Education in Washington, D.C., in 1895. She had begun teaching in that school system in 1887. Terrell became the first Black woman to hold this type of position. She resigned from the school board post in 1901, but was reappointed in 1906 and served on the board until 1911.

Active in the women's rights struggle, she zealously organized minority women in the fight against racism and sexism. In 1892, she headed a newly formed group called the Colored Women's League. That organization combined with other Black women's organizations in 1896 to form the National Association of Colored Women.

Terrell was elected the first president of the group, which established kindergartens and day-care centers for Black working mothers. The organization also pushed for economic opportunity and voting rights for Black women. That work led Terrell to join forces with Susan B. Anthony and Jane Addams in the suffrage movement. Women were finally legislated the right to vote in 1920.

Terrell was also important in the international women's movement; she represented American delegations at congresses in Berlin, Zurich, and London. Usually the lone African American at these gatherings, she impressed fellow delegates by giving her addresses in fluent German and French, as well as in her native English.

Terrell was poised, intellectually gifted, and articulate. These characteristics put her in great demand as a speaker, a vocation she successfully enjoyed for about 30 years. Terrell spoke eloquently on a wide variety of topics, ranging from racial injustice to crime and culture. Writing these speeches led Terrell to write articles on the same themes, which were published both in America and abroad. The culmination of her writing career came in

1940 with the publication of her autobiography, *A Colored Woman in a White World*.

In 1909, Terrell was one of two Black women at the founding meeting of the NAACP. She also attended the 1910 meeting, which formalized the organization, and for many years served as vice president of the Washington, D.C., branch. During the presidential campaigns of 1920 and 1932, the Republican Party appointed Terrell to organize minority women in the East. However, her three crowning accomplishments didn't come until 1949, when Terrell was 86 years old.

She chaired the National Committee to Free the Ingrams, a family of Georgia sharecroppers accused of the murder of a White man. The incident was obviously self-defense. Terrell appealed to the United Nations and Georgia's governor. The Ingrams were eventually freed. That same year, after a three-year battle, Terrell gained membership into the Washington, D.C., chapter of the American Association of University Women. Her membership ended the group's policy of excluding Blacks.

Finally, in 1949, Terrell chaired the newly organized Coordinating Committee for the Enforcement of District of Columbia Anti-Discrimination Laws. The "Lost Laws of 1872–73" prohibited discrimination in restaurants, but owners often ignored the laws. The group fought through the press, in negotiation, by picketing and boycotting, and in court to have the laws enforced.

For almost a year, Terrell had her group boycott department stores whose restaurants refused to serve Blacks. At the age of 90, supported by a cane, Terrell herself headed the picket lines. Several stores finally yielded, and in 1953 the U.S. Supreme Court upheld the laws thus forcing other restaurants to comply. Terrell had won.

She died shortly thereafter on July 24, 1954. Many schools and women's organizations throughout the country have since been named in her honor.

WILLIAM MONROE TROTTER

William Monroe Trotter was one of the first major militant Black leaders of the 20th century. Editor of *The Guardian* newspaper and cofounder of the Niagara Movement, Trotter was a vigorous foe of White supremacy and conservative, accommodationist African-American leaders such as Booker T. Washington.

While turn-of-the-century Whites elevated Booker T. Washington as the "good Negro," *The Guardian* newspaper editor William Monroe Trotter was the militant Black leader at the time. He blossomed from a burgeoning newspaperman to become a significant thorn in the side of segregation and the champion of his people.

After President Woodrow Wilson said segregating government employees in federal bureaus was "in Blacks' best interest," Trotter, on November 12, 1914, marched into the White House. Trotter felt that for the president to say this at a time when there were many lynchings and other increased attacks against Blacks was not only calculating but downright "insulting." Virginia-born Wilson reportedly dismissed Trotter for shaking his finger at him.

Trotter had an interesting history for an African American at that time. He was born April 7, 1872, in Chillicothe, Ohio, but was raised in a predominantly White suburb. There he was steeled in the traditions of abolitionists.

Trotter's father, James, the Mississippi-born son of a White slave owner, was a federal officeholder under President Grover Cleveland. Trotter's father was successful in real estate and his mother was a fair-skinned woman related to Thomas Jefferson.

Raised in an upper-class Negro household, young Trotter was constantly admonished to do better than Whites as a means of breaking down color barriers. The lessons he learned from his parents helped him develop into a human rights activist filled with Black pride.

He started his work early. Trotter was the only African-American student in his high school class. He led the class academically and was elected student body president. His studiousness won him scholarships to Harvard College, which he entered in 1891. He was elected Phi Beta Kappa in his junior year—the first African American to earn that distinction at Harvard.

Trotter entered the real estate business after graduation. Racial problems encountered while pursuing that career led to his growing militancy. The Jim Crow segregation laws that swept the country at the turn of the century forced Trotter to move his business several times. He also had to make other frustrating, race-based concessions.

In 1901, to rail against such injustices, he started *The Guardian* newspaper in Boston with Amherst-trained George Forbes. Their newspaper was in the same building that housed William Lloyd Garrison's *Liberator,* an abolitionist newspaper that had the same message of total equality and total struggle.

Trotter launched his activist journal in part to show a viable alternative in Black leadership to the accommodationist Booker T. Washington. Trotter felt that Washington, the most high-profile Black leader of the day, was a traitor to the African-American cause. He believed that Washington consistently tried to paint American race relations and opportunities for Blacks in a better light than reality indicated.

Trotter would constantly bash Washington in *The Guardian*, portraying him as a self-serving political hypocrite. Subsequently, he was able to agitate considerable public criticism against Washington in the Black community. Washington, in turn, filed several lawsuits against Trotter, while funding another newspaper that he hoped would be a rival to *The Guardian*.

This personal feud escalated and culminated in July 1903, when Trotter organized a disturbance, including hecklers, at a speech given by Washington in Boston. The disturbance turned into a riot. Trotter was arrested and served a 30-day jail term.

Washington's intimidation seemed to work in reverse, though, firing up this incendiary activist even more. He helped make Trotter a hero in the Black community among those favoring Trotter's more militant views over the accommodating leanings of Washington.

Trotter teamed up with W.E.B. DuBois, another Harvard-educated Black, and African-American feminist social worker Ida B. Wells. Together, they formed the Niagara Movement in 1905 in Niagara Falls, Ontario. It became the forerunner of the NAACP. Trotter and DuBois's work also reinvigorated the Black press and was a key influence in reviving the protest movement among African Americans.

Trotter, with his editorials in *The Guardian*, and DuBois, with his columns in *The Crisis*, were two men of letters who created a new, intellectual-based journalism.

Trotter attended the founding conference of the NAACP in 1909, but never embraced it. Although DuBois became an instrumental force in the organization, Trotter could not go along with the White money and White leadership that directed the NAACP. Instead, he founded the National Equal Rights League. However, as the NAACP grew, Trotter's leadership declined.

He died on his 62nd birthday in 1934. He left his mark as one of the 20th century's first militant Black leaders.

SOJOURNER TRUTH

Wearing her trademark turban and
sunbonnet, ex-slave Sojourner Truth
crossed the country for 40 years,
drawing on her experiences and deep
faith to preach against the cruelties of
slavery and to support human rights for
African Americans and women.

Sojourner Truth was an ex-slave who used her experience and her faith to convince others of slavery's cruelties. She will best be remembered as an abolitionist, suffragist, and feminist. For more than 40 years, Sojourner Truth was also a preacher and a teacher. The great and the near-great sang her praises and quoted her strong and striking utterances.

Truth believed it was her Christian duty to further the cause of Black people. That sense of duty won her an au-

dience with President Abraham Lincoln. Ushered into Lincoln's presence October 29, 1864, she showered him with unabashed praise. Truth assured him in a deep-toned voice that he was the greatest president this country ever had, a man to be likened unto Daniel, the biblical standard of courage and faithfulness.

Sojourner Truth and Harriet Tubman were twin mountain peaks of the tradition of Black women. These deeply religious women practiced what they preached. They honored the human rights of Black people, many of whom were held in the bonds of slavery.

Born Isabella Bomefree in Ulster County, New York, in 1797, Sojourner Truth had a succession of cruel slave masters. One took her away from her parents; another sold her youngest child away from her. He illegally transported her son to Alabama.

Truth showed her resiliency and strength of character by attaining the assistance of Quakers in Ulster County, who helped her successfully sue to have her son returned. This was one of Truth's first and most dramatic efforts to show that she would not be broken by the tyranny of slavery. The next year, 1827, Truth herself became free under New York's Gradual Emancipation Act.

Experiencing a religious conversion the same year, she joined the African Zion Church and became an inspired preacher at camp meetings around the New York area. In 1843, tiring of urban life and feeling the need to spread her message to a larger audience, she walked out of New York City. All she had was a bag of clothes, 25 cents, and a new name: Sojourner Truth.

"The Lord," she said, "gave me the name Sojourner because I was to travel up and down this land showing people their sins and being a sign to them. Afterwards I told the Lord I wanted another name 'cause everybody else had two names; and the Lord gave me Truth, because I was to declare truth onto people." That is exactly what she did for four decades.

On a platform, Truth was amazing. Though illiterate, she had the persuasive power that reduced seemingly complicated matters to their essentials. On one occasion, a proslavery heckler told her, "Old woman, why I don't care any more for your antislavery talk than I do a bite from a flea." Truth smiled and candidly replied, "Perhaps not, but the good Lord willing, I'll keep you scratching."

She refused to let antagonists stop her. In doing so, Truth helped define womanhood in a way that embraced the African-American women's experience. "Nobody ever helps me into carriages, or over mudpuddles, or gives me any best place!" she declared at a women's rights convention in Akron, Ohio, in 1851. "Ain't I a woman?"

Another famous incident in which she proved her womanhood occurred in 1858. She stood up to a heckler who asked whether she was a man or woman; he believed she was far too smart to be female. Truth opened her blouse and referred to her work as a slave wet nurse.

Wearing her trademark turban and sunbonnet, Truth walked the land for more than 40 years. She supported herself through lecture fees, the sale of personal items, and the sale of the book *The Narrative of Sojourner Truth*. The book was written by abolitionist Olive Gilbert, and Truth published it herself.

Sojourner Truth proudly broke the taboos about women speaking in public by preaching, teaching, and testifying about the rights of both African Americans and women. Truth had a stunning presence and a searing message. She died November 26, 1883, in Battle Creek, Michigan.

HARRIET TUBMAN

Harriet Tubmam, later dubbed Black
Moses, was the most famous of all
the conductors on the Underground
Railroad. Her courage symbolized the
abolitionist movement, and she risked
her life 19 times to bring more than
300 slaves to freedom without ever
losing a passenger.

Probably best known for her altruistic efforts as a conductor on the Underground Railroad, Harriet Tubman's
life was dedicated to achieving one thing—freedom. With
stops in the South, the Underground Railroad operated
primarily in New England and the Ohio Western Reserve,
where secrecy in helping runaway slaves was essential in
the pre-Civil War era.

Tubman also was the first and possibly the last woman to lead U.S. Army troops into battle. Working in South Carolina and other states, Tubman organized slave intelligence networks behind enemy lines and led scouting raids.

A graphic account of the battle she led appeared in the *Boston Commonwealth* July 10, 1863. In glowing language, the article noted how Colonel Montgomery and his gallant band of 150 Black soldiers, under Tubman's guidance, dashed into the enemy's country. They destroyed millions of dollars' worth of commissary stores, cotton, and lordly dwellings, "and struck terror into the heart of rebeldom, brought off near 800 slaves and thousands of dollars worth of property, without losing a man or receiving a scratch."

Despite working for four years off and on in the service of the Union Army as a nurse, spy, and scout, Tubman was never duly rewarded after the war. Yet she was never bitter. She was a true humanitarian. A big-souled, God-intoxicated, heroic Black woman, Tubman's mission was saving others. She spent the last two decades of her life, however, in virtual poverty. She was a woman with a mission—that mission guided her to freedom and back into slave states where she brilliantly planned and executed escapes for hundreds of slaves.

At great personal risk, Tubman led many to freedom with an operation that she funded primarily by her work as a domestic. In doing so, Tubman inspired peers and future generations of African-American women to continue the long-standing tradition of self-help and self-improvement prevalent in the Black community.

Dark-complexioned and short, Tubman had a full, broad face and she often wore a colorful head bonnet. She developed almost extraordinary physical endurance and muscular strength as well as mental fortitude. She was unpretentious, practical, shrewd, and a visionary. A deeply religious woman with a driven sense of purpose, she credited the Almighty and not herself for guiding her through her many dangerous journeys. She also had a superstitious side, believing deeply in dreams and omens that seemed to put a constant protective umbrella over her perilous exploits.

She was born on a slave-breeding plantation in Maryland about 1821, one of 11 children of Harriet and Benjamin Ross. Originally named Araminta, she was renamed Harriet by her mother. In an attempt to stop a nearby runaway slave, Tubman's master threw a two-pound weight on her head as a child. The weight crushed her skull and caused her sleeping fits and headaches that later plagued her all her life. After the master died, it was rumored that the slaves were to be sent to the Deep South.

Fearing the often deadly consequences of such a move south, Tubman and two of her brothers decided to escape. Fearful of what would happen if they were apprehended, her brothers turned back but Harriet kept walking to freedom. She later returned to get three of her brothers and returned again to get her mother and father. Infuriated slave masters offered a $40,000 reward for her capture, dead or alive.

Said Tubman: "There was one or two things I had right to, liberty or death; if I could not have one, I would have the other; for no man should take me alive; I should fight for my liberty as long as my strength lasted, and when the time come for to go, the Lord would let them take me."

For her heroic work, Tubman received many honors, including a medal from Queen Victoria of England. When she received a $20 monthly pension for her nursing services during the Civil War, she used the money to help needy, elderly freed men and women.

Tubman died in Auburn, New York, on March 10, 1913. After her death, a campaign was launched to collect funds for a monument in the town square. The monument stands in testimony to her indomitable will.

HENRY McNEAL TURNER

Henry McNeal Turner was an
abolitionist minister, a chaplain to
Negro troops during the Civil War,
one of the earliest African-American
elected officials during Reconstruction,
and later an AME bishop in Atlanta.
He found refuge in Pan-Africanist
theories and believed that ex-slaves
should be paid for their labor so they
could return to Africa.

The Black church has always been and probably always
will be the most autonomous institution within the
African-American community. Never was the influence
of the Black church so powerful as during the late days
of slavery.

It is said that of all the groups and individuals working with the missionary movement to aid southern Blacks, none were more important than the northern churches of free Blacks. Not only did they collect money, clothes, and food, but they also sent social workers and teachers to their downtrodden brothers and sisters languishing under the harsh dictate of southern slavery.

One of the most famous leaders of the Black clergy was the Rev. Henry McNeal Turner of Israel Church in Washington, D.C. He was born in Abbeville, South Carolina, in 1834. Like most militant Black intellectuals at the time, Turner was educated in the North. He studied to be a minister. Turner used his pulpit to urge his parishioners to join the Union Army. In 1863, shortly after Turner's historic report about the jubilant effect of President Lincoln's Emancipation Proclamation on Blacks and Whites, Lincoln made him chaplain of the Black troops. President Andrew Johnson made him a chaplain in the Regular Army in 1865.

Following the end of the Civil War, Turner went to Georgia, working in the African Methodist Episcopal Church—a church founded by Blacks who were denied worship by Whites. After the passage of the Reconstruc-

tion Acts, he became a member of the Georgia State Legislature, but only after a bitter fight, which lasted from 1868 to 1870. The fight left him battered publicly, but he was still defiant. Turner was finally seated in the statehouse as a Republican despite attempts by White Democrats to prevent it. In defense of himself and 23 other Black representatives who were temporarily being denied their rightful seats in the Georgia legislature, Turner made a historic speech before the body that began at 9 A.M. and ended six hours later. He said, "We are told that if Black men want to speak, they must speak through White trumpets!" Turner and the others were finally admitted in 1869. But by 1876, radical Reconstruction in the South was dead.

In the next few decades, disenchanted with the increasing White supremacy, Turner and others found refuge in theories bandied about by Pan-Africanists who felt life for Blacks in America was futile. He and other emigrationists, including Edward Wilmot Blydon, called their concept "Africa for the Africans." Turner called for "two or three million" Blacks to return "to the land of our ancestors, and establish our own nation, civilization, laws, customs, style of manufacture, and not only give the

world, like other race varieties, the benefit of our individuality, but build up social conditions peculiarly our own." Despite his passionate leadership in the back-to-Africa concept, Turner preferred the word "Negro" to "African" when speaking about Blacks in the Western Hemisphere.

Refusing to die on American soil, Turner died in 1915, in Windsor, Ontario, Canada.

NAT TURNER

Nat Turner was either a hero or a madman. In 1831, Turner led a violent insurrection against Whites in Southampton County, Virginia. The repercussions led to the major debates over slavery that eventually ignited the Civil War.

Nat Turner said he felt the pain and horror of slaves like him who were kidnapped, raped, abused, and tortured. So he set out with his band of insurgents and killed 60 Whites. That insurrection stirred slave owners to increase atrocities on slaves to teach any would-be Nat Turners a lesson.

To some, he avenged the Holocaust bestowed on his fellow Blacks by Whites who were profiting from human flesh. To others, Turner was a demented madman who left

a trail of terror in which he and his followers killed about 60 Whites in a rebellion in Southampton County, Virginia, in 1831.

Ironically, Turner, who was born a slave in Southampton County in 1800, managed to escape when he was 21. But he returned to his master, he said, because of religious convictions.

Like most men with a mission, Nat Turner came to the view early in his life that God chose him for a purpose. He believed that purpose was to lead an uprising against slavery. To prepare himself for his mission, he kept to himself, fasted, prayed, and avoided crowds, tobacco, liquor, and money. By the time he reached maturity, he was well respected among slaves.

He was known to pray by the plow, and some say he saw visions and heard voices. One vision showed Black and White spirits fighting in the sky until the sun darkened and streams ran with blood. What happened that day was a solar eclipse, but Turner believed it was his sign to begin the uprising.

Turner chose his disciples, and after much preparation and prayer, he met them in a wooded retreat near his cruel slave master's farm. Under the cloak of darkness on the

morning of August 22, they attacked the slave master, named Joseph Travis, hacking him and his family of five to death.

For the next 40 hours, the group, originally consisting of seven slave rebels, rampaged. They went from house to house, village to village, gathering more slave warriors on the way as they liberated several zones in Southampton County. They sent slave owners and traders to hell, while gleefully singing the praises of their bloody insurrection. No Whites were spared except poor families who owned no slaves.

News spread quickly over the state of Virginia and surrounding areas. Soon, some 3,000 armed Whites, including soldiers from as far away as North Carolina, converged in Southampton. The troops committed atrocities, slaying innocent Blacks at will—as many as 200 in Southampton alone. That was apparently the point—not to put down the insurrection but to terrorize the slave population so they would never rise against their White masters again.

In fact, on September 3, 1831, the Richmond *Constitutional Whig* verified that fact. An editorial said that if another such insurrection should happen, it will be a "sig-

nal for the extermination of the whole Black population."
Slave revolts could be directly linked to laws that legalized branding, burning, hamstringing, amputation, and death to slaves who resisted captivity.

Turner was finally caught on October 30 of that year. On November 11, this bold Black man, who some called Prophet, dangled from a tree as if he were a strange fruit.

Turner's death was a turning point in America. The major slavery debates raged from that point on until the abolition of this inhuman practice was ended by a bitter war that tore the nation in two. The same year that Turner's insurgents spread Black hope and White fear, William Lloyd Garrison established his inflammatory *Liberator* newspaper. Abolitionists also organized the New England Antislavery Society that year.

Twenty years later, a White man with a mission named John Brown would set out on the same path as Turner. He bellowed Nat Turner's name as he traveled freedom's road only to find his liberty, like Turner's, at the end of a rope.

THE TUSKEGEE AIRMEN

The Tuskegee Airmen were brave
Black fighter pilots who had to
fight discrimination at home as well
as Nazi aggression abroad. They
helped win on both fronts.

The incredible story of African-American aviators in
World War II began on a lone Alabama runway at
Tuskegee Army Air Field on March 21, 1941, with the
activation and construction of a segregated airfield for the
99th Pursuit Squadron.

On March 7, 1942, five pilots stood on the runway at
graduation exercises, poised to take their place in aviation
history. First Lady Eleanor Roosevelt took a flight with
Black pilot Dr. Charles Alfred Anderson to show her official support for the program that detractors said would
never get off the ground.

This airfield came at a time when African Americans were shackled by legal White supremacy in the South and racial exclusion in the North, and any act of so-called disrespect could result in injury or death. Learning how to fly, to many Whites and a few Blacks, was one such act of disrespect.

African Americans up to that time had routinely and rudely been excluded from the Army Air Force because there were no established Black units. There were persistent myths that Blacks were incompetent to fly and also lacked the intellectual skills to do so. Yet, there were more than 100 Black pilots at the time. Two bold Black pilots 20 years prior, Eugene Bullard and Bessie Coleman, had learned to fly in France. They inspired a whole new generation of African-American aviators. At least two Black schools developed: the Bessie Coleman Aero Club in Los Angeles and the Coffey School of Aeronautics at the Harlem Airport in Oak Lawn, near Chicago.

Under the leadership of Lieutenant Colonel Benjamin Davis, Jr., the Tuskegee Airmen had their first taste of combat against the highly fortified island of Pentelleria. The successful attack of the island proved that Blacks could be triumphant in battle.

Subsequent successful battles in Europe and Africa proved the Tuskegee Airmen's talents and abilities. They also substantiated the Black aviators' contention that given the opportunity, Black fighter pilots could be every bit as good if not better than their White counterparts. Captain Luke Weathers scored two victories in one day. Another of the many heroes was Lieutenant Clarence D. Lester, whose bomber formation was attacked by 30 or more ME-109 and FW-190 enemy planes on July 18, 1944. Piloting a P-51 aircraft en route to enemy installations in Germany, Lester engaged with the enemy planes. He destroyed three enemy fighters "thus materially aiding in preventing the enemy from making concentrated attacks on American bombers," Lester's citation read, when he was decorated for outstanding bravery in battle.

On July 26, 1948, President Truman issued two executive orders desegregating the military, thanks in part to the heroic efforts of the brave Black Tuskegee Airmen.

ALICE WALKER

Alice Walker won the Pulitzer Prize
and the American Book Award
for her epic novel *The Color Purple*.
The book was developed into a
movie, which garnered 11 Academy
Award nominations.

Writer Alice Walker paved the way for both Black and female authors when her Pulitzer Prize-winning novel *The Color Purple* was developed into a Steven Spielberg film. It received 11 Academy Award nominations. Her books have sold millions of copies and have been translated into two dozen languages.

While the controversial and popular book *The Color Purple*, which examines the effects of domestic violence and racism on three generations of southern Black farmers, is her most famous work, it is one of many important pieces penned by this self-described "womanist" writer. Other noteworthy works include *The Temple of My Familiar, The Third Life of Grange Copeland*, and *Possessing the Secret of Joy*. A more recent title, *Crossing the Same River Twice*, which had received favorable reviews and lots of attention—something Walker enjoys professionally yet shuns in her personal life—is a collection of essays and journal entries that explores her personal suffering and awakening.

She was born the youngest of eight children in 1944, in Eatonton, Georgia. Her father was a sharecropper and her mother was a maid. Walker said both her parents were strong storytellers, and she remembers her mother toiling to make their humble shack spotless.

Like other important writers, Walker's childhood had pivotal events that changed her forever. At age eight, she was shot in the eye with a BB gun by one of her brothers. Because her family did not own a car, Walker was forced to wait a week before a doctor examined her. The doctor then told her she was permanently blind. Self-conscious and shy, Walker, who had been an outgoing youth, retreated to a private world of words, ideas, and books. She started writing poetry and became so proficient she was

awarded several fellowships. She was also offered the opportunity to have her poems published.

Some critics speculate that Walker's own mutilation helped her identify with Tashi, the main character in *Possessing the Secret of Joy.* Tashi is a tribal African woman who was genitally mutilated by the tsunga's knife and severely traumatized because of the experience. She spends the rest of her life fighting madness and is treated by disciples of both Freud and Jung, and even Jung himself. Finally, she regains her ability to feel. This book has generated much controversy—critics of Walker say African cultural rituals are not America's concern. Feminists and many others say mutilation of women is not about culture but about control of women.

After high school, Walker attended Spelman College in Atlanta and Sarah Lawrence College in Bronxville, New York, where she graduated. Her first job after college was working in the Welfare Department in New York City. She hated the job and wrote feverishly at night. After leaving the Welfare Department, she was writer in residence and professor of Black studies at Jackson State College and Tougaloo College in Mississippi. Her night writing paid off in 1970 when she published her first novel, *The Third*

Life of Grange Copeland, about sharecroppers. She would soon revisit the same theme with *The Color Purple*.

Walker continues to write. Her most recent work is a collection of essays inspired by her ever-growing interest in political activism, entitled *Anything We Love Can Be Saved: A Writer's Activism: Essays*.

MADAM C. J. WALKER

Madam C. J. Walker revolutionized
the hair-care industry for Blacks in the
early 1900s when she invented a hair
straightening process. She employed
more than 3,000 sales agents and
amassed a fortune that made her
America's first Black millionaire.

After 38 years of a humble life where she and her daughter lived virtually hand-to-mouth, Madam C. J. Walker perfected a hair-care formula. It was so popular with African Americans of the early 20th century that she became this country's first Black female millionaire and a pioneer in the cosmetics industry. Although she became one of the most famous African Americans of her time, sadly, she enjoyed her business success for only 14 years before her death.

She was born Sarah Breedlove in Delta, Louisiana, on December 23, 1867. Her parents were poor farmers and former slaves. She lived in a run-down shack on a plantation on the Mississippi River. The house had no toilet or running water, and the family slept on the dirt floor. Walker picked cotton from sunup to sunset until she was orphaned at age seven. She then went to Mississippi, where she lived with an older sister.

At the age of 14, Walker married to escape the cruelties of her sister's husband. Her own husband was killed when she was 20, leaving her alone to raise her two-year-old daughter, A'Lelia. For the next 18 years, Walker worked as a washerwoman in St. Louis to support them. Although she could not read or write at the time, she saved her small earnings and sent A'Lelia to Knoxville College. Despite her future success, this single act remained one of her proudest accomplishments.

Walker found herself going bald and she began experimenting with medicines and secret ingredients to try to nurse her hair back to health. In 1905, she developed a formula, with sulphur as a main ingredient, that not only stopped her hair loss but also enabled her hair to grow back quickly.

Walker always said that the formula came to her in a dream after she prayed to God to save her hair. Some ingredients in the recipe that appeared to her in the dream were grown in Africa, so Walker sent for them. She prepared the concoction and after applying it, she found her hair growing back in faster than it had fallen out. Walker then began selling this pomade preparation, which she called a "miracle hair grower," to friends and neighbors.

After moving to Denver to live with her sister-in-law, she continued to sell her product to local Black women. Then, with only $1.50 to her name, she decided to buy the necessary chemicals and begin manufacturing her pomade in jars. Walker was now a businesswoman.

She soon met newspaperman Charles Walker, whom she married. He brought his expertise in advertising to the operation. Now known as Madam C. J. Walker, she put ads in Black publications and also began a profitable mail-order arm of her business.

Personally showing her styling methods door-to-door throughout the South and East, she opened beauty schools and trained agents. These agents started their own businesses selling her products. Walker also developed a steel comb for Black hair that could be heated on a stove.

The success of her hair-care treatment system rested in the versatility of styling that it offered African-American women who wanted different hairstyles. The Walker System became an international success when Josephine Baker (who sang mostly in France) used it. This success prompted the French to develop their own pomade.

Walker and her daughter became wealthy and opened cosmetic colleges in Pittsburgh and New York and a plant in Indianapolis. They built and lived in a mansion in New York called Villa Lewaro.

The Walkers gave more than 3,000 Black women the opportunity to leave domestic work and become entrepreneurs. These sales agents learned how to set up beauty parlors in their homes, keep business records, and become financially independent.

Though Walker and her daughter became prominent socialites and patrons of the arts, they used much of their money to benefit others. Madam Walker contributed freely to the NAACP and funded scholarships for young women at Tuskegee Institute.

Madam Walker died May 25, 1919, at Villa Lewaro.

BOOKER T. WASHINGTON

Booker T. Washington will always be
fondly remembered as founder of
Tuskegee Institute, a Black college in
Alabama that launched the careers of
thousands of Blacks. Washington was
an ex-slave who may have been the
most powerful Black man in
U.S. history.

At the turn of the century, Booker Taliaferro Washington was simultaneously the most powerful and the most controversial Black leader of his time.

His supporters say he tirelessly toiled for Black pride and educational and economic advancement and that he used his influence with White industrialists to get huge amounts of money for Black colleges. His critics say he cozied up to the White power structure, using federal patronage and the favor of White philanthropists to create his own political machine. Historians agree with both.

Washington was born a mulatto slave in 1856 on a small Virginia farm. He spent his early years of freedom working in coal mines and salt furnaces. He attended Freedmen's Bureau School and Hampton Institute, then a secondary and industrial school.

In 1881, Washington founded Tuskegee Institute in the Black belt of Alabama—something many cite as his crowning achievement because of the thousands of Blacks whose careers were made possible thanks to the opportunity they were afforded at Tuskegee. The school specialized in vocational and agricultural careers—jobs nonthreatening to an increasingly hostile White workforce.

Washington spent the next 15 years building this landmark institution by accommodating local Whites and raising money from northern ones, who were attracted to his emphasis on thrift, hard work, and good moral character. They viewed industrial education as no threat to southern White labor.

At this time, militant abolitionist Frederick Douglass was deemed the most articulate Black spokesman. Douglass died in 1895, the same year that Washington catapulted into national fame with a speech known as the Atlanta Compromise Address delivered at the Cotton States and International Exposition. In Washington's speech, he implied a scaling back in Black voting rights in favor of White support for Black business. He used the parable of the open hand and the empty bucket to illustrate his point.

His accommodationist, self-help philosophy was clarified in *Up From Slavery*, his autobiography published in 1901. The book became a best-seller and Washington a household word. He was constantly hailed as a "credit to his race." It even earned him a White House audience with President Theodore Roosevelt that same year, and he remained an important advisor to the president. Washington then perfected his political prowess by building an organization that more often than not yielded principle to expediency. Washington secretly funded lawyers and pressed court suits to protest segregation in public transportation and prevent Black sharecroppers from being driven from their land. He maneuvered bad situations and made them work for him—perhaps his greatest skill.

His program of industrial education and promotion of small business as the primary way Blacks could move up the ladder might have seemed pragmatic, given the racial hatred that existed at that time. But critics then and today cite it as taking people of African descent several steps backward. One critic of the Atlanta Compromise speech was noted educator John Hope. "I regard it as cowardly and dishonest for any of our colored men to tell White people or colored people that we are not struggling for equality."

Others praised Washington's industrial philosophy. Industrialist Andrew Carnegie and feminist Susan B. Anthony were among the most prominent speakers who appeared at Tuskegee Institute. Washington's biographer Louis R. Harlan said that Washington "worked unceasingly" for Black pride, material advancement, and every kind of education. "He did these things more by private action than ringing declaration."

Washington's most vocal critic at the time was W.E.B. DuBois, the Harvard-educated philosopher-activist-writer who called for "ceaseless agitation" as opposed to Washington's "go along, get along" line. According to DuBois, "It wasn't a matter of ideals or anything of that sort. With everything that Washington met, he evidently had the idea: 'Now, What's your racket?'" Washington's rule was "bossism." He rewarded his friends and punished his enemies. He used spies, bribes, and anything else short of violence to bring down opponents, who mainly came from the progressive quarters of the Black community. Meanwhile, poverty, lynchings, and other assaults to the human dignity of Blacks flourished at the hands of southern and northern Whites who in the 1890s began a movement to take back all the rights Blacks had achieved.

A little known fact about Washington is that in his final years he addressed many of the civil rights questions that the NAACP had raised and he had previously rejected. In his last few years, Washington differed from their approach but not their goal.

Washington's supporter, William H. Lewis, memorialized his mentor by saying: "He knew the Southern White man better than the Southern White man knew himself, and knew the sure road to his head and heart."

At age 59, Washington died after a long illness at Tuskegee. Three days after his death, one of the largest crowds in the Institute's history gathered to honor him.

Washington's successor was Robert R. Moten, his former secretary. Moten was more accommodating to the protest movement, signaling that it might now be acceptable for some of Washington's old supporters to join forces with the NAACP. Ironically, in the Depression era of the 1930s, W.E.B. DuBois, Washington's old antagonist, advocated economic policies similar to those proposed by Washington. This caused a spilt between DuBois and Walter F. White within the ranks of the NAACP.

Washington will forever remain a controversial figure. Each small community and hamlet would create their own Washington, a Black man who could speak to his community and for his community as the voice of Negro opinion. On the other hand, Washington remains admired by many Black nationalists and Black radicals, who view him as a symbol of Black empowerment, "doing for self."

IDA B. WELLS-BARNETT

A journalist and civil rights leader,
Ida B. Wells-Barnett fearlessly fought
for Black self-reliance and against the
violence and economic repression that
had kept African Americans and
women in oppression.

Ida B. Wells-Barnett was a formidable force in the battle
for equality and economic parity for Blacks. She was nicknamed a "crusader for justice" by the people. Wells-Barnett's scathing editorials against lynching and White
violence against Blacks alerted the country to the atrocities that were common in the post-Reconstruction South.
Wells-Barnett spent her life lecturing against discrimination and injustice—in America and abroad— and she ex-
horted Blacks to use their economic power to change
racist White behavior.

In 1862, Wells-Barnett was born a slave in Mississippi to a family with a strong faith in education. Her parents died of yellow fever in 1878, and the young teenager began teaching so she could care for her siblings. Later, Wells-Barnett moved to Memphis, Tennessee, which turned out to be the beginning of a lifelong quest for equality.

In 1884, Wells-Barnett refused to accept a seat in a Jim Crow car, then filed an unsuccessful lawsuit against the railroad company. Her militant actions, along with some editorials critical of inadequate African-American schools, caused her to lose her teaching job. Wells-Barnett then launched a career of using her mighty pen to call the country to task for its treatment of Blacks.

After editing and writing for several small Black papers, Wells-Barnett became part-owner of the Memphis *Free Speech and Headlight.* In 1892, three Black men were lynched because their business was competing with a White firm. Wells-Barnett fired off a series of blistering editorials, accusing Whites of using lynching to punish financially indepedent African Americans. She declared that "neither character nor standing avails the Negro if he dares to protect himself from the White man or become his rival." Furious Whites burned down her paper's

presses and threatened her life if she returned to the South.

Undaunted, Wells-Barnett moved to New York, continuing her angry attacks on lynching at militant journalist T. Thomas Fortune's *New York Age.* She published pamphlets on the lynching problem and traveled overseas, drumming up international outrage.

This tireless crusader helped form and worked with many important groups, including the National Association of Colored Women, The Ida B. Wells Club, and the Negro Fellowship League. Wells-Barnett was also instrumental in creating the National Association for the Advancement of Colored People (NAACP).

Wells-Barnett moved to Chicago in 1893, where she published a pamphlet denouncing the exclusion of Blacks from the World's Fair. She continued to fight against lynching, and in 1895, she published *The Red Record,* a statistical report on lynching. She also became active in the issues of segregated schools in Chicago and the importance of Black female community involvement.

In 1895, Wells married lawyer and *Chicago Conservator* founder Ferdinand Barnett, and together they were formidable champions for Black civil rights.

A forceful speaker of courage and conviction, Wells-Barnett's voice was finally silenced on March 25, 1931, when she died in Chicago of uremic poisoning. She remains a jewel in the crown of the struggle for equality.

PHILLIS WHEATLEY

Phillis Wheatley was a slave who was originally from West Africa. She became the first African American to publish a book and the second woman in the United States to publish a collection of poetry. She is considered the mother of the African-American literary tradition. Her writing abilities shocked Whites of her day.

A young slave stolen from her native Senegal village in Africa at the age of seven or eight, Phillis Wheatley is the mother of the African-American literary tradition. She was the first Black to publish a book—a collection of poems—and only the second woman in the United States to publish a book of poetry. In the process, she became almost an icon to abolitionists trying to prove that Blacks and Whites were intellectual equals if given equal opportunities.

Twas mercy brought me from my Pagan land,
Taught my benighted soul to understand
That there's a God, that there's a Savior too:
Once I redemption neither fought nor knew.
Some view our fable race with scornful eye,
"their colour is a diabolic die."
Remember Christians, Negros black as Cain,
May be refin'd and join th' angelic train.

Wheatley's poem "On Being Brought from Africa to America" was part of a series of works published in her 1773 book, *Poems on Various Subjects, Religious and Moral.* Except for a poem published in 1760 by Jupiter Hammon, another slave, Wheatley's book was the first published by an African American. She often wrote her poems, mostly elegies and honorific verse, to commemorate the life and death of friends, famous contemporaries, and important events. She wrote her poetry in a style and with references that reflected her African heritage.

Wheatley's writings set off a storm of criticism, both by those who couldn't believe that a Black woman was capable of creative thought and by those who saw her as a Black genius and proof that African Americans were not intellectually inferior to Whites. Before *Poems on Various Subjects* was first published, the fact that Wheatley had written it was considered so extraordinary that 18 of Boston's movers and shakers questioned her to prove that she had written the poems. When *Poems* was published in 1773, it began with a signed "Attestation" by these men, including John Hancock and the Massachusetts governor, Thomas Hutchinson, asserting that a slave woman had written the book. The book was published in England with the help of Wheatley's patrons, the Countess of Huntington and the Earl of Dartmouth, after publishers in Boston refused.

Wheatley is believed to have been brought from West Africa by a slave ship called the *Phillis*, which landed in Boston in 1761, when she was seven or eight. There, the wife of a wealthy local merchant bought her and taught her English and gave her a classical education. A child prodigy, Wheatley was observed trying to write letters on walls with chalk shortly after her arrival. She was fluent in English within 16 months of her arrival.

Wheatley, a frail young woman, published her first poem in 1770. On the advice of doctors, she sailed to England in 1773 with her mistress's son when her book was about to be published. She received a celebrity's welcome. In fact, Wheatley was so well received her owners were shamed into granting her freedom.

After her former mistress died in 1774, Wheatley tried to publish another volume of poetry, this time in America. She failed despite public praise.

Wheatley married a free Black man, John Peters, in 1778. During the political upheaval that followed Boston's fall to the British, Wheatley lived in poverty with her husband and three children. Two died. Wheatley died at age 31, in 1784, trying to support herself and her last remaining child.

WALTER F. WHITE

Walter F. White administered the NAACP during its most significant period of growth and its rise to become the nation's preeminent civil rights organization. Under White, the NAACP's legal defense committee won the historic *Brown* v. *Board of Education* case, in which the Supreme Court outlawed segregation in public schools.

Thanks to Walter Francis White's outstanding organizational and administrative skills, the National Association for the Advancement of Colored People (NAACP) grew from a small group to the preeminent civil rights organization in America.

Under his leadership as secretary from 1931 to 1955, the NAACP greatly increased the number of its local branches, consolidated the dominance of African Americans within its body, and created the legal division that won so many key court battles that spurred the advancement of the Civil Rights Movement by ending legal segregation.

White's NAACP turned America's attention toward equal voting rights and the horrors of lynchings. It helped end all-White election primaries, restrictive housing practices, and legally sanctioned public discrimination.

It was under White's stewardship that the NAACP's legal division won the landmark *Brown* v. *Topeka, Kansas, Board of Education* Supreme Court case in 1954, which outlawed segregation in public schools. The *Brown* case precipitated other court rulings that eventually ended all forms of public segregation and led to the enactment of civil rights legislation that championed equality of rights and opportunities for African Americans.

White was a blue-eyed, blonde-haired man who could have enjoyed a comfortable life passing for White. But he fought hard for racial justice because he was victimized several times in his life because he was African American.

In fact, his father died of neglect in a Georgia hospital while doctors argued about whether or not he was Black.

White was born in Atlanta in 1893. At the age of 13, during an Atlanta race riot, White and his father sat inside with guns drawn as a mob threatened to invade their home. In 1916, after he graduated from Atlanta University, the city's school board was moving to limit public education for Blacks to sixth grade, while Whites could go on to high school. Atlanta's Black community formed an NAACP branch, with White as secretary, to combat the board, which eventually backed down on its plans.

White's actions caught the attention of James Weldon Johnson, then field secretary for the national organization. Johnson was influential in getting White a position in 1918 as assistant secretary.

Because of his complexion, White volunteered to investigate lynchings in the South since he could pass for White. He gained valuable information, even though he was almost lynched himself on one occasion. In 1920, White published his highly regarded *Rope and Faggot*, a major indictment of lynching in America.

In 1935 and again in 1940, as NAACP head, White lobbied to introduce federal antilynching legislation, which was defeated both times by proposed Senate fili-busters. But those efforts turned national attention to the atrocities of lynching in the South and helped the NAACP become politically influential.

White organized the defense for innocent Blacks in-volved in the 1919 Chicago Race Riot. After Johnson be-came the NAACP's first Black secretary in 1920, White worked with him for a decade. The organization flour-ished and White became invaluable as an administrator. He succeeded Johnson as secretary in 1931, the position he held until his death from a heart attack in 1955, when he was succeeded by his assistant Roy Wilkins.

DANIEL HALE WILLIAMS

Dr. Daniel Hale Williams was a physician and surgeon who performed the first successful surgery on the human heart in the world. He founded Chicago's Provident Hospital, the first interracial facility in the country, and started training programs for African-American nurses and interns.

Dr. Daniel Hale Williams was a pioneering surgeon who saved the life of a stabbing victim by performing the world's first heart surgery. He founded Provident Hospital in Chicago, Illinois, because other area hospitals refused an African-American woman a nursing education. Provident is the nation's oldest freestanding Black-owned hospital.

Williams created training programs for African-American nurses and interns, and was the only Black in the charter group of the American College of Surgeons. He also helped organize the National Medical Association, a professional organization for Black doctors.

Williams was born in Hollidaysburg, Pennsylvania, on January 18, 1856, one of seven children. At 17, Williams worked part-time in a barbershop while living with one of his sisters. He took a two-year apprenticeship with Dr. Henry Palmer, a legendary surgeon and former U.S. Surgeon General.

In the 1800s, many doctors began practicing after two years of training. But Williams went on to graduate from Chicago Medical College (later Northwestern Medical School) in 1883, opening his first office at 3034 South Michigan Avenue in Chicago. He was on the surgical staff at several institutions, taught anatomy, and in the late 1880s was appointed to the Illinois State Board of Health and was surgeon to the City Railway Company. Williams was the first Black to hold that position.

African-American doctors often performed surgery in people's homes at that time because hospitals refused to appoint Blacks to their staffs or to train Black nurses. So

Williams pulled together a group of prestigious African-American and White doctors and founded the Provident Hospital and Training School Association in 1891.

In 1893, on a hot July day, Williams saved the life of a stabbing victim by opening his chest and suturing a wound to the pericardium. The man lived for 20 years after the surgery. That same year, Williams was appointed Surgeon-in-Chief at Freedmen's Hospital on the campus of Howard University in Washington, D.C.

In 1899, Williams was visiting professor at Meharry Medical College in Nashville. After returning to Chicago, Williams took a position on staff at Cook County Hospital from 1900 to 1906.

Ironically, leadership at Provident Hospital had passed to Dr. George Cleveland Hall, Williams's longtime antagonist. As a response to the increased segregation of Black life, the hospital board, under Hall's direction, required all physicians to bring all their patients to the hospital. Because many of Williams's patients were White, board policy severed his relationship with the very hospital he founded.

In 1913, Williams became the first Black appointed as associate attending surgeon at St. Luke's Hospital in

OPRAH WINFREY

Oprah Winfrey is living proof that
the American dream is possible. She is
an actress, television talk show host,
and businesswoman who has spent
her career trying to help women and
Blacks increase their self-esteem
and self-reliance.

Oprah Winfrey is an Emmy award-winning talk show
host, an Academy-Award nominated actress, and one of
the highest paid entertainers in America. She uses her position as the country's best-known talk show host to tackle
issues affecting people's daily lives. *The Oprah Winfrey
Show*, now handled by Winfrey's own production company, deals with social problems ranging from sexual
abuse to racism and is watched by more than 17 million
people daily. Winfrey is a testament to the resilience of

the human spirit in the face of adversity and to the heights reachable through hard work. Her strength is her ability to make her guests and audience feel at home. Her emotional empathy for their problems is genuine.

The bubbly, voluble Winfrey had a stormy childhood. Born in a small Mississippi town to unmarried parents, Winfrey spent her early childhood with her grandmother. She was an exceptional child, making her first speaking appearance in church at the age of three. At age six, Winfrey moved to Milwaukee to live with her mother, Vernita Lee, but didn't fit into the subsistence-level existence Lee eked out on welfare and domestic work.

Winfrey lived briefly in Nashville, Tennessee, with her father, Vernon, but soon returned to her mother's home. The next few years were among the darkest in Winfrey's life. She was repeatedly sexually abused by a cousin and friends of the family. Vernon Winfrey brought his daughter back to Nashville, and she began to bloom under his strict guidance.

Despite her troubles, Winfrey was destined for great things. She was reporting the news for WVOL radio in Nashville before graduating from high school and continued in broadcasting as she started at Tennessee State

University. She became the youngest and first African-American female coanchor in town when she started at WTVF-TV. A few months before graduation, Winfrey moved to WJZ-TV in Baltimore, Maryland.

The talented Winfrey found her niche when the station made her cohost of its morning show, *People Are Talking*. Winfrey continued her meteoric rise in the field with a move to Chicago in 1984 to host WLS-TV's morning show, *A.M. Chicago*, which became the top show in the market within three months. The show was renamed for Winfrey, went into syndication, and consistently gets phenomenal ratings.

Winfrey has also expanded into film, with both Golden Globe and Academy Award nominations for her role in Steven Spielberg's movie, *The Color Purple.* She also received accolades for her performances in *There Are No Children Here* and *The Women of Brewster Place.* Both films are inspirational stories portraying strong, determined women who represent triumphs of the human spirit.

As one of America's highest paid entertainers, Winfrey has contributed $1 million to Morehouse College, one of her many philanthropic contributions to the community. She also uses her own company, Harpo Productions, to

develop positive projects dealing with women and African Americans.

Winfrey has received numerous awards, including the prestigious Peabody Award, both for her talk show and for her philanthropic work. She currently lives in Chicago along the lakefront.

CARTER G. WOODSON

A historian, Carter G. Woodson
created Negro History Week in
1926 to call attention to Black
contributions to civilization. The week
he selected in February contains the
birthdays of Abraham Lincoln and
Frederick Douglass, two pivotal players
in African-American history. Negro
History Week has since become
Black History Month.

Carter G. Woodson arguably did more for the accurate study of Black Americans than any other historian. He opened the long neglected field of Black studies to scholars and also popularized the subject in Black schools and colleges.

Ironically, studying anything was something Woodson had to put off for quite a while. Born December 19, 1875, in New Canton, Virginia, he was the oldest of nine children of former slaves. Woodson could not attend school because his parents needed the money he earned in the coal mines.

Though unable to attend high school full-time until 1895, when he was 20 years old, the self-taught young man made up for lost time by graduating in less than two years. Admitted to Barea College in Kentucky, he earned his degree in 1903. Two years earlier, he had already earned a teaching certificate, which he used to teach in West Virginia high schools.

Through periodic semesterly visits and correspondence courses, Woodson received his bachelor's degree from the University of Chicago in 1908. Meanwhile, from 1903 to 1906, he was a school supervisor in the Philippines and then spent 1906 and 1907 studying and traveling in Asia, North Africa, and Europe, including a semester at the University of Paris. In 1912, Woodson received his Ph.D. in history from Harvard University.

It's not clear why he had such an intense interest in the field of Black history—there were no courses in the subject offered during his collegiate work. Perhaps that was the reason. Still, in 1915, along with several other associates, Woodson formed the Association for the Study of Negro Life and History (ASNLH) in Chicago to encourage scholars to engage in the intensive study of the Black past.

Previously the field had been grossly maligned at the hands of White historians who accepted the traditionally biased perceptions of Black involvement in domestic and world affairs.

The ASNLH was primarily committed to historical research, training African-American historians, publishing texts about African-American life and history, collecting valuable or rare materials on the history of the race, and promoting that history through schools, churches, and fraternal groups.

From 1916 until his death in 1950, Woodson edited the *Journal of Negro History*, one of the premier historical publications in America during its time. From 1919 to 1920, Woodson was dean of the School of Liberal Arts and head of the graduate faculty at Howard University. From 1920 to 1922, he was dean at West Virginia State College. While there, Woodson founded Associated Publishers to produce accurate, scholarly books on Black life and culture.

In 1926, the stern and demanding academician founded Negro History Week to focus attention on Black contributions to civilization. The week was observed nationally and expanded into Black History Month in 1976 by proclamation of President Gerald Ford as part of the nation's bicentennial.

Woodson was writing a six-volume *Encyclopaedia Africana* at the time of his death. He died of a heart attack on April 3, 1950.

RICHARD WRIGHT

Richard Wright was one of the first
writers of protest fiction decrying
White mistreatment of Blacks in
America. His most noted work is the
novel *Native Son,* which detailed the
life and death of Bigger Thomas, a
Chicago Black man who accidentally
kills a White girl. The 1940 best-seller
won Wright the NAACP's
Spingarn Medal.

An important writer of the 20th century, Richard
Wright was one of the first and most forceful authors to
call attention to the consequences of racial exploitation
of Blacks through his striking works of protest fiction. His
existential writings explored the recurring theme of how

Black Americans live in a country where structural racism denies their very humanity.

Wright's most compelling argument of this came in his 1940 novel *Native Son,* the raw and powerful story of Bigger Thomas, a young, Black man in Chicago who accidentally kills a White girl. Thomas then learns the depths of hostility that the White world harbors against Blacks.

Native Son was an international best-seller that quickly sold more than 300,000 copies; it was translated into six languages and it became a Book-of-the-Month Club selection.

Wright also turned the work into a powerful Broadway play starring Canada Lee and staged by Orson Welles. In 1941, he won the Spingarn Award—the NAACP's highest book honor—for his novel. The book earned him fame and encouraged him to pursue a lifelong writing career.

Wright had come to the public's attention two years before with his *Uncle Tom's Children,* a collection of short stories released in 1938 that won the author a Guggenheim Fellowship. In these stories, Wright explored racial tensions in the rural South that most often ended in violence. With *Native Son,* he shifted locales to the big north-

ern ghettos, where the same tensions culminated in the same results.

In 1945, Wright published his autobiography, *Black Boy*, which has become an American classic. Also selected as a Book-of-the-Month Club selection, *Black Boy* was translated into six languages and outsold *Native Son*. The story is about Wright's early childhood in the South and his young adulthood in Chicago. The book examines the painful workings of the racist social order.

Wright was born near Natchez, Mississippi, on September 4, 1908, and grew up in poverty in orphanages and with various family members. It was a dismal childhood that gave him a dark outlook on life.

He had trouble adjusting to southern racism and Jim Crow segregation. He determined that if he was to survive, he had to go North to live. Wright moved to Memphis in 1925 and two years later he moved to Chicago, where he worked odd jobs until being accepted into the Federal Writers Project during the Depression.

After the success of *Black Boy*, Wright, disturbed by American racism and having found more freedom in his travels abroad, left America for Paris. He continued to write, publishing titles such as *The Outsider* and *White*

Man, Listen!, which was compiled from a series of lectures given in Europe. In 1977, his autobiographical *American Hunger* was published posthumously.

Wright lived the rest of his life in Paris, where he died of a heart attack November 28, 1960, at the age of 52.

MALCOLM X

As the primary spokesman for the
Nation of Islam for a dozen years,
Malcolm X captivated the country
with his passionate speeches about the
anger and frustration felt by Blacks
because of the devastating effects of
racism. He forcefully challenged
White dominion, demanded change,
and helped inspire racial pride in many
African Americans.

Perhaps no one else in the Civil Rights Movement gave
as forceful a voice to the rage and frustration of Black
Americans as Malcolm X. As he passionately spoke to
America, Malcolm brazenly challenged White domina-
tion and demanded change. In so doing, he struck a nerve

with a large segment of the Black population, many of whom began to find self-respect and racial pride.

Malcolm's style and message stood in stark contrast to his leadership peers in the Movement, who favored non-violent protests and integration to end discrimination. Malcolm believed in fighting back if attacked, calling it unmanly not to do so. He also felt that integration was demeaning; that it would lead to only token accommodation by Whites. He believed that it would have no effect on the urban Black underclass.

Malcolm was a nationalist who believed in Black self-reliance—that African Americans should control their own institutions, economy, and politics. He preached that this self-determination would have to be realized "by any means necessary."

He rose to prominence as the national spokesman for the Nation of Islam, a Black separatist group (also known as the Black Muslims) led by Elijah Muhammad. The Muslims taught that Blacks were the original human race with an impressive culture and civilization until they were enslaved by Whites. Black Muslims taught that only by returning to their true religion, Islam, could Black Americans recapture their rightful heritage.

As the Nation of Islam's representative for a dozen years (1952–1964), Malcolm was a brilliant, powerful orator who attracted huge crowds on the university lecture circuit and had a constant media following. He increased Muslim membership by traveling the country and telling African Americans about their previous rich culture, which he said had been taken away by Whites who had then brainwashed Blacks into a mentality of self-hate. Malcolm pointed to the Muslims and Islam as the way to a better life, using his own life as an example. He proved it was possible to readjust one's life path.

He was born on May 19, 1925, in Omaha, Nebraska, as Malcolm Little. His family was forced out of Omaha by White vigilantes who burned down the family's house. The Littles resettled in Lansing, Michigan, where, in 1931, Malcolm's Baptist minister father was killed, supposedly by Whites. After his mother was institutionalized from the strain of trying to raise her family, the children were separated and sent to various foster homes.

Malcolm went to Boston to live with a relative, but fell into a life of crime—selling and using drugs, running numbers, and organizing a burglary ring. These activities landed him in jail for six years at the age of 21.

While imprisoned, he was introduced to the teachings of Elijah Muhammad; those teachings allowed him to vent his anger at the way Whites had treated his family and denied him opportunities.

Malcolm began to accept Muslim ideology, which stresses fastidiousness of mind and body and allows no unclean habits. He improved his intellect by copying every word of the dictionary and reading voraciously.

After his parole in 1952, Malcolm intensified his Muslim studies and dropped the last name Little and took X, the Muslim designation for an African American's original lost African surname. In 1954, Muhammad, whom Malcolm at first worshiped, made him a minister. Through the years, Malcolm headed Muslim mosques in Boston, Philadelphia, and Harlem and organized dozens of temples around the country. He also founded *Muhammad Speaks*, a newspaper that would later denounce him.

But Malcolm's growing popularity became a source of contention within the Nation, and his discovery of Muhammad's alleged immoral personal behavior created a schism. Malcolm left the Muslims in 1964.

He organized two groups of his own, the Muslim Mosque Inc. and the Organization of African-American

Unity. To undergird his religious beliefs in opening his own mosque, Malcolm took a pilgrimage to the Islamic holy land of Mecca, Saudi Arabia.

Malcolm encountered worshipers of all colors who embraced him in brotherhood. This made him reconsider his indictment of all White-skinned people as being evil "devils," and he revised his separatist notions. After this pilgrimage, he changed his name to El-Hajj Malik El-Shabazz.

Upon his conversion to orthodox Islam and his return to America, Malcolm denounced Muhammad, which led to an increasingly bitter and open feud. He expanded his interests in civil rights to include human rights worldwide and even sought to make partial amends with leaders of the Civil Rights Movement, especially Dr. Martin Luther King, Jr.

But on February 21, 1965, just one week after his house had been firebombed, Malcolm X was assassinated.

WHITNEY M. YOUNG, JR.

Whitney M. Young, Jr., almost
single-handedly put the National
Urban League at the forefront of
the struggle for civil rights and
Black economic equality. Young
worked within the system to
create jobs and bring financial
support to the organization.

Whitney M. Young, Jr., was a calming voice in the midst
of the militant Civil Rights Movement of the 1960s. As
executive director of the National Urban League, Young
worked to keep communication open with White America's centers of financial and political power. He did so in
order to give concrete help to African Americans. Critics
feared Young had too many close ties to Whites. Yet he

brought millions of dollars to the Urban League, increased the number of branches, and gathered government support that might have been lacking.

Young was born in Lincoln Ridge, Kentucky, on July 21, 1921. After getting his bachelor's degree at Kentucky State College in 1941, he taught briefly before joining the U.S. Army during World War II. Young then studied electrical engineering at the Massachusetts Institute of Technology. His experiences with racism in the military turned Young toward the civil rights struggle.

Young received his master's degree from the University of Minnesota and started working with the Urban League. He worked at branch offices in two states at a time when the organization was focused more on housing and health issues than with civil rights. In 1954, Young became dean of the Atlanta University School of Social Work. The articulate, personable Young spent a year at Harvard University under a Rockefeller Foundation grant in 1960, then began a brilliant career as executive director of the National Urban League.

Before Young's involvement, the group was training Black social workers to fight for improvements in housing, sanitation, and other self-improvement issues. It left the civil rights fight to more militant African-American organizations. Young leaped with both feet into the fray. He dealt with social problems by influencing White decision makers and becoming part of the process for change.

Critics called Young an "Uncle Tom," but he increased the Urban League's budget from $250,000 and a staff of 34 in 1961 to $3,500,000 and a staff of 200 by 1968. He created jobs and opened 90 new regional branches. Young, fighting to keep his credibility among Blacks, proposed a national Marshall plan in 1963 to help African Americans catch up. His book, *To Be Equal,* documents his vision. One quote from his book is an example of that vision, "Good race relations—race harmony—is more than the absence of conflict, tension, or even war. *It is the presence of justice.* Nothing is more immoral than the suggestion that people adjust to injustice or that we make a god of 'timing.' The time is always ripe to do right."

During the sixties, American leaders turned to Young and leaders such as Dr. Martin Luther King, Jr., to calm the voices of more militant Black leaders. Young stayed at the front of the struggle, helping to organize the 1963 March on Washington, D.C. Young published *Beyond Racism: Building an Open Society* in 1969, which explained that the Black power era could help the nation move toward a more democratic society.

Young's brilliant career was cut short when he drowned in 1971 in Africa, while attending a conference.

INDEX

PSYCHO

Stuart Pearce

The Autobiography

with Bob Harris

headline

First published in 2000
by HEADLINE BOOK PUBLISHING

First published in paperback in 2001
by HEADLINE BOOK PUBLISHING

10

A catalogue record of this book is available from
the British Library

ISBN 0 7472 6482 1

Typeset by
Letterpart Limited, Reigate, Surrey

Printed and bound in Great Britain by
Mackays of Chatham plc, Chatham, Kent

HEADLINE BOOK PUBLISHING
A division of Hodder Headline
338 Euston Road
London NW1 3BH

www.headline.co.uk
www.hodderheadline.com

DEDICATION

To my wife Liz and daughter Chelsea

ACKNOWLEDGEMENTS

Stuart Pearce and Bob Harris would like to acknowledge the help of Liz, for her patience, Stuart's family, Kevin Mason, Jonathan Harris, Ian Marshall, Lorraine Jerram, and all at Headline.

contents

There was no mention of a penalty shoot-out. The prospect had simply never crossed the minds of the players and I'm not even sure whether it crossed the mind of the manager. It wasn't just another game. This was a big one, a very big one, and all of our thoughts were on the 90 minutes ahead. Every player was focused on what he had to do, his role in the team.

In that situation, you just think about the game and nothing else. When the 90 minutes comes to an end, and there's still another 30 minutes of extra time to go with tired minds and tired bodies, that's when mistakes are made. The concentration has to be even stronger. When the referee blows the final whistle, the winding down process begins immediately, the jangling nerves begin to relax. The game is over. You have given it your best and it has finished as an honourable draw. Then the realisation dawns – penalty kicks. Everything you and your team-mates have worked for over the past months rests on five individuals taking penalties and a goalkeeper who you hope is going to stop at least one of the opponents' spot-kicks.

In those two or three minutes before the penalty-takers

are announced, you suddenly have to concentrate, regain your focus as quickly as possible, especially if you are chosen or put yourself forward as one of those under the microscope, as I did.

The players gather in the centre circle, encouraging, showing solidarity for each other. There is anxiety among the chosen five and a perceived relief among those who do not have to shoulder the responsibility. The goalkeeper is away at the end of the ground where the shoot-out is to take place, bouncing around knowing that he, above anyone, has nothing to lose and absolutely everything to gain.

I keep my socks up and my pads in to try to stay in game mode. Others prefer to lie down and draw a deep breath, relax those cramping muscles but I stay on my feet, take a drink and keep my mind as sharp as I can. The job isn't over yet; it's only finished when we have won on penalties and that is now all that matters.

All you need to do is walk 50 yards, take a penalty and score. That's the worst part of it, that bloody walk from the halfway line. Why do they make you stand there, so far away? God only knows which masochist decided that. It is clearly someone who has never been in this nerve-jangling position because it heightens the tension to an unbelievable degree. The stadium is a complete blur as you take that seemingly endless walk. I was not aware of the crowd or of anyone talking to me. I had already decided in which direction to shoot. But you talk to yourself. You tell yourself not to sidefoot the ball to give the goalkeeper a chance. It is now down to the simplest of equations – you against him.

2

When you are in a tight corner like this, a crisis situation, the usual decision is to go for your best penalty, to play your strongest card. Drill it, because even if he goes the right way, if there is pace on he might not be able to keep it out. After this basic concept there are two other choices to make – whether to aim straight down the middle allowing for the certainty that the goalkeeper will move, or whip the ball across him.

Suddenly you're there. While you have been making the long walk there has been a feeling of detachment that only disperses when you grab hold of the ball, which is either bouncing around or, more often than not, thrown with unnecessary pace by the goalkeeper who is trying to gain a psychological edge. The nerves which have been racking your body disappear when you finally reach the penalty area and pick up the ball. You are on familiar territory, like the seasick sailor who at last sees the land ahead.

But it is still a dream world. There are no individual noises from the crowd, just a muffled blur. You try to flood your mind with positive thoughts. You tell yourself that you are the favourite, that you are 12 yards out with everything stacked in your favour. Make a good strike and if the goalkeeper picks the wrong way it will look like one hell of a penalty.

The pressure is truly on. No one has missed so far and the burden of not only your team-mates and your family, but also an entire nation is weighing heavily on your shoulders. Football is supposed to be a team game but now you're on your own. There is no hiding place in a football stadium for a penalty-taker in a shoot-out.

You put the ball on the penalty spot. It's only about six

inches in diameter and you put it on the extreme edge nearest the goalkeeper. Silly as it sounds, it gains an inch and every player does it. Much more important is to find a high point. The last thing you want is a sunken penalty spot and you quickly seek an upgrade. You look for every possible advantage, no matter how tiny.

Having finally placed the ball, you walk back, totally ignoring the goalkeeper, taking nothing in, keeping the mind focused. I know where I'm going to put the ball and I won't change my mind. I never have before and never will, no matter what the circumstances. Any hesitation now is lethal.

I know that the goalkeeper will be hoping for that unnerving eye contact. He has nothing to lose and you have everything. I have to take a quick glance when I reach the end of my run, just to make certain that he isn't standing by one of his posts or hasn't gone for drink. You will look a fool in front of the world if you run up and shoot without looking and are called back to do it again. But there is no searching for his soul through his eyes. In most cases during 90 minutes and extra time, I am more than happy to stare into someone's eyes and throw down the challenge but all I want to see now is his profile. Come penalty shoot-outs, I'm more than a bit shifty. If I look in his eyes, that would move the advantage to him. When you are in combat, you have to play your strongest hand.

I walk back to the edge of the penalty area, just far enough to be able to get the right pace on the ball. Then, at last, you are on your run up, and there is no going back. Half a dozen steps between you and glory or abysmal failure. I know what my job is. I know exactly where I want to hit it. Keep your eye on the ball . . . keep your eye on the ball. One . . . two . . . three . . . four . . . five . . . six . . . and strike. It's like a golf shot, the moment you make contact you know whether it's good or bad, hit or miss.

the penalties

Turin, Wednesday, 4 July 1990

The ball flew straight and true and German goalkeeper Illgner dived to his right but he was aware enough to get his legs in the way and the ball rebounded back into play. My world collapsed. I had been taking penalties for as long as I could remember but now I'd missed the most important penalty of my life, in the semi-final of the World Cup.

If the walk from the centre circle had been long and nerve-racking, the walk back was a nightmare as the first onrush of tears pricked at my eyes. I had given away our advantage. We had won the toss and elected to take the first penalty, which Gary Lineker tucked away. Peter Beardsley and David Platt scored, but the Germans were unshakeable. Brehme, Matthaus and Riedle beat Peter Shilton. Now at 3–3, the advantage swung heavily towards the Germans. All I could do was pray that Thon evened the balance and missed his. He didn't, of course, and it was up to Chris Waddle to keep us in it and at least force the Germans to take their fifth penalty. He put the ball into orbit and we were out of the World Cup, facing a third-place play-off against Italy instead of the final in Rome against an Argentinian team we felt sure we could beat.

I don't blame Chris. I don't blame anyone but myself. It was my fault that England were not in the World Cup final. Friends surrounded me; special friends including Des Walker along with my other Nottingham Forest colleagues Steve Hodge and Neil Webb. But it scarcely eased the pain. Mark Wright was the first to come up, quickly followed by Terry Butcher. They put their arms around me and told me not to worry. My Forest team-mates knew me better than the others and knew that I would be in no mood to talk.

I noticed as I walked off that Gazza and a few others had gone over to the fans to applaud them for their support. I would normally have been there with them because I appreciate the effort the fans make, the time and money spent, to come and watch England play. I am from a working-class background and I know it means a lot when the players go over to say thank you. But on this occasion I couldn't do it. I felt guilty because I'd let them down. Neil Webb threw me a towel because I was sobbing my heart out. I had it over my head like a convicted criminal leaving a courthouse. I had never cried on a football pitch before. The towel hid the tears. I didn't want them to be seen in public; crying is something you do behind closed doors. Once Chris had missed and I knew that we weren't going any further, it was a case of getting away from the arena as quickly as possible. I wasn't running away to hide because I'm not that way inclined. It was just that I could do no more, we had lost, we were out and I didn't want to shed my tears in front of the cameras and the thousands in the stadium.

As I reached the touchline, our manager Bobby Robson was there. I had let him down too. He was gutted like the rest of us. We all knew that this was our final; get through this one and we would win the World Cup. We knew we had enough about us to go all the way. The confidence was building game after game following a bad start. Bobby came over, gave me a tap and said, 'Unlucky, son.' But it's not always words. Des Walker, who knew me better than most, came over and he didn't have to say anything to me. He knew how I felt and I knew what he was thinking. It wasn't a case of 'how are you doing' and 'don't worry'. Of course I was going to worry. It made no difference that Chris Waddle went on to miss as well. I was the one who missed first and piled all the pressure on him. As far as I was concerned, it was my fault, my responsibility that we lost. Chris Waddle's penalty was irrelevant. As soon as I missed, if the Germans scored twice we were out.

To this day I admire everyone who goes up to take a penalty in those circumstances, especially the Germans. Every time we have come up against them they have held their nerve, even in our own backyard. Credit to them, it shows a lot of mental strength. I don't know whether mental strength helps you score a penalty or even whether practising does, but you have to admire teams who manage to hold their nerve more often than not in something they call a lottery. It is not such a lottery for them.

I took penalties for my club so I had not bothered practising. Anyway, in those days penalty shoot-outs were the exception rather than the rule. It changed, of course, as time went on with penalty kicks deciding cup matches at every level from European Cup finals to World Cup finals. As they became more frequent, managers became cuter, putting on good penalty-takers in the final minutes as substitutes.

I could practise 100 penalties in the morning but it wouldn't help me score from the spot at ten o'clock that night when it mattered. There was a lot of criticism levelled at Glenn Hoddle for not insisting his team practised spot-kicks before the World Cup against Argentina in France eight years on, but I'm not sure that was justified. If I were to level a criticism it would be that the penalty-takers and the back-up were not named before the game. Then it would be up to the individual to go off with a goalkeeper and practise if that was what he wanted. To my mind, a match situation cannot be recreated no matter how hard you try.

In Italy I volunteered to take the third penalty but Bobby Robson felt that the fourth was the most important and wanted me, as a regular penalty-taker, to shoulder the responsibility for that one. The team's penalty-taker, in our case Gary Lineker, takes either the first or the last. What you need most of all is five people who want to take the penalties, without having to break their arms to persuade them. Then you have to look around for others if it goes beyond there.

The five penalty-takers that summer's day in Turin really picked themselves. Bobby knew and we knew who would be taking them – Gary Lineker, Peter Beardsley, David Platt, myself and Chris Waddle, all confident in our own ability to score from 12 yards. I don't think Paul Gascoigne wanted to be one of the five, although he would have taken his place afterwards, offering to take the sixth – a brave option. Des Walker wouldn't have wanted to take one, not because he was scared but simply because he was not a good penalty-taker. He readily admitted that he had scored just one goal in his entire career. No one in the team had a bigger heart than Tony Adams but he, like Des, wouldn't be one you would expect to take a penalty. No one has his guts but you would say to yourself surely there is someone better than him. There were those who did and those who didn't and we all knew who they were without going into great debates. That was not what happened with Glenn in France. His five penalty-takers weren't the logical choice. But ask anyone close to the team in 1990 and they would say that we had the correct five.

I have often wondered what would have happened had we put Dave Beasant in goal in time for the penalties. He's a big bloke, fills the goal. He had come out as a replacement for the injured David Seaman and brought with him a great reputation for saving penalties, including in a Cup Final at Wembley against odds-on favourite Liverpool. On the other hand, I couldn't remember the last penalty Peter Shilton had saved.

Who knows? Maybe the day will come when there's a specialist goalkeeper on the bench and you bring him on in the same way that you bring on a penalty-taker in the last few minutes. Imagine the psychology of the situation. It would certainly give the opposition food for thought because the move would be a very obvious one and they would be thinking, 'Oh, oh, what have we got here?' They would see this big monster coming on and the first-choice goalkeeper, captain as it happened, going off. I know I would be thinking the worst.

Martin O'Neill did it for Leicester City in the League Cup when he brought off injured Tim Flowers and sent on Pegguy Arphexad who had saved penalties in the competition before. He is shrewd is Martin O'Neill. I noticed on the way to winning the competition he made late substitutions to send on penalty-takers.

But it would have been a brave manager who took off Peter Shilton for that reason. He had been magnificent for England for 20 years and had more than played his part in taking us as far as the semi-finals. I still wonder if big Beasant might have saved one of those spot-kicks. Peter claimed he went the right way for every penalty but you can do that once the ball has hit the back of the net! He could offer an even better argument by saying England would have had a better chance if they had taken me off.

As I was leaving the field in Turin, Thomas Berthold, the German right wing-back whom I had been up against for the last two hours, came up and wanted to swap shirts. I wasn't in the mood to do it there and then and I told him to come into the dressing-room afterwards and I would look after it then. The last thing I wanted to do was to wear a German shirt as I walked off the pitch.

I was massively disappointed for myself and seeing the look on Bobby's face did not help. It was his last chance with England and he must have thought that he was about to emulate Sir Alf Ramsey and win the World Cup. I had let the nation down, but most of all I had let him down. He was and is a good man. Everyone who knows him and especially those who played for him like him and I have never heard a bad word about him.

As I reached the sanctuary of the dressing-room there was a tap on my shoulder and Doc Crane was telling me that I had been picked for the drug test. My immediate reaction was to hell with it. I won't do it. I'm not getting involved in that. But it was just the Doc doing his job.

The dressing-room was like a morgue. There were a lot of tears. Myself, Chris Waddle and some of the others were sobbing. I sat there thinking that I had let them all down even though it was evident that they were not thinking that way. The grieving was interrupted when a couple of the Germans came in, including Berthold. They were most civil and polite but a couple of our lads took offence. Steve Hodge shouted at them, 'Fuck off out of here.' He was distraught and thought they had come to rub our noses in it but I told him to leave it and exchanged shirts as promised.

Peter Shilton was the other England name to come out of the hat for a drug test and, having taken on board extra fluids, we went to the medical room where we joined the two Germans who had been nominated. Had an outsider walked in they wouldn't have known who were the winners and who were the losers. That's how respectful the Germans were. There was no question of them gloating over their victory. Shilts was lucky. He walked in, had a pee and walked out again leaving the three of us sitting there waiting for something to happen. The two Germans said nothing about the missed penalty; they just kept their own counsel and respected my silence. I appreciated that for I was in no mood for chitchat. I wasn't just low, I was double low. I'm not sure that the English would have behaved as well. I guess if the roles had been reversed, we would probably have been jumping around, laughing and celebrating. I appreciated their professionalism when I thought about it later. They had achieved a massive honour but, at the same time, they clearly knew how I felt. I had my head down all of the time and didn't take in their faces. I couldn't say who they were, but right now I would like to thank them.

I learned a good lesson. When we beat Spain on penalties in Euro 96, I celebrated the goal but when we won I went up quietly and shook hands with the Spanish players who had missed. I didn't want to be rubbing it in. I also congratulated the Germans when they beat us one match later. I cried then, not just because we had lost but because I had made up my mind that I was going to retire whichever way the result went. I thought it was my last international game.

It took the two Germans almost half an hour to give their samples but I was so dehydrated that still nothing happened. I was in there for a good hour and a half and still not able to take a leak. We were probably losing six pounds a game during the World Cup in the heat of an Italian summer, and despite drinking litre after litre of water I was just soaking it up like a sponge. In the end, I walked around the deserted stadium with Doc Crane for company, just the pair of us walking around having a quiet chat. Seventy-five minutes earlier I had been on that pitch in the midst of the action, and here I was now with my belly swollen and sloshing round with water. What I really wanted at that moment was to be with the rest of the team, commiserating and supporting, a group of blokes together in a time of mutual despair that only we could fully appreciate.

When I did finally have that long-awaited leak and returned to join them, they were all sitting on the coach waiting for me. I can't even remember whether I apologised to them. I was gone. The first to come up to me again was the manager who told me to keep my head up and not worry. I sat down on my own and Terry Butcher came and sat by me. I cried all the way back to the hotel. I was glad that it was Butch. I knew what he said was coming from the heart because he had the same attitude and passion for the game as me. It must have been hurting him as well; he knew that this was his last tournament. Even so, I would have preferred to sit on my own in my abject misery but he sat there for a good half an hour talking to me and doing what he thought was right.

There was a meal laid on at the hotel when we returned but I just went straight up to bed. I was rooming with Des Walker, as usual, and for once it wasn't him keeping me awake with his incessant chatter. We were old room-mates. He liked to stay up late and talk and I liked to go to sleep. I would usually doze off, wake up every half an hour or so and say 'yes Des', 'no Des' until he went off to sleep. But it pays to have a friend alongside you to share the load. He knew when to talk and when not to talk – and boy could he talk. This time he kept silent and that tells me volumes about the man.

I couldn't get to sleep anyway thinking about the game, and having started to pee I couldn't stop. I was going every half an hour and I didn't want to keep Des awake. After going half a dozen times I got hold of one of the old tin wastepaper bins and put it by the side of the bed. Every time I wanted to go I just rolled over and urinated out of the bed straight into the tin. Poor Des, it must have sounded like a machine-gun at first and then a waterfall. All you could hear was the noise made by the tin and come the morning I had virtually filled it. All I can say is that it was a good job that the bin had a good seal on it! Des claims he slept through it all.

The next day the management had arranged for the team to meet up with our wives and families at another hotel. I had not seen Liz or my father and mother, Dennis and Lil, since before the game. I apologised to them when we met and immediately filled up again. But that was to be the end of my tears. Football beckoned with a third-place play-off game against the hosts Italy in Bari.

It is always a massive let-down for a player to face what is a consolation match when you feel you should be in the final and this one turned out to be an even bigger disappointment for me because Bobby Robson decided to leave me out. Had I been a bit more experienced and a bit older I would have stood up to the manager and told him forcibly, 'There is no way you are going to leave me out of this game after what happened to me.' Certainly Peter Shilton did. Bobby was going to play Dave Beasant instead but this was going to be Shilton's last game. He said he wanted to play and was reinstated. He had 125 caps and had the right to say it. But I was young and had too much respect for Bobby Robson to start throwing my weight around and he decided for his own good reasons to leave out both me and Chris Waddle, saying that he wanted to give the patient Tony Dorigo a game and that Chris was looking tired.

It concerned me that people would think I had wanted to be left out and was hiding after missing the penalty. Quite the opposite was true. I wanted to go out and show how well I could play. I wanted to prove to everyone that I wasn't afraid. I believe that had I said so, Bobby Robson would have played me for at least part of the game.

It would have been selfish of me not to let Tony Dorigo play. He had been with us all the way through, his parents were there and he was especially keen to play against the hosts because of his Italian ancestry. Nevertheless, it remains a regret, and I missed a cap.

We all stripped and sat on the bench anyway. The pressure had gone and it was a carnival atmosphere, although we lost 2–1. At half-time we stayed out and had a kickabout and it was so relaxed that I walked over to the touchline and talked to Liz in the crowd.

There was another twist to the tale when the physio came on to the pitch and gave me a shout that I might be going on. Bobby and all the staff were in the medical room with Mark Wright who had one of his socks and boots off. I heard Bobby say, 'I don't give a fuck. Get your boot back on and get out there for the second half.' It was not the first time Mark had complained on the trip and Bobby was adamant that he should go out and run it off. I should have said then, 'Get him off and get me on. I'm desperate. He doesn't want to play. I do.'

It was back home the next day and I thought that Chrissie and I were going to be lynched when we arrived back at Luton airport. We had heard a whisper that there were a lot of people waiting for us and I was dreading it. All I wanted to do was to go home to Nottingham because I knew that with my relationship with the people and the football fans I would have no hassle. Nottingham is not a hotbed of football and they would let me get on with my life, leave me alone and let me have my own time.

An open-topped bus was waiting to take us from the airport to the Hilton Hotel at Junction 11 on the M1. Both Chris and I sat downstairs out of the way. We were taking no chances. But we need not have worried. There was not one bad word from anyone. The support was tremendous. What should have been a 15-minute drive took us almost five hours so dense were the crowds. Talking to Chris about it now, it is still unbelievable the way people rallied round. I am sure it is the British spirit. It was just incredible; everyone got behind us and I couldn't understand it because I expected to be hammered. In Italy, we were insulated from how people were feeling about the World Cup. I am not much of a newspaper reader and, anyway, things are hyped up.

When we realised there wasn't a lynch mob waiting, Chris and I quickly made our way to the top of the bus. People had turned up to say well done and that we had been unlucky the way we went out. It would have been rude to stay downstairs. At least I wasn't wearing a pair of plastic tits and a false bum like Gazza at the front of the bus; I preferred to be a little more sedate at the back.

I don't think you should glorify losers but I have to admit that reception gave me a huge lift. Maybe it was because we lost gloriously and went out trying. I must have received over 500 letters of support and I replied to every one. It was the least I could do but it was still a total surprise. There was not one nutcase nor a single anonymous slagging. I expected at least one from Chris Waddle telling me that it was entirely my fault.

Admittedly, some people made up for it the following season with chants of 'Pearce is a German' and I was the one with the target on my back. But I had taken something positive from that dreadful time and had by far my best season for Forest, in fact my best season in football. I scored 16 goals with not a penalty among them; Nigel

Clough was taking them successfully at the time. He took over before we went to Italy.

Brian Clough didn't say a word about the World Cup when we returned. His main concern was that the four of us would come back from Italy thinking that we were big hitters. I can't remember having any dialogue with him other than asking for some extra days off as there were only eight days between the day we returned and going back to pre-season training. He told me that I couldn't because he had signed a contract committing us to a trip abroad.

I thought I had cleansed myself of that penalty miss in Turin long before my goal from the spot in the shoot-out against Spain in Euro 96 but watching the video now, I'm not so sure. My emotional reaction was the culmination of several things – scoring a goal for England; the competition being on our own soil; and thinking the tournament was going to be my last for England. Perhaps there was also something lingering deep down from Turin.

When Terry Venables first rang me up, I'm sure he hoped I would retire when he told me that I would not be his first choice left-back. I responded that if he thought I was good enough to be in the squad, I was prepared to sit in the stand if necessary and wait for my chance. I think that shook him. That was in 1995 and I spent a lot of time watching Graeme Le Saux play at left-back. He played reasonably well for his country and it was only his injury that got me back in. I was lucky. I wouldn't wish that on anyone but so often in football one person's downfall is another's bonus. I would much prefer to stand up, fight my ground and put him out of the team by my own form.

Terry left the door open for me to walk away from England but I'm glad I never did. Come that penalty against Spain I was well pleased that I had hung around on the off chance.

This was a completely different situation from that warm, pulsating night in Turin. When I was walking up this time I knew that the entire stadium was behind me. It was tangible. The whole of Wembley was buzzing. But I was also aware that half the people in the stadium were thinking, 'Oh no, not him again,' while the other half were probably saying to themselves, 'Don't let him miss this time.'

Afterwards Liz asked me why it always seemed to be me on the spot. My response was that I would rather take one than send a mate of mine up for him to miss. Liz was sitting with her brother and they apparently just looked at each other when I made my way to the penalty area. Neither said a word. No one knew I was going to take a penalty that day, not even me.

Terry had told us to practise spot-kicks prior to the game but it hadn't been sorted out who would take them and in what order. Practice was crazy anyway and far too light-hearted to be of any real use. One of us would put the ball down to take a penalty and Paul Ince would steal up and hit it. It ended up with Incy taking more penalties than anyone else. The only thing we knew for sure was that Alan Shearer would be taking one because he was the nominated penalty-taker. When Terry came off the bench to sort it out, I made a beeline for him and said that I wanted to take the third one.

'Are you sure?' he asked.

I had never been surer of anything. If he had said no I

would have fought it. I don't know whether I surprised him but I felt that I had, just as I did when I said I was prepared to sit in the stand and wait my chance.

When I scored, my reaction wasn't stage-managed. It was a release of pressure and if you looked around the stadium you could see the relief and joy on every English supporter's face. Like me, they probably celebrated that particular penalty more than any of our others. It was a great feeling of elation but after my initial celebrations it was a case of being a bit humble, remembering how proper the Germans were.

No one deserved credit more than David Seaman, the Arsenal goalkeeper. Not only did he make the save that took us past Spain but he was also our best player throughout the tournament. I congratulated him quickly but didn't get involved in the mêlée. I went off to find the Spanish lad, Nadal, who had missed and shook his hand, trying to keep a civil head on it because I remembered what had happened to me. I drew the line, however, at going into their dressing-room. I hadn't been invited and sometimes it can be misconstrued, as it was by Hodgey when Berthold came in for my shirt.

When we went back to the training pitch on Monday morning to prepare for the German game, I already knew my strategy if it went to penalties. I told Terry Venables that I wanted to take the third one again. It would have been extreme cowardice to score against Spain and then not take one against the Germans. I knew that the Germans would be thorough. They would have watched every video of every penalty-taker and noted in which directions they shot. It was my belief that the German goalkeeper, Andreas

Kopke, would dive the way we took our penalties against Spain. I sought out our penalty expert Alan Shearer and explained my theory to him and asked him, 'Are you going to change direction if it goes to penalties?'

'I'm not going to tell you,' he replied.

'Well, cheers mate,' I said. 'I'll watch you anyway as you take the first penalty.'

Maybe he had heard the chants around the grounds that I was a German and didn't trust me after my miss in the 1990 World Cup.

Of course, it went to penalties. I was sure that my theory was right because a German goalkeeper would be so professional that he would know which way he was going to dive against each penalty-taker. If a player took one which went to the goalkeeper's right against Spain, he would dive to his right.

Alan took the first and he chose the opposite corner to his penalty against Spain; the goalkeeper went the other way. I thought that was going to throw a spanner in the works. If the second penalty-kicker, David Platt, went for the other corner as well, what would the goalkeeper think then? I was in a quandary until Platty took the penalty. He went the same way as before – the goalkeeper guessed right but failed to save it. That put my mind at rest and I went up thinking if I went in the other direction I would score.

Don't get me wrong, the pressure was on – it always will be at that level – but in David Seaman we had a goalkeeper who was playing so well. He had already saved Gary McAllister's penalty against Scotland as well as Nadal's against Spain and he was such a colossus I just couldn't see him being beaten. That's not meant as any sort of slur on

Peter Shilton six years earlier; it was just that Seaman was in such prime form I couldn't see us being beaten if we scored our penalties. I simply couldn't see him letting five penalties in and even now when I watch it on the video I cannot believe he did not stop one of them.

To be honest, the pressure had lifted in comparison with the game against Spain when I felt the weight of the world on my shoulders. The pressure was still there but it was different, and I had convinced myself that provided I changed corners I could even sidefoot it in. That's how confident I was of scoring.

I went through the usual routine and hit the penalty with far less force than usual. In fact, if Kopke had gone the right way he would have saved it; it would have been a doddle. He could almost have headed it out. The BBC's Barry Davies said on the commentary, 'What a penalty! What a great penalty!' It was not a great penalty; it was a shite penalty but the goalkeeper had gone the wrong way. I had done my homework and it had paid off. It was a great feeling that it had worked. I knew that this time the advantage was mine. It gave us a chance of going to the final but it didn't give me the same feeling as the goal against Spain.

Hassler, Strunz, Reuter, Ziege and Kuntz took tremendous penalties and although Dave Seaman got near to a couple he couldn't save any of them. Our first five were rattled away with equal authority as Shearer, Platt, myself, Gascoigne and Sheringham all scored. Then came Gareth Southgate. How my heart bled for my young friend.

Before we came together with England, we didn't know each other at all but straightaway we hit it off. He is an excellent professional and that's something I admire in a player. The way he talks is very mature and he is not a beer-swilling player who is going to be a bad influence on the game. I was impressed with Gareth. He puts his heart and soul into his profession and we struck up a good friendship.

So when he missed his penalty, I went straight up to him to console him. Andy Moller completed the *coup de grâce* with another fine penalty and we were out. He even showboated a bit, puffing out his chest in a parody of Gascoigne. Who could blame him? They had come in the three lions' den and bitten our heads off again. I have to give them total credit. They came into our backyard and scored six out of six penalties. You have to applaud their bottle.

I swapped shirts with winger Thomas Hassler and joined the others in a lap of honour that gave me my best footballing memory. Euro 96, with my family there, the atmosphere in the stadium and the closeness of the team, brought a joy greater than I had ever experienced, and walking round Wembley thinking I was never going to do this again or represent my country again brought the tears. I was there as understudy to Graeme Le Saux and only played because of an injury. Every time I pulled on an England shirt it was a bonus to me.

I hadn't gone straight from school to a football career. I had worked for a living and I walked around Wembley thinking to myself, 'I'm an electrician and here I am at one of the great football moments in English history.' This was something I loved doing. It wasn't a game of football; this was my life. I have a wife, Liz, and a daughter, Chelsea, but this was different and the pride I had in playing for

England and the thought it would never happen again made me very emotional.

Gary Lineker made a statement when he retired saying that he had more important things in his life – his wife and his family – and that football was just something he had done. I am not like that at all. I find that attitude as alien as probably he finds mine of football being something far more than just a game that you play for fun. People might find that attitude odd but I'm convinced a lot of supporters and players share it. Anyway, I'm not sure I totally believed Gary. He loved the game. I suppose some love it more than others and some of us have a great passion for the sport. Looking back on my career, I still have that great surge of passion and pride.

We saw our families to commiserate and then we boarded our bus. Just before we pulled out from Wembley I asked Terry if I could say something over the microphone. I told the other lads it had been an honour and a privilege to play with them, it was my last game and that I was retiring. As a footnote, I added that I wasn't retiring from football and would still be around the Premier Division to kick shit out of them.

Back at the hotel, we ordered beers. Our football had finished, there was no third-place play-off, so we were on holiday. We stayed up for most of the night. Sleep was impossible after that with so much adrenalin still flooding through our bodies. Terry told us we could go home if we wanted to but we all stayed, had a meal together and then got drunk together.

Gareth went straight up to his room to telephone his family and then came and joined us in the bar. As he walked in, Tony Adams booed and hissed at him and that broke the ice. Gareth was under a cloud, an awful cloud, and Rodders (Adams) had done the right thing. Everyone laughed and it lightened the atmosphere.

As everyone finished their dinner and drifted out to the bar I was left talking to Gareth. We had a long chat and I hope it helped him having me there. The others could only imagine what he was suffering but I knew for sure.

There were more than a few who took offence when Chris Waddle and I joined Gareth in a television advert that raised a laugh out of the three of us missing crucial penalties. As far as I was concerned, the penalty trauma was in the past. The ghost had been vanquished and banished when Pizza Hut asked me to do the advert, offering me £40,000, a considerable sum of money for what amounted to one day's work. I couldn't really turn it down. To be honest, if it had been straight after the 1990 World Cup I wouldn't have done it. Wild horses wouldn't have dragged me within a mile of television cameras.

But in 1996, for me it was just a spin-off of being a professional footballer. I found it very amusing and so did Chrissie. I think Gareth did as well. He had his doubts about doing it but the two of us persuaded him. 'It's old hat,' we said. 'Everybody misses penalties. Go for it.'

Call me a hypocrite or worse – when he asked me if I would have done it just after the 1990 World Cup, I told him I would. In my defence, in 1990 the entire issue of penalty shoot-outs was new. They hadn't happened that often. By the time Gareth missed his, there had been lots of such dramas all around the world at every level. Also, if he hadn't agreed, there would be no fees for Chris and me!

Selfish? Maybe, but most people took it the right way and I don't think it harmed Gareth at all. Sometimes in our game you have to laugh at yourself and this was some sort of relief for all of us.

It was hardest for Gareth in every sense – he was the butt of the joke and he was the one who had to keep eating the pizzas. The pizza he was seen eating in the advert had to look hot and steamy so someone kept blowing cigarette smoke on it. Imagine how awful that was for a non-smoker and fitness fanatic. Chris and I kept cocking it up on purpose so that he had to take yet another bite. We had him on about 20 takes before we relented.

The advert was shot in a studio in Park Royal starting at eight in the morning. I left at seven in the evening. It was exhausting. Gareth had more to do than the rest of us. Chris finished his part and shot off, and when I left the poor boy was still hard at it, shooting the scene where he stood up and walked into a post. He had to stay for another two hours, bumping into two Germans, and he finally went home at around nine, tired and feeling sick from all the pizzas he had to eat.

Of course, the simple way out would have been not to volunteer to take penalties in the first place. Certainly that was Liz's feeling. Why, she asked, did I continually put myself in this position? It was because I had been taking penalties for so long and I did so because I could strike the ball well. It dated back to my childhood. When you are a kid and you hit the ball firmly, you tend to take all the free kicks and penalties as I did from schooldays onwards. It is also part of my character and I have always wanted to do it.

At most of my clubs I have also been captain and it is a natural extension of that responsibility.

It's easy enough to take a penalty when you're 3–0 up but the higher the stakes the harder it becomes. One of the first misses I remember was in the County Cup in a Sunday league for a very strong team called Bourne Hall. Apart from me, we had John Humphrey who went on to play for Wolves and Charlton, and Gary Waddock who played for Queens Park Rangers. Most of the others were attached to Watford. I was one of the lesser lights in the side. That day the pitch was thick mud. We were awarded a penalty, I didn't hit it hard enough and the goalkeeper saved it. To this day the coach will remind me that I missed a penalty that cost us a game when he would have put money on me to score.

At Wealdstone when I was 18 and in my first season, we played AP Leamington with so much on it that the winners would stay up and the losers would be relegated. It was a bigger deal than normal because who went into the newly formed Alliance Premier and who didn't depended on the result. It was even more massive for me as I was being paid £15 a week for doing something I loved. It was a baking hot day, the last game of the season, we were 1–0 up and cruising. We had a lad on loan from Millwall named Jimmy Swetzer. I had not heard of him before and I have not heard of him since. He missed a penalty; we lost and went down.

That was my first experience of what a missed penalty could do. Had he scored we would have been two up and we would never have lost but he was on loan and probably didn't care too much one way or another. The rest of us were stuck with the outcome and I was there for 12 months trying to get out of the Southern League and back into the Alliance.

There was a repeat scenario when I was playing for Coventry. We needed to win our last three matches in the 1983–84 season to stay in the top division. Nowadays every game finishes at the same time on the last Sunday but it was not the case then. We beat Luton 1–0 when Brian Kilcline scored a goal in the 82nd minute, thundering one in from the edge of the box. We went to Stoke in the next game and I scored from the spot in the last ten minutes, whipping one across the goalkeeper like the one I took against Spain. Then Ian Painter had a penalty at the other end. He took a long run up, smashed it against the underside of the crossbar and it bounced up so high that our goalkeeper Steve Ogrizovic caught it on the way down. Had that gone in and the game finished in a draw, we were down regardless of our last result.

On the last day we were due to play the league champions Everton on a Sunday at Highfield Road. Everyone else had finished so we knew that a win would keep us up. We won 4–1. You could smell the booze on the breath of the Everton players. We were sure that they had been out on the Saturday night to celebrate. We were trying our hearts out but if the game had been played a month earlier when they were chasing championship points, they would have wiped the floor with us. They had lost seven games all season. We won three games in the last week and yet previously we had won just 12 games all the rest of the season. In retrospect, the two penalties in the Stoke game proved to be critical.

Another crucial penalty in the Stuart Pearce scrapbook

was in the quarter-final of the League Cup against Arsenal in the late eighties. We were 2–0 down at the time and I missed from the penalty spot. We scored after that and were playing well enough to have taken something out of the game. I thought we could have won if I had scored. I can be the most philosophical player in the world when someone else is taking and missing penalties.

Free kicks are all part of the same thing but without the pressure of taking a penalty. You are expected to score from the spot but if you score from a free kick outside the penalty area you are hailed as a hero. There is nothing I relish more than a free kick just to the right-hand side of the penalty area. At Forest, Nigel Clough was brilliant at winning free kicks in that zone. He wanted the ball to feet and when he was touched from behind he would go down. We set the wall up so that we had someone masking the ball from the goalkeeper, so I got in a lot of strikes and goals at that time. I scored from one in the semi-final of the League Cup against Coventry City. I curled the ball in from wide and it hit the underside of the bar, beating Oggi. It put us in the final and gave that particular Forest team the first bit of silverware for Brian Clough.

In those days we were being awarded two, three and sometimes four free kicks in good positions every game. Even if the goalkeeper saved from them, more often than not there would be the pickings for the others to follow up on. Nigel wasn't a diver but he was very clever. He was ahead of his time because that's how it's played now when, at the merest contact, down the forward goes. You have to be cute.

I hear and understand the arguments about cheating and

diving but to me it's clever play. I never take a dive and if I did I would probably look such an idiot the referee would laugh and play on, or book me. Much of the time, as the laws stand now, if you are stupid enough to make that lunging tackle, you have to expect the worst. When Paolo di Canio goes down and wins a penalty for West Ham, I would never ever criticise him or any other player for diving. If it were me who conceded the penalty, I would probably blame myself more than the forward. I would probably have a little moan at him at the time but you have to think to yourself that if you can't win the ball then don't make the tackle.

People used to say that I wouldn't be able to cope with the new interpretation of the rules at either club or international level, but you have to learn and adjust. In the end, it makes you a better player.

yak jensen, the three-time loser

I was never a big lad. If anything I was a bit small and skinny and, consequently, there was no queue of top clubs knocking on my parents' door in Kingsbury, a free kick away from Wembley Stadium. In fact, I was a pretty normal sort. I played semi-professional football at Wealdstone on a Saturday afternoon, went down to the local pub on a Saturday night and turned out for my mates' team, Dynamo Kingsbury Kiev, on a Sunday morning.

I wasn't supposed to play for them because of my contract with Wealdstone but these were my best mates, most of them schoolmates, and I didn't want to miss out on the fun. We cooked up the scheme that I would play in goal under the assumed name of Yak Jensen. I had to look the part, of course, and I wore a spectacular tangerine and black goalkeeping kit complete with an embroidered number one along with the name Jensen. A pair of long black shorts that came down to my knees completed the outfit. It was hardly a case of hiding my true identity – if I wasn't spotted in that get-up I certainly was when I went upfield for corners and free kicks. I did lots of stupid things like standing on the penalty spot to take crosses with four defenders on the line. I would also throw the ball out to the wing and then chase it myself, taking on opponents because I was confident that I was better than most of the players in that league.

Not everybody appreciated this colourful 'Russian' interloper and now and again someone would take offence, come across and whack me down as I tried to push the ball past them. 'That will teach you to come out of your goal, Jensen,' I heard more than once. I knew that if I had played under my proper name, sooner or later I was going to get collared. Even so I was taking a risk but I enjoyed every minute and one season I even finished top goalscorer in the team with seven. It was a great laugh and was simply an extension of Saturday night out with the lads.

All good things have to come to an end and, sure enough, one winter Sunday morning one of the rivals caught up with me. I had come to the edge of my box and was caught on the side of the leg. I didn't think much of it at the time and carried on playing even though it was a bit sore. Wealdstone's training was called off on Tuesday because of the bad weather and it wasn't until I went in on the Thursday that I began to realise that something was wrong. It was still icy so all we did was run up and down. The leg was worse but I said nothing. We were due to play at Runcorn on the Saturday and when I went out for the warm-up it became obvious that it was far more serious than I thought. As I went to turn, it felt as though someone had thrown a lump of mud at the back of my leg with quite a smack. It turned out that I had fractured the small bone, the tibia, and when I turned it snapped completely.

I limped into the dressing-room and told the manager, 'I think I've broken my leg.'

'What?' he said.

'I think I've broken my leg. I thought at first it was one of the boys messing around and throwing something at me but there was no one near. I think it's broken.' He wasn't convinced.

'We've only got one substitute with us. Do you think you can go out and give it a go? See how it goes.'

I agreed. It was only a small bone, not load bearing, so I thought I could get away with it. I lasted five minutes before I had to give it up and as I limped back to the bench along the touchline one of the Scousers leaned over the barrier and yelled, 'You soft Southern twat.' He thought I'd gone off because I'd bumped into someone.

I went off for an X-ray and the hospital confirmed my worst fears. I was out for six weeks and that was when I decided that Yak Jensen should hang up his goalkeeping gloves and return to the anonymity of the Russian plains.

I really missed the Sunday football; not that it stopped me meeting up with the lads. We continued to sink our pints together at the Plough in Kingsbury, usually going on to the Preston in Preston Road. We used to drink a fair bit and lads being lads we got into the odd scrape or two. I have to hold up my hands and confess that I was as bad as the rest of them. I blotted my copybook enough to have three convictions against me.

The first offence was taking and driving away a car. A group of us had been to a nightclub in Acton and left so late that there were no tubes and we couldn't get a cab for love nor money. In our weak defence it was not like the modern car theft, which is a serious offence and a real stigma, but more of a minor misdemeanour. We were desperate to get home and when we spotted an ancient Escort, we piled in. We thought that when we got home we could telephone the police anonymously and tell them where it was, or even drive it back to where we had found it the next morning. As jack-the-lad teenagers you tend to think silly things like that.

The three of us jumped in the car, turned the ignition using someone's house key and shot off. We were so naïve. We were only a couple of miles from home when, sure enough, the Old Bill saw these three kids batting along in an old motor, flashed us to stop and nicked us. I took control of the situation and said to the other two not to say a word and under no circumstances to tell them our real names. They nodded but as soon as the copper asked, 'What's your name?' I immediately replied, 'Stuart Pearce, sir.' So much for the hardened criminal.

I was gutted. I went to Harrow Magistrates Court where I was fined £100 and handed a year's ban from driving. I was thoroughly ashamed and very grateful that my parents hadn't heard about it. But I hadn't thought that one through either and, sure enough, a brown envelope popped through the front door with Harrow Magistrates Court emblazoned across the back. Naturally, my mum and dad opened it and discovered that their son was a convicted criminal.

The boys down the pub, who had been through the experience before, told me that the secret was always to take your chequebook with you to court so that you could pay the fine on the spot. That way no bumf is pushed through the front door. It was a little late for all that good advice and I suffered a serious grilling over the escapade from my parents with my dad even calling round my eldest brother Ray to try to find out if I was truly going off the rails.

It would be nice to say that I learned my lesson and trod the straight and narrow afterwards but I didn't and shamefully admit I was done twice more, once for being drunk and disorderly and then for criminal damage. At least I learned one lesson and neither my mum nor dad knew anything about offences two and three – well they didn't until they read this!

My mates to this day will say that there are two Stuart Pearces – the footballer and the lad they know. Certainly I proved that I could be as stupid as the rest of them. The difference now, however, is that I am a professional in the limelight and I know that I have to watch my step even though I still have a few beers, a laugh and take the piss with the best of them. They don't let me forget how I became a three-time loser.

As usual, the demon booze was at the heart of the matter and my second brush with the law came after a visit to a local nightclub when a friend of ours, behaving a bit over the top, had his collar felt. Showing admirable solidarity, we followed him down to the nearest police station. When we arrived he was already banged up in the back. Undeterred we approached the duty sergeant and asked if Mr Mitchell was there. When he confirmed that he was, we politely asked for the waiting room only to be told that there was one but we couldn't use it. With that the sergeant turned his back and disappeared into his office. Of course, we found the waiting room and went in to sit it out until they released our mate. We were soon discovered by a constable.

'You lot can't wait in here,' he said.

'Why not?' I asked. 'It says waiting room and we're waiting for our friend.'

He didn't like our attitude. 'One more word from any of you lot and you're nicked as well.'

Sure of my rights, I answered indignantly, 'You can't do that.'

He could and he did. He pointed at me and said, 'You'll do,' and promptly nicked me for being drunk and disorderly. I wouldn't have minded but I wasn't even drunk! I couldn't believe that I'd been arrested. It was embarrassing to be done on such a charge when all I wanted to do was sit in a waiting room.

That is not the end of this sorry tale of criminal activity. A week later the Sunday team went out for our usual dinner dance. That was a fancy name for meeting down the local, in this case the Green Man, where we each chipped in a fiver, more than enough to start the kitty with pints at 50 pence. I was delegated to collect the whip, make a note of the drinks and fetch them from the bar. On the way, I had a bright idea. I suggested to the barmaid that since every time I came up it would be the same order, if I paid her the same amount as the first round each time, it would save us both a lot of time and trouble. She was happy with the arrangement unaware that I had a little scam going. I paid the 13 or 14 quid for the 20 or so drinks and the next time I simply read off the list but added myself a drink at the top, another in the middle of the order and a third at the end and still paid the same money. I would take up one of the boys, ask him what he was drinking, and we would stand there and enjoy the first one on the house while she filled the remainder of the order.

Needless to say, I was several drinks ahead of the rest when we finally lurched out of the pub and staggered down Wembley High Road, past the Hilton Hotel and into the Greyhound on the corner. Football supporters will confirm that it is a rough-and-ready pub now but it was even rougher in those days. They had a live band and we played up to it, doing forward rolls on the dancefloor and generally larking around.

The dinner part of the evening followed at closing time, when we were uncorked into Wembley High Street to look for a curry house or fish and chip shop. It was then that, in my wisdom, I decided to climb a traffic light. Don't ask me why because to this day I haven't a clue. As if that wasn't daft enough, once at the top I decided to remove the little plastic cone, all under the surprised eyes of two policemen who watched the entire cameo. So I was nicked again, caught as they say 'bang to rights'.

I should have been set for a night in the cells to sleep it off but there were about 20 of us and the others followed us down to the station. Clearly the police were worried that they might have a minor riot on their hands and they let me straight out in response to the football-like chant of 'let him out, let him out' at the counter of the Wembley Police Station. They charged me to attend Harrow Magistrates Court, would you believe, on the same day that I was due to appear at the same place for my alleged drunk and disorderly charge!

I duly went to court and was asked whether I pleaded guilty or not guilty to the charge of being drunk and disorderly. I answered, 'Well, to be honest, I'm not guilty but I have got to plead guilty because I can't afford the time off work to fight the case.' The magistrate was clearly perplexed at this unusual response.

'I can't work this out. Are you pleading guilty or not guilty?' he said.

'I'm innocent but I'm pleading guilty.'

This was real John Grisham stuff but he wasn't impressed with my innocent look and, trying to hide his smile, he banged his gavel and fined me £25.

There are six or eight courts at Harrow and I thought that the chances of me going back to the same court and appearing before the same judge were remote in the extreme.

Who says that lightning doesn't strike twice? Thirty minutes later I was back in front of the same magistrate. The look on his face was worth the price of the first fine alone. It was a picture. He asked me what had happened this time and I answered that I had enjoyed a few drinks and climbed a traffic light and lifted the top off and that I was very sorry. Criminal damage sounds really bad when you are up in front of the beak but when you have had a couple of drinks, or more, and climbed a traffic light, it's not the worst offence in the world. Is it?

The magistrate asked me what had made me do it. Having just fined me for being drunk and disorderly he had hardly any need to ask and I mumbled the facts again, that I had had a few drinks and that I was sorry, really sorry. I was ready for him to throw the book at me for this, my second charge in half an hour, but he fined me £15 and added 77 pence for the cost of the part I had 'damaged'. I was much relieved and immediately wrote out a cheque totalling £40.77 while blessing a magistrate with a sense of humour and a grasp of reality.

My parents never did discover about that double whammy and I didn't class myself as a bad person even though I had a triple strike against me. Drunk and disorderly, stealing a car and criminal damage makes me sound a real tearaway, an absolute rogue and a hard case but I wasn't at all. What I was really guilty of was being all too ready to act the fool and be distracted – just as my old school reports said.

Strangely my football remained totally professional, believe it or not, and nowadays it's only once in a blue moon that I go past my limit and never when football is in close proximity.

Fortunately, I was never one for getting involved in fighting or anything physical like that. One or two of the lads were known to the local police and, later, when a fight broke out in a pub where we were drinking I slipped out of the door and was stopped by a couple of the local policemen, who knew I played for Wealdstone. They warned me not to get involved with that particular crowd, as they would surely land me in trouble. I took that advice to heart. I had been in enough grief.

The ones I meet up with every year were certainly not the worst of the worst but friends I have remained in touch with since our days together at school. Everyone is grown up now and a lot more sensible . . . most of the time. What amazes me is that none of this has come out over the past 20 years. Obviously my mates aren't into the kiss and tell business with the tabloid newspapers.

It was all part of growing up and while it's not something to be proud of, I can look back and laugh about it. I can relate to some of the young footballers who land themselves in trouble nowadays.

Although I liked a drink I can't say that I was ever a big drinker. We had a drink on a Saturday night like everyone did in my age group and it was the company and the laughs that meant more than the alcohol. It was all part of my background and I only did what most of the other kids did in those days. Some were caught and some were more fortunate.

I was born in Hammersmith Hospital on 24 April 1962, the youngest of four children. My eldest brother, Ray, is 17 years older than me, my sister Pamela is 14 years older, and my other brother, Dennis, ten years older. Dennis is the only one I can remember being at home.

Dennis is not sport-orientated at all, and neither is Pamela. Pamela is a child of the sixties. She was into women's lib and stuff like that and quite a headache for the old man by all accounts. When he asked her how she got home from school, more often than not she would tell him that she had hitchhiked. He was a bit old-fashioned and that sort of gay abandon tied him up in knots at times. As far as he was concerned, she was a girl and he couldn't treat her in the same way as her brothers. Now she teaches at Tottenham Tech.

Ray, on the other hand, is heavily into sport. He played football but his real love was boxing. He was a London ABA champion. My father was very disappointed when Ray got his girl pregnant and packed up boxing to marry her. He thought Ray had a real chance of making something in the fight game; it was not so much the pregnancy that upset him but the fact that Ray gave up boxing! That was when Dad started pushing me into football. He pushed me hard because he wanted me to do well but also because he's like that anyway – a bit obstinate.

I have never gone into details with Ray over why he quit. He was matter of fact about it at the time. He enjoyed boxing but once he had the responsibilities of a wife and family he packed it up and started taking an interest in football refereeing. He progressed through non-league into the Football League and ran the line in top matches. The big age difference between us meant that when he was asked the usual questions about whether he had any relatives in the game he answered quite truthfully that he had not.

In fact, a trivia question that would flummox even the most knowledgeable football fan is when did two brothers take part in the same game with one playing and the other officiating? It happened to us when he ran the line in a Nottingham Forest League Cup tie at Brighton. He disallowed a goal for Brighton! I had no fears, however, about his honesty. He would have erred on the side of Brighton rather than favour me.

No one knew, apart from the Forest team. It was funny running up the wing and having my brother alongside me on the touchline. He could have booked me because I kept taking the mickey out of him – 'Oi, you ginger dickhead,' is one thing I remember calling him. Perhaps it was a good thing that he never became a league referee because it would have come out eventually that he was my brother.

As can be guessed by the age gap I was an accident, something my parents have told me many times. It must have been quite a shock. Once you have had the kids and seen them grow up, I'm sure that the last thing you want is for another one to come along with the nappies and all the other things you thought were long gone.

We lived in a terraced house in Latimer Road, Shepherd's Bush, with an outside toilet. We were not on the poverty line and I'm a million miles from being a deprived child but it was bloody cold going outside to the toilet in the middle of winter and when I had a bath it was in a tin tub in front of a coal fire. Other than that, I can't remember a great deal about Shepherd's Bush or the fact that we were so close to Queens Park Rangers' ground. The odd thing sticks in the mind, though, like waking up in the middle of the night and finding Mum and Dad not there. I ran out into the street to the next-door neighbour who took me to the local pub where my parents were having a drink and a game of darts. They took me home and put me back to bed. I must have been very young but the memory is etched vividly on my mind. If that happened now, there would be hell to pay but in those days they weren't the only ones to leave the front door on the latch and ask the neighbours to keep an eye out.

We moved to Wood Lane, Kingsbury, near Wembley, when I was five, which was an ideal time for me as it coincided with me going to Fryent Primary School. My father worked hard, clocking up the overtime to ensure that we lived as well as possible. He was a waiter up in London, working on the railways, at Quaglinos and at other restaurants, but he found time to play football for a Waiters' XI. If you listen to both my father and my father-in-law, they were both the iron men in their teams but then I have yet to meet someone of 50 or 60 who owned up to being the little farty one on the wing, the one who used to scream when he was tackled. They were either a great goalscorer or the iron man of defence. I find it quite comical. My old man loved his football, was honest and a grafter but never progressed beyond the waiters' team.

Dad worked hard to pay off the mortgage in Kingsbury. He would be up in London as early as six in the morning, travelling either by train or, if he was lucky, being dropped off by my mum. Sometimes he didn't finish until midnight. Ridiculous hours. There were times when Mum would have to get me up in the middle of the night, and drive me up to the West End to collect Dad because he couldn't get home any other way. Mum worked as well. She was a dinner lady at my primary school; that suited me because I always got extra chips.

Dad's belief was that you paid your mortgage off whatever the circumstances. John Beresford, whom I knew at Newcastle, told me that there was a young striker he played with at Southampton, James Beattie, who was bought as a reserve from Blackburn Rovers. He had a Porsche and a half share in a boat but rented a flat! We were laughing about it because we were both brought up by parents who force-fed us their own ideas, like all parents do. Sometimes when you reach your 30s you think what a load of rubbish they talked, but there was some good advice in there. I'm with my dad all the way where bricks and mortar are concerned. It has always been my philosophy, too, to get the house paid off.

As soon as the mortgage was settled, Dad packed in the job in London. It was the only reason he had worked so hard and as soon as it was done he became a postman in Wembley. He used to work on the post in the morning and come to watch me play football in the afternoon. In fact, both Mum and Dad would regularly come to watch me play. Dad couldn't drive so Mum used to take him in the Morris Minor and they would both watch whether it was a school match or a district match. Dad was marvellous the way he backed my football. He was so keen to see me get on that if he was doing nothing he would even clean my boots. With my brother no longer boxing, my football became the focal point of his life. He was living the football through me. The important factor was that both my parents were very supportive and helped me whenever they could. As I grew older, I sometimes played and trained with Ray but it was my dad who put his hand in his pocket to buy the boots and other equipment I needed. He even wrote off to our old local club and got me a trial.

'How would you like to play for QPR?' he asked me one day. I told him I would love to and he broke the news. That was very exciting for a 13-year-old kid.

We were very successful at Fryent Primary in Kingsbury – champions of London one season, losing just one match in the year. We also won the League and Cup in Brent but lost the Middlesex Cup 3–2 with the opposition's games master refereeing and being a bit liberal with the timekeeping.

At that time I always played centre-half – never, ever at left-back – but the first medal I won was as a goalkeeper in the third year of primary school, before I got into the school team. It was in a six-a-side tournament with third and fourth years. Each side had to have at least one third-former in the side and I was picked to play in goal.

It was my first medal and the feeling was unbelievable. I took it home and just looked at it. I guess that's when I developed my taste for winning trophies. Winning that medal really meant something. Times have changed. When I do presentations for kids these days, I find myself giving out so many trophies. When I ask did they win the cup or the league, the answer invariably is that they won neither; they are just awarded a trophy each year. There are medals for the Most Improved Player, the Leading Goalscorer and even for Turning Up Each Week and so it goes until these kids walk away with armfuls of cups. I had to play all season to win a trophy if we were lucky, and we were also given a medal.

I still have that first medal along with all my other school medals. They are side by side with my World Cup medal, all together. Obviously some mean more than others do but every one has its own personal memory. Sadly, I don't display them anymore because the police warned that things like that might attract burglars. I could lose a video or a television but I couldn't stomach losing an England cap, my World Cup medal or Littlewoods Cup winner's medals. It's a shame I can't show them but I can't take the risk. Other players have pictures of themselves in this game and that covering the walls but I suppose I have grown beyond that. I would rather have a nice print of a horse on the wall. It is more traditional and better for the room than a picture of me kicking a football.

I won about 70 cups and medals while I was at school – and not just for turning up. At my senior school, Claremont High in Kenton, we never lost a single home match. Quite a few of us went together from junior school to senior school so we had a good understanding and a very good spirit. We had a pretty decent side but I was the only one to come through and make it at professional level. Gary Waddock was the only other one from my district to make the paid ranks. It wasn't ability; it was dedication.

When I was at school I was very small, probably the smallest in our team. That was probably what held me back in terms of being spotted. Who wants a tiny centre-half? I couldn't win all the headers so I had to make up for that by trying to win everything on the ground. That was when I started left-back for the county team. I was always one of the better players in all the teams I played for – not the best, but one of the better players. I put that down to pushing from the old man plus a lot of self-belief.

Dad bought me a briefcase when I went to senior school, which was probably the worst thing he could have done as you were immediately seen as a wally kid. That soon had the shit kicked out of it not only by other kids but also with some help from me to make out I wasn't one of those wallies!

Football was everything to me in senior school. We had one or two matches a week. They used to kick off at around 2.30 so the team used to miss the afternoon lessons, especially if it was away from home. All sport meant a great deal more to me than my academic work and as well as football I was picked to play in the school rugby team. Although I was very small, I could kick the ball over the posts for the conversions and penalties. Rugby wasn't really my game but I didn't mind because it meant I missed more classes. This sometimes happened three times a week with two football matches and a rugby match all during school time! In the summer I threw the javelin for the athletics team and I admit now that I did most of it to avoid as much school as I could.

Yet I never bunked off. I never missed one day of school when I was able to go and, in fact, I quite enjoyed it. I loved history, as I do now. We studied the twentieth century and even now I am a keen student of the Second World War. Looking back, I wish I had taken a little more notice of geography because of my love of travelling and visiting different countries. I also wish I had learned cookery for the times when I lived on my own. I gave maths my best shot but it was far from being my best subject, and if I had known I was going to be an electrician it would have been useful to do carpentry.

Dad wanted me to do well at lessons and all that but it was football where he most wanted me to succeed. Out of the four kids, Ray is an electrician like me and intelligent. He sometimes belies that by acting the fool but he is bright. If any tricky jobs had to be done, a big boiler house or anything like that, the council would call him in straight-away. He taught electronics at Willesden Tech. Dennis joined National Cash Registers from school and is still with them now. He is heavily into computers, working at Lloyd's of London as I write. With Pamela also teaching, I am so far from them intellectually it's untrue. I don't know whether the old man knew that.

I am one of those people who have kept my old school reports. (Without seeming too pathetic, I've also got the match reports of games I played in. I don't know whether that says something about me or not.) Every year my school reports were the same – maths C, English C, games AA. The comments were pretty standard, too, with 'too easily distracted' and 'too ready to play the fool' the most common. Lessons didn't mean a great deal to me and when you are not that intelligent you seem to slip even further away from it.

Both my parents were very understanding and I have no doubt that their support helped me come through.

Watching me play became something of a hobby for them. You wouldn't know what the other parents looked like because they would be working when the games were on. Mum and Dad continued to watch as I moved on to Sunday football and then non-league with Wealdstone and into the professional game.

As a teenager I was a firm QPR supporter and went regularly to Loftus Road. My hero was that brave aggressive defender David Webb. This was just after the Rodney Marsh era under Dave Sexton, with Don Givens, Stan Bowles, Dave Clement, Gerry Francis, Ian Gillard, Frank McLintock, John Hollins, Don Masson, Phil Parkes and the rest. I could name the whole team and the substitutes.

They finished second in 1975–6. I watched them a lot that season and was there for the last couple of games they needed to win to take the championship. Although we beat Arsenal and Leeds at home, we missed out when we lost 3–2 at Norwich, which allowed Liverpool to nip in and take the title. We had a small squad and needed one or two more to have won it.

I had friends who supported Leeds United and I would regularly watch them, too. We travelled to Elland Road and to games in the Midlands and all over London, of course. They were a fantastic side under Don Revie and I loved watching them. They were so good, it's hard to pick out favourite players from the likes of Jack Charlton, Paul

Madeley, Terry Cooper, Allan Clarke, Paul Reaney, Billy Bremner, Norman Hunter, Johnny Giles, Eddie Gray, Peter Lorimer and all the rest. I remember having tears in my eyes watching them lose to Chelsea in the FA Cup final replay at Old Trafford when Dave Webb scored with a far-post header. He was no hero of mine that day! I even used to wear sock tie-ups with Peter Lorimer's name on them because I fancied I had a big shot like him.

I eventually left school at 16 having earned a CSE grade one in social studies and CSE in geography. I was never going to be academically gifted. I was average. It was hardly preparation for the big wide world.

I started work in a warehouse and attended day-release classes to become a qualified electrician. After the problems of school, I really enjoyed going to college and doing the work. I applied myself a little bit more and sailed through it, probably doing a lot better than some of the others in the class. I began to realise that maybe I was not so daft as I thought I was at school, especially compared with some of the others.

I qualified not just as an electrician but as an advanced electrician. That, however, was as far as I got. I became a little lost in the advanced mathematics that followed and, as it became a bit like hard work, I tailed off my studies.

As I got older, I became a lot closer to Ray. As I've mentioned, we used to play football together, especially in the Rolls-Royce six-a-side competition. He had that same instinct to win at all costs that I have and he could be a bit nasty in the tackle when he wanted; worse than me.

Mum is very relaxed and laid back, the same star sign as me and fairly quiet until something rouses her. I think I took some of that from her and the strong will to succeed from my dad. The old man is a bit more serious; my mother is more of a fun person, always ready for a laugh. They played an equal part in my development in their own way.

They were there for my first game at Coventry and followed me through the years, especially the big games. Once I moved to Newcastle it became more difficult and they stopped coming regularly. It was a long way for them to come from their home near Bury St Edmunds where they moved about a year after I joined Coventry.

The family have remained close without having to talk to each other every single day. It can sometimes be weeks between calls but the relationship remains solid. My parents see a lot of my brothers and sister and we all get together when we can. That's difficult at traditional family times such as Christmas because I tend to be playing, training or preparing for a game.

I probably have less in common with my sister than with Ray or Dennis but that is understandable because she has little interest in sport and is a college lecturer. I go to concerts with Dennis and talk football with Ray. I guess we are a pretty normal family.

I realise now how lucky I am that I have been able to do something for a living that I love and to get paid enough to fulfil some of the ambitions of my life. I know full well that had I been an electrician I would be working on a building site, probably married to a different girl.

I appreciate what the game has given me. I was good at football but I believe that it was my professionalism that dragged me through even at school level, then on to non-league and the professional game. I think I was born with it because I can see it as a family trait. Dad and Ray were my role models. I believe I could have been taken away from the bosom of my family and still have developed in the same way because it is within me. You are what you are and you have what you are born with. I guess I was lucky that the very thing I loved doing could also provide me with a well-paid career.

I have experienced a lot of different things because of football, travelling and meeting people who would otherwise be well out of my sphere, such as the Sex Pistols. I know some would say who the hell would want to meet them but they were my heroes when I was a boy because I loved their music. Now I can go and see bands, go backstage and have a laugh and a joke with them, but if I was not a footballer I wouldn't get that opportunity and they wouldn't want me.

I am privileged to have this life. Once I became a footballer, my horizons opened up and these experiences shape you.

to hull and back

My first taste of football with a professional club came when I was 13. It was also my first experience of rejection!

I was offered a trial by Queens Park Rangers after my father had written to them and after they had watched Gary Waddock and me playing for our district side. We trained at a gymnasium in Eastcote on a Friday night under a coach named Brian Eastick. Mum drove me there and back every week. It lasted for six months.

I was invited back for the following season and given the time, date and venue, but when I arrived at the training ground on the given date there was no one there other than Chris Geeler, one of the staff coaches.

'Oh, it's not today,' he said. 'We'll let you know when it is.'

It was the classic case of don't call us, we'll call you. But I was far from devastated; I didn't really enjoy those Friday nights. A few of the lads were a bit cocky; they thought they had already made it. I felt more comfortable playing for the school and with my mates on a Sunday morning.

I also had an option to go to Arsenal about the same time, again after being spotted with the district side. Some of the boys went to QPR one week, Arsenal the next and Crystal Palace in between, but I felt that one club at a time was enough. I told them that I was already training with QPR.

After the west London club gave me the elbow, I never really had a sniff. I find it quite strange looking back that it all went so quiet because I didn't suddenly become a bad player. I can only assume that I was improving with age and my physique developed. I reached the end of my schooldays having achieved quite a bit, winning lots of medals and going almost to the top in local representative terms, just failing to make the London team after reaching the final 22. But that was it. Suddenly there I was, a 16-year-old in love with the game and no team to play for. I can understand how so many players drift away from the game at that stage when work, women and booze begin to intervene.

I have to confess that it hit me with a jolt when I left school. I found I no longer had any real belief in a career in football and hadn't a clue what to do with myself. It was evident that A levels and university were not an option. Initially I was interested in joining the police or one of the armed services because they offered an active, outdoor life that fitted in with my interest in sport and lack of interest in desks and offices.

As the time approached to make a decision, we had career talks at school and as a result I went for interviews with the Old Bill – this was before my convictions – and with the army. My priority was the police but the army interview came up first and I went off to Brentwood in Essex for a weekend of tests that I cruised through, especially the physical tests over the assault course. The only mistake I made was that I was too honest. I told them that I couldn't make a decision at that moment because I had an interview with the police the following week and if I passed that I would join them and if not I would join the army. The recruitment officer didn't like this at all and told me that clearly I wasn't interested enough and turned me down there and then. At the time they were overwhelmed with recruits and could afford to be selective. Nowadays they drag people in off the streets from what I hear.

I went to the police recruiting as planned, passed all the physical tests and failed the interview! It was a lot harder to get into the police force at the time and to this day I don't know why I failed. Maybe it was my lack of confidence or my shyness that counted against me. No one bothered to tell me. What I did know was that I was up the creek without a paddle as my two chosen careers had been blown away in the space of a week.

I had left school by this time so I had to do something. Then I spotted an advert in the local paper for a spares clerk at a warehouse in Stonebridge NW10, working for the Binatone Radio and TV Company. I got the job but I was far from convinced that it was right for me.

In fact, on the day I was due to start work I went back to the school. It happened to be the day when those who wanted to stay on enrolled and I went back to see what was going on. On the second day, I went in to work and told them I had been ill. Some start to my working life!

I didn't have a clue what the job entailed until I started. I was a spares clerk for about a month and then they moved me to another department. I was basically the odd-job warehouseman. In those days, school leavers tended to stay in their first job but this was a dead-end job, manual labour with no real future.

Fortunately, my sister came up with the idea of going to

college to qualify as an electrician like Ray. She advised me that if I applied, the firm couldn't turn me down. It was a real crossroads in my life. When I started, I found I was one of the brightest there, something I had never been at school. I was there because I wanted to be there and not because I was made to go.

There were other boys from the firm on day release, studying radio and television engineering as that was what the firm specialised in. It was only when my half-term report came in that they discovered I had taken a different course in electronics. But my report was really good with 100 per cent attendance and excellent marks, and when I suggested that perhaps there would be jobs with the firm as an electrician, thankfully they allowed me to carry on.

It would have been so easy to walk away from serious football then, as so many youngsters do when they leave school. There were other attractions – the pub, music, girls. I suppose I was a year away from just playing for a Sunday pub side. Luckily, Geoff Carson took a hand.

He was the school caretaker. He had a daughter in our year and took a keen interest in the football team, often ferrying us about. He recommended a few of us to local club Wealdstone. Someone from the club took a look and invited us to go down there. Had it been just me on my own I don't know that I would have even bothered. There's no doubt that it was Geoff Carson who put me on track.

When you finish school and you have no club to go to, you have a job and maybe a bit of private work on a Saturday, then football tends to be pushed into the background and standards drop. Even though I was playing for the youth team and occasionally the reserves, it was a big club and not football to be taken lightly.

My perspective on life now is due in no small part to coming through the non-league set-up. It's probably why I don't make a song and dance of what I have achieved. I certainly don't see myself as a big-time Charlie and the fans do seem to identify with me. I'm a tradesman who has struck it lucky. People are still surprised that I can do things other than play football. We had a man in fitting a washer and when a socket needed changing I told him to leave it and that I would do it. He was amazed when I told him that I was an electrician.

I count myself fortunate that I have travelled the entire journey, missing out virtually no stops in between other than perhaps not having played in the lower divisions. But five and a half years of non-league more than makes up for that. I have seen every level and I thoroughly appreciate what I have – it's all the sweeter for having started at the bottom.

I attended a Wealdstone dinner recently and I was surprised when I was told that I had played 242 games for them in those five years. Add that to the 600-plus as a professional and it makes for a long time in football.

If I hadn't gone to Wealdstone I don't know what I would have done, probably gone and played with the rest of the lads in the pub team on a Sunday morning and watched QPR on a Saturday afternoon.

Come the end of that first season there was the usual massive backlog of fixtures and the old pros didn't fancy taking days off to travel to all points north and south. It meant the team was short of a left-back and I was told I was making my first-team debut away to Dorchester at barely

17 years of age. This was the breeding ground for the player who was to develop some years later. These weren't friendly kick-abouts. They were very, very physical. It wasn't a case of me kicking the winger, more the other way round. The old pro against the young whippersnapper – they used to kick the shit out of me. You had to learn to look after yourself at places like Altrincham where it was very rough. I was a bit quick but also a bit naïve.

I couldn't have been too bad, though, because I ended up being offered a two-year contract by manager Alan Foggarty when that first season ended. It was £15 a week plus bonuses – an absolute fortune at the time and a massive addition to my salary as a warehouseman.

I passed my exams at college and applied for a job with Brent Council. Ray was working for them at the time. I went for the interview confident that with that year at college and my good results – not to mention the fact that my brother worked with them – I would have a good chance. I was right and I was taken on board. It was a blinding job because I could always get away to play for Wealdstone in their midweek games. If we were playing at somewhere like Scarborough, the team coach would leave at lunchtime and they would not only let me off but would put a couple of hours' overtime on my timesheet.

While I was ducking and diving between Brent Council and Wealdstone I was invited for a trial at Hull City, who were managed by former Welsh manager Mike Smith. I hadn't been in the Wealdstone first team for much more than a season when the rumour machine began to suggest that I might have a chance of picking up a league club. I let it be known that I might be interested and the next thing I knew John Watson and I were invited to travel north for the trials.

John was the Wealdstone and England non-league captain. He was 27 at the time and pretty settled in his ways, while I was around 18 and very unsure of what might lie ahead. John had a good job, also with the council, as a stonemason. He had family in London and was earning a good wage with Wealdstone. I had my doubts about whether he would be interested and when I couldn't find him at the station in London I assumed that he had backed out and I began to wish I had done the same. Being a shy young lad, I wasn't that keen on going on my own. But when the train arrived at Hull, he stepped off it two carriages away.

We travelled up on the Tuesday and trained that day. We trained again on Wednesday before playing away to Grimsby in a local derby. John was brilliant, absolutely superb, head and shoulders above everyone else on the pitch. He always was whenever he played in any big game. I was average.

We had dinner with Mike Smith on Tuesday night and went to his office at Boothferry Park on Thursday morning to talk about signing. I chatted to John first and he wasn't that keen because of what he had back in London. I decided there and then that I was going to say no as well. Mike Smith did his best to persuade me, even offering to find me a job on the local council when I told him that I wanted to keep on with my trade! But I had made my mind up and turned it down. Then when John came out he told me he was thinking about it! I thought I had done it all wrong because had John said yes I would have gone as well. In the end, neither of us went.

In my first full season at Wealdstone we were relegated and Alan Foggarty, the manager who signed me, was sacked. He was a nice guy from Birmingham. He had been around for years, a cigar smoker and a spitter. We used to have our team meetings on the back of the bus where we would all gather round and he would say things like, 'The centre-half has just split up with his wife. I live near him and I know he's upset about it so have a pop at him about his missus.' Another time, he said about a useful opponent, 'He's just lost his job. Have a go at him about being out of work.' He knew bits about everyone and was always ready to make use of it, or rather have us make use of it by winding up the opposition.

I was sorry for him, devastated for myself. What if the new manager didn't fancy me? I remember vividly Alan Foggarty coming round the dressing-room to say his good-byes and saying to me, 'I will see a lot more of you.' I hadn't a clue what he was talking about; I thought that maybe he was going to invite me around for dinner or something. I felt very sad because I liked him, looked up to him, and he had given me my chance. But he was a survivor and I still see him from time to time, scouting for managers including Dave Bassett.

It was certainly an experience playing at Wealdstone. I recall a trip to Bangor in North Wales. It was too far to go by coach and so we all travelled up together by train instead. We played the game and afterwards four of us collected a whip and slipped off to find a pub so we could get crated up with lager for the train journey back home. We were in our suits and club ties and walked straight into a pub full of bikers. We weren't going to turn round and walk away so we brazened it out, expecting a hiding at any minute. Perhaps we were too brave because we had a few beers, picked up the crates – and missed the train by five minutes! The porter told us that there was no other train back to London for three hours, so what else was there to do but go back to the bikers' pub and carry on drinking.

We finally caught the later train to London with enough lager for nigh on 30 young men. It proved to be a monster journey. There had been a derailment outside Crewe and this delayed our train so badly that it was eight o'clock in the morning when we arrived. We didn't care. In fact we had drunk so much beer that we didn't care about anything until we turned up for training on Tuesday when we were slaughtered by the rest of the team for missing the designated train. To make matters worse, the team had travelled back in a train without a buffet so they had nothing to eat or drink, fuming at the thought of the four musketeers with their money and their beer.

That was the joy of non-league football. It was full of characters. Roy Davies was one of them, a bit of a lad who was always pulling stunts. Roy went from Hayes to Torquay and on his debut on the left wing for his first league club he picked up a woollen bobble hat thrown on to the pitch by one of the fans, carried on his run and got on the end of a cross from the other wing with a diving header with the bobble hat still on.

You can imagine what an influence he was on us at Wealdstone with a mind like that. When we had a testimonial match for his big mucker Wally Downes from Wimbledon they had a couple of mackintoshes and streaked across the pitch. I was a bit impressionable and this incident stuck in my memory. When Brian Roberts had a testimonial at Coventry I thought that I would resurrect the stunt. Our manager Bobby Gould was getting ready to come on in the second half as a bit of a gimmick when I collared our 6ft 3in centre-forward Brian Withey, another former non-league man who went from Bath to Bristol Rovers before joining us, and told him to meet me in a few minutes. We both put on flasher's macs, skimpy white briefs and old men masks. We waited until the ball went near Gould and raced on, flashed him and raced off again. It was quite impressive; we probably looked naked from the stands. Gould knew very well that it was his players involved but, because of the latex masks, he didn't know who. Such was the interest that the local newspaper, the *Coventry Evening Telegraph*, ran a competition to name the two flashers for a prize of a couple of tickets for our next game (which someone did win!).

At least that was all a bit of fun. The same could not be said about some of our non-league encounters. One time at Scarborough for instance we were involved in a very rough match indeed. It has to be said that we were giving more than we were taking. The tackles were becoming naughtier and after one particularly evil one our captain John Watson jumped up, chinned an opponent and was promptly sent off. A Scarborough player slid into our goalkeeper who was carried off just before half-time with concussion and took no further part in the game. With only one substitute there were precious few options open to us and I finished up in goal for the second half, reviving memories of the Russian Yak Jensen! We were two goals down by that stage but still playing and trying to squeeze a result from an impossible situation. I was watching a corner at the other end when I spotted our centre-half whack their centre-forward on the halfway line. Unfortunately for us I was not the only one; a linesman saw it as well and off went our central defender. Then there were nine.

It was quickly getting out of hand. After another bad tackle, another of our players had gone and there we were with me in goal behind seven outfield players. I conceded two more goals, one a screamer into the top corner, and we lost 4–0. As we trailed off towards the dressing-room we were being booed and jeered by the local supporters when our manager Ken Payne, who was under pressure for his job at the time, ran on and headed straight for me.

'Well done, son,' he said, 'you've grown up today.'

I didn't know what he was on about. We had been hammered, had three players sent off and here he was telling me I'd grown up. Then, as we walked along the touchline, he turned round and started shouting at the home fans, 'Fuck off, you wankers,' and waving two-handed, two-fingered gestures in their direction. I couldn't wait to get off the pitch. Just another day at the office.

On another occasion we were playing Barnet in a traditional Boxing Day game with a morning kick-off. This was another nasty one. Before I arrived our big annual punch-up was with Wimbledon before Wimbledon went into the League. The lads told me that you could guarantee a 2–2 draw and six sent off. Barnet had taken over as our grudge match and on this day the linesman had given decisions which hadn't delighted the home manager, a certain character by the name of Barry Fry. Barry, hardly a shy retiring flower, finally had enough and set off up the line after the linesman carrying a bucket of ice-cold water and tipped it over him. It's the sort of thing you don't see anymore. Nowadays he would be banned *sine die*. Barnet was always a flashpoint game but that day we were united in our mirth at Barry's antics.

We managed to hoist ourselves back up into the Alliance only to be relegated again, leaving the way for the renowned Allen Batsford to take over. He was a strict disciplinarian and his reputation preceded him, having taken Wimbledon into the League. Everyone was dreading him arriving but I have to admit that he did a lot for me. There were a couple of ex-league players who thought they were Jack-the-lads and I ended up being influenced by them, messing around. Batsford quickly pulled me and told me that it was high time I got out of my pram. It was only when I thought about what he had said that I realised the message he was putting across. He was right; it was about time I grew up. So I did and it was Batsford and his joint manager Brian Hall who sold me into the League.

Batsford was deaf in one ear, caused when he was caught on the ear during practice, some say deliberately. The boys reckoned he could tune into Radio Luxembourg on his hearing aid and, in typical football fashion, they used to get on his deaf side to give him some verbals without fear of reprisals.

When I tell people I played against Alex Stepney they are amazed but he was in goal for Altrincham when they won the Alliance twice. He was about 41 then and I was 18 so there was a massive age difference. He has always been my trump card when footballers gather together and swap stories about who they have played against. When I drop Stepney's name in they reckon it makes me around 90.

We were all PFA members at Wealdstone. Every year we would put on our hired dinner suits and head off for the annual Professional Footballers Association awards dinner to brush shoulders with the big stars. The tables were seeded so we were almost out in Park Lane, so far away from the action it was ridiculous. It became a standing joke. It was almost as if we were at a different function. We were, of course, in awe of the big stars who, in those days, attended in numbers. Nowadays there seem to be more hangers-on than footballers. I haven't gone for years because I end up signing more autographs than after a Premiership game. But it was good in those days and after the speeches and awards we would all mix together and have a drink. One day Allen Batsford said to me, 'I want you to come over and meet Kenny Sansom. He's a friend of mine.'

As much as I admired Kenny, I wasn't that keen, as an electrician and a non-league left-back, on being introduced to the current England left-back and a superstar of his time. But Batsford insisted and introduced me, saying, 'This is Stuart Pearce. He's a good left-back.' Kenny stood there with a bottle of champagne in an ice bucket in one hand and his glass in the other, waiting to join his mates. He was very good but it became even more embarrassing a few seconds later when Batsford added, 'He'll have your place soon.' It was a flippant remark and Kenny must have been thinking, 'Yeah, sure he will.' The great irony was that when I did break through into the England team, it was Kenny whom I replaced. I never did remind him of that embarrassing conversation at the Hilton Hotel in Park Lane.

I didn't make the non-league England team. I came close after we won the double of Southern League and Southern League Cup to get back into the Alliance. We had a good team and the next season we finished third and could have won it but for giving away silly points. The chairman was so confident that he told us he had put £500 on us to win the League at 14–1 and if we won he would take us all to Florida for an end-of-season jolly on the proceeds. We had a saying as we ran out of the dressing-room door on a cold Saturday afternoon: 'Win today – Tampa Bay.' But we ended up blowing it.

I had a fairly good season and I heard that the England selectors were having a look at me in an FA Trophy tie at Wycombe Wanderers. It was a heavily sloping pitch at Wycombe and in the opening minutes one of their players came flying down the hill towards me. I put my head in to clear the ball and he just missed taking my head off with a flying boot. He would have caught me if I hadn't pulled my face away sharply. It was nasty and Roy Davies promptly chinned him while I stamped on him for good measure. There was an instant free-for-all as the referees ran up to sort it out. He sent Davies off having seen him throw the punch, but he hadn't spotted my indiscretion and said nothing. I had got away with it but the crowd had seen and every time I went near the ball they gave me plenty of stick.

This incident clearly sowed seeds of doubt about me with the selectors but they invited me, all the same, for a trial at Nuneaton where we played a Combined Universities side. A mate of mine, a wages clerk at the council, drove me to the Midlands so I could sleep on the way. I had a good game and the only moment of indiscretion was when I bollocked one of my team-mates for not giving me the ball. They were all very proper and the manager told me that there was no need for that. I was pretty pleased with myself all the same and thought I had given myself a chance. When I went into the bar to find my mate who was driving, I discovered he had bumped into the manager of South Liverpool and some of their team who had come to give support to a couple of their players. He was out of it, absolutely steaming and I finished up having to drive him all the way back. What's more, I didn't get picked, probably partly because of the stamping at Wycombe and partly because I had mouthed off at one of my own players but mainly because Altrincham, top of the League at the time, had a left-back named John Davidson who, quite frankly, was better than me. I was up and coming and might have pushed him the next season if I hadn't turned professional but there was no doubt in my mind that he earned his place.

In fact, my disciplinary record in what was a very tough league was pretty good. I learned to look after myself not only then but even before that when I used to play in the park against older boys. I was small and had to learn to protect myself. I am what I am. I haven't manufactured myself. I have always been that way and able to punch my weight. I grew a little more when I left school but I had to be able to handle myself in a physical league.

The dream of every non-league club is a run in the FA Cup. It not only brings in much-needed money but also puts the players under the national spotlight. I was in the Wealdstone side on both occasions when we reached the FA Cup first round proper, drawing Southend one year and Swindon Town a couple of seasons later. We lost both times. We tried to rough them up a bit to even the balance and both of the professional teams moaned that we were too physical. Many years later when I was at Newcastle we played Stevenage Borough and they moaned that we were too rough. Things certainly seem to have changed since my day. I suppose Alan Shearer was a bit physical at the time but it was still a surprise how the wheel had turned.

We lost 1–0 to Southend in a very good game when we missed our chances. Two years later at Swindon there was a very strange incident. It was a massive game for us and we took about 1,500 supporters to Wiltshire. We were playing quite well and were a bit unlucky to be losing 1–0 at half-time. Just after the break I tackled Swindon's golden boy Paul Rideout. He was the up-and-coming star, a leading light in the England youth team and tipped for the top. I'll never forget what he said to me – 'Get back to your fucking nine-to-five job.' A few words were said and I doubt that he would even remember having an exchange with an electrician from London. But I remembered and two seasons after that I was playing for Coventry and he was on the bench for Aston Villa. I can't say how tempted I was to go over and say, 'How's the nine-to-five now? You can't even get a game.' But I didn't. I bit my lip and let the moment pass.

It still happens. When things become a little fraught on the pitch, the professional will often turn round and ask the non-league player who has been bugging him just how much he earns. It's a pet hate of mine because I've been there. I remember Garry Birtles did it when we played at Forest. We had gone to a non-league ground for a game to mark them getting floodlights. Garry was kicked and he turned round to this plumber and told him to get back to his proper job. I thought it was rich coming from a former carpet layer and I turned on him and told him to behave himself and grow up. He was out of order, especially as he had been through the mill himself.

I enjoyed my non-league days and I am glad that I came through that route. I wouldn't have it any different. I feel that I served my apprenticeship. I don't know whether I would have carried on playing football for so long if I hadn't had those five years. In a strange way I thought to myself that as I missed five years at that end of my career I would make up for them at this end.

One thing it taught me was the value of a £10 note. Even now if I am driving on empty I will pass a petrol station that is selling petrol at 84.9 if the next one is selling at 83.9. I could afford to go to any garage and pay whatever price they're asking, but why should I? I would rather go to the guy who is going out of his way to sell his petrol cheaper.

When I joined Coventry I became very pally with Trevor Peake, to such a degree that he was best man at my wedding much later on. He had played non-league at Nuneaton until he was 21. You could tell by their attitudes who had been non-league players. Kirk Stevens and Cyrille Regis were classic examples. There was a mile of difference between them and the kids who joined straight from school. Others such as Graham Roberts, Ian Wright and Andy Townsend had done the rounds. They made it late in the game and fully appreciated what they had.

Big clubs should scout around the non-league for the better players. They could pick them up cheaply and if they don't make it, the chances are that they could still sell them on, usually for more than the initial outlay.

When I was briefly manager at Nottingham Forest I tried to sign a young non-league player called Courtney Naylor, recommended to me by an old Forest team-mate Steve Wigley who was then manager of Aldershot. Steve had played against Naylor in a game against Dagenham. I trusted Steve's judgement so I rang Dag's manager Ted Hardy and asked if he would be interested in sending the player to me for a month. I thought that if Courtney Naylor had half the attitude I had when I joined Coventry City, he would be worth it. Ted Hardy wouldn't even consider it. Whether he wanted me to dive straight in with a couple of hundred thousand I don't know but he gave that impression when he added that in a year's time a big club would come in for the player and pay a lot of money. I asked him to let the lad know that a Premiership club was interested. By one of those strange coincidences I was at Dagenham with the England Under-18 team a couple of years later and I asked after the player. I was told he had gone off the boil a bit and had been sold on to Enfield or somewhere like that for a few quid. Who knows what might have happened had the manager allowed him to spend a few weeks at Nottingham Forest and he had impressed me?

I put myself in his place and wonder what would have happened to me if no one had told me that Coventry were interested in buying me. They paid £25,000 and although it was good money it wasn't the difference to the club between collapse and survival but to me it was everything.

There had been plenty of rumours but I ignored them until we played an evening game at Yeovil. Our centre-half came up to me and told me that the Coventry manager was there to look at me. He told me that our manager knew and so did most of the team but they weren't sure whether to tell me or not and he had taken it upon himself to let me know.

I doubt whether it spurred me on because I always gave my all anyway. On the Friday of that week, Bobby Gould was in touch with the club and offered them £25,000 for me. I learned later that Gould had originally asked his scouting staff to find out who the best left-backs were in non-league. It was a position where they were lacking; in fact, they had no left-back.

The connection was Brian Eastick whom I had trained under at QPR as a kid. He told Gould I was the best – the right age, 21, and as good as he would get. Gould lived down the road from Yeovil and took his wife to the game to run the rule over me personally. The story he tells is that he watched me for 25 minutes, saw me kick the winger over the stand and said, 'He will do for me.'

Coventry were playing Arsenal at Highbury that weekend and he took the opportunity to pop round to our house in Kingsbury to talk to my dad and me. I think he was concerned that now it was out that he was after me, someone else might step in. They didn't.

I was the recipient of well-meaning advice from all the old pros at Wealdstone – Ray Goddard, a goalkeeper for Millwall for 500 games, Paul Price from Arsenal, in fact almost everyone in the team apart from me had league experience. They all had something to offer, mainly to ask for a £25,000 signing-on fee and a king's ransom for wages.

I sat down with Gould and I told him what I was getting from the club and council, adding up to £230 a week, and that I would like £250 a week and a £25,000 signing-on fee.

Gould looked up and said, 'There's the door – use it.'

I thought, 'The bastards didn't tell me this at Wealdstone. What do I do now?'

'I don't give signing-on fees,' Gould said. 'I never got one so I don't give them to anyone else.'

There were no agents then and here was me, an electrician who was being given the chance to play against the likes of Liverpool, Manchester United and Arsenal. He knew that. He knew that if he offered me a tenner a week I would have grabbed the paper off him and signed it there and then. It was not really about money. After all, how could I go back to the council and tell them I hadn't signed because I couldn't agree terms and could I please have my job back as an electrician.

It was Bobby Gould's second season at Highfield Road and he had signed a load of players, including Trevor from Lincoln, Terry Gibson and a lot of others who were desperate to play in the top division. I discovered later he had used the same line on all of them, apart from Ashley Grimes whom he signed for £200,000 from Manchester United. No one else got a signing-on fee from Bobby Gould, just the chance to make it at the top level. The rest of us had to swallow it and take what was offered.

It was rumoured that there were other clubs watching me but Bobby Gould was the one who took the gamble. Certainly if I go back into management I will look around for non-league players. I would want players of the right age and with the right attitude. I would give them a chance because I was given that chance myself.

CHAPTER 4

sent to coventry

Going from Wealdstone straight to Coventry in the First Division was beyond my wildest dreams. Of course I heard the whispers but my yardstick was the trial at Hull City. If I was going to turn professional, I expected it to be with a third- or fourth-division club, another step on the ladder. Allen Batsford called me into his office and said, 'We have just accepted an offer from Coventry City of £25,000 for you and you go with our blessing. Good luck to you.' It finally struck me that I had achieved Utopia in one step. All of a sudden, it was actually happening, the bid had been made and by the Monday the deed had been done. I was a professional with a first-division club. I had been sent to Coventry in the nicest way possible.

It was case of take it or leave it – £250 a week and a two-year contract. I bit Bobby Gould's hand off once we had overcome that initial misunderstanding. Effectively, it was a 20-month contract and that, I suppose, represented something of a gamble on my part, giving up a steady job and leaving home. But in truth it was no gamble at all. How could you finish your life as a sparky knowing that you could have been a professional footballer? What's security when you're 21, single, living with your parents and paying your mum £30 a week? Where was the gamble? I was committed. In fact, I couldn't have written a better script. I'd got my qualifications, had experience of a job and if my tilt at full-time professional football failed not only did I have a trade to fall back on but also my governor at the council told me that he would keep the job open for me if things didn't work out in Coventry.

My first game was for the reserves under John Sillett at Blackpool. We drew 1–1 and afterwards Sillett told Gould that I was the best player on the pitch and recommended me for a step up. It suited Gould because he wanted to fast-track me if he could, having no left-back. So after one reserve game I was promoted to the bench for the game against Stoke. There was only one substitute permitted in those days so I was that close to the team and my debut. I didn't get on. We won 3–1.

Gould came specifically to watch me at Rotherham in the reserves and because I didn't play very well he decided not to pick me for the away game at Birmingham that coming weekend. But he gave me my debut in the next game on 12 November 1983 at home against, of all teams, Queens Park Rangers – the team I had trained with as a kid and supported as a youngster. That wasn't the only coincidence, for up against me was Gary Waddock with whom I had played in my district team.

I couldn't tell you whom I marked but on the Monday we watched a video of the game. I had a shot from about 40 yards and if the goalkeeper hadn't come out to collect it, it wouldn't have reached the goal. Everybody laughed and took the mick out of me, this raw, new professional trying to shoot from so far out and not even reaching the goal. We won 1–0 and I found myself involved in an unbeaten run that eventually stretched to nine games, including a 4–0 win over the mighty Liverpool, lifting us up to fourth place, high enough for a nose-bleed for Coventry. Terry Gibson scored a hat-trick against Liverpool and it was one of the upsets of the season.

That was my fifth first-team game. It was ridiculous. It felt easier than playing at Wealdstone and I was thinking to myself that this wasn't bad and I had settled in quite well. My feet were still firmly on the floor, however, as John Sillett, knowing my background, soon had me wiring up his stables. 'Sparky,' he said, 'come and do some work for me.'

In truth, it was not as easy as I pretended. Sure I did fairly well, but I found the step up to training every day instead of a couple of times a week very tiring. I ended up suffering a stress fracture of the shin in my second season, which kept me out for three months, and I am convinced that it was the change in training and playing routines that caught up with me. It was a pity because I had settled in so well, kept my place apart from the odd injury and quickly felt that I belonged. How different it might have been if I had walked into a losing team.

Results-wise I was brought down to earth as we slipped badly in the second half of the season. In fact, after the sensational win over Liverpool we won just one of our next 19 games and we needed to win three of our last seven matches to stave off relegation, a regular feature for Coventry then as it is now.

Around Christmas time in that first season, we hit the wall. We could not win a game to save our lives. We nicked the odd point here or there which just kept us in or around the relegation zone and our finish meant that Birmingham went down with 48 points instead of us. We drew at Luton, lost at Liverpool as they avenged their earlier thrashing by hitting us for five, and beat Norwich while Birmingham drew their last three matches. It was so tight that season that we were fourth from bottom with 50 points, the same as Stoke City and one fewer than four other clubs – Norwich, Leicester, Luton and West Bromwich Albion.

In that first season, I had already played for Wealdstone in the preliminary round of the FA Cup. I thought nothing of it until we drew Wolverhampton Wanderers in the third round. Then I realised that my game against Basildon four months earlier had cup-tied me. I was gutted. As a non-league player I had never gone beyond the first round. I was thinking surely this doesn't count. I can't miss a game like this. We won against Wolves after two draws and went out to Sheffield Wednesday in the next round. I sat in the stand and hated every minute of those four games.

Some of the reserve-team players at Highfield Road never went out of their way to make friends with me, and one or two of the first team seemed to resent my sudden arrival and immediate elevation. Trevor Peake wasn't the first to come up to wish me well but I discovered that those who came up first were also often the first to drift away. I later discovered why Trevor had been a bit cool to me when he told me that they had heard that I had turned down third- and fourth-division clubs waiting for the big one to come along. It wasn't true but that's how rumours get around, bits in the newspapers and whispers here and there. Trevor and I got on like a house on fire after I explained that the rumours were absolute rubbish. It had all started because I turned down Hull City as a raw kid. Sometimes you meet someone and you get on with them straightaway because you think along the same lines and have the same sense of humour. We just clicked and we will always be on the same wavelength.

Trevor and his wife Haddwyn put me up for a while when I was struggling for somewhere to live. It was a worthy gesture as Haddwyn was pregnant at the time. I had been punting about for digs. I stayed at a hotel for a couple of weeks before I was recommended to go and stay with a dear old couple who offered me a place. They were really good. I was no trouble and half the time I was travelling back to my parents' after the game down the M1. But the age difference meant we had little to talk about and, inevitably, I became bored and decided to move on.

I moved in with Dave Bamber, who scored the only goal on my debut, but we were chalk and cheese. He was horse-racing mad and used to record any race on television. Every video in our house was of horse racing and he would watch all of them. He was ringing bets through rather than going to the bookmakers and as a non-gambler I discovered that was a sign that you were well into the business. Dave did the cooking and I did the washing-up. He wasn't a bad cook but I suppose most of it was Marks and Spencer, usually served with a huge mound of mashed potatoes. Despite our different lifestyles we managed to rub along quite well but when he was transferred to York City I didn't fancy keeping up the place on my own and once again I was on the lookout.

I had a spell in digs with Ian Butterworth and a Scot named Jim McDonald. Jim was a staunch Catholic and had a picture of the Pope above the bed. We had single beds next to each other and I would mess around with his picture when he was out. He was not too happy about that, but generally we got on well. Ian, with whom I eventually moved to Forest, was good fun and kept us all amused.

I went home at the end of the season and when I returned I was again having trouble finding somewhere to live until Keith Thompson, brother of West Bromwich Albion's Gary Thompson, invited me to live with him and his family. It was one of those casual statements when he remarked that if I was struggling I could stay with him. Unfortunately for him, I'm one of those people who take things at face value and I turned up at his house in Birmingham with my bags one day.

Eventually I found myself looking round again because of the drive in and out of Birmingham with its attendant heavy traffic. When I mentioned it to Peakey, he told me to come and stay with him and his heavily pregnant wife in a new house they had just moved into. Again it was probably one of those offers that was only half meant and I think it may have caused a bit of friction between them. But I made myself useful and, being a bit of a handyman as well as an electrician, I was able to help out about the place, mainly fixing things like scales and electrical things to walls.

It worked quite well until I was due to make my come-back after the three months lay-off with the stress fracture for the game at Leicester City two days before Christmas. I was due to ease my way back into the team as substitute. We did all the public relations bit about me returning and I was pictured in the local paper on the Friday holding up the number 12 shirt.

After all that nonsense, we trained and, of all people, I did Peakey going for a 50–50 ball in our usual north v. south match. It all became a bit spicy in the tackle as usual and he ended up on crutches with me driving him home. He couldn't even drive his car never mind play the next day in what was a critical match with us languishing a couple of places off the bottom.

We walked in through the front door and Haddwyn, preparing for Christmas, said, 'What's happened to you? Who did that?' Then I walked through the door and she said, 'It was you, wasn't it?' All I could say was, 'It was an accident. It was an accident.'

I finished up not only wearing Peakey's number 6 shirt at Leicester but also his captain's armband and what made it worse was that we were absolutely annihilated. We lost 5–1 and the man I marked scored twice. He was some raw, young kid named Gary Lineker. Happy Christmas! And it didn't get any better.

I missed the Boxing Day game with injury – we lost 2–0 at Luton – and then I was back in the side as we went down 2–1 at home to West Ham, which left us struggling in 20th place. In typical Coventry fashion, just when everything looked bleak we bounced back to beat Stoke City 4–1 at home on New Year's Day and then we beat Manchester United 1–0 at Old Trafford in the next game.

In those days, the season didn't all finish on the Sunday at the same time. If you were behind with your fixtures, quite often you would play after the final Saturday. We had three games left – Stoke on the Tuesday, Luton on the Thursday and the champions Everton on the Sunday. We were on 41 points and Norwich had finished their fixtures with a win against Chelsea at Stamford Bridge taking them to 49 points. It looked as if there was no way out for us this time.

As is recorded elsewhere in this book, we won the first game 1–0 when I scored with a penalty near the end, and Stoke's Ian Painter missed a penalty, hitting the bar; our centre-half Brian Kilcline scored from outside the box in the 83rd minute against Luton; and on the Sunday we beat the league champions 4–1 in a farcical game with the Everton players stinking of booze. I almost felt sorry for Norwich manager Ken Brown who was pictured walking his dog while our last game was being played. He had every right to feel that the gods were against him.

Coventry was a good, family club. I was pleased that I went there for my first taste of professional football. Even though they were first division, Highfield Road was a friendly place and I'm glad I went there before I joined Brian Clough at Forest. I was there for 20 months and it allowed me to bed down and get used to the pace of league football before the onset of pressure.

Bobby Gould was given the sack while I was there and the dour Scot Don Mackay took over. He was the one who eventually sold me to Forest. Brian Clough originally came down to look at our centre-half Ian Butterworth and finished up buying both of us.

Before that, we played a game at Nottingham Forest and a couple of us were down injured at the same time which meant that the Forest physiotherapist Graham Lyas came on to treat me. While he was bent over attending to my injured leg, he whispered out of the side of his mouth, 'How old are you, son?'

'I feel about 38,' I groaned.

'No, seriously, son, how old are you?'

It transpired that this was the first or second time Brian Clough had seen me and he took a liking to me. When he had the chance to send on his physio, he told him to find out how old I was. He never missed a trick that Brian Clough. I couldn't believe what I was hearing. It was the sort of stunt that Clough pulled but he was only doing his job, even if it was a little unusual.

I still find it unbelievable that Coventry didn't nail me down on a longer contract. Even though there was no such thing as freedom of contract in those days, no one bothered to come and talk to me about staying or a new contract. I suspect that the changeover of managers was the reason. It was not until March, when I had a couple of months of my contract remaining, that they started talking to me.

Soon after that I was accosted walking up King Richard Street to the ground. I had parked my car round the corner, ready for a quick getaway after the game against Liverpool, when some fellow sidled up behind me, tapped me on the shoulder and said, 'I'm Alan Hill from Nottingham Forest. Would you be interested in joining us?'

I couldn't believe it. It was like something from a bad movie and just yards from the ground and a couple of hours before one of our biggest games of the season.

Then he said, 'Can I have your phone number? Brian Clough wants to talk to you.' If that was naïve of him, I was even worse because I gave this man I didn't know from Adam my home telephone number!

I played the game – which we lost 2–0 – and thought nothing more about it until one evening the telephone rang and there was the same man, Alan Hill, telling me to hang on because Brian Clough wanted to talk to me. Clough came on the phone and said, 'Hello, son, do you want to play for me?' I muttered something about my contract being up at the end of the season and that I would love to play for him.

'OK,' he said. 'Ta ra,' and he put the telephone down. That was the extent of our conversation.

Luton, Leicester and Forest had all shown an interest in me but the only concrete offer I had was from Forest.

I wasn't at Coventry long enough to gain a full rapport with the fans but I really enjoyed my time there. We were blessed with a lot of good professionals and although on a bigger scale, it was a bit like Wealdstone in many ways. At Wealdstone, we had a lot of old players dropping out of the League; at Coventry, Bobby Gould trawled around for experienced players. He brought in seasoned performers such as Kenny Hibbitt from Wolves, Peter Barnes the old Manchester City and England winger from Leeds and big Cyrille Regis from West Bromwich Albion, and he brought Bob Latchford back from Holland. These were people I used to watch as a kid down at Loftus Road, and Bob Latchford was a cult hero when he was with Everton and England. They were massive names in the game and they came to join us at Coventry. I learned a lot from them in a short time.

We used to go out for a warm-up before games and when I asked Kenny Hibbitt if he was going to join us for a loosener, he looked up at me and said, 'Look, I have got to run around for an hour and a half out there. I don't need to go out for an extra twenty minutes beforehand.' He probably won't remember the conversation but I do. I never went to warm up after that. I could understand the logic – Why shatter yourself before a game? If it was good enough for him, it was good enough for me, and I followed that philosophy thereafter. The only times that ever changed was when there was a brief romance with plastic pitches and when I played for England under Graham Taylor. Graham insisted on all the players warming up together. I told him I didn't like to but as I was his captain I went out at Wembley for two minutes. Then I went back inside to do what I always did. I'm so regimented it's frightening.

My routine gradually moulded itself and, once set, rarely changed. It went like this:

* Arrive at around 2 p.m. Sit down to read the programme.
* At 2.15 start to get changed.
* 2.20 stretching routines.
* 2.30 find a quiet wall to kick a ball against to get a feel of it.
* 2.35 sit down again, flicking my legs out to stretch a little more.
* 2.40 work a set routine with the physio on yet more stretches.
* 2.45 pads on, prepare for the game and sit quietly getting my mind right.

Well, fairly quietly – the music came in to it, while the others were out warming up. I brought the tapes into the dressing-room at Forest so I played what I wanted (captain's prerogative). I also introduced the music at Newcastle until I heard Ruud Gullit outside the dressing-room door. The music on that occasion wasn't particularly heavy, not even punk rock, but clearly he didn't like it. I heard him say, 'What thee fook is thees shit?' I knew that was the end of the music in the Newcastle dressing-room but I didn't realise it was the end of me as well.

Musically Ruud and I were incompatible. Basically, I played it when the others were out and once I had finished with the physio. I would listen to the Clash, Stranglers and bands like those but a lot of people don't like that music so I compromised with Big Country, Oasis and Spear of Destiny. I would never sell out with crap like garage. At 2.50 prompt it was music off and mind on football with no distractions.

When I went up to Newcastle with West Ham, I popped into the dressing-room to see the Newcastle boys and Alan Shearer pulled me aside and said, 'Listen to the music they play now.' It was soul and I looked at him in disgust. 'You've sold out,' I said. I was tempted to go and confiscate the machine but I suppose with Bobby Robson there they were lucky it wasn't Frank Sinatra or Vera Lynn!

I bumped into Bobby Robson and he was like a kid in a sweet shop. He asked me how my leg was (I broke it the day he started at Newcastle) and he took me out to look at the new stand. When you think of all the big clubs where he has been, he was clearly as proud as punch to be manager of Newcastle. What a nice man.

One of the most significant events during my stay at Coventry was meeting Liz, the lady who was to become my wife. When she left school, she worked in a hotel for a while in her native Wiltshire. Then she had the opportunity to work for international showjumpers Ted and Liz Edgar at Kenilworth in Warwickshire. While she was there she groomed for showjumpers Nick Skelton and Lesley McNaught. When Lesley moved on to join Paddy Lynch, Liz followed her. Paddy Lynch owned a big construction company in Birmingham. He was also Pat Cowdell's boxing manager. His daughter owned ponies and up-and-coming horses. When Lesley left, Liz stayed on at the Lynch house. I met Liz when Lesley dragged her along to a function at Coventry City. Lesley liked football but Liz had no interest. We met, got chatting and I have been with her ever since.

Up until then my social life wasn't that good. I moved around between digs and went back home whenever I could. It took an hour and ten minutes in my brand new Capri, a lovely thing which I still have. It cost me five grand for a spanking-new, black, two-litre S Capri; it was my pride and joy. My mother-in-law Mary drives it now.

The garage put a sticker in the back saying 'Sold and Serviced by . . .' For a game against Luton I pulled into the car park next to their coach. Their players looked out of the window and, according to Kirk Stevens who joined us later, they thought it was a sponsored car that I had been given after being at the club for just two weeks.

That car has been a lucky omen for me. Mary loves it as much as I do and calls it Cruella. It was a bit temperamental for me, a devil to start in the winter but for her it goes first time every time.

Until I met Liz my main pleasure was just the same as it was when I played for Wealdstone – having a drink with my mates in the local in London. In those days, Britain seemed huge and even the short run home seemed to take an eternity.

I met Liz in the February and in May Lesley said that they were off to Barcelona for a show and why didn't I join them. I said I'd love to and, being one of those people who tend to do what they say, I made the trip, much to Liz's surprise. She had taken the horsebox a couple of weeks earlier and driven through France and Spain, stopping in Gijon for a minor show before moving on to Barcelona where I planned to meet up with them.

I booked my ticket with a local travel agent and arrived at Heathrow nice and early for a 1.30 p.m. flight. I must have looked a right 22-year-old Jack-the-lad in my tracksuit, with my streaked blond hair, listening to music on earphones and having a few beers. I didn't look exactly like one of the horse set.

I began to get worried when the flight did not register on the departure board and at 1.20 decided it was time to ask about it. The steward on the information desk looked at the ticket and told me the flight was leaving from Gatwick not Heathrow, observing as he looked at his watch that I wasn't going to make it. He took pity on my plight, telephoned the travel agent and told them they had given the passenger the wrong information and that while he could put me on another plane, they would have to foot the bill as it was totally their fault.

There was another flight a few hours later and with time to kill I was lucky to bump into a friend who worked at the airport who pointed out that if I wanted a cheap beer I should follow his directions to the bar where all the porters drank. By the time my flight was called I'd had a good drink and I eventually arrived in Barcelona at around 6 p.m. a little the worse for wear and suddenly aware that I hadn't a clue where I was going. My only instruction was to go to the showjumping in Barcelona.

I spent the next hour looking for people who spoke English and asking them where I could find the show-jumping. Eventually Air France gave me the address of a polo club on the off chance that it might be there and if it wasn't they could probably tell me where I could find the event. As luck would have it, they directed me to the right place and I arrived at this very fancy establishment in my black Sergio tracksuit, earphones around my neck and sports bag over my shoulder.

Despite sticking out like a sore thumb, I paid my entry fee and sat in the stand, looking round for where I might find Liz. I eventually saw Lesley sitting in the VIP area and immediately made my way across the seats calling out her name. She saw me and told me later that she said under her breath, 'Oh, my good God.' She quickly shuttled me out the back to where the horseboxes were parked and the horses stabled and then wisely washed her hands of me.

I found Liz and she was equally startled to see me. Clearly neither of them had thought for a minute that I would take them up on their casually offered invitation. I realised that if I hung around I was going to be in the way so I set about looking for things to do. I even managed to find a local greyhound track where they had an evening meeting. The way the locals looked at me they clearly thought that I was gay. I had a couple of beers and a bet and returned to the showjumping for a few more beers.

Liz was obviously embarrassed to have me there and continued to have as little to do with me as possible. I slept the first night on a settee in the horsebox while Liz had a bed with the horses where they were stabled. The second night I arrived back to find the horsebox locked. There were people sleeping everywhere so I found a sunbed by the swimming pool in the club leisure centre and slept there.

The rising sun and some irritating itching woke me in the morning and I jumped up to find that I was covered in insects and flies. I was startled to hear laughter from across the swimming pool and looked up to see all the grooms eating breakfast and falling about laughing at me. That didn't exactly raise me in Liz's esteem.

The next night Moët et Chandon, who sponsored one of the jumpers, Nelson Pessoa, threw a party and all the grooms were on the free champagne in one of the horseboxes. I came out of there in a very happy mood and made my way back to our horsebox, where I slapped on a Bob Marley tape. Suddenly a head came up from the horse section and one of Liz's colleagues slaughtered me for waking her up.

That was the last night in Barcelona and rather than fly back on my own Liz asked if I wanted to travel back through Spain to Lyon in France and then on to Calais. By this time, I was wearing a white Sergio T-shirt, white Sergio shorts and a pair of trainers with no socks. I looked more like a tennis player than someone connected with show-jumping or even football. We arrived at the border and the driver offered up the horses' passports and all the other documentation needed. Liz was out watering the horses and I was sitting with my feet up in the cab, earphones on, chilling out. The border guard appeared, opened the door and said, 'Move this wagon. It's in the way.'

I shrugged and told him I couldn't drive it but he was so insistent that he took his gun out to back up his request. I still shook my head and he demanded my passport. I reluctantly handed it over and he disappeared with it. I told a groom what had happened and he told me that I should go and recover my passport as quickly as possible because once they had received clearance they were gone and I would be left behind. He suggested I stay with the customs officer who had taken it. I did a man-for-man marking job on this Spaniard all around the control post. He kept looking over his shoulder at me, eventually telling me to go away. I turned but the moment he made his move I was back up beside him again. He turned round again, took out his gun and pinned me up against the wall, demanding that I leave him alone. I was only just in time with my passport. I think he was glad to get rid of me in the end.

We made our way to Lyon and a lovely racecourse setting, then on to Calais. They dropped me off at Dover and I made my way back home.

Despite the Barcelona experience and although Liz didn't have much time for football, or for my punk rock, we hit it off and got on quite quickly but the real catalyst was the move to Nottingham. By that time she had left her job as a groom and was nannying. I told her I was going to Nottingham and planned to buy a house, and I asked her if she would like to move in with me.

At that time I was off the road because of a drink-drive conviction, another unwanted entry on my CV. We had played at Norwich on 30 March and lost 2–1. On the way back in the coach I suppose I must have had three large

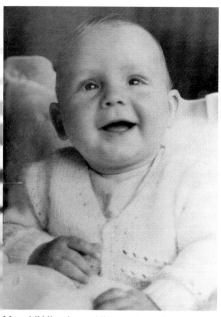

The perfect throw: practising the essentials.

More dribbling than tackling: me in my first year.

Hardly Psycho: me as an angelic schoolboy.

Silverware and long hair: the Fryent Primary School team and some of our trophies. That's me fifth from left on the back row.

Still me to come: my parents with Pamela, Dennis and Ray.

The original hard man: eldest brother Ray, who quit boxing and took up refereeing.

Putting on the style: brothers Ray and Dennis all set for a trip to the West End.

Making my mark: my first Player of the Year award with part-timers Wealdstone.

Champagne and cigars: manager Alan Batsford enjoys a puff as Wealdstone celebrate winning the Southern League.

Someone even older than me: Coventry City keeper Steve Ogrizovic and I go for the same ball. (*Coventry Evening Telegraph*)

Going blond: a moment of madness saw me dye my hair just before my trip to see a surprised Liz in Barcelona. (*Popperfoto*)

Turning it on: even after I joined Nottingham Forest, I still advertised my services as an electrician in the match programme. (*Nottingham Evening News*)

Of all people! John Aldridge, never my favourite player, settles our fate in the 1988 FA Cup semi-final at Hillsborough with his second goal. (*Colorsport*)

Wembley here we come: the end of a cold, wet semi-final against Bristol City at Ashton Gate, celebrating quietly with manager Brian Clough and the ever-present Alan Hill.

Derby day: yet another tussle with my old Derby County rival Ted McMinn. (*Popperfoto*)

The tragedy unfolds: when the problems began at Hillsborough during the 1989 FA Cup semi-final it was all at the far end of the ground, so the Nottingham Forest players were not really aware of what was going on until much later. (*Popperfoto*)

No quarter: a battle with rival defender and England team-mate Steve Foster in the 1989 Littlewoods Cup final against Luton Town. (*Colorsport*)

And again! Celebrating retaining the Littlewoods Cup, this time beating Oldham. (*Colorsport*)

The old one–two: celebrating another Stuart Pearce goal courtesy of my mate Nigel Clough. (*Bob Thomas*)

Beauty and the beast: I introduce Princess Diana to manager Brian Clough before the 1991 FA Cup final against Spurs. (*Empics*)

Take that! Lee Glover moves Gary Mabbutt out of the wall to give me space to score the first goal of the final against Spurs after Paul Gascoigne's injury. (*Popperfoto*)

cans of lager. In those days when we arrived back in Coventry we invariably went to a pub, and I had another drink, this time a lager shandy, before driving Micky Adams home. I was doing 40 in a 30mph zone and was pulled up for speeding.

The two policemen asked me if I had been drinking and I told them truthfully that I had had three cans of lager during a three-hour trip from Norwich. They tested me and I was fractionally over the limit. When Micky saw this he said, 'I'm all right from here. I can walk home,' and cleared off leaving me to handle the problem on my own.

I had originally planned to drop my car off and go out for the night. I was not a drink driver, even though it was not treated quite as seriously then as it is now. A lot more youngsters did drink and drive. I went down to the police station because they said that if I went for a blood test I might well pass positive because it was so close. On the way, I thought of a cunning plan. I was too clever for them, far too clever. I told them that I didn't like needles, I thought that if I went back to the club, I could pretend that I was on some form of medication that had pushed me over the top to get off any charge. I went to the club and asked the physio what I could say but he looked at me as though I was stupid and told me that there was nothing. I was gutted because I might have got off if I had gone through with the blood test. I ended up losing my licence at the worst possible time, when I was moving an hour further away from Liz.

Fortunately, Liz packed up her job and moved up with me. It was difficult for her and she found it hard at first. She is an independent girl and had been living away from home for a while and working with horses. Horses had been her whole life. When she joined me in Nottingham, she had no involvement with horses at all and sat around with nothing to do. That was just not her style. Both of us would admit to the fact that it was an awkward time.

I'm sure that it was fate that we met in Coventry, not hometown for either of us. I liked her as soon as I met her. I'm still a bit baffled about why she reciprocated. It certainly wasn't my music; she hated it. She was interested in horses and the country life while I knew nothing of either. Indeed, when it came to horses, I was scared to death of them. I was a bit of a Jack-the-lad, a city boy from London, thinking I was smarter than anyone else in the world. We had nothing in common but I seemed to have the ability to make her laugh. She was very shy, as I am until I get to know people when the guard comes down and exposes the real me. She is more homely than I am and while I love a holiday and travelling she is just as happy pottering about at home or in the stables. Give me the slightest excuse to climb on an aeroplane and I'm off. She may take a little persuading but once away she loves it as much as I do. The hard part is getting her there.

Not long after we arrived in Nottingham we took a retired racehorse on loan, an absolute lunatic. His name was Last River, hence his nickname Swim. He had been pulled out of racing because he wouldn't start, quite a drawback in that game. He would stand at the start and when the other horses went forward he went backwards. He was some character, completely barmy, but Liz loved him. We stabled him up the road and spent a lot of time with him. That started my interest in horses and once you get to know them you fall in love with them.

We had a little flirt with horse racing and had a horse in training with Jenny Pitman for a couple of years. Once you lose the fear, it's fine but never lose the respect for them because you don't want to be kicked.

I also have to help out. I can't let Liz deal with the horses while I watch television. It takes two to tend to a sick animal of that size and when one of our horses contracted mud fever – that's developing little scabs on the backs of the heels when the ground is wet underfoot – I had to hold the horse while Liz treated the scabs. You have to be prepared for that sort of involvement or not have horses at all.

It's worked well. Horses provide a welcome relief from football and its attendant pressures. Managers seem to have the cares of the world on their shoulders. They think of nothing else but the job, walking round with it on their minds every waking minute. I remember the brief time I was in the job; I was in a permanent daze, thinking only of football. Sir Alex Ferguson and Kevin Keegan have both found a release in horses and I have followed that same route.

Fortunately, Liz appreciates that football is my life and, like most women, she says that I put football before her!

It made me laugh watching an interview with Manchester United and England defender Phil Neville and his new bride on their wedding day. The interviewer asked him if this was the biggest day of his life or was it winning the European Champions League. He was immediately on the backfoot. Every professional footballer watching knew that winning the European Cup was the biggest day. To be fair to him, he didn't say that getting married was the biggest day of his life;

instead, he hummed and haa-ed. If I had been him, I would have lied. He finished up trying to wriggle out of it saying, 'The European Cup was a one-off.' That made me laugh and I asked his image on television, 'So your wedding isn't a one-off then?'

But when your life, and I mean your whole life, is football, winning a European Cup or a World Cup has to be the biggest thing. It would be like me asking Liz if she would swap all involvement with horses for the marriage. She could not and it would be unfair to ask.

We were together for a long time, around nine years, before we eventually tied the knot. I asked her to marry me a couple of times and she turned me down, saying she wasn't ready. Then Nottingham Forest beat Spurs in a League Cup semi-final to reach Wembley and when I arrived home that night I opened a bottle of champagne and asked her to marry me. This time she said she would. It was third time lucky and I mean lucky!

She has long been aware that football means everything to me and she has been prepared to adjust her life accordingly. On a Saturday morning, for example, if the telephone rings she knows I won't answer it, whoever it is, even if it is my mother or my dad. I don't talk to anyone on matchday mornings.

If we have friends coming to the game and they call at the house, Liz sees them and I stay in bed. I'm resting and I get up when I'm ready. Even with friends, I get into the car, turn the punk music on, have no conversation with them. They sit in silence while I continue to get my mind right. Football is on my mind, nothing else. Liz understands that and she deals with it.

Sometimes I listen to other players' wives and they don't understand exactly what their husbands require to give of their best. My diet and preparation routines have been in place for years. A football wife has to be aware of all that. There are routines I have picked up as I have gone along over the years. I have always been in bed by 10.30 on a Friday night whether it is at home or in a hotel. Sometimes you can hear the boys still chatting at midnight. Maybe that's what they do every night, but it's not what I do and I expect everyone to respect that. Trevor Peake used to have four cans of lager every Friday night before he played. He had done the same thing at Nuneaton, Lincoln and Coventry where he was one of our best players and close to an England call at one stage. When I went to live with him and his wife, he asked me if I wanted a beer and was surprised when I declined. I'm strong enough to know what's right and what's wrong for me. I personally thought that he was wrong but that was his business.

I learned quite a few bits and pieces from England coach Glenn Hoddle that he, in turn, had picked up from Arsene Wenger when he was manager at Monaco.

Mary, my mother-in-law, gave me a good tip. She put me right when she said, 'A horse wouldn't have a meal three hours before a race. So why do some athletes?' She was right, of course, and gradually I worked out a diet that suited me. When I'm away on the day of a game, I have a raw carrot, raw broccoli and beans on toast for breakfast. The others might have a fry-up. Nutritionally, that's rubbish but it's what they have always done. A lot of it is down to habit. I have a pre-match meal at the same time every matchday – for a three o'clock kick-off it will be at 10.15 on the dot – and

I have been doing that for a number of years now. Previously I was like all the others having my pre-match meal at 11.45 because we knew no different. Everyone is looking over his shoulder at what the next man is eating and you end up having what everyone else does so as not to be different. As you get older you become wiser.

The game is changing quickly, though. That came home to me when I went with the West Ham United team to Newcastle for a league game. There were a lot of youngsters on the trip including a player the Hammers had signed from Arsenal. Arsene Wenger is meticulous about what players eat and what vitamin pills they should take and this lad had been at Highbury since he was 14. But when he came down for breakfast at the hotel, he saw the older players having a fry-up so he followed suit. The physio spotted it and asked him if he would have done that at Arsenal. He, of course, admitted that he wouldn't but when he was asked why he was eating it now he said, 'Because it's there and it looks nice.' You have to be strong and he wasn't.

Liz knows how professionally I take my job and, in turn, I know how she is in dealing with horses. I wouldn't say I am like that in everything I do in life but in football I have to be prepared properly and she understands that. You go into the players' bar after a game and there will be players' wives there who don't know the result and don't care. They don't even know which way the teams are kicking. I used to go away from there and tell her I couldn't live with someone like that. She appreciates how I am and it has rubbed off on her. She knows that if we have been stuffed or if I have played badly, it is no use saying that it's only a game and suggesting that we go out for a meal or a few drinks. She is aware that I will have the hump and won't feel like going anywhere.

In some ways we are not compatible in our backgrounds, our hobbies and many other areas but in other ways, such as attitude and professionalism, we are totally on the same wavelength. I am thankful that I have someone alongside me like that. People may say I have a one-track mind or that I am a chauvinist but even the strongest person needs some support and she has been brilliant for me.

Another important factor was that we didn't have children until we were well into our 30s. I have never understood how players can be focused on their careers when they have a family. At times I find it very demanding and hard work.

When Chelsea came along it was a bolt out of the blue. We had not planned or tried for a family. When Liz discovered she was pregnant it once again emphasised the support I receive from her. She discovered on the Thursday that she was carrying but because we were playing at home against Arsenal on the Saturday she didn't tell me until the Sunday in case it put me off my game. I appreciated that. It represented real support.

On the Sunday morning she said, 'I have something to tell you.' I said, 'What's that?' expecting she had spent more than she thought she should have done on a coat or some such thing. She stunned me when she said, 'I think I'm pregnant.' There we were, two 36-year-olds who had been round the block once or twice, and I was so staggered that I did not know what to do or say. It was so unexpected. I started laughing, that nervous laugh that just sometimes happens.

She asked me what I thought and I said, 'Ask me Tuesday. It's done me up. I need a couple of days to think about it.' It wasn't the best or the most thoughtful of responses and Liz, understandably, burst into tears. We had our own lives and although there had been children around, we had never considered it. We had all the excuses. It knocked the pair of us for six for a while. It wasn't that we didn't want children but for both of us it was always later, let's think about it later. Both of us were terrified.

When Chelsea was born, I loved her to bits but I couldn't have done it when I was 21. Physically, I would have coped but I don't know what detrimental effect it might have had on my career.

Brian Laws at Forest used to go swimming with his kids on the morning of a game. I couldn't have done that. Even when I was young I would stay in bed on Saturday morning and my parents and later Liz knew that I was preparing myself. Even now that I am further than the back end of my career, I wouldn't dream of doing anything on the morning of the game.

I'm not saying that young players should not have children but I'm convinced it must have a negative effect on their careers. For a start, there is no doubt that when you have children your diet suffers. You end up having burgers and chips because it's easier.

Liz is an outstanding mother. I knew she would be simply by the caring way she tended the horses in her charge, not that she hoses Chelsea down or puts a cold pack on her leg when she is poorly. I have to confess that I'm a doting dad. I used to take the mickey out of other couples with kids, telling them that they ruled their lives. I joked how I hated those little boys who come up to you, shove a scrap of paper under your nose and say, ''Ere Pearce, sign this.' Now the boot is on the other foot and they are poking fun at me. The funny thing is that I don't mind.

When the baby finally arrived it was a case of finding a suitable name. We were a bit stuck at first as most parents are. We produced a short list with the names we both liked. I liked Tallulah but Liz thought it sounded like a street-walker. I also liked Toulouse but that was put on a back shelf as well. In contrast, I also liked the traditional name of Victoria and, when we looked at a baby book, the name Milan caught my fancy.

I was slightly worried about the football connotations with Chelsea and Milan but then I thought what the hell. I was nearing the end of my career and in a year or two no one will think twice about it. It is just the names I like, not the football clubs, and I never once thought of calling her Queens Park Rangers or Nottingham Forest. They didn't roll off the tongue like Chelsea.

There is no doubt that Chelsea has changed our lives. What a different sort of love a father gives to a daughter. I see bits of Liz in her, I see bits of me and I see her own individuality. It is all very exciting.

I was lucky to have a solid home life with my parents and then moved almost straightaway into an equally solid home life with Liz. She doesn't go to as many games now we have Chelsea but she was a regular at Forest and I think she enjoys football. She will even watch it on television although she prefers it when someone she knows is playing.

When I broke my leg the first time, I didn't want her to hear it on the radio. I telephoned and just told her I had broken my leg. There was no panic. At least she didn't have to call the vet to have me put down.

We have discovered a common bond in travel, although as I said, she sometimes takes a little persuading. For me it started with Coventry when we went on a pre-season tour of Scandinavia. I thought to myself that this couldn't be bad, being taken to Sweden to play football, all expenses paid, and drawing a wage at the same time. But my interest in having my passport stamped was really aroused when I joined Forest a year later. Brian Clough would have us pack our bags at the drop of a hat. If he had an 'earner' (a friendly that paid the club good money) he would tell us on Friday that we were flying to the Middle East immediately after playing the league game on Saturday. It was phenomenal. Two years earlier I had been changing fuses for Brent Council and now someone wanted to take me to Tenerife for a mid-season break or to Saudi Arabia to play football. More of that please!

Football not only put pages of stamps in my passport but also gave me the bug for travel. I quickly decided that the world was too large to go anywhere twice and I vowed that I would always take my holidays in different places every year. I have been to Bermuda, for example, and while I loved it I don't feel the need to go back. I want to go somewhere else. Liz wasn't too enamoured when I first started dragging her round the world with me, but now she appreciates it.

We are too protected from what is going on elsewhere in our comfortable homes in Europe, and it is an eye-opener in many respects when you start widening your boundaries. One of our most fascinating trips was when we went to

Zimbabwe on safari. Because of what we had been force-fed on television and in magazines, we were of the belief that all animals should be preserved, especially as we are both animal lovers. I didn't believe that they should be hunted down or culled. What we didn't know about was how a herd of elephants might trample through a village, destroying precious crops and wrecking people's homes. A television documentary doesn't tell you that. Travelling gives us both sides of the argument and the opportunity to make up our own minds. It doesn't mean that I now believe all elephants should be shot but I can see someone else's point of view.

The attraction of travelling is that you see people in their own environment and can begin to understand why they behave as they do. As soon as we walked out of the airport in Sri Lanka it was a real culture shock. It was India without quite so much poverty. We travelled to our hotel in a minibus and instead of being held up by traffic jams we were stopped because there was an elephant in the middle of the road. That's the norm there. Driving into the capital Colombo, there might be a herd of cows sitting in the fast lane of the dual carriageway. Then a bus will go careering past with people hanging off the sides, doors and roof. When I drove to work from my Wiltshire home to West Ham, there might be an eight-mile traffic jam because a horse had escaped or because there was a sheep on the hard shoulder. It's a different world and I want to see as much of it as I can. You don't see anything if you stay at home.

I can never understand it when I hear people in their 30s saying that they have never been abroad. I know that I am fortunate in having a career that has made me financially secure and given me the opportunity to travel, but I would say to everyone, if you get a chance to travel – go! Just going to an airport is exciting. I love the buzz, the atmosphere, the coming and going. You can sit in a bar in an airport and see the whole world go by. The place has a special feeling. I'm so sad I get excited just flying out to Dublin or up to Glasgow.

My favourite spots in the world so far are Zimbabwe and Sri Lanka. Bermuda was idyllic with beautiful weather and beaches, but the other two places offered so much more, particularly when you sit in a safari camp with perhaps 14 other people swapping stories. The experience is imprinted on the memory. On our first night in Zimbabwe we were in our high single beds by around nine o'clock because of the early start and lay there terrified, listening to the noises of the night. It was like being in Jurassic Park. It didn't help the next morning when we emerged into the sunlight to find cheetah paw prints going through the camp.

The camp was on the edge of Lake Kariba. We got up at six, went out with the guide until eleven, then back for breakfast followed by a little rest, out again at around 3.30 and finally back before the light went for dinner at six. We sat round a big table under the stars in the jet-black sky, chatting to the guides and the other guests – a couple of South Africans and a group of Europeans.

One guide, Steve, used to work for the government before he acquired his own camp and he told us tales that made our hair stand on end. When he was on the anti-poaching squad for President Mugabe's government, protecting the rhinos, elephants and other endangered species, he claimed that he had shot and killed 14 poachers while doing his job. He further claimed that he left the job because the last poacher he shot was a relative of the President! True or not, it beat sitting around and watching soap operas on television.

Sri Lanka was also a great experience with lovely people and wonderful sights. The people are also lovely in Mauritius. That is, in the main, a beach holiday but I had the experience of going horse racing while we were there. They are fanatics. The crowds were incredible. The place was full of Indians, Chinese and Africans with the only white faces belonging to the jockeys, the owners and us. The two things they care about on Mauritius are their horse racing and English football. It suited me because I love both and add that to the fact that the people of Mauritius are probably the most racially integrated and friendly in the world and you can guess we had a pretty good holiday.

With our growing interest in horse racing, Liz and I have also been making an annual pilgrimage to Ireland, combining holiday with hobby. We look around all the studs with friends of ours who buy and sell horses.

There is, of course, a vast difference between going on holiday and travelling with a football team where the strict regimen means that access is restricted for the most part to airports, hotels, training pitches and the match ground. In any case, footballers are basically lazy bastards and even when there is time to spare on tours, they prefer room service in the hotel and a wine bar for entertainment. I have been incredibly fortunate to travel to China, Hong Kong, Australia, New Zealand, Thailand and many of the football-playing European countries, but I didn't see as much of them as I would wish. Things are changing slowly and players opening their eyes to the outside world.

When we went to China we were taken to the Great Wall as a squad and walked round. That evening Gareth Southgate, a couple of FA officials and I asked Terry Venables if he minded us hiring a taxi to go and look at the infamous Tiananmen Square. He gave his blessing and asked the rest of the squad if they wanted to join us. Everyone else blanked it. We had a look around the Secret City and the place where the students were massacred, and while it was chilling, it was a phenomenal experience. I found the attitude of the others very blinkered. They were happy to sit around the hotel and do nothing. If I thought the sightseeing would take away from my job, I wouldn't have done it but it was a couple of days before the game, involved a short taxi ride and a minimal amount of walking. What's more it keeps the mind fresh rather than stagnating.

With Brian Clough, we ended up going away an average of four times a season, usually a couple of times to Cala Millor on Majorca where he had an apartment. They were just jollies, a couple of beers and some rest and relaxation. These were also the money-spinners I've already mentioned, flying out to somewhere exotic, playing a game and flying back again. That was a ridiculous way of preparing for a league match but it made the club, or someone, a lot of money so we did it.

The players got blasé about it all. One time we had played about four games into a new season when he called us down to the hotel bar.

'Skip,' he said. 'The players are looking a little jaded. They need a trip.' The season had only just started and he was obviously poking fun but I responded.

'I think you're right, Boss.'

'Right,' he said. 'We'll go to Tenerife. That's what we'll do. Who wants to go?' I was always up for a trip and was first in line with just four others out of a whole squad of 20, including a fair number of single boys. Clough looked in dismay and spat out, 'I can't fucking believe you lot. Fuck off, all of you.'

Then he turned to the five of us and asked, 'Do you want to bring your wives?' That was even better as far as I was concerned. Liz would always think of a million and one reasons why she couldn't go before actually agreeing, and off we went, five players, their wives, Clough and some of the staff.

I thought it was unbelievable that when someone was prepared to give you a few days off with the sun on your back, in the company of your wife and pay for it all, people turned it down. It was alien to me. I don't understand that mentality. It wasn't the only time it happened. The players made excuses and said that it was because Clough would be in their face all the time and they would prefer to do their own thing. Bad excuse. In five days away with Liz, I would hardly see the manager. If you wanted to stay away from him, you could, and it was no problem having dinner together, especially if his wife was with him.

Moving to Forest was great for me. Brian Clough collared me at the right time. Even when I went to Forest, I was still unsure of myself and whether I could make it as a professional footballer. There was always that nagging doubt.

At Coventry, Bobby Gould was a big influence on my career. However, all the Coventry managers of that era were so busy looking after their own jobs that they didn't have much time to help others. When Bobby was replaced with Don Mackay, he was instantly under the same pressures. Coventry were always down among the lower clubs. But I was happy there – as happy as I was at Forest – and if they had offered me another contract I would have bitten off their hand. I could just as easily have played at Highfield Road for 12 years.

It was not until after a couple of years at Forest and the England Under-21 call-up in 1986 that I was finally convinced that I had made it as a professional footballer and that no matter what happened I would be able to find myself another club. The question mark hung over my head all the time I was at Coventry. I had a two-year contract and no one was talking to me about extending it.

I remember telephoning a friend when I signed for Forest and saying that I had signed a three-year deal and if it did not work out, well, I would have had three years. I carried on with my electrician's work; it was a common-sense thing to do.

forest fire

Football was definitely a gamble in those early years of my professional career and I was glad that I had my trade to fall back on in case I flopped or was struck down with injury.

I kept my hand in at Coventry, doing some work for John Sillett, Peter Barnes and Kirk Stevens. Kirk wanted a light fitted in the bedroom. On the face of it there were no problems. It was a bowl-shaped fixture with a chandelier effect hanging from it, to be fixed to the bedroom ceiling with three screws. I did the job, jumped off the bed and said to Kirk, 'There you are, mate, a lifetime guarantee with that little lot.' No sooner had the words left my mouth than the whole lot came crashing down on to the bed where, a few hours later, Kirk would have been lying with his wife discussing the mysteries of the universe. I had over-tightened the screws and they cracked the glass so that the screws stayed up but the light fitting did not. We both fell about laughing and it all turned out well as the shop replaced the fitting because they thought it was faulty.

The work for John Sillett was a little more robust. He lived out in the rural part of Coventry and he needed to lay an armoured cable down his drive and into the stables.

When I moved to Forest I thought to myself that if I started a little electrical business it would be security in case the football didn't work out. I had been a professional for less than two years and nothing was certain. I went to Brian Clough and told him what I had in mind and asked whether he would mind if I advertised in the matchday programme. He had no objections and it brought in a few bits and pieces, so much so that after a few months it became too much with all the training and playing demands at Forest. The little jobs were not a problem but I rewired a friend's house in Coventry and the effort of training and then travelling to and from Coventry plus working on my own became a bit of a strain. In the end, I asked Forest team-mate Brian Rice to come and help me out and I paid him a daily rate for working with me up in the loft.

I also worked in a hotel where I met a builder who offered me some contract work with him. He looked after a chain of banks and hired me to clean all the light fittings in a local branch. Again it was too much for one person and I pulled in another of the Forest players, Billy Reilly, to assist me for the accepted daily rate.

After we had played Brighton in the League Cup at the City Ground I took a call on my business line from a Brighton supporter who wanted to know whether it was THE Stuart Pearce. He was an electrician himself and was delighted that I was in the same business earning an honest living as well as playing football.

Far from putting any obstacles in the way, Clough brought in his iron and his kettle for me to repair, although when I told him it was cheaper to buy a new iron rather than replace the element he began to doubt whether I really was an electrician. Mind you, it could have been some Clough master plan to rebuild the club from the inside because as well as me, he took on Gary Crosby who was a carpenter and Garry Birtles, a carpet fitter.

My first season at Forest involved not just bedding into a new club but becoming used to a completely different type of management under the colourful Brian Clough. Within a year I was captain. It was basically a very young side. With hindsight, I was a natural choice for captain – there was no one else on that bus whom he could have approached and asked. Even though I was a professional of less than three years, I was still a senior player.

My stature grew in the dressing-room over the years, far more than it did with Clough. It was never a nice, friendly partnership – I was his captain and left-back and he was the boss. It was a working relationship. My reputation grew within the club without me even realising it.

Like Mark Hughes, I am a different person on the pitch compared with off it. I like to do my shouting on the pitch during a game, although I have had my moments off it! Your career shapes your personality, especially when you are in the limelight. I enjoy the way I have done it and I agree with Mark's approach, fiery on it and quiet off it. I am not an Ian Wright type with all that cockiness and confidence in themselves. Sometimes I have my doubts about that type of character and, when I meet someone who is outlandishly over the top, the first thing that springs to mind is to ask myself what they are trying to hide. For some, that's how they are but my feeling is why are they giving it big? Why not let your football do your talking for you? But that's just the way I am.

I may have been quiet away from the ground by this time, but the dressing-room was my court and once I had my feet under the table people came in under my terms and if there was any mickey-taking I would be at the forefront.

Even at Coventry I was organising the odd function, bringing my non-league roots with me. After a couple of years at Forest, I was involved in everything. After a while you know everyone at the club and you become happy with the workplace. My rapport with the fans was great. It was a lovely place to go to work. To me that meant a lot. If you're happy with your surroundings, you're happy in your life and I was.

Of course, I was concerned that we weren't winning league titles. We finished third in 1988 and 1989 and thought we could go on from there. It was only Liverpool, who were the big side at the time, keeping us out and we expected to move on. But we didn't. In my first six seasons we never finished lower than ninth, but we could not push on. While we were successful in the cups, we were short of a couple of international quality players such as John Barnes or Peter Beardsley who were both around and available at the time. We needed a couple of individuals of that stature. But when Liverpool went in for players, they usually got them ahead of us.

Make no mistake, we were big with four players in the England side. We were short of players in the same way that clubs are now. Aston Villa, for example, are the modern-day equivalent. Gareth Southgate took so long to ask for a move because he felt that Villa were only one or two players short of being a top side. It's the old story. They are not far away but the difference between winning titles and being a decent side is vast.

Clough brought in some foreign players including Johnny Metgod and Hans Segers, but I'm not sure that was the answer. What we needed at the time was another midfield player – keep Neil Webb and add a proven striker of quality. We were a young squad and lacked depth when things went wrong or when we suffered injuries. What we didn't have were a couple of 30 somethings to come in and settle the ship when things were going wrong.

But if you listen, every club in the country is a couple of players short. We were good enough for me to enjoy being there. I was getting international recognition and we were doing well in cup competitions so I had no regrets about not seeking to improve my lot with a so-called bigger club. Forest remained a strong side, very competitive and always challenging until we were relegated out of the blue.

Perhaps it was the success in the cups that took our attention away from what should have been the major target. In fact, sometimes when we went to Wembley it papered over the cracks of the team not being strong enough. We thought we had got away with a bit when we had the League Cup standing in our cabinet, one of only three domestic trophies available.

Everything hit the fan in a big way in 1992–93. There were never any real signs of us going down but the house collapsed like a pack of cards. On the other hand, someone should have realised because neither were we realistically challenging for the title. After a sequence of finishing third, ninth, eighth and eighth, we went from losing 1–0 to Manchester United at Wembley in 1992 to being relegated a season later in 22nd position.

It is nothing you ever plan, to do well in cups. It is often inexplicable when you see Brighton taking Manchester United to a replay in the Cup final and being relegated in the same season. Where is the logic? Even now I still cannot say why we did so well in cups but the reason why we did not push on in the League was because we were short of a couple of top-class players. Here was a side who, 13 years earlier, had lifted back-to-back European Cups, relegated out of the top flight. A lesson to anyone but a lesson that never seems to be learned because you can never see it coming until the day it arrives. Just ask Manchester City.

Our best finish in the League while I was there was third and, give or take one or two better players, we might have been a bit closer to pushing a tremendous Liverpool side all the way. Had they not been as good as they were, we would have undoubtedly won more.

Brian Clough was clearly building a side for a tilt at the title. We finished eighth in my first two seasons there, 1985–86 and 1986–87, and third in the two following seasons as Des Walker emerged, Nigel Clough came in and Neil Webb proved to be a sensational buy. Garry Birtles came from non-league and did well, as did Dutchman Johnny Metgod. But, as I say, we were still a couple of players short of having a serious go and we couldn't get near enough to Liverpool for love nor money. We weren't good enough to get past them. They were head and shoulders above everybody at the time, although we gave them good games and beat them on occasions at our place.

There was a lot of bad feeling between the two teams, certainly there was on my part. It was probably jealousy where I was concerned because they always seemed to be in our way.

From my point of view, I would have played in Europe on three or four occasions but for the behaviour of some Liverpool supporters at the Heysel Stadium in Belgium, as a result of which we were all banned from playing in Europe. Personally, I thought that was very unfair. Liverpool should have suffered for what went on at Heysel, not Nottingham Forest or Norwich City, who hadn't put a foot wrong. That was an injustice.

We lost FA Cup semi-finals to them in 1988 and 1989 and what was really annoying was that had we been drawn against any of the other semi-finalists we would probably have beaten them and reached the final but both times we drew Liverpool. It stirred up a lot of feeling between the two sides because of the intensity of our meetings. Before the first of these two semi-finals, I was sitting in my car in the Forest car park with the radio on waiting for the draw. It was our luck. We had been drawn away in every round, beating Halifax, Leyton Orient, Birmingham City and Arsenal, but the semi-final was to be played on a neutral ground and we felt that if we could avoid Liverpool and draw either Wimbledon or Luton Town we would make the final.

We went up to Hillsborough, which we didn't mind, especially when a whisper went around the dressing-room that the Sheffield Wednesday groundsman had asked our club how we wanted the pitch: did we want it wet or dry?

We were a young side with Des Walker, Nigel Clough, Franz Carr and me, against the likes of Bruce Grobbelaar, Alan Hansen, Peter Beardsley and John Barnes.

Some say that the worst thing is to lose in the final but as far as I am concerned the first round is the worst. I would rather go as far as I can every time and if I am going to lose, make it the final. We just weren't good enough to get there. John Barnes caused havoc. He was up against Steve Chettle who had been tucked up by a journalist in the previews to the game. He was playing out of position and was asked how he fancied reaching the final. He said that he was looking forward to it. Then when he was asked what he would have for his breakfast on the morning of the match he replied, 'Beans on toast.' The headline the next day was: 'I will have John Barnes on Toast'. It wound up John and he ran Steve ragged; not that Barnes needed stoking up. He was the best player in the country at the time. That individual battle was one of the main factors in the result.

It was a very tight game. They scored first through John Aldridge who then got a yard on me and scored a second. Nigel pulled one back for us and we gave them a couple of hesitant moments. But it was not enough and once again Brian Clough was left wondering about the FA Cup.

Clough could be calm or livid in defeat; it varied according to the performance. On that day he couldn't say a lot because we played as well as we could and were beaten by a better team. It was straight back on the coach, as ever.

I often wondered what would have happened, how the club would have risen in stature if we had won that semi-final in 1988. We were sniffing around the cups in the eighties and early nineties – semi-final, semi-final, third round, final, quarter-final in the FA Cup in successive years from 1988 to 1992. That's a good run for any team and on top of that we won the League Cup back to back in 1989 and 1990.

We were back at Hillsborough exactly a year later, hoping this time that we could overturn them. We had been playing for five or six minutes when people began spilling on to the pitch from the Liverpool end and my first thought was, 'Bloody Liverpool supporters again.' I am not ashamed to admit that because it's what I thought as the referee took us off the pitch. We didn't realise what was going on and all I could think of was that Liverpool and their supporters were stopping me from plying my trade in Europe and now they were keeping me from playing in a semi-final. We were protected from the horror of it; we didn't know what was going on out there.

The semi-final was eventually played at Old Trafford. Brian Laws scored an own goal and once again Liverpool got right up my nose as John Aldridge ruffled Brian's hair in mock congratulations. Little things like that, added to the fact that they were in a different class from us, riled me no end. When we beat them in the League, not one of them wanted to shake our hands but when they beat us they were in our face, wanting to shake hands and pat us on the back.

Everyone was saying to us that there was no way we could win the semi-final at Old Trafford and that even if we did, everyone wanted Liverpool in the final. That wasn't my attitude. I wanted to beat them even more than before the aborted Hillsborough semi-final. People will probably say what a hard bastard and that is taking football beyond sport. But having been banned from Europe for so long, I was aggrieved that they had stacked the entire nation on their side, again through no fault of ours.

Not long afterwards we went to Anfield for a league game and lost to a late John Aldridge penalty. Before the game Aldridge apologised to Brian Laws for rubbing him on the head. The game was a bit nasty to say the least with a few tasty tackles flying round and I was guilty of losing my head on one or two occasions. Ironically, it was Laws who brought Aldridge down to concede the penalty. Unbelievably, Aldridge rubbed him on the head again after apologising only a couple of hours earlier. I told Laws that I wouldn't have accepted that. I would have chinned him there and then on the pitch.

John Barnes recounted the story when we were both at Newcastle and according to his version Lawsy was having a go at Aldridge when Pearce came running up shouting, 'Never mind Aldridge, forget about him . . . get fucking McMahon, get McMahon.' It was true that I disliked Steve even more than I did Aldridge!

After the penalty, I was chasing a ball out to the sidelines and just couldn't get to it. Already steaming at the injustice of the whole thing, I smashed the ball into the crowd as hard as I could. I am not a good loser at the best of times. A few days later the Nottingham Forest secretary brought me a letter from the fellow I had hit. Apparently, it had knocked him out cold and he came around just as the whistle went. He went on to add that the guy sitting next to him suffered with a heart condition and that if the ball had hit him it would probably have killed him. He was complaining that my attitude was a disgrace. We are in this game to win and sometimes you can go over the top in the heat of the moment.

I understand that Liverpool were a good team and like

most top sides they had a nasty edge to them. They could look after themselves just as the current Manchester United side can. It's part of being winners. In 1989 we got to Wembley in the League Cup and won, beating Luton Town 3–1, and once you get a taste for it you get a little nasty streak because you want to win again. We were young lads and we weren't used to winning but once we'd got there, it seemed a lot easier to get back. Statistics show that to be true for lots of clubs. Whether you grow in stature or you get used to it I don't know. But after my experiences against Liverpool, win, lose or draw, whatever the game, I leave the pitch straightaway. If someone crosses my path and wants to shake my hand I will do so but I won't go out of my way, purely on what I saw John Aldridge and other Liverpool players do. That to me was not sportsmanship. It was hypocritical. I am of the opinion that while I will try to kick lumps out of opponents, I can accept it without whingeing when they do it back to me.

Brian Clough was funny about Liverpool, as well. His opinion was that they were the sort of club who put things in your tea. He used to tell us, 'Don't drink the tea. The cheating bastards probably put something in it.' At Liverpool, he wouldn't drink anything that wasn't sealed.

The ill-feeling between Liverpool and Nottingham Forest culminated for me in a little spat at the end of the 1988–89 season. Arsenal took the League at Liverpool in that memorable 2–0 win at Anfield. I was in Scotland at the time with the England team for a friendly. We were preparing to play Poland at Wembley in a World Cup qualifier. We won that game but afterwards I had an argument with Steve McMahon. He was a spiky little devil who was not afraid to leave his foot in; mixed with my natural aggression it proved to be a strong cocktail that sometimes went to the head! It was a minor incident, soon forgotten. For my part, I put it down to losing those two FA Cup semi-finals. I was bearing a grudge because twice I had been a gnat's whisker away from reaching a Cup final, the only trophy Brian Clough had never won. I make no excuses and no apologies.

In fact, if I was asked what I regretted most it would have to be losing four semi-finals, those two, the World Cup in 1990 and the European Championship in 1996. If I could have any results changed, it would be those four to give me a tilt at winning the World Cup, the European Championship and the FA Cup. Each time the same teams thwarted me – Germany and Liverpool.

The first time we reached Wembley in the League Cup final, in 1989, we beat Bristol City in the semi-final. At Bristol in the second leg it was freezing cold and pouring with rain, the coldest conditions I have ever played in. We had drawn the first leg 1–1 and we squeezed through with a goal from Garry Parker in extra time. Before we left the pitch, we went over and clapped the crowd. As I went down the tunnel, Clough, back at Wembley for the first time in ten years, grabbed hold of me and said, 'Son, son, come with me, come with me,' and promptly took me back to our supporters. He wanted to give them a clap but didn't want to go on his own. Make of that what you will. It was a proud moment for me because I was his captain and we had taken him back to Wembley.

The key word for him was respect and I had that in abundance. Of all the good names I have worked for I held him in the greatest of respect. Ted Edgar, Liz's former employer, was very similar in his approach – unpredictable, having a go when you least expected it and holding back when you thought he would have a go.

Clough was a good man to work for. At Forest I had eight years under him, six as his captain, and then four years with Frank Clark. The press drummed it into us all the time that Clough had never won the FA Cup and being his captain I would have loved to have won it and said, 'This is for you.' Pictures of the European Cup winners were scattered all around the club and, indeed, all around Nottingham and I would have been ecstatic to have added ours with the FA Cup. I would have liked to have said to him, 'Here you are. The others couldn't win that for you.' Although I wasn't there when Clough won back-to-back European Cups, in 1979 and 1980, I was still very proud of the achievement. I know that some players and managers have no time for the past but without history you cannot have a present.

I have the same feelings about the achievements of an individual. When Brian Clough did what he did for the club, they should have named a stand after him straight-away and not waited until he retired and was in ill health. It was the same with Bobby Moore at West Ham. He was the captain of the winning World Cup team and the most famous player in West Ham's history. Why wait until he dies to honour him?

There is no accolade that the city of Nottingham or the club could have bestowed on Clough that would have been over the top. He put them on the map as much as Robin Hood did. They could have named the entire ground after him. He did more than any other manager at any other club, apart from perhaps Bill Shankly at Liverpool.

When we reached the League Cup final for the second time, in 1990, we played Coventry in a two-legged semi-final. That was a big deal for me against my old club and I scored a goal in the first leg from a free kick in the inside-right position. It went in off the underside of the crossbar and gave us a slender lead to take to Highfield Road. We drew at Coventry and were overjoyed at reaching Wembley. We arranged to go round to goalkeeper Steve Sutton's house for a party to celebrate and it was the early hours of the morning when I finally rolled home.

The next day we could hardly move and Clough was furious, perhaps because we hadn't included him. He made us do five laps of the pitch as a punishment and he was screaming at me to run harder. I couldn't resist shouting back, 'I got you to Wembley.' He ignored me.

When Forest went to Wembley, nothing was organised in terms of big celebrations. Whether that was based on superstition, I don't know. I went to Wembley twice with Newcastle and there were parties after both games. At Forest, if anything was arranged it would be by the players meeting in a pub and having a few sandwiches laid on, or a few drinks in the boardroom. That was the case even after the 1991 Cup final when Tottenham beat us 2–1 after extra time. There was another club I hated losing to but we always had good open games against them. We often won at each other's ground because both teams' style suited the one playing away.

The 1991 Cup final was a big day with Princess Diana and Prince Charles as the guests of honour, particularly in retrospect with the sad events that were to follow.

I believe Clough picked his favourites instead of the best side that day and I was not alone among the players in that belief. We were surprised at his choice, particularly as in the past Clough had even selected his strongest teams for testimonials. Nigel Jemson was a bit of a loud mouth but was playing well at the time; Clough dropped him in favour of Lee Glover. Jemson was not even selected on the bench and he was in tears on the morning of the final. I think Clough did it because he thought Jemson was a bighead. He certainly always called him that. Jemmo always had a lot to say but it was softened because he was funny with it. Clough probably thought that he was teaching him a lesson.

He also left out Franz Carr. Forest were in negotiation over a new contract with Franz's agent and his father. Clough didn't like agents at the best of times and he showed it. Franz's dad didn't like Clough's attitude and from what I understand stood up to him when Clough bad-mouthed him, and told him forcefully, 'How you talk to my son is up to you but if you talk to me like that I will sort you out.' That was the background to poor Franz being dropped and the suspicion is it was the reason he was dropped. We felt he could have given Spurs problems with his explosive pace. Clough also left out Steve Hodge, another who was playing well at the time.

It was a bad day for a lot of people, that final. The game hinged on Paul Gascoigne. Because of him the hype for the final was incredible, much more over the top than I could remember before. Our manager had never won the FA Cup and Gascoigne was playing his last game before going to Lazio for £8.5 million in a high-profile transfer. The expectations were high but, in truth, it wasn't a very good game at all. It will always be remembered for what Gazza did, not for the brilliant football of which he was capable. His tackle on Garry Parker was so bad that he caught Garry in the chest but it was nothing compared with the horrific challenge on Gary Charles. He should have been sent off rather than carried off but that wild tackle had a massive effect on his career. It put him out for a year and God knows what effect it had on his electric pace. He was never quite the same player afterwards.

The first tackle on Parker gave an indication of what lay ahead. Everyone should be up for a Cup final but he was way over the top. I knew Gazza and I knew what he was like. He had a remarkable run in the competition that season. He took them to the final almost single-handedly and few will forget the two goals he scored in the fifth round to put Portsmouth out. He was the player we were most worried about because we knew he could turn a game on its head. We started quite well for the first 15 minutes. Then Gazza was carried off and his foul gave me the chance of a free kick on the edge of the box that I buried – 1–0. But after that we didn't play. The game was finding its feet for the next half an hour; they were trying to settle down after losing their best player while we thought it was too easy.

Nothing was said in the dressing-room. We were one up, Gazza was off and we felt all we needed to do was to play the second half out. I don't know whether it was complacency or whether we thought we had something to hold on to and sat back. We ended up letting them back in the game. Paul Stewart equalised in the 54th minute and then, in extra time, Nayim, who had replaced Gazza, took a corner. It was touched on by Stewart and Des Walker, our best player on the day, headed through his own goal.

Receptions to glorify a defeat are not my scene, but I told Liz I would see her back in the boardroom at Forest where something was laid on. The players' coach arrived back first and I was having an orange juice when the directors' coach arrived. They had sunk a few beers and were well on the way. I remember saying to John Hickling, who came in smoking a cigar as happy as Larry, 'It's fucking small-minded bastards like you who make this club what it is.' I liked John and bore him no malice but I couldn't understand someone being happy when we had lost. He was talking about how he had met Princess Diana, what a good day he had had and all the rest of it. It was a red rag to a bull.

By the time Liz arrived I was in a towering rage. I was captain and I had gone to Wembley to win. I guess I was just a bad loser. I said my piece and got it off my chest. Fortunately, John was understanding and apart from telling me to calm down took it no further. At some clubs I would have been given my cards.

We didn't see Clough at the back of the coach. He sent a few messages down to us, one of them telling us that we need not go in for training until Thursday. Had we won, we would probably have been in the next day just to keep our feet on the ground. That's what happened after winning the League Cup.

If we had won the 1991 FA Cup, Clough could have retired then at the top instead of waiting to be booted out when the club was relegated two years later. He would have gone out the complete hero having won everything. He is still a hero to most in Nottingham but relegation somewhat tainted his image.

I collected autographs in a book when I was a kid and when I looked at it a couple of years after joining Forest, I saw I had Margaret Thatcher and Brian Clough on one page. There were two people with the same attitude and aura about them – strong characters. It was dated 1974 and I have no real recollection of getting the great man to sign my little book. I was a ball boy at a Vase final and I took my autograph book to the Banqueting Suite after the game. The Prime Minister and Brian Clough were there among all the other celebrities, so it must have been then. It must be rare to have two such diametrically opposed people, in terms of their political leanings, on the same page.

We all knew how much Clough would have liked to win the FA Cup but he never spoke about it to the players. In fact, the games he was most revved up for were the East Midlands derby matches against his old club Derby County. He hated losing to them. I can understand that in part – I don't like losing to clubs I used to play for. It was emphasised for him because of the bad feeling when he left the old Baseball Ground.

He was always desperate to win that one and in all my time at Forest we lost to them just once and that was 1–0 at the Baseball Ground the year Derby were relegated. It is amazing how it becomes instilled in you that you must win a particular game because of the manager's attitude. Even in the short time I was manager at Forest I told the boys that whatever happened in the rest of the season we couldn't lose at Derby, and we nicked a 0–0 draw. I was passing on what I had learned from Brian Clough.

The old Baseball Ground was tight and compact and the touchline was very near to the crowd. So much so that when I took a throw-in I would have coins thrown at me and was regularly covered in spittle. This wasn't a group of wild teenagers or louts in their 20s; this was all sorts ranging from little old ladies down to six-year-old boys. I loved it. It stoked me right up. People ask me if I find certain grounds intimidating and I can honestly reply that I have never once felt intimidated at a football ground. I love a hostile atmosphere. No one is going to come on and kill you, so what have you got to fear?

I hear people outside the game say that places like Turkey and the old Eastern Europe must have been scary. What rubbish. It may be for the spectators who are unescorted in the city before games but the players are shepherded to the ground, escorted into the dressing-room and policed on to the pitch. It might not be brilliant for goalkeepers, who have things thrown at them from behind the goal, but for the rest of us, we stand more chance of being hurt by a bad tackle than by an angry supporter.

At Derby you could sense the hatred from the home supporters and I would wind them up by running straight over to the Forest fans before the kick-off to give them a clenched fist salute. They would respond with a massive cheer while the home supporters would chant 'Bastard Stuart Pearce'. Old ladies, whom you would normally help across the road with their shopping, would call me things that would turn a navvy's face red. The tension and the hostility were tremendous, much better than playing in a nicey, nicey atmosphere.

It was just like that one day when I was marking Ted

McMinn, a tall, leggy Scot. He was on the wing and I was full-back, so we spent a great deal of the game confronting each other along the touchline. I went sliding in for a typical tackle right on the touchline and we both crashed to the ground in a heap, him on top of me with my head level with his chest. It was a spur of the moment thing but I couldn't resist the target staring me in the face. I bit him right on the nipple as we lay on the ground. Ted jumped up and screamed at the official, 'Ref, he's just fucking bit me!' I looked at him and started laughing. He saw me out of the corner of his eye and he started laughing as well. The whole thing was just too ludicrous for words. This, I hasten to add, was pre Tyson biting off Evander Holyfield's ear. That little episode gave my kind of love bite a bad name and only a fool would try it now.

It reminded me of stories my brother Ray would tell of when he played for a working men's club in Harlesden. The centre-half would go up for a corner, head the ball and land in a heap on the ground with the centre-forward attached to his leg by his teeth. Maybe I took a bit of that with me. In my younger days when I played with Ray, if anyone tried to sort me out he would go and take care of them, even though I would protest that I could look after myself. The game has changed a lot since those days when local football was a lot more robust.

Nowadays if a player was caught biting another player the way I did, he would be called uncivilised, a savage, an animal and mad. It makes me laugh. When Tommy Smith scythed someone down it was brilliant but when Vinnie Jones did the same thing he was an animal. It's that nostalgia thing. Why is one brilliant because it was in the old days but the same thing terrible now?

Two incidents occurred within weeks of each other when David Beckham was sent off for a powder-puff tackle in a tournament in Rio while Robbie Savage could have broken Kanu's leg when Leicester played Arsenal, but he escaped. I don't support tackles like that and I would have shed no tears if the Leicester player had received a ten-match ban. It was what the tackle deserved.

At club level when two teams who are at loggerheads clash, even players with no knowledge of past conflicts pick up on the hostility and are soon joining in, saying, 'C'mon. Let's have some!' This sort of game, particularly local derby matches, creates extra tension between the two sets of supporters.

When I went in to see Forest chairman Irving Scholar about leaving Nottingham Forest, he expressed a concern that I would go to Derby or Leicester. Kevin Mason, my agent, butted in, 'With due respect, you have no idea of the politics of the area. If you think Stuart would play for Derby after leaving Nottingham Forest you are seriously mistaken.' I hadn't said a word to Kevin but he was a man who was born in Derby and now lived and worked in Nottingham so he knew the intensity of the feelings.

He had it spot on. If I didn't have a club to go to and Derby was my only option, I would rather go on the dole than join them. I do not mean to be derogatory to Derby and probably if I had played for Derby for 12 years the situation would be reversed. The longer you are at a club the more those rivalries become ingrained. If I had said to those 24,000 supporters who attended my testimonial that I was going to join Derby in the future, a great many of them would not have bothered to attend and pay their money to see the game. I could never walk in Nottingham or go to the ground again if I signed for Derby. I am sure that the Nottingham fans respect me staying when we were relegated and I can still go there and not have a bad word said about me. They are not concerned about Newcastle United or West Ham. Some have made the switch – Archie Gemmill and Steve Sutton – and that is their choice. I couldn't kick those Nottingham fans between the legs by playing for Derby. Liverpool, yes . . . Derby, definitely no.

Scholar couldn't understand that. I doubt whether anyone outside football would understand it. Football, even though it is now plc, is not company business. It is about flesh and blood, emotions and feelings.

Despite my loyalty, if I were playing against Nottingham Forest in the last game of the season I would be desperate to beat them even if it meant sending them down.

I had my opportunities to leave the City Ground long before I did with two of Britain's biggest clubs making overtures to me. Just before the 1990 World Cup in Italy, my contract was nearing its conclusion. England captain Bryan Robson spoke to me as we were preparing for the tournament and told me that Alex Ferguson was interested in taking me to Manchester United the following season. Graeme Souness, who had recruited several top English players four years earlier before the Mexico World Cup, also told me that he would like me at Rangers. It sowed a little seed, not a big one because I was settled and happy at Nottingham Forest.

As a result I went in to see Brian Clough and hammered out a very good five-year contract that would carry me up to ten years' service with the club and a testimonial. We were getting to Wembley regularly; Manchester United were winning nothing at the time. We were an up-and-coming side ready to challenge for the major honours while United were not the side they were to become ten years later. It was even rumoured that Alex Ferguson was under severe pressure for his job.

Rangers, on the other hand, were winning everything but I wanted to play my football on the competitive battle-ground of English football and not have just the occasional high-intensity game north of the border. I was happy living in Nottingham, as was Liz, and I was contented with life at the City Ground.

On the reverse side of signing a five-year deal, I had a problem three years down the line when wages accelerated that much that I was left behind; not massively because I was well paid but significantly enough for the long-serving captain of the side, who was also captain of England.

I was first named captain on the 1986–87 pre-season tour of Sweden. Ian Bowyer, the previous long-serving captain and a player whom I held in the greatest regard, had left the club at the end of the season having been through all the glory years. We jumped on the coach to take us to the airport and Ronnie Fenton made his way down to the back. 'The gaffer wants to know if you would like to be captain,' he said. I was well pleased. It was an honour but it might have meant just a little bit more had the man himself asked me. Even so, I was as proud as punch. He obviously saw in me someone who could lead on the pitch. I had something to say for myself, although not too much when Clough himself was around. Without being boastful I think he made the right choice. I enjoyed the responsibility and organising. I am always ready to do my fair share.

A high for me was the rapport I had with the fans at Nottingham Forest. Arguably the support I had from them during the highs and lows was as good as any player who's ever played the game. I could walk off the pitch having had a stinker and no one would complain. I think most people realised that I was not the most gifted player in the team but I have a fair amount of ability and I always give 100 per cent. I'm totally committed to any team I play for.

I also have a theory that the fans see a little bit of themselves in me – a bit of a park player, a bit of this and a bit of that. Forest supporters knew I had the love of the club at heart and put them first. I gave the same to every club I played for but because I was at Forest so long that relationship grew and grew. It has never ever been just a job of work. You are representing people who have hopes and dreams for the club. There will always be fans at the City Ground. It's a lifetime thing for them.

I listen to a radio talk show while I'm driving to West Ham and one morning they were discussing how hard it is for some players to settle at a new club. I can't understand that. I don't think I could ever go to a club and not settle. At Newcastle I had a bad time under Ruud Gullit but I loved the North East and I loved being part of Newcastle United Football Club. If you go to a club and don't settle, it's down to the player, no one else. You have to be open-minded. If things are not going right on the pitch, you have to work to put them right by your performances and not blame managers, surroundings or the other players.

Coming back from the World Cup having missed that

penalty, I could not believe how the fans supported me; and not just fans from Nottingham but from all around the country – even though a few weeks later those same people slaughtered me with chants of 'Stuart Pearce is a German' from the stands at Chelsea and Derby among others. When I came back all I wanted to do was get out and play for Forest. Even now I still have a massive mailbag from Forest fans. I have a soft spot for the club and the supporters, but not necessarily for Nottingham Forest plc.

Liz seems to think that I am the unluckiest footballer around. With some players it seems as though their careers are scripted, but Liz and her brother Chris think I'm jinxed. To them, it's bad enough being on the losing side in a World Cup semi-final but it's worse to miss a penalty in the same game. Losing in the semi-final of the European Championship reinforces that theory as does reaching Cup finals with Newcastle and Forest and losing them both. Liz calls me the 'nearly man'. She says, 'You're nearly a legend but you're not because you keep messing up at the final hurdle.'

The fact is that I can get a big high out of winning 1–0 in what to others is a meaningless league game. I have been on the winning side in semi-finals and the atmosphere has been really quiet. At Newcastle it was almost an anticlimax when we returned to the dressing-room after beating Sheffield United at Old Trafford. I remember saying, 'Come on, lads, it doesn't get better than this.'

Reaching the League Cup final and going to Wembley for the first time in 1989 was memorable. Going to Wembley was the next best thing to winning the League. To me it didn't matter what competition it was. Clough had the same attitude and we went to Wembley for some of the most obscure Cup finals ever to be played and won most of them. There was the Mercantile Credit Trophy in 1987–88; the Simod Cup the next season; and in 1992 the Zenith Data Systems Cup, the same year we were runners-up in the League Cup final to Manchester United. We even took part in a Wembley tournament to mark the Football League's Centenary Year, and won that as well. In all, we went to Wembley eight times and won all the games but two. Unfortunately, one of them was the FA Cup final.

Give us an obscure Cup final and we would win it because Clough would always play his best team and demand that we play it for real. We were on no bonus scheme for trophies like the Simod Cup – we had never heard of it and so it wasn't written into our contracts – but I seem to remember Clough buying the wives a box of chocolates each, almost certainly from his own shop!

We won the Guinness Soccer Sixes two years out of three and reached the final the third year; and he took the Nottingham Senior Cup seriously, lifting that as well. Clough would never belittle any competition the way Newcastle did when I was there. Newcastle played a reserve side, of which I was a member, in the Northumberland Shield, as most teams would. I was taking my coaching badge at the time and the FA coach supervising the course would laugh when I had to shoot off early to play at somewhere like Scarborough, which was important to me because we wanted to stay nine points clear in the reserve league. When I told him I was off to play Blyth Spartans in the Northumberland Shield he fell about. I told him not to laugh; I wanted a winner's tankard to put next to my medals from the Simod and the Mercantile Cups. Play to win, otherwise why play at all? I probably have the finest collection of obscure medals of any professional playing at the moment thanks to Clough's philosophy.

Before the FA Cup final against Tottenham Hotspur, we were all concerned not to get injured but the flipside when Clough was about was that if you weren't trying you would be out of the team. Clough had promised that he would play Notts County in a testimonial across the Trent on the Monday before the Cup final on the Saturday. He took the full team and played us for the full 90 minutes. What's more, he spelled it out that if we didn't play and didn't play well, we wouldn't be appearing at Wembley. What other manager would do that five days before the Cup final? Fortunately, we all came through safely.

I'm not saying he was wrong because his philosophy worked. Footballers are creatures of habit and there is no better habit than winning games. It came home to me many years later at West Ham when Igor Stimac was one booking away from being suspended for a possible League Cup semi-final. He played in the reserves instead of the quarter-finals and was booked. But we were knocked out in the quarter-finals and so he missed an important league game. When you start planning ahead and being smart you invariably land on your backside.

If I start thinking to myself that I haven't been injured for a time, I can guarantee that something horrible will be lurking around the corner for me. The old saying about taking every game as it comes is worth taking note of, and the one about the important game being the one you are playing in. That's what I tell anyone asking for advice.

Never look down the fixture list because it always works against you.

You can be successful in your own little world. For me playing for England counted as one of my greatest successes. Being the most capped player while at Forest made me very proud and it was one of the reasons I preferred to stay at the club. I was player, captain, union representative and manager, I scored and led the side to a 2–0 win all during one day at Nottingham Forest. There was only one way after that – downwards! There wasn't much else I could have done for that club. I didn't sweep the dressing-rooms but that was only because I didn't have time.

When we beat Aston Villa 6–0 at home, Clough came in at half-time and pulled me to one side. We were three up with the game won, but he said, 'Dip your bread.' I asked why I should keep steaming forward when there was a chance for other players to express themselves. He looked at me and repeated, 'Just dip your bread. When you can, dip your bread, dip your bread.' His message was clear – keep playing to the best of my ability and never let teams off the hook. If you have scored three, go on and score four and so on. As a youngster, you don't appreciate these things.

Some people can coach for hours to get across the same message; Clough could get it over in one sentence or even a couple of words. It is another little thing to pass on. It teaches you the game and your job if you are prepared to listen. It's great coaching to my mind.

My best feeling is to do a good day's work, go home and put my feet up. The older I get the more satisfaction I gain from it. I prefer not to go out on the town, have a few beers and glorify the victory with every sycophant in town. It's nice to go home, walk round the garden and enjoy the moment.

Going to Wembley was success because it had to be earned the hard way. The first time I went there was to play Luton Town in the 1989 League (Littlewoods) Cup final. Luton were no pushover; they had been there the year before in the same competition and beaten the favourites, Arsenal. Few of us at Nottingham Forest had played in a Wembley final before and, in that respect, we were the underdogs.

I have always maintained that to reach Wembley you need the luck of the draw. For those two FA Cup semi-finals against Liverpool we believed the luck of the draw had denied us a Wembley appearance. In the finals we did reach, generally the draw was kind. If a club the size of Forest draw Arsenal or Manchester United away, the odds are that you are going to go out. In 1988–89, we played Chester City home and away, scoring ten goals in the process; then beat Coventry City 3–2; Leicester City 2–1 at home after a goalless draw away; QPR 5–2; and Bristol City on a 2–1 aggregate over two matches in the semi-final. They were hard enough games but there was no real bummer. We would settle for playing any team from outside our division in the semi-final, especially over two legs.

We reckoned we were a better team than Luton and so it proved with Nigel Clough scoring two in a 3–1 win. It was a great atmosphere and to go as Clough's captain and finally break that barren spell for him was special to me. It was also the first major triumph for the club since the European days and it meant so much to the club and to its supporters.

It was the start of a succession of visits to the famous old stadium and not just for those small cups.

It always makes me wonder when players and managers belittle the League Cup. They go out of Europe, out of the FA Cup, can't win the League and suddenly they wish they were back in the old League Cup again. The League Cup final was, to me, as important as the FA Cup final.

I find cup finals strange days. There is so much pressure on you. Often younger players do better than established players. They can go and enjoy it. People don't remember a youngster having a shocker but the club captain or an established player feels the weight of the club's and fans' expectations.

We were lucky. We won that first one fairly comfortably, beating Luton with something to spare. The next year, we wanted to succeed even more, having gone out at home to Manchester United in the third round of the FA Cup. The draw wasn't particularly easy. We beat Huddersfield on away goals; Crystal Palace 5–0 in a replay; Everton 1–0 at home; Spurs 3–2 away after a 2–2 draw at the City Ground; and my old club Coventry again 2–1 on aggregate in the semi-final. That left us facing Oldham in the final, again a team from a division below us. We won 1–0 and although it was hardly a classic it was another win.

With no banquet, as usual, I arranged a little session in a local wine bar near the ground. We had a few glasses of champagne on the coach back; then I persuaded all the lads to chip in £50 each to cover the food and drinks and to subsidise the young players. The youngsters were soon at it and when they realised it was free they were ordering up champagne and anything else that they could think of. I made certain it was all going well and then Liz and I slipped quietly away. I was knackered. When I went in to the ground the next day I discovered that the bill had gone over what we expected and I quickly had another whip round of a tenner each to cover the extra costs. Everyone put in except Tommy Gaynor. Even though he had played in the final and picked up his £6,000 bonus, he refused to pay the extra because, he claimed, he had eaten only a chicken leg and drunk a couple of Budweisers. I told him I had probably had about the same and it wouldn't hurt to help pay for the youngsters. But he wouldn't hear of it and no one else was prepared to back me on the issue.

The nearest we came to an official party was when we went to the Council Buildings a couple of days after the 1991 FA Cup final. None of the players wanted to go after losing to Spurs, but it was one of those events that Clough decreed as compulsory. To make it worse, they organised an open-topped bus ride. I have only been on three and all were after losing! They are nightmares. It's the last thing you want and it should have been organised on the proviso that if we lost it would be cancelled. The fans turned up in their thousands and that was terrific of them, but I would have happily gone to Market Square on foot and signed autographs as a thank you. To go on an open-topped bus around the city was an embarrassing farce.

I vowed I would never go on one again but, sure enough, Newcastle organised one after we lost in the Cup final. I was sorely tempted to say no but I realised that it would have put our manager Kenny Dalglish in a terrible position had one of his players refused to go. So I swallowed my pride and tried to smile.

Sometimes I remember the bad times more than the good times. I can recall more about the three times that Clough substituted me than I can about the four major cup finals we played in. The good times can look after themselves; you have to work harder to eradicate the bad.

One of the biggest disappointments was the 1990–91 FA Cup final, losing 2–1 to Spurs. We had quite a history with Spurs in cup competitions, having beaten them on the way to our second League Cup victory. Those two games had a total of nine goals. With such open games, it always seemed that the away side had the better chance but this was different. We were playing on neutral territory.

On the run of play we probably didn't deserve to win. It was an uninspiring game, dominated by Gazza's injury. People remember that and not the fact that I scored direct from the free kick on the restart. I doubt whether a neutral would remember any of the three goals. It will always be remembered for Paul Gascoigne and his extravagant fouls. That guy was always likely to do something ridiculous one way or the other – getting himself carried off or being sent off through overexcitement or winning the game on his own.

At the time, we were pleased to see him go. I am not aware of any of our players visiting him, but why should they have done? I was friendly with him but I can't say I really knew him well. We had no idea of the extent of his injury and, in any case, sympathy was a bit short as he had tried to maim two of our players.

It was one of those situations, like Hillsborough, where you are focused on your own job and I was oblivious to almost everything else. I certainly didn't rush over and ask him if he was all right. I am not the most compassionate of players, especially when I am in the heat of battle and about to take a free kick from the edge of the box. If I had spoken to him it would have been to shake his hand and say thanks for the free kick that was right in my zone.

We went home with what we deserved – nothing at all. The dressing-room was deathly quiet.

Whether Brian Clough lost or won in finals he stayed quiet. I can't remember him whooping and hollering around the dressing-room when we won and it was the same when we lost. He might have come over and kissed Des on the head after the Tottenham defeat or he would come and have a word with me as his captain. He was a past master at building players up and motivating them; he also stuck by his players in times of crisis. When Gary Crosby was the fans' whipping boy and his form and body language cried out for him to be dropped, Clough stuck by him and kept playing him. Whether it did the lad any good in the long run I don't know; it didn't always help the team. Clough would say, 'I don't care what thirty thousand fans are saying. I pick the team not them and if I say that Gary Crosby is playing, he'll play.'

But if things were going well, he loved to put you down. If I did well in the England side, I knew he would be after me; and if I gave a big interview to the press, he would ask me if I thought I was a big hitter. Yet no one manipulated or used the press the way he did.

I don't think he enjoyed his players talking to the press. He preferred to do that himself and he was a regular columnist in the *Sun* whenever there was anything to say about Forest or, come to that, football. I don't suppose he did that for nothing.

In the end I got used to him. He was predictable in his unpredictability. If you lost a final he would be quiet and polite and likely to give you the week off but if you won he would be down the back of the bus telling you to turn the music off and to report for training the following morning, even if it was a Sunday. If you lost he would be there to help you out and lift you up but if you won he would be banging on your door trying to keep you down.

Des Walker was certainly down after the FA Cup final defeat, shattered by the experience and there wasn't a lot Brian Clough could do to lift him that day. Des was there for me in the World Cup when I needed him and this time I wanted to be there for him. I appreciated his support just by being there and I hope that in some small way I repaid him that day. We didn't say a lot. We didn't need to.

We walked off the pitch at Wembley as a team and our thoughts were that we had been beaten 2–1 and not that Des had scored an own goal. If he hadn't got his head to it someone else would have been there behind him. He was distraught, absolutely gutted. I told him that we were in it together. It was a year on from when he did the same for me. It must have been even more difficult for him in Market Square the next day. God knows the rest of us were pissed off but for Des it was murder because in his own mind he had to face thousands of fans thinking he had cost us the game.

The person that the press and the public know and the Des that I know are two vastly different people. With the media and in public he is silent and almost forbidding whereas to me he never stops talking and can be a bit of a smartarse who is never wrong. But he is a terrific friend. When I lost my licence, it was Des who drove me to and from London, dropping me off to see Liz in Coventry on his way back. We got to know each other pretty well through that and through learning together at Forest, even though I am a little bit older than he is. We have grown up together in football terms not only with Forest but also with England and I suppose I have played more games with him than anyone else. When we went to the 1990 World Cup he was almost certainly the first name on Bobby Robson's sheet. In other words, he was a very good, very consistent player.

We are both from London but more importantly we respect each other as professionals. I can't get on with someone I can't respect. With Des it hurts him to be beaten as a footballer even though he appears a bit unemotional on the pitch. He likes to come to work, get the job done by giving it his best shot and then go home. He loves football when he is playing it, and when he is away from the game he doesn't particularly want to talk about it.

Outside football his passion is for cars and his latest fad, motorbikes. He scared Liz and me to death when he roared up our drive dressed in his black leathers, helmet and biker's gear. We didn't know anyone who rode a motorbike and couldn't think who it was until he took his helmet off. Typical of Des he not only had a motorbike, he had the fastest motorbike, the only one made in the world, and he had just come from the local airfield where he had been doing wheelies at 120 miles per hour.

Without any doubt he was the best player I played with at Forest in the five years we played together. He left for Sampdoria a year before we were relegated and that speaks volumes. He was a huge loss to the club.

Going to Italy was a great move in every way for Des.

He was career-minded and he wanted to play in the best league in the world, as it certainly was then. He wanted to see how good he was and he enjoyed playing against the best players in the world. He did as well as any defender in Italy. He didn't endear himself to the Italian press because he didn't bother talking to them. We were of a similar mind.

I had been tucked up once or twice early on with misquotes and silly headlines and it turns you sour. I thought to myself that if they were going to do that I wasn't going to play their game. Just before the 1988 European Championship I had been out injured and when I came back in a pre-season tour of Italy a journalist collared me coming out of the hotel and asked me how the injury was. I told him that it was coming on fine. He asked me if I would be playing soon and I answered that I sincerely hoped so. When I telephoned Liz she told me that her cousin had called her about a piece in the *Sun* under the headline: 'I want your place Kenny'. Kenny Sansom was the current England left-back. It went on to give the quote I gave which had no mention of Kenny Sansom. The headline had nailed me to the wall and made me out to be a bigheaded bastard. I wanted no part of that, with my family and friends believing that I had gone over the top. It annoyed me. As far as I knew, the journalist was at fault. I didn't realise at the time that someone else wrote the headlines.

So I shut off from the press and, to be honest, it suited me. I did not elbow the media completely. I built a working relationship with the Midlands *Daily Express* writer John Wragg after warning him that if he messed me up a single time our relationship would be over. I wasn't asking for someone to say I had a good game when I had a bad one, I just wanted him to be honest and in return I gave him an interview when he wanted one. He knew the boundaries – be honest with me and I would be honest with him. We worked well together and if it had been like that across the board I would have been quite open and I'm sure that goes for a lot more professionals.

Five or six years later, the *Sun* carried the same headline only this time it was Tony Dorigo who was supposedly wanting my place. I looked at it and burst out laughing. I knew Tony and I knew what he was like and I thought to myself, 'You've been tucked up just as I was.' And so the cycle continues.

It is annoying but the older and hopefully the wiser you get the more comical it becomes because you know exactly what's going to happen. Build the player up and when he is selected knock him down and start promoting someone else. I have been through that not once but several times.

When I made my international comeback at the age of 37, I made a personal appearance for the England players' pool at the Nationwide Building Society with Gareth Southgate. England had just been drawn against Scotland in the Euro 2000 qualifying play-off and a flood of journalists turned up looking for a good quote. I was ready for them and, sure enough, one of the Sunday tabloid writers started on a line of questioning which suggested to me that he already had his story written in his mind and just wanted a comment, preferably from me, to stand it up. I fenced with him until he finally had to ask me outright, 'Can you make it? Tell the fans, can you make it to the European Championship finals?' I knew he wanted me to stick my head out at the age of 37 and tell the world that not only would I help knock out the Scots single-handedly but I would be in the finals. Having been around the block several times I just looked at him and laughed. Ten years earlier I would have fallen right into it and answered yes, leaving the way open for him to add his words. This time I wasn't biting and eventually he realised and gave up. He probably wrote it anyway.

That sort of interrogation displays not only a lack of professionalism but also a lack of originality of thought. But it goes on and will no doubt continue to do so.

Of all the highlights I enjoyed at Forest my most memorable was the evening of my testimonial match against Newcastle United in May 1996. Obviously, if we had beaten Spurs in the Cup that would have been it, but we didn't and while the other Wembley occasions were big, they could not overshadow that night of my testimonial.

I wanted it to be a big event, not just for the money it would bring but for me to thank the Forest supporters who had backed me so brilliantly over all my years at the club. I wanted the best possible opposition for them, and for weeks I talked to Walter Smith, manager of Glasgow Rangers, and always there were excuses about the police not allowing it because of security reasons. So eventually I cleared it with the Nottingham police myself and they promised to back me, but then the excuse was that the police in Glasgow wouldn't stand it. I thought I had sidestepped the excuse but I hadn't.

It was a wasted couple of months and when I was stone-walled by Walter I had to look around for someone else. I suppose Rangers must have hundreds of these requests because they are a massive club but a straightforward and quick no would have been a much bigger help.

I telephoned Kevin Keegan at Newcastle United around January and he agreed. At the time Newcastle were 12 points clear of Manchester United and I had my fingers crossed for them to win the League. Having dealt initially with Kevin, Arthur Cox took over. I was as nervous as hell, particularly when their lead at the top began to crumble. All the tickets had been printed and sold and I kept ringing Arthur to make sure it was still on and he kept saying, 'If Kevin has said he'll do it, he'll be there.' The pair of them were so good to deal with and despite losing the title to Manchester United Kevin not only honoured his word but brought the full side to play – everyone including Tino Asprilla and David Ginola. Unfortunately, my England team-mate Peter Beardsley was injured but such was the support that he came down on the night anyway. What's more, both Kevin and his assistant Terry McDermott came on as substitutes and made cameo appearances. Nigel Clough and Des Walker returned to play for Forest and Coventry's Gary McAllister made a guest appearance.

Newcastle being there helped fill the ground. The kick-off had to be delayed for a quarter of an hour to get everyone in. I had been with the club for 11 years and it was all the good times encompassed in one night. Even the local radio stations were telling people that if they didn't go to another game, they had to go to this one because of what I had done for the club. It was nice and touching and it made it my biggest night. I had a nervous build-up, rushing around trying to keep everyone happy. A couple of the guys from Madness turned up to present me with one of their platinum discs. The score was 6–5 and while players weren't busting a gut, it was semi-serious and a lot of good football was played. The big crowd appreciated it. That night was as much for me to say thank you to them as it was for them to say thank you to me. To cap it all my brother Ray refereed the game with a couple of his friends running the line; that just tied everything up nicely. By the time the game was over and I'd had a couple of drinks, I was knackered and ready to go home.

To put it in perspective, in the March of that year we played Aston Villa in the sixth round of the FA Cup and had 23,000 fans through the turnstiles. When we played Newcastle in my testimonial we had over 24,000! Ian Bowyer, European Cup winner, league champion and the rest, had 6,000 or 7,000 against Derby when he was the beneficiary, and goalkeeper Steve Sutton was the next to be honoured with the same number turning up, again against Derby, the club he was playing for at the time.

It all started to go wrong at Forest long before we were relegated. We had a real high from 1988 up until the 1991 Cup final when things began to wane. Then Des Walker left and we started papering over the cracks. Selling Teddy Sheringham after he'd scored 20 league and cup goals in his first season was a monumental mistake in my opinion.

Clough was Clough. He ticked along while the fans were demanding he sign new players and we realised we had lost too many quality players to maintain our previous high standards. In typical style he ignored the demands and the obvious failings. It wasn't until March that he brought Neil Webb back to the club where he had made his name, but he wasn't the Webby who had left us to go to Manchester United. Clough also signed striker Robert Rosario and, to be honest, that didn't work. Robert simply wasn't the sort of goalscorer to lift us out of trouble.

I suppose the fact that we reached the 1992 League Cup final – losing 1–0 to Manchester United – put off the inevitable. Two weeks earlier we had won the Mercantile Cup at Wembley, beating Southampton 3–2. I was injured in that game in a tackle with Glenn Cockerill after about 20 minutes. I carried on for a quarter of an hour but every time I sidefooted the ball I suffered a searing pain. It transpired that I had damaged my knee ligaments. I didn't play again that season so I watched the League (Rumbelows) Cup final from the bench sitting behind Brian Clough. On the other bench was Manchester United's injured captain, Bryan Robson.

That was when I knew the writing was on the wall. Teddy Sheringham hadn't set the world on fire in that first season but it was obvious he could score goals. The potential was clearly there, as he has gone on to prove. Had he stayed and achieved the same level for us in a second season, we would have stayed up.

I thought Brian Clough was stronger than any man or board member at Nottingham Forest, so to me it was never inevitable that he was going to be the one to go. I didn't think that there was a board member strong enough to even suggest he should be sacked. People at the club conspired behind his back because they were afraid to do it face to face.

In the dressing-room, the players knew that things were going badly with no signs of getting better. I couldn't see a way forward. From Christmas onwards we were a relegated side. We were miles adrift and there was no way we could catch up. We seemed to go without a fight.

Even so, the sacking came out of the blue. It was terribly sad coming on the back of the Championship, the European cups and our revival in the eighties. Now we were facing the unthinkable of relegation. People were saying that we were too good to go down but in truth we were shocking. We weren't good enough to stay up.

The only bright spot for the club was the incredible form of the young and versatile Roy Keane. When he was playing centre-half it meant we lost a great midfield player and when he played in midfield we lost our best central defender. I can't speak highly enough of him. He was a young, up-and-coming player who was new to the club. When he first played for Forest, I didn't know who he was. I was injured and missed the fixture at Liverpool. We lost 2–0 and the next day when I asked the physio what had happened, he told me that Roy Keane had played on the right wing. I assumed that he was a Liverpool youngster as I had never heard of him and asked why Ray Houghton hadn't played! Roy had been signed just the week before from Ireland and, because I was injured, I had never even trained with him.

Basically, he stayed in the team from that moment on and he was brilliant. He is a strong character and that showed through even at that early age. I had the impression that he didn't listen to Brian Clough or the senior players much but it didn't affect his form. He was outstanding.

Maybe by then Brian Clough didn't have the same aura about him. His powerful influence had diminished and players were no longer frightened of him. Things had changed dramatically. I heard on the car radio that Clough had been sacked.

The last home game of the season was against Sheffield United and the atmosphere in the ground was creepy. I had a really eerie feeling and I've never worked out whether it was just me or generated by the crowd. I was in the stand watching with Liz and there was a real buzz around the ground and a tingle when he came out. Here was an institution and this was his last home game after 18 years or whatever it was. Suddenly it was all over. We lost to a team managed by Dave Bassett, the man who was eventually to take over from me. I was very aware that this was a momentous occasion and the end of an era.

I'd had my problems with Clough but nevertheless I found it all quite sad. We were down months before but our relegation was rubber-stamped that day. It was unfortunate that such a great man who had done so much for the city should go out on that note. It says a lot about going out, if you can, while still on top. I didn't go to the final game at Ipswich but thousands of our fans did and they turned the wake into a carnival.

hillsborough

Hillsborough, Sheffield on Saturday, 15 April 1989 remains strangely remote in my memory. It was something that happened to someone else in some other place, not to me.

That, of course, was the day when 96 Liverpool supporters lost their lives, most of them just a few yards away from the dressing-room where I sat, or rather paced about waiting in vain for our FA Cup semi-final against Liverpool to restart.

We didn't have a clue what was going on. All we knew was that referee Peter Williams had called both teams off the field after six minutes as supporters began to pour over the fence behind Bruce Grobbelaar's goal. As far as I was concerned or knew, it was another case of football hooliganism. As I've explained elsewhere, I was always ready to hear and believe the worst about Liverpool because they were our nemesis, so much better than any other team in the country, a constant barrier between Nottingham Forest and silverware.

I must say that I wasn't best pleased when, on the Monday lunchtime after our quarter-final win at Manchester United, I listened to the draw on my car radio in the club car park, just as I had done the previous year. Bloody Liverpool again.

Why couldn't it have been either Everton or Norwich, two teams we fancied we could beat? I drove away trying to convince myself that sooner or later we were going to beat them. After all, hadn't underdogs Wimbledon beaten them at Wembley the year before? But I knew that, if anything, that defeat probably made them even meaner. They were still winning everything in sight but we were a year older, a year more experienced and we were very, very hungry for success.

The venue was to be Hillsborough again and, with its good pitch and the high terracing behind the goal where our supporters would be massed, that was fine.

Liverpool began well and Peter Beardsley soon hit the crossbar. The nerves were twanging but the game was gradually beginning to sort itself out. Then I saw one or two spectators come on to the pitch behind the Liverpool goal from the Leppings Lane end, then a few more. I was cursing the Liverpool fans under my breath as the referee took us off the pitch.

From the far end where I was stationed, it looked like no more than another of those frustrating pitch invasions, a blight on our game for a few years. As a player that was one of my pet hates. I am so dogmatic and careful about my preparation for games and when referees started coming into dressing-rooms and telling us that kick-offs had been delayed it threw me. Mentally I wanted to be ready to go out five minutes before the kick-off, fresh and ready to go bang like a boxer coming out for a fight.

This, if anything was worse because we had already begun, the adrenalin was pumping and the muscles becoming loose. We were told that there was going to be a delay of ten minutes and the instructions were to keep warm, keep loose and not let the delay blunt the competitive edge and take our minds off the game. Then someone else came in and told us fifteen minutes more. We still didn't have a clue what was going on outside. All we knew at that stage was that Liverpool supporters had come tumbling on to the pitch and forced us off.

There we sat in the dressing-room, still in our kit, waiting for an hour. It was five o'clock by the time we had bathed, changed and climbed into the coach. During that time I never left the dressing-room and no one had explained why such an important game was being delayed for so long and then called off. It was only when our centre-forward Lee Chapman boarded the team coach that the first grains of doubt were sewn. He said that he had seen scenes of devastation, with people injured, and been told that there might even be some deaths. He was very upset but, to be honest, most of us took this news with a pinch of salt. People didn't get killed in English football stadiums, at least not since the Bolton disaster way back on 9 March 1946 when 33 fans perished while the game played on. This was a football match, not a war; as far as I was concerned, it was a silly rumour. Perhaps I didn't want to believe it. I was still livid because I had turned up to play in one of the biggest football matches of my life and my own eyes told me that some supporters from the Liverpool end had caused the game to be cancelled. Had I been convinced that it was that serious, I would have been worried for Liz's safety. She had gone to the game with a friend of mine from Coventry, Jim Connolly.

I rang Liz on the way back to see that she had got home safely and it was only then that she told me what she had been watching on television. Liz had watched the incident develop from her seat in the stand. Jim, wisely, had quickly summed up the situation, decided that the game was not going to restart and driven them both back to Nottingham.

It was only when I watched it on television that I saw what had been going on while we were in our dressing-room as bodies were carried away on makeshift stretchers and placed side by side in the club gymnasium. It was surreal, like watching an earthquake in Russia. Was I there? It didn't feel as though I had been there at all because I didn't see any of it. I felt strangely detached from it all, even then. It was as though I was watching something that had nothing to do with me. I had seen none of this.

At no stage did Brian Clough tell us anything of what was happening out there. There were two different reactions – Lee Chapman and one or two others had heard that supporters had died and they were devastated while others like me could only think that Liverpool, who had stopped us playing in Europe, had now halted a semi-final. That was the only information I was taking in. The anger was building in me. We were told to stay in the dressing-room but Chappie ignored the instructions and found someone to tell him what was happening. He went down the tunnel and glimpsed the dreadful scenes. Me? I was, as usual, cocooned in my own world trying to maintain my concentration in case the game restarted. I was annoyed because I didn't know the facts. Brian Clough had a go at the

Liverpool supporters after Hillsborough and I felt the same way until I read all the accounts and began to understand what went on and how many had died. Clough should have kept his mouth shut until he knew all the facts. I was glad that I did.

Those chilling facts emerged slowly, the deaths of innocent men, women and children. People were giving their versions and the blame, in those early days, was spread around. Some said the police were at fault, others blamed the fans themselves; for a while, drink was suspected to be the main cause; an accident on the motorway caused spectators from Liverpool to be late, a gateman opening his gates to let the crush of latecomers in. You paid your money and took your choice. I felt it was unfair at the time to heap all the blame on to the police. In our society that happens all the time. If you are in trouble or your house is broken into the first people you ring are the police, yet they get it in the neck.

It was horrific but I cannot say that I was affected or mentally scarred by it. Most people there saw a hell of a lot more of what happened than we did and even those who watched the horror unfold on television as it happened knew more about it than us. That is why on the Monday morning I found it ridiculous that the police came to interview us about what went on. I felt aggrieved at the waste of police time, going through the charade of questioning all the players, none of whom knew anything about it. The police interviewed me, when I saw nothing, but didn't want to talk to Liz who saw everything. I was up in arms about it and considered refusing to co-operate. I felt that they wanted to interview me just because I was Stuart

Pearce; it certainly wasn't because I was an eyewitness. They knew full well that we were in the dressing-room for an hour and a half but sometimes these things are done for appearances, just for the sake of it. Interview the journalists from the press box, the stewards, the programme sellers, all of them will have seen 98 per cent more than any of the players.

I wouldn't say I am a particularly religious person and when Liz and I attended the memorial service in Nottingham I told Liz I felt a bit of a fraud being there at all. But I appreciated that if the captain of Nottingham Forest or the manager had not attended that would have been pounced upon by the media who, not unnaturally, were wallowing in the tragedy. There were television cameras in the church and I felt that I was there for their benefit. I didn't want to be seen doing things for the sake of doing things. I was never one to court publicity. It was a strange scenario.

I didn't have the same emotions that Lee Chapman had or those who had witnessed it. I felt that I was paying lip service. I don't want to give the impression that I didn't care. I did. But I felt the same emotion that I would have done if it had happened at some other game on some other ground, desperately sorry for the bereaved and for the game of football but not personally involved. I am not a heartless person. I saw nothing. I had no first-hand knowledge of what had happened. I felt great sadness that innocent people had been killed in an incident at a ground where I was plying my trade.

The game was eventually played at Old Trafford on 7 May and between the tragedy and then all kinds of options were offered, everything from cancelling the competition for that season to giving the FA Cup straight to Liverpool. I was in a Catch-22 situation. I wanted to win the game even more. As a professional sportsman that was only right. Yet the whole nation wanted Liverpool to win as a mark of respect. I found that unfair on Nottingham Forest, just as unfair as our ban from Europe after Heysel. I had total sympathy for the Liverpool supporters and the bereaved families but to say that I didn't care whether I won or not would be lying.

Within the club, I tried to stoke up my colleagues so that we wouldn't go out and lie down if and when the replay took place. The game and the football public deserved more than that. Some may say that it went beyond sport but if that was the case then they should have scrapped the semi-final altogether and given the Cup to Liverpool as some suggested. It was not right to use us as stooges. I pleaded with the players not to go through the motions when we eventually played and told them not to give up the game because of what had happened, something which was not only out of our control but out of Liverpool Football Club's control as well.

The atmosphere at Old Trafford was terrible. There was a dull edge to the game that made it a bit of a non-event. We did not play well but we tried and Liverpool won on merit, which was the right way. How would the Liverpool players have felt if we had rolled over and let them win? I can't imagine one of them would have enjoyed that. Maybe everyone was relieved in the long run and Liverpool went on to win the Cup.

There were no instructions from anyone to take things easy in view of what happened and that was right. My game is built on aggression; it is one of the aces in my armoury. I am not pacey and I am not blessed with an abundance of skill. For someone to tell me not to overdo it in a semi-final against Liverpool would have been akin to telling me not to play at all. We were there to beat them and get to Wembley and in the end we were beaten by a very good side and, apart from the needle over the Aldridge business with Laws, it was played in the right spirit.

Afterwards I asked myself what I would have felt like if the boot had been on the other foot. Had it been the Nottingham Forest supporters who had died, I would have been devastated. I can understand the sadness and I thought the mourning of those people was phenomenal, the flowers and the work by Kenny Dalglish and the players with the bereaved were exceptional. But I couldn't share it with them because I didn't see it; I can't lie about my feelings and pretending would have been an insult to those innocents who lost their lives, youngsters and adults who had arrived at the ground early and were there to see a football match.

Chappie remained the one most affected by it all. On our end-of-season tour he was in tears talking about it in a bar with Steve Hodge and me. Had I looked out of the tunnel and seen what he had seen, I might have felt the same.

I didn't have those tears inside me and I was annoyed that we hadn't won. That's not being the hard man. I have cried over football and I have cried over a few other things in my life.

Sport may get nasty at times but the beauty of it is that it has all the emotions of life. It was a tragedy that so many people were killed; things like that shouldn't happen at

old big 'ead

Did I want to play for Brian Clough? Did I want to play for the twice European Champions Nottingham Forest? Is the Pope a Catholic? Of course I did! They sent a car to collect my Coventry City colleague Ian Butterworth and me at the end of my second season as a professional but I would have walked and, just as when I joined Coventry, money was never a consideration.

Brian Clough was a managerial colossus and, as a kid, when he wants to sign you, you sign. To be honest, he scared the life out of me as he did most of the squad, even the million-pound superstars. Trevor Francis used to hide from him in the laundry room or the boot room.

When I first walked into the office at Nottingham Forest with my Coventry manager Don Mackay, my first impression was the difference between the two men. I liked Don and whenever I see him we still have a chat but that day it seemed as though he was in awe of Clough. After we had signed, we travelled back to Coventry in the car and we couldn't stop talking about the charismatic Clough, repeating over and over, 'That's a manager, that's a manager,' until Mackay threatened to turn us out on the roadside and let us find our own way back. But you could see on his face the same admiration for the man that we had. This was a giant. When he walked into a room, people stopped talking. That was the strength of the aura surrounding him.

It was not only Ian and I waiting to see Clough but also Neil Webb from Portsmouth. Webby was a lot more worldly wise than me. He went in first and knowing that Aston Villa and other teams were after him he had bargaining chips. When he came out smiling I asked what he had asked for because I hadn't got a clue what I should be saying. He wouldn't tell me what deal he had struck (I later discovered he signed for £300,000) so when I went in I told Clough that Coventry had offered me a £25,000 signing-on fee (strange that it should be the same figure I had originally asked for when I first joined) and £500 a week and if he matched it I would sign for him. I had already decided not to tell him that I had a drink-driving conviction and was currently banned from driving before putting my name to the contract in case he decided not to sign me. He clapped his hands and said, 'Done!' I suspect I was.

Once I had signed I plucked up the courage to tell him about my latest offence. He jumped on me straightaway. 'Have I signed a drinker?' he said, and, 'Shall I get you a bucket to drink out of?' He told me that he wouldn't have signed me had he known but then suddenly asked if I had a girlfriend. I told him I had, wondering where the conversation was going. He asked me if I was going on holiday that summer and I told him that I was going to Disneyland in America.

'Are you taking your girlfriend?' he asked.

'No,' I replied, 'I'm going with a mate.'

'What's the matter son?' he came back. 'Are you a queer or something?'

He had only just signed me but in a matter of minutes he had hammered me for being a lying bastard, for being a drinker and now for being a homosexual. I explained that Liz was too busy looking after horses and couldn't get the time off.

He signed five of us that pre-season – Scottish international John Robertson came back from Derby; Neil Webb was the big-money signing; Brian Rice came down from Hibernian; Ian Butterworth, an England Under-21 international; and me. By the time he added his son Nigel, although not quite ready for the first division, he had bought half a new team. Another one coming through was Des Walker who was a kid, a 17-year-old pup who was about the place but on the way.

We were all together on the ten-day pre-season tour of the south coast with the colourful Robertson immediately earning cult status among the new boys by turning up with a toothbrush in his back pocket and no clothes other than those he stood up in.

Clough tried to label me with the boozer tag but gave up after a couple of months when he realised how wide of the mark he was. He switched his attention to Webby who was much more a couple of glasses a wine man than I ever was. Maybe because Neil had cost the most, Clough gave him no respite; he hammered him. He was on his case all the time as if he was trying to make or break him. Selfishly, I was grateful because it took the pressure off Butty and me.

If you went away with Clough and he picked your name out of the hat, it became easy to see why some players wouldn't want to go away to Tenerife and other places with him. He could make life sheer hell. He would accuse his latest target of being a drinker, an idiot, a fool and worse; it was as though the rest of the team didn't matter and he was on to the one player all of the time. He was cute because he rarely dug out more than one player at a time and would play off the rest against his stooge. Ian Bowyer was his captain and a very well-respected player. Clough would have a go at Webby through him, saying while Webby was in earshot, 'Ey, Bomber, he's a fucking idiot. He doesn't know his trade.' It could have worked either way and often did – it made Neil Webb a footballer, an international footballer at that, but he had to suffer for a full season before relief came in the shape of another patsy.

My turn arrived unexpectedly and I could have cheer-fully chinned him as he got on my case during a ten-day pre-season trip to Holland. He would stand there at the side of the pitch shouting, 'Stand up and tackle. You are always on your fucking arse,' 'You are an idiot,' 'You cockney bastard, always stealing this and that.' He would tell me that I ran funny, that I had a lopey stride, that I was always on my backside and so it went on. It was a nightmare. He made my life a misery. Why? I don't know. Little things seemed to annoy him.

I learned what it was like to be the butt of his comments and what he could really be like. It made me angry and I desperately wanted to fight back and prove him wrong but there were others who left the club because they couldn't stand that sort of abuse. It makes or breaks you. I hated him and there were times when I rang home and told Liz that it was a nightmare trip, club and manager and that I hated all of them. Every player went through it to some degree or another, even Des Walker whose standards were always so high. He was the most consistent player I have ever played alongside. If he had played for a more fashionable club or a London team he would have been in the England squad three years earlier. If he had a bad game it was memorable. Tony Cottee once scored a hat-trick against him at West Ham and Clough never let Des forget it, taunting him that he couldn't get near the little striker and doubting his lightning speed.

Des has the same footballing mentality as I have. We are different animals but he wants to do well at his job. Maybe he is not as dedicated as I am in certain ways but what he wants to achieve in the game spurred him on. For four years he was brilliant and then he had one bad game and Cloughie was down his throat for a week or two.

It was a myth that Clough wouldn't let Des go over the halfway line. I was flying down one wing most of the time and Gary Charles or someone would be flying down the other flank. Someone had to stay back and sort things out. That was usually Des. It became comical because Clough would talk about Des getting a nosebleed if he got too far forward. Before Des went to play in Italy for Sampdoria he did start venturing forward a bit more and, because he had never done it in the past, it became a big joke to the manager and the fans.

Not everyone suffered the barbs from Clough's sharp tongue. When I had been there for four years or so, Lee Glover forced his way into the team. You could name just a couple of players in the eight years I was with Clough whom he liked and respected. Lee Glover was one and Peter

Davenport the other. They tried to do the right things, hold up the ball, turn and all the things that he preached daily. It suited them because that was their natural game. He loved Davenport; Peter never had to come in on a Monday when he pulled the rest of us in for extra training.

I had been Clough's captain for three years when, one day, I went in to see him in his office. Lee Glover happened to be with him at the time and, although he was no older than 17 or 18, he was telling the boss that he didn't want to play for the youth team and added what he would rather do. I waited for the explosion but it didn't come. Even as his captain, I would never say anything like that to him because he would have had me for it.

I don't know whether he liked me or not. It was impossible to tell. I did a job for him, sometimes I did it well and sometimes I didn't but I assume that he thought he needed me at the club for what I did professionally. He accepted me and that was how it was. There were times when I hated his guts and not just on that Holland trip. Sometimes you loved him for the things he did, like buying those tickets for me to go to America, and sometimes he would go out of his way to niggle you.

Because I was captain, he would always give me the players' complimentary tickets to hand out to the boys. I was late getting in one day before a game against Luton Town and Des Walker, being the vice captain, handed out the tickets instead. Tommy Gaynor asked him if there were any spares. Des replied that the only ones he had left were mine. Gaynor promptly told him that I had said that he could have my tickets so Des gave them to him and he put them on the door for his friends. When I finally arrived I asked Des for my tickets only to be told that Tommy Gaynor had claimed them. Des laughed because he thought I was winding him up but this just happened to be one of the occasions when I did need them.

By now I had the hump and when I demanded my tickets back, Gaynor just laughed at me. That was a red rag to a bull. I marched him up to the office and reclaimed my tickets off the door. Five minutes later I passed him in the corridor. He was standing with Franz Carr and as I walked past he laughed at me so I promptly threw a punch at him, missed him by a mile and he grabbed me in a headlock. It was over in seconds but when Clough came into the dressing-room before the kick-off he had been told that we had been seen having a scuffle and asked, 'What's been going on then, Skipper?'

I told him Gaynor was out of order but that it was a storm in a teacup and it was all over. He glared across the dressing-room at Gaynor and said, 'If you need some fucking help, Skipper, let me know.'

He almost certainly said it to me because Tommy Gaynor was more expendable than I was at the time. All the same, I appreciated his backing.

My respect for the manager, despite our ups and downs, was immense. He makes you into a player and if your standards fall he will have you out of the team. He would do it if you were a senior player to spite you. He substituted me three times during our years together when I was playing badly and every time he would hold the board up with my number on instead of leaving it to the assistant manager or the physio, as was the norm.

I can even remember the games, the memory is so vivid.

The first was away at West Ham when he was up on the touchline making a big show of holding up my number. When I came off I tried to look him in the eyes but he wasn't paying attention; he was back in the dug-out. I was livid and he knew it. I count it as a personal insult to be taken off even if I am having a stinker – and I was. No one plays well all the time and I have had my share of stinkers.

Another occasion was on the last day of the season at home against Leeds and the other was away at Wimbledon. He was right. I was woeful in every one of those games. The substitution served its purpose: he was not only showing everyone who was boss and that he could take his captain off when and how he liked; he was also posing the question to me, asking me if I could still do it. He knew that I would want to prove him wrong. It worked because every time I would roll up my sleeves and come back in the next game, even if it was the first game of a new season, to show him that he couldn't do that to me. It was brilliant psychology.

There was an FA directive some years ago which stated that the captain had to go to the referee's dressing-room at 2.15 to present the teamsheet and receive instructions. I loved going in with Brian Clough because the referee and his linesmen would be wetting themselves. That was the power of his presence. I would still be in my tracksuit because my habit was to get changed at 2.20 but any number of the captains would be half-changed and turn up in their flip-flops. That was fatal with Clough; he would deliberately stand on a bare foot. We would be there for three or four minutes and, throughout the entire time, Clough would stand there with his foot nailing down the opposition captain who would be too embarrassed to say a word.

The officials would also be very deferential to him but he would not reciprocate. He would say, 'I don't want any shit from you lot. They have a shithouse playing for them who kicks my centre-forward.'

I was glad I had him there with me. He wasn't an extra player but having his presence was a lifting factor because you could never let your standards drop when he was around.

Forest was totally dominated by Clough in the time that I was there. He dominated a succession of chairmen like no other manager at any club. Sir Alex Ferguson is clearly the boss at Manchester United while Don Revie was all-powerful at Leeds and Bobby Robson ran Ipswich from top to bottom but none of them ruled a club in the way that Clough ruled Nottingham Forest. If he had wanted, he could have got rid of the chairman because the club didn't even have a proper board of directors at that time. He was the boss.

Certainly players who stepped out of line or who didn't fit the bill were out on their ears no matter how much they cost or what their potential was. Before I arrived, Gary Megson arrived with a fanfare but lasted just a couple of weeks because Clough was forever in his face. He couldn't stand it and had to move on. I saw it at first-hand when he signed Dave Currie from Barnsley. He lasted for no longer than a month. I knew what was coming the day I was in an away dressing-room with Currie, Clough and a handful of others. Clough turned to Currie and said, 'Ey, son, have you got yourself a house yet?' Currie said, 'Not yet,

Boss.' Clough gave him the all-time put down. 'Don't bother!' he said.

It made Currie laugh because he thought Clough was joking but the lads who had been around a long time knew differently. I looked across the dressing-room at Des Walker and we both knew he meant it. Sure enough, Currie was soon on his bike.

John Sheridan was another. He joined Forest from Leeds United and was there for a couple of months before Clough decided he was wrong for the team and moved him on.

The offending player would do something that convinced Clough he was not suited and Clough would blame his assistant, Ronnie Fenton, for signing him. All the bad ones were Fenton's fault. Teddy Sheringham was a classic case. He signed in 1992 and scored 20 goals without playing particularly well. He eclipsed Nigel with his goals. In those days he didn't play the link role as he does so brilliantly nowadays; he was a penalty-area player who wanted the ball on his head. You couldn't argue with his goal record. However, Clough had made up his mind about him that season and again I knew that Teddy was for the chop.

I was injured just before the 1992 League Cup final and sat behind Clough on the bench at Wembley listening to him criticising Teddy non-stop from start to finish. He was unrelenting, saying things like, 'He shouldn't get in my reserve team never mind play at Wembley.'

Teddy was still with us on our pre-season tour of Ireland, but there were rumours that he might be going to Tottenham. He was still there for our first game of the season and curled one into the top corner to help us beat Liverpool 1–0. He played one and a half more games and he was gone, sold to Spurs. That year we were relegated and Clough was sacked. It was all because Clough had made up his mind that Teddy couldn't play and sold him before he had sorted out a replacement.

It also worked the other way, of course, and he was just as quick to decide when someone could play. He made his mind up about Roy Keane in an instant when he arrived from Ireland as a raw kid, because he was so good in the air. Clough's philosophy was that if you could head the ball you could play. I don't know where he picked up that idea, whether it was from someone else or simply from watching the game. Keane was one of the best headers of the ball I have ever seen and Clough decided that he was his man and put him into the team as soon as he arrived. No one else had heard of him.

Clough helped to make Roy a rounded international, as he did with Neil Webb. In the couple of seasons before he went to Manchester United, Webby was scoring 20 goals a season from midfield, including a spectacular hat-trick against Chelsea. In fact, Webby was the first of our little group from Forest to be called into the England squad by Bobby Robson. He was playing so well he couldn't possibly be ignored. He was in the England squad for a year and a half before I was selected. That was what Clough was like. If you were career-minded and prepared to take some flak he could make you. In many ways he made me.

He never lectured but would suggest things, instead, asking if maybe you should have done this or that. Then he'd leave you to think about the wisdom of what he had said. I equate it to a couple of young horses we have at the moment. When you are breaking in young horses, you give them a short lesson, finishing on a good note and turning them out into the field. The same applies to young footballers. You don't have to preach to them until they get bored. Instead you plant the seed, let them think about it and then get them back. If they are any good they will come back with the right answers.

A typical team-talk would be for Clough to throw a towel in the middle of the dressing-room ten minutes before the kick-off. By then everyone had done his warm-ups and stretches and was ready for the game. You could hear a pin drop as we waited and anyone walking in at that moment would think we were at a wake or saying our prayers. He would then put a ball on the towel and say, 'This is what we play with. Go and get it.' That was it. You could feel the tension vanish. One of his big thoughts was that you could not play if you were nervous.

Brian Clough was no great organiser and often we would start the season not knowing who was in the wall or who was picking up whom. Sometimes we would work it out ourselves or one of the coaches, Liam O'Kane or Archie Gemmill, would pull us to one side and try to arrange basic things. But if Clough spotted them he would shout across, 'What do you think you're doing? What are you telling them?' It was all very strange. Most of the time we played off the cuff and got away with it because there was so many good players. But it hit the fan in 1993 when we didn't have enough good players and suddenly discovered that we could no longer get away with it.

Clough didn't coach; he ruled by fear. But the few words he used and the little throwaway phrases were better at times than hours of coaching from another manager who could not get his point across so succinctly. When early on he told me to stay on my feet, he did not labour the point on the training ground but it was something he might scream at me one week and say quietly the next. I went away wondering what he meant; then I would dive in and the winger would nick it past me. The realisation hit home and I knew what he meant. I could make ten good sliding tackles, miss one and he would have me for the missed one. That was his way of coaching. If I laid the ball off first time and it went astray he would say, 'Stop the ball.' Because I was in awe of the man, the penny dropped, quickly. He would have had me soon enough if it hadn't.

The little line he would throw at the forwards was, 'When you get the ball, turn.' He wanted them to turn all the time to face the goal. Once a forward has turned, he has half a chance, and I can vouch for that as a defender facing them. Little things like that I will certainly take with me into management.

You can't work for eight years with a man of his domineering personality and not learn something. Tactically he was very cute but I would never say that the man was a great coach. Coaching sessions on the training ground were unheard of. Basically, our training sessions comprised a few sprints, a warm-up and a five-a-side. You found your own level. If you were good enough in his eyes, you survived; if you weren't, your feet wouldn't touch the ground.

Only Clough could arrange the sort of pre-season we had at Forest. I came back from the 1990 World Cup with only an eight-day break between the last match in Italy and our return for pre-season training. I went to see him and asked if I could have an extra week off, explaining I was fully fit and just needed a rest rather than a hard pre-season.

'I have signed the contract. We are going to Sweden and you will be there,' was his response. 'But what I can do for you is give you the week off before the season, when we go to Italy.'

Play on a Saturday and he might say he would see you next Friday for training. Come in Friday, play Saturday, if that was what you wanted. It didn't suit everyone's needs and some would ask Liam O'Kane to put on a session for Tuesday. Liam would come in and we would please ourselves. It wasn't always like that but if the players looked tired or jaded or the performances weren't as good as they should be, Clough would give players time off instead of pulling them back in for extra work the way other managers did. The worse the performances, the more he would go the other way. It takes a strong man to follow that route.

Clough probably had it right. Come Christmas, everyone was as fit as players in other teams. You have had enough games by then, whatever the pre-season arrangements.

Players who say they weren't scared of him are almost certainly lying. Many were relieved to be out of his way and avoided him if they could. Look at the strong players he dominated even before I arrived, including Larry Lloyd and Kenny Burns, big names and hard men. But if Clough saw a head-to-head conflict in the offing, he would sidestep it. A classic example was when he took the first-team squad to Porto Benuese in Spain for a six-day break. There was rarely a curfew and normally it was very much come and go as you pleased. This time he said that he wanted everyone back at the hotel at ten o'clock. It was unheard of. But what the man asked for, the man got and at 9.30 we were all gathered in a bar, before heading for the coach that was picking us up. Fifteen minutes later, we struggled to our feet ready to go, all that is except Garry Birtles who, having had a few drinks, said belligerently, 'I'm not moving. I have a wife and three kids and I'm old enough to make up my own mind when I go to bed.' Ian Bowyer tried to persuade him but he refused point blank and shouted after us, 'You're a load of fucking boy scouts.'

We knew Clough would miss him and, sure enough, he was waiting for us at the pick-up point and immediately asked where Birtles was. Garry received a reprieve when the coach failed to turn up and we all trooped back to the bar where he still sat nursing his drink. Instead of walking up to the bar and hammering the still aggressive Birtles for going against him, Clough joined the rest of us for another drink and ignored Birtles completely. He knew that Birtles was a stubborn guy and if he had confronted him, there would have certainly been a row that he might not have won in the circumstances.

It was the same when he used to substitute me. I would walk off muttering obscenities loud enough for him to hear but he would avoid all eye contact with me and would never jump up and ask what I had called him. He wouldn't always sidestep but he knew when to take someone on and when not to.

At the end of my first season, we went away to Cala Millor. I lived in the same village in Nottingham as Neil Webb and we had the crazy idea of reporting to the airport in Bermuda shorts and flip-flops with hair greased back and sunglasses. It was raining cats and dogs and cold when we drove to the ground to catch the team bus to East Midlands airport wearing all our gear including mirrored sunglasses so that Clough wouldn't be able to see our eyes when he confronted us. Clough was going straight to the airport and when we climbed on the coach Ronnie Fenton said, 'Good joke lads, now take the stuff off or he will go mad.' We stood our ground and said it was a holiday and end of season and even though it was May and freezing cold, there was little we could do about it as all our stuff was in our cases.

We queued up at East Midlands airport shivering and everyone thought it was hilarious, except Brian Clough.

'What are those fucking idiots up to,' he raged. 'What the fucking hell do they think they're doing?'

He wanted to send us home there and then but Ronnie and Liam managed to persuade him that we were just having a bit of fun at our own expense.

The Walsall team were in Cala Millor at the same time as we were and early one evening they joined us at our table where we were playing music and having a few beers. A short while later, Clough and the coaches arrived. There were no spare seats so our manager just pulled the chair from under Walsall striker David Kelly. He yanked it so hard that Kelly shot across the road and landed on his backside. Clough sat down, reached over and turned off the music. Kelly leapt to his feet not knowing whether to hit him or keep quiet. Wisely, he chose the latter course of action. It might not have been his manager and he might have been seriously wronged, but this was Brian Clough. We were all half-cut having been there for most of the day enjoying the sun and the beers. Clough sat there silently for 20 minutes with no music and not a word said. Just as suddenly as he had arrived, he stood up, said, 'See you later,' and shuffled off into the night. The music came back on and everyone just sat open-mouthed, amazed at what had happened. No one blamed Kelly for not reacting and the Walsall players were as much in awe of the man as we were.

One time, when we had just beaten Queens Park Rangers in the quarter-final of the League Cup, a group of supporters ran on to the pitch celebrating. Clough hated supporters on his pitch and he lashed out at them, landing punches on two or three of them. Those lads made a big fuss, threatened to sue him and have him arrested. In typical fashion he invited them into the club on Monday morning where they met the players. If they thought that they had been called in for an apology they had another think coming. Clough laid into them, telling them that they shouldn't have been on the pitch. He didn't apologise but they did.

Who else would have got away with that? Instead of being pilloried, he received letters of support from a chief of police and Labour leader Neil Kinnock, and the FA offered to hold the resultant tribunal in Nottingham instead of London! He was fined and briefly banned from the touchline.

However you look at it, he was a remarkably successful manager with two unfashionable clubs. He won the League championship with Derby and reached the semi-finals of the European Cup, and at Forest he won the League and, most incredible of all, back-to-back European Cups, taking on and beating the multi-million pound giants of Europe.

That's what makes him the man he is – the success he has achieved.

Local derbies between Derby County and Nottingham Forest were always fierce affairs on and off the pitch. The local rivalry was intense. Brian Clough is among the few who made the switch and after his acrimonious departure from the Baseball Ground he had more than enough reason to be all fired up whenever the two clubs met.

One midweek in the early nineties before a home game against Derby he was worse than usual and instead of posting the team up in the morning he told us to come in at 6.30 and he would tell us then. When I arrived in the dressing-room the boys were laughing and when I asked them what was up they nodded towards the showers and told me to look for myself. There was Brian Clough, one of the most feared and respected managers in the game, sitting in the tub fully clothed.

I asked Liam O'Kane what the team was but he shrugged his shoulders; he still hadn't been told. We ushered the players out to look at the pitch, leaving Liam to try to glean the information from the boss but when we returned things had gone from bad to worse. He had moved from the bath to the sauna, still fully clothed, and he had a big yard shovel, the sort the ground staff used to clear the snow, by his side. What he had the shovel for God only knew but I suppose he might have been using it as a sort of walking stick or a crutch.

The unpredictable things Clough did, when analysed later, often showed not just his eccentricity but his brilliance as a motivator. One such occasion was when we were going to play Millwall at the old Den in the first division. At the time Millwall were under the spotlight because of some crowd disturbances and, sure enough, they had some hard supporters who could look after themselves. A mile from the ground Clough ordered the driver to stop the coach and told us all to get off. He led the way and strode on, swinging his walking stick as he made his way through the hordes of Millwall supporters down Cold Blow Lane. We are thinking, 'What's going on? I don't want to be here.' The supporters were just amazed. He marched us through. The message was that they might have a reputation but they weren't going to intimidate him or his team. At the same time he was telling us that there was nothing to be afraid of.

We had no hassle at all and the Millwall supporters seemed to enjoy it. Mind you we kept close to the manager; no one wanted to tail off in case they suffered a rogue one! It was clever psychology and all part of the Clough mystique.

On another occasion we were driving to London when he saw a truck driver with his cab down looking at his engine. He called to our old driver, Albert, to pull over and took a plate of sandwiches, prepared for after the game, to the stricken driver on the hard shoulder. He stuck his head under the hood and said, 'Can I help you?'

'Fucking hell, you're Brian Clough,' said the amazed driver.

'That's right, young man. Can I help you?'

Clough knew nothing about repairing a broken-down lorry and he must have been quietly relieved when the bemused driver said he could manage. Clough gave him a couple of salmon sandwiches, got back on the coach and off we went. As we drove off we could see the lorry driver watching us, shaking his head and obviously thinking that his mates down the pub would never, ever believe his story.

Albert had more points on his licence than any other football coach driver because Clough would be forever telling him to get us to the game on time. If the police stopped us, he would tell them, 'Get off my fucking bus. We're late for the game.' Even the police were frightened of him, but unfortunately not of Albert. If Clough had told him to drive over the grass verge and through the supermarket he would do it – or get the sack.

Motorways seemed to bring the worst out of Clough. Albert once broke down on the M1 on his way back to Nottingham after a game at Tottenham. The engine was spluttering and sounding very unhealthy, forcing him to pull over on to the hard shoulder. Albert made his way up the middle of the coach to climb through the trapdoor to get at the drive shaft. When he was up to the waist down the hole the bus suddenly started moving off. We thought he must have left the brake off but when we looked down the aisle there was our manager driving the bus up the hard shoulder with the needle creeping past 30 miles an hour. The police were quickly on the scene and when he spotted them Clough put on the brakes, jumped out of the driver's seat and back into his own just behind it. Albert was struggling back up the coach when the police came knocking. I don't know whether they knew it was Clough driving but the boys were rolling about on the floor laughing.

I had a friend with me that day, having asked the manager for the favour of allowing him to ride on the team bus, a rarity for me because I didn't like owing the boss favours. He didn't believe what he was seeing and even those of us used to Clough's peculiarities were stunned. It scared Albert. I don't think he was laughing too loudly.

Clough did lots of things that normal people just wouldn't do. Having arranged a trip to Spain a couple of weeks hence, he suddenly decided that the coach should pull off the motorway at junction 24 so that we could drive past East Midlands airport and wave. 'We'll be there in two weeks' time, Skipper. Give it a wave, give it a wave,' he said. All we wanted to do was get back to Nottingham and we'd gone half an hour out of our way just to wave at an airport. What's more, it wasn't the only time we did it. Imagine grown men sitting on a coach waving at an airport.

The peculiarities extended way beyond our frequent coach journeys. He was in the habit of taking the boys for a walk on the morning of a big game and would suddenly come across a tree.

'This,' he said, pointing at the tree, 'is a punch tree. You have got to punch it. It's lucky.'

There was never a boring day, never a dull moment. Often he would invite you to join him for a drink at the oddest moments. He liked having people around him. When I first went there I would have half of Guinness so as not to upset him. Clough didn't mind if his players had a decent drink when they were at the bar at his invitation. Neil Webb liked a drink and he would occasionally down a bottle of red wine over dinner. He was playing well and claimed it relaxed him so Clough took no notice. When Webby went to Manchester United and Alex Ferguson found out that he was drinking a bottle of wine on a Friday night, he was not impressed. Personally, I thought it was unprofessional. It was down to Webby but I have to say he was magnificent when he played for us that first time around. Had he not played well Clough would have held it against him.

When we played at home we used to play deep; I thought that was wrong. I felt we should push on and if they had a throw-in near their corner flag, push in, squeeze it and win the ball early rather than let them bring it out and play. I had the nerve to mention it to Clough and it worked for four or five games. Then we were caught out and lost a match. He turned on me.

'You twat. Push on, push on, idiot, idiot,' he shouted.

He didn't mind when I told him but he used to store things up and turn on you when it went wrong. He always liked someone else to blame. He has an incredible memory and I had given him a noose to hang round my neck by opening my mouth. I thought it was for the good of the side. I didn't suggest anything again.

One evening before our first away game of the season he rang round our rooms and invited us all to join him in the bar for a drink. Chris Fairclough, Ronnie Fenton, Neil Webb, Nigel Clough and I were there with others. He always let us drink whatever we wanted, a Guinness or a glass of wine. I would have an orange juice and sit with him for half an hour before slipping off to my bed. But on this occasion as we sat chatting among ourselves, one of the customers, who had been sitting with his wife having a drink, came over and said, 'Hello Brian, you have put on a bit of weight.' I looked at Chris Fairclough and we started counting one, two, three, four . . .

'What the fucking hell did he say to me, Skipper?'

He knew exactly what the man had said because he was

standing right next to him but I repeated it. Then he turned to the unfortunate fellow.

'What did you say to me?'

The man started to splutter something but Clough cut him short.

'What job do you do?'

'You don't want to know what I do.'

'What fucking job do you do?' Clough repeated a couple of decibels louder.

'I'm an undertaker, Brian,' he eventually ventured.

We were biting our lips by this time, trying desperately not to fall over laughing as the manager gathered himself for his riposte.

'Well, fuck off and die then.'

The man returned to his wife and said loudly, 'What a fucking rude man he is.'

Just because he had seen Clough on television he thought he knew him but it was like going up to someone in the street and saying, 'You are a fat bastard.' You just don't do it.

Celebrities used to pop into the dressing-room now and again. When Elton John was chairman of Watford first time round, he always used to come in whenever we were at Vicarage Road. After one particular game, Clough had gone to have a bath and was all lathered up when Elton popped his head round the door. Ronnie Fenton shouted through that Elton was here to say hello. Elton was chatting to one or two of the boys when Clough bellowed back, 'Tell the fat poof I'll be out in a minute.' All the players started laughing and, to be fair, so did Elton. The next minute Clough appeared, naked but for the soapsuds, and gave Elton a big cuddle. For all the players, Elton was a massive star and we were in awe of him – but not Clough.

I have been to see Elton in concert and backstage and I really do like him. He is definitely a man of the people and I liked the way he took Brian Clough at face value when other so-called superstars might well have been upset and walked out.

Geoffrey Boycott came into the dressing-room once to see Clough. We were playing Sheffield Wednesday at Hillsborough. He walked in after the game and you had the feeling that both were talking and neither was listening to the other.

'Eh, by 'eck, that centre-half of yours is a quick lad, isn't he?' said Boycott.

'Do you mean Dessie?' asked Clough.

'Aye,' said Boycott. 'He's quick – but I'd still run him out though.' That brought the house down.

As I've said, I don't think that Brian Clough liked his players talking to the media. He never came out and said as much but we got the drift that this was his province and for us to leave it alone. Neil Webb and one or two of the others liked having their names in the paper, but I didn't and neither did Des Walker, Nigel and a few of the others. If anyone said anything ridiculous in print or on radio or television, he would pounce on them and leave them in no doubt that they were fools to be trampling on his territory.

What he did say to me and to others was that we could use him as an excuse for not speaking to the press and that suited me. It was easy to say that the boss had banned us from talking and, knowing him, everyone believed it.

When I went with England for the first time he repeated

the instructions and that delighted me. I didn't want to talk to the press before such a big game – it was against Brazil in the old Rous Cup – and have them turn something against me to upset my preparations on the morning. They were already building me up as the hot head, saying that it was a big risk to play me in an international. I knew I was in for my first cap because Kenny Sansom was injured. I just didn't want to worry what they would write if I commented.

The big story the next day was that Brian Clough wouldn't let his captain talk to the press. That was fine. He had done me a big favour, shielded me from what could have been a difficult situation. Not that he was particularly generous about my international call-ups. When I was first pulled into the squad by Bobby Robson he called me into his office.

'Son, you're in the squad, are you?' he said.

'Yes, Boss.'

'Do you think you'll play?'

'I don't know, Boss,' I replied, knowing that I would.

'Do you think you're good enough?'

'I don't know.'

'I don't. Get out.'

He meant it. He didn't think I was good enough to play for the country. In fact, he didn't like his players playing for their country much anyway because he thought we came back as smartarses, comparing wages with other players from bigger clubs and, of course, for that period we were outside his influence. But he never tried to stop anyone playing. He would tell them that if they didn't want to play he would back them up by reporting that they were injured, but in my experience he never once told anyone, 'No!'

One time I was due to head out for Saudi Arabia with England for a friendly. Des Walker was injured and pulled out, as did Steve Hodge and Neil Webb, leaving just me from Forest and I had just had a nightmare of a game. It was the one against West Ham in which I was substituted. I was gutted and Clough offered to pull me out if I wanted. I was tempted but I quickly put the idea out of my mind. It would have meant giving up another England cap for one thing and a trip on Concorde for another, not to mention a first visit to a new country. Those were three good reasons to go. I went, played well, got my passport stamped and travelled on a great aircraft.

It wasn't the best game. We scrambled a draw thanks to a late goal from Rodders, but I had a decent game and safeguarded my place for the next one. Bobby Robson took the flak for our performance. The press climbed all over him with the memorable and unfair headline: 'For the love of Allah, Go!'

That taught me the greatest lesson of my international career. I was a total idiot for even considering pulling out and I told myself never, ever to consider it again. I never did. It annoyed me to this day that I even thought of backing out.

A lot of players do back out. Talk is cheap. When they say it's a pleasure and an honour to play for England, that's lip service. Some pick and choose their games, especially when they know they are not going to play. I spent two years sitting in the stand waiting for my chance to come back when Graeme Le Saux was in the team. Terry Venables gave me the chance of retiring honourably, indicating that I wasn't going to get back in his team. I remembered my lesson, bit the bullet and stayed patient. As long as he picked me in the squad I was going to turn up and if Brian Clough had suggested different we would have had a row.

I don't know how the physiotherapist Graham Lyas coped with Brian Clough at times. Clough may have been happy to back up any international who wanted to cry off with an injury but if too many players were in the treatment room he would sometimes lock the door. The players would roll up, get changed and set off for the training ground. As we walked down the corridor, there would be the physio and the injured players standing around kicking their heels outside the locked door. When we came back from our training session, they would still be waiting. Two or three times while I was there Clough locked the treatment room for up to a week, stopping the physio attending to the injured players.

Graham became numb to it in the end; it just ground him down. He joined us from the County Cricket Ground next door and in the end he came in, did what he could and went home. If the door was open he would work; if it wasn't he had to find something else to do with the injured players.

I'm sure there was the odd shirker but I doubt whether Clough's ploy to get them out of the treatment room and back on to the pitch worked. Most players want to play and for someone whose career was terminated early through injury you would have thought he would have had a little more understanding, but it was in character.

Contact with the manager, even for the club captain, was limited to say the least. I went in to see Clough in the summer of 1992 about a new contract. When I asked him about the prospects he shouted across the table, 'Do you want to leave the club, son? Do you want to leave the club?' No, I didn't. I had simply gone into his office to ask about upgrading my contract. The last thing anyone does is to go into Clough's office and demand anything. His reaction took me aback. I told him that I wanted to stay. My point was that I thought my contract was a bit outdated to which he replied, 'I do as well, son. I do as well. Come back and see me in the week.'

It was a week before the season began and there was a ruling in force at the time that if you signed a new contract it had to be done before the season started. I probably had it wrong but that was firmly in my mind so I told him and we arranged our meeting accordingly. The next thing I heard was that he had cleared off to Spain for a week, which carried us into the season. I was furious. I telephoned the PFA and the FA and asked for dispensation as it had been agreed that I would have a new contract but I had to wait for the manager to come back from his unexpected holiday. They appreciated the eccentricities of our unusual manager and agreed.

Clough then arranged for me to meet him before a reserve game at 6 p.m. I was there on the dot but there was no Clough and not even Ronnie Fenton knew where the gaffer was. He was nowhere to be found. We sat waiting in his office for an hour before Ronnie shrugged his shoulders and said to come back at half-time.

I had no intention of going back at half-time; I had been at the club for seven years and his captain for five of those. He had cleared off on holiday when he had arranged to meet me without bothering to cancel the appointment and now he was swanning around the ground somewhere and had left me waiting again. That was plain bad manners. The least he could have done was be there.

It was all building up inside me as I made my way home. I told Liz what had happened and said that I wasn't going to go back at half-time as Ronnie had suggested. We put the answer machine on and, sure enough, the phone rang exactly on half-time. We leaned over the machine and we could hear Ronnie saying, 'He's not in, Brian.' Then I heard this voice shouting in the background, 'Not in? Not fucking in? What do you mean, he's not in?'

I turned to Liz and said, 'That's going to cost us a lot of money.'

Clough and I never talked properly again. I blanked him because I felt that I had been treated like dirt. I had never fallen out with a manager before, but once I have made up my mind I am obstinate. I would walk past him in the corridor, he would say hello and I would ignore him. That went on for an entire season and my form suffered because of it. From February until the end of the season I was out with injury, a groin strain that needed an operation. We were relegated that season, my form was rubbish and he was given the sack. It didn't help either of us.

He had lost me by then. In his autobiography he slaughtered me. Certainly his recollection of events is very different from mine.

Away from home, the coaches, the manager and me in the dressing-room made for a frosty atmosphere, but I was as stubborn as he was. At Maine Road before a game against Manchester City, he said to me that we should sort things out. I told him there was nothing to sort out, he hadn't bothered to turn up, and so the standoff continued until he left. When he went we were still not talking and there was still a bad atmosphere, certainly from my side. I felt aggrieved and hard done by and judging by his comments he thought I was a greedy bastard.

Everyone has their own side of the story. I can only tell it as I saw it and maybe I'm off the mark somewhere. But I was mad with him for that entire season and afterwards as well. I told him he had messed me up and messed up my family. I have mellowed a bit since then.

When Frank Clark took over, he not only had the problem of Forest being outside the top division but also the problem of me and my contract to solve. The chairman, Fred Reacher, obviously knew that there had been a massive gulf in that last season between the captain and the manager and, naturally, he wanted to sort it out. It hadn't helped that he and the other players had witnessed Clough saying, 'Hello Skipper,' and me ignoring him. No one blanked Clough – but I did. I wasn't trying to be the big shot because I couldn't touch the manager in terms of stature and achievement; I was just being true to myself, right or wrong.

This wasn't the Brian Clough I knew. He wasn't in the best of health but the saddest thing was that the club was going to be relegated and he seemed to do nothing about it. He had sold Teddy Sheringham at the start of the season and not only had he not replaced him, he had not signed anybody at all until March. We went slowly down and down and were relegated without a fight.

I have to hold up my hands and admit I was part of the cause. I played poorly up until February and then played no part at all. Clough, in his book, suggested that at the time they thought I was shirking and it was only when I went into hospital for an operation that he realised how serious my injury was. I don't believe that the situation would have developed a few years earlier when he was still on top of the game. Things were allowed to fester all season whereas he would have sorted it out or kicked me out. I'm not proud of it and have to take my share of the responsibility for Nottingham Forest being relegated. Nor was it the way I wanted to end my association with Brian Clough, a man and a manager I had respected above all others. I was mad at the time but it is water under the bridge and with time I have recovered my respect for the man.

I have stayed in regular touch with Nigel and I always ask after his father. I'm sure Nigel knows the problems I had with him, but he is diplomatic and lives his own life. We have always got on well together with a great deal of respect and no animosity. If I get a job in football management, the first person I will ring is Nigel Clough. It was the first thing I did when I was caretaker at Forest.

There is plenty of contact there but none between his father and me. But then I never really had any social contact with him before. He managed and I was captain. We were never friends, I was never invited to his house and we didn't even swap Christmas cards. He was my boss and I was his workman. That was hard and fast and it suited both of us. I'm sure he didn't want me as a friend and I wouldn't have been comfortable sharing confidences with him. I was always on my guard with him because he was that sort of person.

I caught up with him at a dinner where he was being

forest after clough

The technical side of my game has improved and the proof of that is that throughout my career I have been sent off only three times. Unless you are technically decent you don't play for England, certainly not the number of times I have played and for so many different managers.

Sometimes when a player is considered over-robust, his technical qualities tend to be overlooked. I am not talking solely about myself but others of the same ilk such as Julian Dicks, Mark Dennis and Neil Ruddock. There is no sweeter left foot than Ruddock's but because the main weapon in his armoury is the physical pressure he puts on other players that quality is often forgotten. He is a strong player who intimidates opponents and that is what has made him such a good professional footballer rather than that superb left foot that can drill 40-yard passes.

You have to be cute, you have to learn and you have to evolve. Technically, I have a good left foot and a virtually non-existent right foot. I have been able to get away with it because my left foot is so good that if the ball is between my feet or to the right, I can hit it with the outside of my left foot and with pace as well. I can comfortably take a corner with the outside of my left foot and whip one in. There are not many of us left-sided players about because of the way the game has changed and that is probably why I stayed involved with England for so long.

For my height I jump well; I don't lose a lot at the far post when it counts. If you are not going to win the header, it's important to prevent the player you are marking from scoring a goal, even if it means having to put your head in his face.

Obviously Clough helped my technique with his odd remarks and observations while Don Howe, a coach with England for much of the time I was there, has a vast knowledge of defensive football. I dipped into that as often as possible. I had respect for Don and once you have that you hang on to every word the coach has to say. He has been around for years at the very top level. I remember coaching sessions when he would be looking after the back four and he was so committed to what he was doing, almost dogmatic, that you could not help being sucked in. I find myself coaching some of the sessions the way he did. That I can remember them after 12 years shows what an impression he made.

As much as the game evolves and technically improves over the years, the basics stay very much the same as they have always been. A player or manager has to change with the times but good play never changes. That was something Clough would always hammer into us. If you are defender, then defend. Don't look where the player is; look where the ball is. The ball can hurt you far more than the player. Midfield players have to win the ball and turn and if you are a forward you have to score goals. If you are in trouble, put the ball in their half of the pitch and don't mess around with it in your own penalty area. There is nothing wrong with putting your foot through the ball and kicking it 80 yards at the right time. These things haven't changed since the game was invented. Heading the ball is a basic and so is playing the right ball, playing it simple, playing what you see, playing what is on.

Watch a video of Pelé in the semi-final of the 1970 World Cup in Mexico against Uruguay. Pelé was the best player the world has ever seen. He was capable of running through ten players but what does he do? He gets the ball, commits a defender, and rolls it to his mate Rivelino who strikes the perfect goal. Pelé saw what was on and played it. If you are coaching youngsters I would say show them that goal first rather than Diego Maradona running through the entire England team and scoring in the Mexico World Cup 16 years later. They will no doubt prefer the Argentina goal but then explain why the first one was better. Pelé took the right option, played the right weight of pass and was aware of what was going on around him. Pelé stuck to the basics that day while Maradona personified the ripples on the top. You can tinker with the bits and pieces of the game, those ripples on the top, but never with the basics.

Respect is the key to coaching and management. Whatever other ingredients go to make the ideal manager is anyone's guess and vary from person to person. Respect can only come with time; it's not something you can order up or simply acquire. Once you have it and the players are listening and want to work for you, you are on the way. If the respect or confidence goes, then there is a problem. The players stop listening.

There is no better example of the dramatic contrast that

there can be between successful bosses than Brian Clough and Don Revie, two totally different characters, yet enormously successful with Nottingham Forest and Leeds United. However, they were not successful everywhere they went. Revie failed as an international manager while Clough did not command the respect of the players at Leeds, the same players who had played under Revie. It's that sort of thing that makes our game so fascinating.

At the clubs where they were successful, the individuals they worked with hung on every word and didn't question what they were told to do. Revie was very dogmatic in his approach; Clough was often perceived as casual. Who was right? The answer is, of course, that they both were. If those two were at either end of the scale, Bob Paisley fitted right in the middle, and he was even more successful than the other two. To copy any of them is to court failure. All three were their own men.

I have learned something from all the managers I have worked for. Some players would not be as benevolent towards Ruud Gullit but despite what happened at Newcastle I still learned things from him and I'll use them when I go back into coaching or management. I'm not too proud to give credit where it's due.

Life at Nottingham Forest after Brian Clough and relegation looked bleak as the team began to break up. Nigel Clough went to Liverpool and the priceless Roy Keane to Manchester United. Nigel had made up his mind to go and many thought he had no choice after what had happened to his dad. One of the directors had placed a derogatory story in the newspapers and dragged Nigel into it as well.

I would be lying if I said I didn't think about leaving. One of my concerns was my England place and I confess that I telephoned manager Graham Taylor to ask him what effect dropping down a division would have on my position as his captain and my place in the team. It was only when he gave me some assurances that I went ahead with a meeting to discuss my role at the club and a new contract. Taylor's only concern was that I was happy at the club and I was able to tell him honestly that I was.

Chairman Fred Reacher and Frank Clark, the new manager, called me into a meeting to sort out my future at the City Ground. I told them that I had felt badly let down by the club, not just by Brian Clough but by the chairman as well because he knew everything that was going on and he sat back and let it all happen. We talked for a long while, resolving the problems that had festered for a year. I finished up signing a new contract and I am not ashamed to admit that I used the situation to improve the terms. I was sorry to saddle Frank with the problem and tried to make it plain that it was more to do with the chairman than him. He sat back while I thrashed out the deal with Fred and once that was done he and I had a talk.

Some players seem to think that when they sign they should be told of all the clubs plans, who they are going to sign and what colour they are going to paint the toilets. To me it's far plainer – sign, play and do your best. Once you start suggesting signing this player or that you are asking for problems. Unless I was asked I wouldn't dream of venturing an opinion. Certainly Frank never asked me. The job is hard enough without me putting my five pennyworth in.

There was a lot of pressure on Frank to succeed from the off as he spent money not just on me but on new players as well. He signed Stan Collymore and Colin Cooper. I had never played against either of them. Stan was an up-and-coming lad with a bit of a reputation and Colin had been earning his wages in a lower division with Millwall. So I really wasn't sure of the quality of the players replacing the engine room we had lost.

Unfortunately, we did not start that well and it wasn't long before we all knew that we weren't going to win the League. By the end of October we had lost five games and drawn four, slipping down to 19th place at one stage. We lost Colin Cooper through injury after just four games.

Millwall beat us at the City Ground on 3 November but after that we turned things around and lost just three more league games all season. We finished second to Crystal Palace, nine points ahead of third-placed Millwall. Steve Stone came into the side and did well, and we also signed Lars Bohinen. In retrospect, staying at Forest and winning promotion was one of the highest points of my career.

I liked Frank. It was a hell of a job taking over from Brian Clough even though he was the man Clough had always said should eventually have his job. Frank had been his captain through some of the glory years, a reliable defender and a student of the game. He was given the job and virtually told to get promoted or get out. That was tough. He is a nice man and I have never met anyone who has a cross word to say about him. He knows his football and he is easy to talk to, as I do whenever I bump into him. Frank coached a little but was more of a manager. Some managers want to be hands on, coaching on the pitch all of the time. I saw Frank as an ideal general manager. As a manager, I could have worked under him a lot more easily than I did Dave Bassett.

We needed a point from our third-from-last game at bottom club Peterborough to be sure of automatic promotion and avoid the lottery of the play-offs. The Posh are not that far from us and we filled their little ground to overflowing as 14,000 people crammed in. The atmosphere was brilliant but the nerves were jangling to such an extent that before we knew it we were two goals down and what was supposed to be a promotion party threatened to turn into a wake.

Stan Collymore scored just before half-time but it was not until about 15 minutes from time that a cross came over, Chettle headed it on and I scored the equaliser with a diving header which carried me into the back of the net. The celebrations were ridiculous and to cap it Stan scored a wonder goal with the last kick of the match. The ball had hardly reached the back of the net before the fans were spilling over the fences in wild celebrations and the referee, wisely, blew for time.

The police eventually came into the dressing-room to tell us that we would have to go out and see the fans or they would never be able to empty the ground. We went up into the directors' box and gave them a wave.

For a nearly man, things worked well for me that day. It vindicated my decision to stay and it was a great occasion, totally satisfying. For everything it symbolised, that game at little Peterborough is one I'll never forget.

To be fair, we weren't a bad side. Stan came in firing on all cylinders and we finished third in the Premier Division the next season, as high as I had ever finished under Brian Clough.

Frank had his work cut out with Stan. I felt a bit sorry for him. He couldn't let things brush past him like Clough could. When Stan first came, he was a bit of a handful but not too bad. Frank had ten other players who would graft, people such as Steve Stone who ran up and down the wing, Colin Cooper who worked so hard that he won himself an England cap and Bryan Roy who came in for that first season back in the Premiership; and I was not playing too badly. All the average players were playing to the top of their form. Frank was conscientious and sensitive, aware of the other players and their feelings, so much so that he came to me on one occasion to ask me what I thought he should do about Collymore and whether he should fine him.

He ended up throwing fines at Stan all the time and I don't think Stan could give a toss about money. Stan is Stan and will do stupid things but for Forest he played phenomenally well for two seasons. I remember saying to Frank, 'I know I have been around the dressing-room a lot longer than most and from my perspective I couldn't give a shit what he does. If he scores me a winner on Saturday, he will be my best friend.' I didn't care what he did with his life or whether he came in for training or not. In two seasons he helped us to win promotion to the Premier Division and get into Europe. I believe we had his two best-ever seasons.

Forest bought him for £2 million and he scored 24 goals in that first season. The next-highest scorer was Scot Gemmill with nine. Promotion made us millions. He scored 25 in the second season, giving us the prospect of earning more millions in Europe, and we sold him on for £7 million to Liverpool. Since then he has not achieved anything. After a good start at Leicester City he was dreadfully unlucky to break an ankle.

He was two-footed, good in the air and, in my opinion, he is one of the best players ever to play for Forest. There are a lot of critics who would pooh pooh that statement but it's fact. Ten of us would defend like hell and when we got it forward he would beat two players and score two goals at somewhere like Sunderland and that would win us the game in our promotion push.

I found Stan bright to talk to and I could never understand why he brought trouble to his own doorstep, especially when things were going so well on the football field. Sometimes he'd do silly things like just not turn up for training and when Frank asked him where he'd been he would throw in a stupid excuse like his grandmother had been poorly! That was the nature of the man. As far as I was concerned, it was thanks for two great seasons and £5 million profit, on you go and good luck to you.

We would have loved to keep him for at least a third season and I honestly didn't think he did too badly at Liverpool where he scored some spectacular goals. But he is not the sort of person to mix the way Liverpool reputedly requires you to do. He is his own man who does his own thing. You have to accept it, although that's easier said than done if you're his manager. Managers have to worry about what other players may do if one is allowed to get away with eccentricities. We used to have a players' Christmas party and Stan would be the only one not to come. What do you do? Get on his back? What was the point? It was his choice.

I wouldn't say we had a great deal in common. I once heard someone ask Sir Bobby Charlton if he got on with George Best, rumours having indicated otherwise, and Bobby said, 'We got on all right but we were totally different people. While he was at a nightclub I would be at home with my wife and family.' It was the same sort of thing with me and Roy Keane and Stan Collymore. We were a different age group and I would go home to Liz while Roy would like to go out clubbing. Stan liked to go back to Cannock and have a beer with his own mates. I always quite liked him and whenever I see him I laugh and ask him, 'Keeping out of trouble, Stan?'

'Trying to, Skip, trying to,' he says.

I'm afraid the game is riddled with might-have-beens and could-have-beens. When I turned professional I drank at a pub where everyone knew someone who was a lot better than I was. To me that does not mean a thing – you have to do it, not talk about it.

The next year, 1995–96, we went into Europe on the back of Stan's goals and enjoyed an incredible run. We played the first three rounds in the UEFA Cup and conceded just two goals. We lost the first leg of the first round 2–1 to Malmo in Sweden, but Ian Woan's goal in the 1–0 second leg was enough to take us through. We followed it up by winning 1–0 in France against Auxerre and drawing 0–0 at home, and reached the quarter-finals by beating Lyon 1–0 at home and drawing 0–0 away. Basically, we just defended. Away from home we were incredible and at home we had the attitude that we were the underdogs. Everyone was playing well, especially our goalkeeper Mark Crossley who was on fire and kept us in it more than once.

The game in Auxerre was the most one-sided game I have ever played in. Steve Stone scored a breakaway goal with what was our only shot of the match. In contrast, they hit the post four times and we cleared three off the line. We hardly got out of our half, particularly in the second half. I walked off laughing because it was ridiculous. Even in the return, we spent the entire 90 minutes defending.

Against Lyon it was not a lot different. The one goal came after my penalty was saved and young Paul McGregor followed up to put in the rebound.

We were eventually found out in the quarter-final against Bayern Munich. I had been out for six weeks with a calf problem and it was only on the morning of the game that Frank told me he wanted me to play after a workout on Bayern's training ground. An hour before the kick-off I discovered that my leg had swollen up and when I pressed my thumb into it, it left a big depression. I showed Frank, who had already put the team in to the referee, and he called in Doctor Jarrett. We went into the showers away from the other players where he advised me not to play. I was almost in tears as the doctor kept telling me he couldn't advise me to play while Frank was insistent that I should give it a try.

In the end, we reached a typical British compromise and it was decided that I should go out and give it a try and if there was any reaction I should come straight off. As it turned out I played for 90 minutes in the Olympic Stadium and we did ourselves proud. Steve Chettle equalised a goal from Jürgen Klinsmann but, ironically, sloppy defending cost us the game when Mehmet Scholl scored what turned out to be the winner just before the break.

We really fancied our chances in the return, as we needed to score only one goal and keep a clean sheet to go through to the semi-finals. We went into a game thinking we had to win and instead of defending as we had done in all our previous games, we went at them and were slaughtered 5–1 with Klinsmann scoring two more. We lost to the much better side and Bayern went on to crush Bordeaux 5–1 in the two-legged final.

We had our chances early on as we lobbed balls into the box where Jason Lee caused havoc with his head and elbows, the famous pineapple hairdo flailing everywhere. If we'd had Stan up there we might have gone all the way. We not only missed his goals but Bryan Roy was not the same player without him. From the time Stan left we began to slip. The average players who had been overachieving went back to being average and worse. Instead of playing to capacity, there were too many players performing below par. We finished halfway that season.

One Friday morning just before Christmas 1996, I took a telephone call from Alan Hill telling me Frank had resigned and the club wanted me to take over as player-manager. I felt sorry for Frank. The club were in the middle of a financial takeover, they were floating on the stock market and there was no money available for him to buy the players we needed. Various parties played tug-of-war, each of them making different promises. They even tried to drag me in, asking for my support but I wouldn't get involved in the party politics.

The players Frank had brought in didn't work. Kevin Campbell from Arsenal was riddled with injuries, Chris Bart-Williams did well to start with but faltered, and we hardly got a game out of the Italian Andrea Silenzi, a 6ft 3in Roman who was bought for ridiculous money from Torino and played one full league game. So Frank resigned and suddenly it was down to me.

To say it was a bolt out of the blue would be understating the situation. It was five days before Christmas and we were playing Arsenal the next day. We were bottom of the table and hadn't won a single league match since the opening-day victory against Coventry City. Hill hung on the telephone waiting for my answer but I told him that I couldn't get my head round it and that I would see him when I arrived at the ground in 15 minutes' time.

Liz was mucking out the horses.

'You're not going to believe this,' I said.

'Frank has just resigned and they have asked me to be manager.' She looked at me as though I was crackers.

I drove straight to the ground and went to see temporary chairman Irving Korn – Fred Reacher had stepped down by then – and I eventually agreed to take over until the end of January.

The players were clearly surprised at this dramatic turn of events, but I had little time to gauge their reaction. The first thing I did after training was to ask Alan Hill to ring Manchester City and sign Nigel Clough on loan. He was doing nothing at Maine Road and it not only meant a new face but it would also mean I had someone on my side.

It was a whirlwind of a day and when I finally arrived home I sat down to try to work out my best team to play against the league leaders the next afternoon. I felt I couldn't go with the same team. I needed to change things if only for change's sake. The team that Frank turned out most weeks was, I believed, our best team but it was simply not good enough. I had Nigel to bring in and I started from there. I made a positive change of tactics by picking three at the back and after trying at least 20 times I finally came up with a team that looked right.

I showed it to Liz and she sat there staring at it for a long while before saying, 'Why have you dropped Mark Crossley?' Of course, I hadn't. I snatched the paper back and realised to my embarrassment that I had picked a team without a goalkeeper. No wonder the team looked strong. I had five at the back, three in midfield and Bryan Roy behind the front two. It was a shambles. I had worked for an hour and a half to come up with a team which covered every eventuality except keeping out the goals.

The next day was difficult to say the least. All of my routine, my careful pre-match preparations, went completely out of the window. I went in early to talk to the coaches, tell them what team I had finally picked and then meet with the players. It looked ominous when Ian Wright opened the scoring for Arsenal in the 63rd minute. Then Wright fouled one of our defenders and was sent off and we took advantage to win 2–1 with two goals from Alfie Haaland. The winner came a minute from time.

The trouble with winning like that is that you have immediately set yourself standards and if I thought that the job was easy I was put right five days later when, on Boxing Day, Manchester United beat the same team and the same formation 4–0 at home. David Beckham and Nicky Butt scored in the first half and Ole Gunnar Solskjaer and Andy Cole in the second. It made me wonder whether I should have changed a winning team for the game. Should I have matched them up 4-4-2? Everything was going through my mind. Liam O'Kane said to me, 'Look at it this way. We have had Arsenal, the top of the League, and Manchester United, second in the League, in the space of five days. Would you have settled for two draws before we played? Of course you would. On that basis, we have one more point than we could have hoped for.' It was good logic and I slept a little better than I might have done.

After that we went to Leicester and Nigel scored the first goal before we slipped behind. But we showed our character and with a minute remaining Colin Cooper scored an equaliser. We followed this up with a trip to West Ham and won that one with a goal from Kevin Campbell.

It is amazing. As a player I could hardly remember one game to the next but I can remember every detail as a manager, right down to who scored the goals and when.

We had built a bit of confidence and that improved even more when we drew Ipswich at home in the third round of the FA Cup and beat them 3–0. Then we beat Chelsea 2–0 and I scored a goal. Bryan Roy scored two to sink Spurs. We also knocked Newcastle out of the Cup. In the middle of all this, I was made Manager of the Month for my first month in the job.

I had to make a decision about whether to stay on. I could have walked away then and everyone would have said I had been brilliant while I sat back and watched someone else get the team relegated. Despite our success, all we had done in this time was to re-establish contact with the other teams battling against relegation. But everything had gone right for us, including a couple of good draws in the Cup and an increase in confidence. I stayed on.

One of the problems I faced was that the chairman Mr Korn was on the telephone to me all the time telling me he had the bank manager on to him and he wanted to sell my players. I told him that if he wanted to sell goalkeeper Tommy Wright and Chris Bart-Williams to Frank Clark, now manager of Manchester City, to go ahead but without my consent and that when the fans asked me why I had sold them I would tell them that it was the chairman not me. I explained that if we sold anyone we would certainly be relegated. He backed off but told me we needed a quarter of a million pounds quickly. Naïvely, I thought that was his problem.

I had signed a new playing contract when I became manager and the club were in such dire straits at the time that they asked me to defer my signing-on fee for a few months until the takeover was complete. As manager I thought I ought to do what I could. So I allowed them to put it off until the spring. It didn't help and the pressure from the bank to sell players grew and grew until one day I went home and stunned Liz by telling her that I was thinking of lending the club some money, around quarter of a million pounds just to keep the bank off our backs and to keep the club solvent.

She thought I was crazy but rather than lose one or two of our better players I was tempted. In the end I decided that it could become too messy with new owners, especially if they decided that they wanted a new manager.

I walked into the chairman's office soon afterwards and he was filling in his lottery card.

'Tell me things aren't as bad as that, Irving,' I said. 'If they are, I hope you have a winner.' At least it raised a smile.

I didn't wave my new title in the faces of the players. I still changed in the same place. I'm not sure all the players liked it, nor did they particularly like having Nigel around because they thought he was my man and would tell me everything that was being said behind my back. But I didn't want to change, especially as initially I thought that I would be doing the job for just a month. Liz carried on sitting in her usual seat with the other players' wives. I didn't use the manager's office, before, during or after the game and tried to run my life as closely to normal as I could.

Joe Royle, then manager of Everton, left a message one day asking me to ring him back and when I called he wanted to buy Alfie Haaland. He knew the player was out of contract in the summer. Alfie had made it clear to me that he was waiting to see whether we were going down. Joe offered me £200,000, pointing out that Haaland would go for nothing at the end of the season. I laughed.

'Joe, to be honest with you,' I said. 'I don't care what you're offering. It ain't my money and I need Haaland or we will definitely go down.'

It was a pity that we didn't have a bit more umph. After beating Spurs 2–0 we didn't score two goals in any other league game for the remainder of the season.

I missed the Cup defeat at Chesterfield through injury but told the players that although they were two divisions below us they would turn us over if we didn't have the right attitude. We didn't and they did! It was a shame because had we won we would have drawn Wrexham at home in the next round and then Middlesbrough, who weren't playing at all well, in the semi-finals. We had the luck of the draw but simply didn't have the players to do anything with it.

It was difficult but I enjoyed the experience. I had always enjoyed the responsibility of being captain and this was an extension of it. Of course, it was hard work and time-consuming. Half the time I walked round like a zombie thinking of teams and training. I was able to take the training as I wanted it done; not jolly up training but stuff that was enjoyable *and* meaningful. I needed to get the enjoyment back into the club because everyone was so down. The morale needed lifting more than anything else.

In March the club was floated and Irving Scholar came in as chairman of the new consortium who were running things. I went in to meet the former Spurs man on the back of a run of poor results. We had lost a couple to Coventry and Everton, drawn with Aston Villa and beaten Spurs. That was to be our last win of the season. We had also gone out of the Cup at Chesterfield.

The first thing Scholar asked me after I had explained that I had promised to stay on as manager until the end of the season was whether I would like someone in to help me. Playing was still the most important thing to me so I saw that as a good idea.

'What about someone like . . . someone like . . . someone like Dave Bassett? Do you think you could get on with Dave Bassett?'

I asked him why he had mentioned Dave Bassett in particular and when he said Dave could be interested, I sat back and laughed.

'You've obviously spoken to Dave already,' I said.

He admitted it and clearly Bassett was primed to come

but Scholar hadn't wanted to walk in, kick me out of the job and appoint a new manager. It was much better for him to have me on board rather than have the supporters on his back but I would have appreciated him being a little more honest.

It was difficult for Dave. He was a seasoned manager and had his own ideas. In hindsight, perhaps I should have said there and then that I would stand down and perhaps the arrival of a new man would have given the players a second wind. If I had thought that Dave could have kept us up, I would have handed over to him like a shot. As much as I enjoyed it, it wasn't an ego trip on my part. Dave ended up coming in and trying not to tread on my toes. He said he didn't want to interfere and that he was there if I needed any help.

He sensibly sat back and if, as happened, the results went badly he wouldn't be the one to shoulder the responsibility. He made sure that when he went into press conferences everyone knew who had picked the team, especially when we lost! He liked coaching and I quite often used to pass over a session to him because I could see he was kicking his heels and wanted to get his teeth into organising set-pieces and the other things that he is good at.

The disappointment at the end of the season was not so much that I had failed in my first effort as a manager but that the club I loved had once again been relegated.

One of the legacies Irving Scholar and I left Forest was a certain Dutch striker, Pierre van Hooijdonk. We were in desperate need of a striker and we drew up a short list with Irving throwing the Dutchman into the equation. He was a lot like Stan Collymore and the club had a couple of good years out of him, helping them out of the First Division. We probably got more out of Stan, who was a better player, but the club couldn't legislate for a player going on strike to demand a move. Pierre helped and we took some decent points in a succession of drawn matches but in our position it was not sufficient to save us. We had left ourselves far too much to do.

When we were relegated I received a call from Dave telling me that West Ham United were interested. The very fact that he felt he needed to pass on this information sowed the seeds. I decided that I was going to leave in the summer. My agent Kevin Mason and I saw Irving Scholar in his London office and told him that I thought it was time to move on. He wasn't impressed. He sat and listened as I explained my reasons.

I had three years left on my contract and I told him that at 35 and with what I had done for the club over 12 years, I would like to go on a free transfer and pick up the signing-on fee I was due in 13 days' time. He agreed to let me go for nothing but refused my other request. I thought that was ridiculous; I could sit on my backside for 13 days, collect my money and then go. I decided not to go down that route, as the obvious retaliation would be for them to try to get the money back via a transfer fee.

There had been rumours around Nottingham that I was being hounded out of the club and, as part of any deal, Irving wanted me to write a piece for the local paper denying it. It wasn't true but I had not bothered to dispel the rumours before by denying them. By the time I left his office he had agreed to a free transfer but not my signing-on fee. When he telephoned me and asked about writing the article to get him and Dave Bassett off the hook, I answered that I would do it if they reinstated my signing-on fee! I thought it was comical but he didn't seem to see the joke. Seriously then, I told him that we all knew the truth and that they should survive on their own merits.

I have never worried about what's written about me in the papers. Providing I'm doing the right thing and can look in the mirror in a morning, I am happy with my life. My philosophy has always been take me for what I am; what you see is what you get.

I certainly had nothing against Dave Bassett and I would say to any First Division club that if they want someone to lift them out of that division they couldn't find anyone better. It is uncanny the way he gets teams up. He signs players at a certain level such as Neil Shipperley who are good First Division players, but, without being unkind to him, when he gets his teams up he carries on buying the same type of player. He doesn't step up. I doubt if he has ever had a world-class player playing for him. He knows the lower leagues like the back of his hand. He has good set-pieces and is well organised.

To prove my point, Dave got the team straight up again. If the board knew we were going down and they brought him in to bring us straight back up, it was a brilliant piece of business.

There was no animosity between the three of us. It was just the right time for me to go, but it was a sad day when I left the City Ground. We lived 15 minutes away and it had been a big part of our lives. I did it the right way. I hadn't gone looking for a club first before asking for a

out of toon

I had been tempted to leave Forest in 1995 when my agent Kevin Mason came to me with an unexpected offer from Japan. The club was in the city of Kobi, scene not so long ago of a devastating earthquake. They wanted me to play for them in the newly formed professional J-League that was booming at the time.

With my love of travelling and the fact that I was unable to force my way into Terry Venables' England team, I gave it some serious consideration. They were offering a million US dollars a season, more than I was receiving in England. I chatted to some of the officials from Kobi and went to see Frank Clark with Kevin. He was none too pleased about me wanting to go, especially as I wanted a free transfer to make the deal worthwhile financially. The Japanese had made it clear that if they had to pay £400,000, they would take that out of the package they were offering. Frank was quite firm. He didn't want me to go and he especially didn't want me to go for nothing.

It was a good opportunity and something that appealed to me, but I was not sure that Liz would be happy living that far away from her family. I liked the idea of going somewhere totally different from everything I had been used to, a different culture and a different way of life. In the end it wasn't a workable situation. I certainly didn't hold it against Frank. I probably got on as well with him as any of the dozen or so managers I have worked for.

When the time came to move on from Forest, I talked to West Ham United as well as Newcastle. Dave Bassett had already told me of their interest. Harry Redknapp was keen, saying he couldn't see anyone coming down the wing with Julian Dicks and me there. I was honest with him and told him about Newcastle. They had been one step away from the championship and they were going to be playing in the European Champions League. I suspected where I would be going.

I told Newcastle that I wanted the same three-year contract and the same money I was earning at Forest. We finished up by agreeing a two-year contract with a year's option. This meant that if they wanted to keep me for a third year, I would stay at an agreed fee, and if they wanted to get rid of me they had to pay a set fee for me to go. It safeguarded my last year. It was a decent deal for both of us, considering they had signed me for nothing.

I had been used to playing for family clubs, Coventry and Forest, and walking into St James' Park was a different feeling altogether. This was big, big business. Kevin, Liz and I walked up to the offices and waited in a reception area before being shown into a private room. Kevin acted as the go-between, going into the office to talk to the secretary, coming back out to talk to me, going back in and so on. It was all very impersonal. In the past I had always gone into the manager's office and talked it out for myself.

Newcastle arguably have the best supporters in the

world. Outside the doors of the ground everyone knows you; inside it was like being in a big city office. No one appears to know you at all.

Having agreed a deal with Newcastle, I didn't want to waste Harry Redknapp's time. We pulled into the first services on the A1 and telephoned him straightaway. He was brilliant and wished me all the luck even though I hadn't given him a chance by going to West Ham to talk to him. But he could have thrown twice the financial package at me and I would still have gone to Newcastle just for the chance to play in the Champions League.

I talked very little to Kenny Dalglish before I signed. Newcastle were playing a friendly in Birmingham and stayed overnight on a Friday. Kevin and I went to their hotel to see Kenny and Terry McDermott. We gossiped and laughed and the only time we talked about football was when Kenny said to me, 'I don't need to tell you how to play football.'

My first game for Newcastle was at home to Sheffield Wednesday and I was amazed. It was a full house, as it always is these days. The ball was on the centre spot and the noise built to a crescendo as kick-off approached. I have played at Wembley and for England in some pretty big stadiums but this was a bit special. It was very uplifting. We were kicking off a new season on the back of finishing second in the League and as I waited for the start I thought to myself how much I was going to enjoy it.

I have played with and against John 'Digger' Barnes over many years. When he was at Liverpool he was one of the best players in the country. But when he, Ian Rush and I went to Newcastle almost together, I felt that I went as a professional to further my career while they went to finish theirs. Ian was given a one-year contract, Digger two and myself three. Neither of them were automatic choices and while John was surprised, I wasn't. The two of them had won everything and had lost some of their edge – and Digger was also looking a little plump around the edges – but I hadn't and this was the biggest club I had ever been to. I still had something to prove and was a regular, apart from injury, in that first season. The difference I suspect lay in the motivation and I was possibly more motivated than either of them; that is probably why I carried on for so much longer in the Premier Division.

Ian played half a dozen times in his year and John wasn't in the team at all when Gullit arrived. He had played up front when Alan Shearer was injured, filled in in midfield and did whatever he was asked, starting in 22 games for his old team-mate Kenny.

If Kenny had stayed, I suspect that I would have been around a lot more in that second season while I doubt whether John would have been. He is a great fellow to have around and I like him immensely. You can talk with him about any subject in the world and he will always have something to say. Whereas some footballers can be blinkered, he has an opinion on anything and everything. I just liked being in his company. I would have loved to have played with him ten years earlier. He was probably the Gascoigne of the eighties. I used to tease Digger that he was the only upper-class Jamaican I ever knew, born with a silver spoon in his mouth. I always liked holding that against him – in fun, of course!

I loved the playing side, the fans and everything about the club except the plc, which was cold and businesslike. It was something I had never come across before but now pretty well every club in the Premier Division is that way.

We started off quite well. We won the first two games against Sheffield Wednesday and Aston Villa, both at home. I was pleased with my form but then in my first European game, away to Croatia Zagreb, I turned and chased someone and my hamstring went. After eight days it felt fine and I was sprinting but on the eve of a match against Wimbledon it went again and kept on going and I was out of action until the end of November.

I had a lump the size of a golfball on my hamstring. It confounded everybody. I had scans and all sorts but no one knew what it was. At the end of three months I was whipping balls over when I felt a twinge again. This time I had a cortisone injection, something I was loath to have but that seemed to clear it up. Even now, the one leg is different from the other. When I showed the physio at Nottingham he had seen nothing like it. It seems as though there is a piece missing.

We qualified for the Champions League proper and I missed out on the opening game against Barcelona at St James' Park. It was an incredible evening with Tino Asprilla scoring a hat-trick and putting on a performance as good as I have ever seen. You can see in their faces when defenders are frightened of a forward and he was running them scared, and this was Barcelona, one of the biggest clubs in Europe.

I also missed PSV Eindhoven home and away. I managed to get myself fit eventually and played in the away game against Barcelona at the Nou Camp, coming on for Darren Peacock after 35 minutes. By then we were already out of it, unable to qualify. The last game was against Dynamo Kiev, the winners of the group, and I scored in our 2–0 victory. This is what I had joined Newcastle for but, for me, it was over before I had started. It was a big disappointment that we didn't qualify.

To balance that we reached the Cup final, which was only the second time that had happened in my career. The draw was kind to us with an ordinary Everton side in the third round, then non-league Stevenage, Tranmere Rovers, Barnsley and, in the semi-final, Sheffield United, all from lower divisions, before we faced Arsenal in the final. It gave us every chance, avoiding the big hitters on the way. You need that help. Newcastle were down the wrong end of the League in the second half of the season, hovering around 15th or 16th place. We had some big, important games and the Cup run was something of a relief.

Unfortunately, on the big day at Wembley we didn't play well and got what we deserved from the Gunners in a 2–0 defeat. Up in the commentary box, Ruud Gullit slaughtered us and talked at length about Alan Shearer looking unhappy and not playing well. What an irony that Newcastle were back a year later under Gullit with Alan Shearer looking even less happy than he had a year before. Gullit was asked what he would do if he was Newcastle manager and went on about how Shearer needed the right sort of service!

We didn't deserve to win the Cup that year. The only decent team we played beat us and we could just as easily have drawn Arsenal in the third round.

I was taken off with about 20 minutes to go and replaced by forward Andreas Andersson as we chased the game. It

No fear: a diving header between the flying feet of two Peterborough United defenders as I score the goal which clinched our promotion back to the elite in 1994. (*TBF*)

Thanks a million: an emotional moment at my testimonial as the crowd show their appreciation along with the two teams. My eldest brother Ray is the referee. (*Empics*)

One of the best: this story may have had an unhappy ending but Pierre van Hooijdonk was one of Forest's best signings as far as I was concerned. (*Empics*)

Another good week: the joys of being a manager – not fit and unable to play I express my emotions in the dugout. (*Alex Livesey/Allsport*)

Gone but not forgotten: although I had left for Newcastle United I was still remembered at Forest as the boys retire my No. 3 shirt to the 'Hall of Fame'.

Happy days: Rob Lee helps me celebrate my goal against Dynamo Kiev in the Champions League. Neither of us were quite so happy six months later.

One in the eye: Arsenal's Christopher Wreh catches me with a leading arm, cutting my eye on a day when little went right for me or Newcastle. (*Colorsport*)

The invisible man: never one who liked to be seen at the bar, I was heavily disguised for this Newcastle United Christmas party.

In action for West Ham in February 2000 following my first broken leg. After my return to the England side earlier in the season, I still hoped I could make it to Euro 2000. (*Empics*)

Not again: I break my leg for a second time during the 1999–2000 season soon after my comeback from the same injury. (*Solo Syndication*)

For the first time: I win the header against Müller to set up the goal for Lineker to mark my international debut against Brazil at Wembley in May 1987. (*Bob Thomas*)

Team-mates: the Nottingham Forest quartet of Steve Hodge, Neil Webb, myself and Des Walker, who were regulars in the England squad but played together just the once, against Denmark in September 1988. (*Bob Thomas*)

That penalty in t
semi-final

Placing the ball on the edge of the spot nearest to the keeper.

Keep your eye on the ball.

The ball flies straight and true...

...but Illgner gets his legs in the way.

If the walk to the penalty spot had been long and nerve–wracking, the walk back was a nightmare.
(all *Popperfoto*)

Peter Beardsley tries to console me.
(*Colorsport*)

Forgiven: thousands turn out at Luton airport and on the route to our hotel to welcome us home after our penalty shoot-out defeat by West Germany in Italia 90.

Captaining my country: leading out England for the first time at Wembley against France in 1992. To my right is Basile Boli with whom I had a coming together a few weeks later in the European Championships. (*Empics*)

had slipped away from us with goals from Marc Overmars and Nicolas Anelka. We changed our system to suit Arsenal and instead of playing with a back three we played a flat back four because the manager was so worried about Overmars' pace and skill.

All in all it was a disappointing season and we had greater hopes for the next one under Kenny. But that might have all become an irrelevance and I might never have played another game for Kenny, Ruud or anyone else after a brush with death.

The team had gone off on a pre-season tour to Ireland and I had stayed at home with a niggling little injury, not enough to worry about but something not to risk unnecessarily before the season started. I was about three miles away from home on my way to visit my accountant. It was a winding road and I suddenly saw a massive garbage truck coming towards me, completely out of control. It was just far enough away to give me time to decide whether to pull over or carry on and try to swerve past it. I stopped but by this time the wagon had toppled over and started rolling, straight towards me. There was a little bit of verge on either side and I could have tried to dive out, or reversed. If I had climbed out I would have been a dead man. Time appeared to stand still; it was a slow-motion replay to beat all slow-motion replays as sparks began to fly, adding to my anxiety as I thought that it had caught fire. I thought, 'I'm going to take one here,' and decided in that instant to lie down flat in the hope that it would roll over the car. Naïve, to say the least, but what do you do when a thing of that size is bearing down on you like a fire-breathing demon from hell? Perhaps I had been watching too many James Bond movies.

Thank God there was no one in the car, particularly Liz who was five months pregnant at the time. I lay down across the passenger seat under the dashboard level and just crossed my fingers that the hit I was about to take would not be a fatal one. Then there was an almighty bang as the truck hit the car. I opened my eyes and looked up to see huge rear wheels on either side of me. The truck's drive shaft had come through my sun roof. Had I been sitting up in the driver's seat, or even leaning to one side, the drive shaft would have killed me.

As luck would have it, the strongest part of the car, the suspension, took one set of wheels and the engine the other. The truck had come down wheels first on top of the car. If it had landed side down, roof down or almost any other way, it would have crushed the car and me. As I was lying across the seats I felt a weight on my back and for a moment I was frightened that I was holding up the entire dustcart. I reasoned in the moment of panic that if I moved it would come down on me. Then I thought I saw flames and all I could think of then was getting out.

The driver, unhurt apart from some nicks caused by broken glass, had come round to the car window, convinced that he was going to find a dead body. The only place untouched was the passenger side; lying down had saved my life. He was pretty shaken himself having been thrown around as though he was inside a tumble dryer.

Having survived the crash, I wasn't going to burn to death and I shouted at him, 'Get me out of here, you fucking idiot.'

I didn't want to open the door in case it was load bearing. The window was slightly open and while I pushed, he pulled until the glass shattered. I scrambled out, ripping my jeans and sustaining a small cut – the only injury I suffered in the entire episode. I went for the driver, thinking he had been reckless, but fortunately calmed down as he apologised before I did him any permanent damage.

In the meantime, another car had pulled up without me noticing and when I saw this other man I went for him as well thinking he had been in the cab. He backed off, saying, 'No, no, I've just pulled up.' I was definitely suffering from a case of road rage.

The police were there very quickly and things had fortunately settled down a bit. I jumped out in front of the police car and told the officer to keep onlookers away from the vehicle in case it went up in flames.

Then I telephoned Liz. In her delicate state I could hardly tell her that a lorry had landed on my roof, so I just said I had suffered a minor bump in the car.

I was taken to hospital in an ambulance as a precaution because I had a stiff neck and felt that I needed a general check-up in case there was anything else wrong, especially if there was a claim to be made. When I returned home having been given the all clear there was a reporter in my driveway and that, with Liz inside the house and pregnant, was like a red rag to a bull. They had given me a neck brace as a precaution, and that excited the man from the *Sun*, although he was probably disappointed that it was not a bit more serious and newsworthy.

The local policeman came round and told Liz that I might suffer nightmares for a while because it had been such a narrow escape, but I was fine. I even took off my underpants and said to Liz, 'Look, nearly killed and no skidders.'

That night I slept like a log while Liz lay awake tossing and turning, thinking how close she had been to becoming a widow with an unborn child.

When I looked at the pictures I also realised just how close I had been to death. Certainly had I sat where I was and covered my head with my hands, the normal reaction, I would not be here now. The cart had gouged a foot-deep hole in the ground just before it had reached me, causing it to leap in the air and come down on top of my motor. It was all a matter of inches where the wheels had landed.

The driver, apparently, had a full load on, hit the curb and started snaking before tipping over and starting to roll. He lost it and so might I have done. I must have been unhinged to think that by lying down the massive truck would have just taken the roof off my car.

My time clearly hadn't come and, for once, I was glad to be the nearly man. But I didn't really think much about it afterwards. I'd had a crash and survived. I suppose I am a bit unemotional about things. I filled in an insurance form and it asked what had happened. I just wrote that I had pulled up to a halt and a garbage truck landed on my roof. There were other silly questions and I thought I should just send a picture and let them see the damage for themselves.

Up until then I had been pretty lucky with all the driving I do. The nearest I had ever come to an accident before that was when we parked in a public car park. On our return from a bit of shopping, I noticed this car with the rear bumper pulled so far out it looked like a rhino horn. I was really sympathetic until I discovered it was my car.

Kenny Dalglish rang me having seen the pictures of the wreck and expressed his wonderment that I had escaped. I went to work in Newcastle the next day, travelling by train, and I sat looking at all the other passengers reading their newspapers with me and my wreck on the front page. Rover were delighted because the car was so strong that it saved my life.

We started off the season by drawing with newly promoted Charlton 0–0 at St James' Park. It wasn't good because they had a man sent off well before half-time and still managed to hold us. Then we had a decent result with a 1–1 draw at Chelsea and suddenly Kenny Dalglish had gone.

Sacked? Resigned? We were only the players and we didn't know. Two games into the season! It was staggering. For that to occur at that time of the season simply made no sense. I don't think he was sacked. He intimated that he wasn't getting the response he wanted from the players and the chairman went off at a tangent and began to look for another manager.

Everyone liked Kenny. He is a great man and good to have around. He has achieved just about everything in football both as a player and a manager, winning the double as player-manager of Liverpool and then taking Blackburn Rovers to the title. But he wouldn't figure on the list of all-time great coaches.

Before we played Arsenal at Wembley there was some concern among the players that we needed to work on one or two bits and pieces, especially our teamwork. There was a lack of depth in this department. You can't just throw 11 players on to the pitch and hope they gel. At Liverpool in Kenny's time there they *were* able to do that because they were all good enough to win most games in which they played. At Blackburn Rovers, Kenny had the good fortune, or good sense, to have Ray Harford alongside him, and Ray took the training, did the coaching and was a good organiser. Blackburn played well within the system they adopted. That was where we struggled. Kenny didn't want to go down that road. At Newcastle, he would have done well in the general manager's role with a good coach to do the other work. But Kenny enjoyed the training and joining in the five-a-sides and was very well liked by the players. If he did ask one of the coaches to organise something, Terry McDermott would be there messing about with Alan Shearer and Dave Batty and undermining what the coach was trying to put on. It was a good, happy camp but at the end of the day we had to get the results.

Even so, Kenny had not been there for very long and it was a bit of a sudden divorce. I didn't realise that it was going to affect me more than Kenny in the long term.

Ruud Gullit arrived and there was no hint of what was to come. He had us all in the office, Alan Shearer, the rest of the senior players, me and others, telling us that we must stick together and that if there was a problem to tell him and generally saying what he thought were the right things. It all sounded very good and matey but personally I wasn't brought up to run to the manager with every little problem. I wouldn't dream of walking into my manager's office and saying we should play this or that formation. I did it once with Brian Clough and had my fingers severely burnt. But I did appreciate it was the way the Dutch players did things, as we have seen over the years – they all have an opinion!

I played the first handful of games under Gullit and we had some encouraging results, beating Southampton 4–0, Coventry City 5–1 and Nottingham Forest 2–0. In fact, I played in his first 11 games. But it was a false dawn. I was to play in only one more league game during the rest of my time at Newcastle United. It was a most frustrating twilight zone of my career.

The catalyst to my future problems came in the game against West Ham United at home on 31 October when I was sent off. The ball was up in the air, I arrived a little late and caught Trevor Sinclair with my elbow. I expected to be booked but Jeff Winter sent me straight off and we went on to lose that game 3–0.

Winter had given a few bad decisions against us in the first half when we were drawing 0–0 and Shearer gave him a hard time coming out of the tunnel for the second half. I was walking alongside the pair of them when Winter turned to me and said, 'That's not fair, is it Stuart?' I just looked at him and blanked him. Three minutes later I'm walking back down the tunnel the other way having been shown the red card. I don't know whether he had the hump with me or not but I hadn't been booked before. It wasn't a deliberate elbow; Sinclair went down but didn't make a meal of it. I was left to wonder what might have happened if I had told him what a good, fair referee I thought he was and supported him against Shearer's tirade. I had disagreed with some of his decisions in the first half but it was Shearer having a go at him, not me.

Gullit called me into his office the night before we were due to play Manchester United and told me that, as I was going to be missing a few games because of suspension, he was going to leave me out of the game at Old Trafford and play Andy Griffin. I told him that was fine, that he was the manager and it was his decision. I went back to my hotel, rang Liz and told her what had happened and that I doubted whether I would play many more games for this manager. Being sent off was exactly the excuse he needed to drop me and I wondered how much longer I would have lasted had I not been sent off. If he thought that I was too old or not good enough, why didn't he put me out of the side straight away?

Andy Griffin played well at Old Trafford in a goalless draw and had one more game before he, too, was left out and another youngster, Aaron Hughes, was brought in only to be replaced by Frenchman Didier Domi from Paris St Germain. In the space of a couple of weeks, I was suddenly a long way down the pecking order. My prophecy to Liz was proving to be accurate. I was training, being picked in the squad and then nothing. I would be named as one of the substitutes on the bench if there was a coachload of injuries but I would never come on.

I played in just the one game, against Liverpool at Anfield, and that was me finished with my first-team career at Newcastle. It was a strange feeling to be discarded so quickly and dramatically.

The older players could not understand what was going on, so much so that one day Alan Shearer came up to me and said, 'What's the matter? Have you been going to bed with his missus or something?' He asked me what we had said to each other and I told him, adding that I assumed the manager had left me out because he didn't think that I was good enough.

It was not going to make a scrap of difference if I went crashing into his office. He was hardly going to say, 'Oh, yes, I forgot you were around. What a good player you are,' and put me back in the team. That sort of thing doesn't happen and all I could do was keep fit, keep my nose clean and be ready if he changed his mind and decided he wanted me.

It was such a ridiculous situation. But I was careful to fulfil my part of the contract – I was always there and always available even though I was basically being ignored. I would wait until the team and the substitutes were posted and if I was not included I would sometimes drive home to Nottingham.

For one game Gullit had so many injuries that he had to pick me on the bench. For once, I went out for a warm-up, joining the lads who were already out there. The fans quickly spotted me and began to cheer and shout. I responded by running round giving them the big salute and causing great hilarity among the other players. I went out at half-time and helped work the reserve goalkeeper and then, with a minute or two to play, one of our defenders went down with an injury. We had already used the one other defender on the bench and Steve Clarke, our coach, told me to strip off in case I had to go on. I was so far removed from my normal, dedicated professional approach that a wicked thought crossed my mind. I wondered to myself what would happen if I took Steve at his word and did not stop at my tracksuit but carried right on until I was standing there in my underpants. The timing was right – by the time I'd completed my strip the whistle would have gone and I could have gone down the tunnel and straight into the bath.

It was almost irresistible but fortunately good sense prevailed. Had it been a few years earlier I might well have done it.

It came to a head at Derby at the Pride Park Ground on 3 April when we had Steve Howey injured along with I don't know how many other centre-halves. I felt this time I had to be given a game because no matter how much he shuffled the pack he was still going to be short in my area. There was simply no recognised centre-half. We had the team meeting on the afternoon of the game. He flicked over the teamsheet and not only was I not in the team, I was not even on the bench although Steve Caldwell, a 17-year-old who had never trained with the first team, was. Gullit had shuffled the pack so much that I had once again slipped out of the bottom without a word said to me.

It was the last straw. I knew that if he didn't want me then, he never would. As we were still living at Nottingham, I had someone drive my car down to Derby behind the team bus. When we arrived at Pride Park I walked down the coach, got off, got in my car, drove down the M1 and then the M40 and arrived at Aylesbury in time to watch our horse Archie run in the 3.30 race at a point-to-point meeting. Liz, of course, didn't know I was going but there I was, the best-dressed man on the course in tie and blazer. Everyone else was in sweaters, green wellington boots and hacking jackets. I confided in her that this time he was taking the mickey out of me and although I was acting unprofessionally, I felt that I couldn't do anymore if someone was prepared to go that far out of his way to exclude me.

In the midst of my problems at Newcastle, I received an

unexpected call from Nottingham Forest coach Liam O'Kane. By this time Ron Atkinson had taken over from Dave Bassett and the club were again in dire straits. I knew what was going on from the local radio and television news and the local paper. My name had been mentioned here and there because I was out of favour with Gullit.

Liam asked me whether I would be interested in going back to the City Ground as a player. I told him of course I would be interested; I needed to play football at my age and not sit around. But there was no follow-up and I heard nothing more until I bumped into Big Ron at the Central Television studios in Nottingham along with Terry Venables. Ron said that he had wanted to bring me in but had found resistance at board level. I can only assume that Irving Scholar did not want me back. It was not surprising if this was the case. I would probably have done the same thing in his place.

On another occasion Alan Shearer had a quiet word with me, saying that a Midlands journalist friend of his wanted my telephone number for Ron because he was interested in chatting with me. That was a laugh because everyone at Forest from the laundry lady to the tea lady had my number and if Ron had looked it was probably on the noticeboard. I certainly did not need to pass it to him through a third party. It wasn't rocket science; if a club wanted me it would have been easy to go through the front door. I was out of the Newcastle team, they would almost certainly have got me on a free transfer and with my record I would have given my all to the Forest cause.

Some days were worse than others at Newcastle. I tried hard to be the complete professional I had always been, but

I have to admit that when Ruud Gullit joined in the training matches I would go out of my way to lump him. The one time I did catch him, he went clean over my back. He was quite good about it – got up and played on. The lads found it amusing and Rob Lee, who was on Ruud's side, offered to leave his pass short to give me another crack at him.

There were times I would go in for training and think to myself what was the point. Gullit had made it plain that I was never going to play for him again and it seemed he was just trying to grind me down. Then there were other days when I went in with a big smile on my face and just enjoyed my training, happy to do what I did best and to be in the fresh air. That was my problem – I did enjoy training and playing football and still do. It hurt not to be playing.

The boys got to the Cup final that year beating Crystal Palace, Bradford City, Blackburn Rovers, Everton and Spurs without me being involved at all. Despite the success in reaching Wembley for a second time, the discord was growing in the dressing-room. A couple of the players had new boots on because of sponsorship deals. Ruud came across in his new adidas boots trying to tell them in his roundabout way not to get carried away with the commercial aspect of the Cup final. He told them how it was when he was with AC Milan and added that nobody won anything wearing flashy coloured boots.

'Apart from Martin Keown,' I chipped in, 'who won the double with Arsenal last year with those red boots of his.'

He said nothing, just walked off. It couldn't hurt our relationship anymore than it had already been damaged and he certainly wasn't going to pick me to play against Manchester United at Wembley. It gave the lads a good laugh because there were more than just me finding the former great Dutch player difficult to understand and get on with.

By the end of the season, we had not discussed the impasse. He seemed content to let me tick along because I wasn't being too disruptive or breaking his door down. I could go with the first team, play in the reserves or not play in the reserves. He left it to me. If his strategy was to try to grind me down, it was working. I felt that I couldn't sit there any longer. I wanted to do something. There was Liz at home with our new baby daughter Chelsea and I was staying in a rented apartment on my own – for what? My professional life had no end product.

But I had served my two years and the option in my contract now came into play. If they wanted to release me they had to pay me up, and if they didn't want to do that, they had to offer me a new contract for the year. I hadn't talked to Ruud about my contract at all but now it was decision time. I needed to know. I hadn't played for the club, apart from one game in December, for seven months. Surely there was no way they still wanted to keep me.

In the week leading up to the Cup final I telephoned the club secretary, Russell Cushing, to ask him what was happening. He told me that there was a board meeting in two weeks' time and he would tell me after that, adding it was nothing to do with him.

I waited. Nothing happened. I waited until the end of May and then telephoned the PFA and explained my position. Gordon Taylor agreed that he couldn't see them offering me a new contract and thought, like I did, that they would pay up as they were legally bound to do and send me on my way. Gordon offered to ring the club and when he came back to me he told me that they had to let me know two weeks after the season ended. But, he said, they had already written to me and sent the letter to my house. I didn't know what he was talking about. What letter? I had seen no letter. It turned out that they had sent the letter to my rented accommodation rather than to my Nottingham home where I had informed them I would be. The letter was telling me, incredibly, that they were offering me another year's contract.

They had made the decision to offer me a slightly higher salary, as they had to by regulations, but clearly more in the hope that I would tell them to stick it. I am nothing if not obstinate and having stuck it out for seven months, I was prepared to wait a bit longer. If they wanted to play cat and mouse, I was game.

I went back for the pre-season at the end of June and finally went to see Ruud. I asked him outright, 'Am I being released or are you giving me a new contract?' He shrugged his shoulders, refused to take responsibility and said that it was a matter for the board. I asked him point blank if he wanted me at the club and he replied that as far as he was concerned he didn't want me at the club. That was fine. It was what I wanted to hear. With that in my armoury, I requested a meeting with the chairman, Freddy Shepherd.

They messed around and the day they arranged to meet me they didn't turn up and didn't bother to tell me. A new date was arranged and this time when they failed to honour it I was told that Shepherd, chief executive Freddie Fletcher and the secretary Russell Cushing were out of the country. When they returned, I stormed in and demanded to know what was going on. I told them that the manager had told me that he didn't want me at the club, so would it be all right with them if I stayed at home in Nottingham and they just sent me my wages.

They laughed and said it could not be done. I had just wanted to make my point. To press it home, I told them that I was the only player in the Premiership who was a non-playing player, the only player in the Premiership this season or any other season who couldn't at any time represent their club. Gullit would never ever play me. I told them, 'Ethically and morally, the decision you have come to by giving me another contract is a pile of shit! You know that as well as I do.'

Shepherd denied it, saying that I was the sort of player they wanted around to bring on the youngsters in the reserves.

'Behave yourself,' I said. 'You know as well as I do that what you want is for me to tell you to stick your contract, walk out and find another club.' They now knew how I saw it so I went on to offer them an alternative.

'Rather than me staying another year, can we sit down here now and organise a payment that is acceptable to both of us if I can find another club, because if I sit here for another twelve months it is going to cost you a lot more than half a million quid.'

If I had followed it through, away from my wife and child for another season, I would have gone off my head but I wasn't going to tell them that.

We eventually agreed on a payment, a little more than half of what I would have been due. That agreed, I said, 'No offence, but I'm not leaving this office without having that in writing. I don't want to come back and tell you I have a club because you will try and get a fee for me.'

I assumed that Ruud had reassured them that I was too old and would never get another club and my agent Kevin Mason had told them that my best chance of continuing my career was with a foreign club. They must have been convinced that I was at the end of the road and they eventually gave me my written agreement.

I immediately got off my backside and telephoned Coventry City, Southampton, West Ham United and Watford and left a message for Aston Villa to which they never responded.

At Watford, my former England manager Graham Taylor hummed and haa-ed after I had spoken to coach Kenny Jackett but decided not to go with me. At Southampton, I talked to Stuart Gray who said they weren't particularly interested in signing me. Gordon Strachan was good at Coventry because he didn't waste my time. I talked to him directly and he got straight back after a couple of days and said what a pleasure it was not to deal with agents but he was sorry he couldn't take me on.

It wasn't looking at all promising and for a while it looked as though Gullit might have been right. I telephoned Liz from the Newcastle flat where I was still living and told her that I would decide on a cut-off date. If I hadn't found a club by then, I would pack it all in.

'I'm staying at Newcastle,' I told her. 'I can't leave and I'm not walking out for anything out of principle because of the way I've been treated. The cut-off date is 7 August.'

I had been sent a training schedule for a month's training in the close season. I did it to the letter, even though I hadn't played for eight months and there was no sign of playing again for another year. It made me feel surprisingly good.

Three weeks before the start of the season, a little castaway group of us who were never going to play while Ruud was there, went off with reserve-team coach Tommy Craig. There was Rob Lee, Nikos Dabizas, Alessandro Pistone, me and a couple of others. Tommy was as fed up as I was. His feeling was that Rob and I shouldn't be playing in the reserves at our ages because we were stopping young kids coming through. We did what we could for him. We'd been playing for him on and off during the previous season and we'd won the League.

Tommy was dreadfully unhappy at the pre-season situation. He would organise a training session for the kids and the pros who weren't in the team and then Ruud would come along and take the kids away to take part in a training match. He did this regularly leaving Tommy with six players, two over age, two foreign pros and a couple of youngsters. He would despair. We ended up doing a bit of training or a bit of head tennis and then we would go off for a walk in the park and Tommy would buy us an ice cream.

I had taken my foot off the gas for a couple of days and was genuinely contemplating my retirement from the game. I had no takers from the clubs I had talked to nor from Forest where I had dropped huge hints that I would be prepared to go back as a player and my deadline was fast approaching.

I thought to myself that if I had no takers by the start of the season I would go down to the Newcastle Youth

Academy for a couple of days a week to help progress my coaching. It would keep me out of Gullit's way and it would also allow me to come and go as I pleased, permitting me to spend a little time with my wife and baby. I went to see the academy coach Alan Irvine, told him of my situation and asked if I could come down and help him out with a bit of coaching. I cleared it with him before I asked the manager or the board. He was delighted for the help.

Tommy Craig was one of the people who kept me sane in those dark days. He really boosted my flagging confidence when he told me, 'I'd love to see you playing in the reserves but if you don't want to, don't. You are a credit to have around. At your age you are working harder than the kids and if I ever need an example to show them I point you out and tell them to look at Pearcey.'

Tommy lived in Newcastle while his family was in Glasgow so he understood my situation. He basically left it to me when I came and went.

I went in for a double training session with Tommy a week before the season started. He was again saddled with our little group and we cleared off to the park with all the mothers and the kids still on their summer holidays and stopped the ice cream van. That was in the place of the morning session and we decided that golf would be a better alternative to the afternoon work. Just as we were preparing for the round my mobile telephone started ringing. It was Kevin Mason to tell me that Harry Redknapp had been given the all clear from his board to sign me for West Ham United – a one-year contract, the same money. It had all been agreed.

To say I was stunned would be to underestimate this

dramatic development. Here we were, eight days from the start of the season and in my mind I was ready to get my head around coaching and wave my playing days goodbye. I telephoned Harry straightaway and it was all systems go. Then I called Liz to tell her that I was no longer a retired professional. Then I started to worry about having done no training for the past ten days. Needless to say my golf went to pot and I played my worst round of the year.

I telephoned Russell Cushing and asked him to telegraph the money to me that next week. I still was wary even though I had it in black and white. They possibly thought I was going to Raggedarse Rovers and when I told him to fax through my playing certificate to West Ham you could hear the astonishment down the end of the line. He sounded gutted that I had a Premier Division club, having to pay me to leave with the knowledge that I was still going to be in the same division to haunt them.

I was staying that night with the physiotherapist Derek Wright and by nine o'clock I was out lapping the local park. It was a crash course because Harry had told me the night before that I would be playing the following Saturday against Spurs in a London local derby.

It wasn't the easiest of times at Newcastle but I loved the football side of it. Even being out of the side I didn't moan or bellyache; I just got on with my job. I kept in some sort of trim by playing for the reserves, not always in the Pontins League, sometimes much lower. Occasionally I would decline to play and have a night back in Nottingham with Liz. I also used the time to study for my coaching badge but the entire situation was weird. I found myself older than the manager, the assistant manager, the coach, the club doctor and the physio. I don't suppose that has happened previously in the top division.

People thought that Ruud and I had had a bust-up but we hadn't. This game is subjective and he had his opinion. We never once rowed about it. Whether he was right or wrong, people will have to judge for themselves but after five games back at West Ham, Kevin Keegan, another Newcastle cast-off, called me up to play for England again.

I was totally committed to Newcastle United and when I first signed I went with the idea that we would move lock, stock and barrel to the north east. It is difficult for us because we can't just pick a house on an estate the way most people can. The horses come first. We need a place with land – more than a big garden, not as much as a massive farm. Finding the compromise between the two is difficult. We looked hard, even searching North Yorkshire. After a month, I moved out of the hotel I was staying in and found myself a nice apartment in Durham. We had a change of heart and decided to stay as we were. I was going home regularly and Liz would come up on a Friday for the home games. It wasn't ideal but it worked because Liz was so supportive.

I enjoyed Newcastle. When I was on my own, I would go to the theatre or try to drag one or two of the staff to see a concert. We even managed a trip to York to see the Stranglers. Theatre was a great night out, much better than knocking around pubs which I didn't really want. I managed to see some Shakespeare and one or two musicals. I would always check what time the curtain went up, arrive as the lights went down and leave while the cast were acknowledging their first encore. No hassle. I even persuaded John Beresford and Warren Barton to come to a couple of Royal Shakespeare Company plays.

Warren and his wife Candy were particularly helpful in showing Liz and me the town and having meals together. Warren had recently moved into a new house and he asked me if there was any chance of helping him fix a couple of lights. He gave me the keys and cleared off, leaving me to it. No wonder. Candy had laid out her chosen light fittings in every room in the house. It added up to more than a dozen. I was out of practice so it took me an exceptionally long time to work my way through them all and I was there all afternoon.

Normally I go into a room, make sure the switch is in the off position and work on it live. But there was one switch that had been taped over. I assumed that the decorators had done it so I untaped it. Immediately alarms went off everywhere. It was a panic button disguised as an ordinary light switch but no one told me. It was me who was in a panic. I telephoned Candy who told me to leave it and it would go off on its own.

That was all very well but the next thing I knew there was a policeman peering through the window, and then hammering on the back door. I went out, complete with my toolbelt round my waist, screwdriver in hand, and said, 'Sorry, mate. I'm the electrician and I've just pushed the panic alarm by mistake.' He couldn't work it out. He looked hard at me and did a double take. Recognition flickered in his eyes but he couldn't nail it down. Who was I? A well-known electrician? A burglar whose picture he had seen on file? He didn't know. He went off shaking his head, having reluctantly taken me at my word.

When Chelsea came along things changed. I'd get back to Nottingham as often as I could. The night before I was due back in Newcastle, we'd be in bed by ten. Liz would get up and do the midnight shift and go back to bed. I would do the four o'clock shift, jump in my car and drive to Durham. There was nothing on the roads at that time and I was back in bed in Durham in an hour and a half, setting my alarm clock ready for training at 11.

I loved the fans and they would always ask if I was playing. I would laugh it off, particularly the week before the Cup final when I told them, 'As he hasn't picked me for the last seven months, I don't suppose he would pick me for that one!' They were kind and sympathetic. But if anyone asked me if I had made the wrong move I would say no. I have to add, of course, that if I had been playing well Gullit would never have been able to leave me out of his side. Usually that's straightforward but on this occasion I feel that the dice were loaded against me. Clearly I was not good enough in his eyes. There was no way forward for me but there was no percentage in looking back. I have never regretted a single move I have made, Newcastle included.

Looking at Newcastle now under Bobby Robson, I know I would have been given a chance. The other three of the ice-cream four, Rob Lee, Nikos Dabizas and Alessandro Pistone have all played a big part in the remarkable revival that my former England manager achieved after starting with seven defeats and a draw.

It reminded me of the time when, after three months out in the cold, Rob was sent over to join us. I said to him, 'Don't tell me you've been left out now?'

'Don't be silly,' he said. 'I'm suspended on Saturday and that's why he's sent me over here.'

It wasn't long after that Rob was relegated to the has-beens. We were both hurt deeply but as I was 35 I could take it a little easier than Rob who was three or so years younger. He had been the club captain before the armband was taken off him and given to Alan Shearer. It was very sad when Rob said, 'To think that a couple of months ago I was in the England World Cup squad – look at me now!'

That's how quickly it changes in football. If you don't keep up your standards you can soon feel the effects but that was not the case where Rob and I were concerned. It was something altogether more personal. I believe that Gullit would have got rid of Shearer as well, if he could. They didn't like each other and he tried to push Shearer into asking for a move. When we played at Everton there was public and press talk of a split and a possible move. Ruud was clever. He couldn't say he wanted him out or just go ahead and sell him, so instead he said things like if Alan Shearer wants to leave it will be his decision. It's the classic way of nudging an unwanted player, pushing them towards the door, tempting them to come in and ask what's going on and have a row that can only end one way.

There was no love lost between Alan and Ruud Gullit, as there was no love lost between a number of players and the manager. It was hard to penetrate Ruud's cold exterior – in sharp contrast to his predecessor with whom the players had a good relationship. Alan was in a similar position to me only he was playing and I wasn't. He is a professional and as long as he is at the club he loves he will play to his best ability. Gullit didn't like him at all, but it was a two-way road. It was no surprise to me that when Gullit left the club, Shearer suddenly found all his old touch under Robson.

It wasn't just me and other players who disliked the man; it was physios and even the boot man, Ray Thompson. That's hardly surprising when the manager would walk into the boot room, toss his shoes at him and say, 'Here, shine these!' Ray does the boots and does them happily but when someone demands he clean normal shoes without a please or thank you, that seemed to me to be sheer arrogance. The same was true at Chelsea from where he was moved on when his demands became too high. I am not sure that he is able to look at himself and see the faults, only the good points.

On the good side, he erected a noticeboard so you could see at a glance what you were doing for the next six weeks, when you were in and at what time. I like to think that I am professional in my outlook and I enjoy having things mapped out for me. I was able to look at the schedule and tell Liz when I would and wouldn't be able to come home.

I also thought he ran the club professionally from the diet to the training. I didn't think his training was bad. It might have been a little too hard, particularly for players who had played week in week out. We would do a running exercise on Monday and for someone like me who had done nothing over the weekend it was fine but for someone like Gary Speed who had worked his socks off for 90 minutes it was tough. He had to pound the ground alongside someone with fresh legs. I would have had Pearce running and Speed resting.

It was only when results were deteriorating that he became dogmatic. He couldn't cope with failure. Local boy Steve Howey ruptured his Achilles and was under treatment for months. Derek Wright and the other physios at the club worked with him day in and day out but one day they arrived to find Steve working out with someone else who was having him balance on a beam, something they thought he was still weeks away from. Derek was, understandably, amazed and confused, demanding to know who this stranger was and what did he think he was doing. It transpired that Ruud had brought in an expert from Holland without telling the physios. For them, that was a real kick below the belt. He did something similar with the club doctor over Duncan Ferguson, sending him to someone else. Assistant physio Paul Ferris was always looking over his shoulder because he thought Ruud wanted him out.

Training became practice match after practice match, particularly trying to sort out the defence. That was probably his biggest downfall because it didn't work. I sat and watched from my place in the stand or on the bench. As a defender, I was aware that we were being run ragged because he hadn't found himself a natural leader. He had the United Nations back there who weren't able to communicate with each other. He needed someone in there to start bullying them. That was me. I could have done that job for him and the club but I was never asked.

Sometimes I would go in early and talk to Steve Clarke, the coach Ruud brought from Chelsea. Steve hardly spoke at all but we did chat now and again, usually at my instigation. I would ask him how he thought a game had gone, just general chitchat. After we had been beaten at Wimbledon he opened up saying that they didn't do this or that and particularly that no one tackled. He said that the team needed someone to stoke them up and get in a few big tackles. I wondered for a minute whether he was taking the mick but he wasn't. The answer may have been sitting in front of him but perhaps he couldn't see it. I just said, 'There aren't many of those about, mate!'

The players had one eye on the Cup final for that game against Wimbledon and Gullit could have played me. I wouldn't have thrown a wobbly because I hadn't played for six months; I would have taken the opportunity to roll up my sleeves and show people that I could still play and make others play. My pride would have ensured that. Only I would have suffered by sulking.

Steve was not the buffer between the players and the manager that Terry McDermott had been for Kenny Dalglish and Kevin Keegan before him. Terry would be in with the players and then in with the manager, conveying what was troubling them and massaging any ego that needed massaging for players who were in and out of the team. Steve rarely said much more than good morning unless you pressed him. Ruud needed something more than that and so did the players.

That was something else I learned. Sometimes you are taught more by a difficult manager than a good manager. One thing, certainly on a personal level, is how to treat people when they are out of the side. Those who are being selected keep rolling along but I learned that you need to talk to players who are not selected and not ignore them. You never know when you might need them.

It was the lowest part of my career. I had gone to Newcastle as a professional footballer and finished up as a professional with the word footballer dropped. It was far worse than being relegated because then at least you are hands on. To sit there and never ply your trade is demoralising. Had they offered me a settlement in January when it became obvious that I was no longer part of the team, I would have quit amicably. But I am obdurate; it is a short career and there wasn't much left. I would certainly have stopped playing had West Ham not come in for me when they did.

The worst time of all was when I played badly for the reserves on a windswept Richmond Park. We looked for a wind machine in case one had been installed at one end of the ground – it was that bad. Imagine playing on a muddy pitch on the Monday after the rugby team had played on it at the weekend. We played Middlesbrough in what must have been the worst conditions for spectators to watch any game. The wind blew straight down the middle of the pitch, gusting so hard that the goalkeeper would put the ball down for a goalkick and then have to chase after it to give it a flying kick. There has never been a good game played in a gale and this wasn't a good game. To make it worse we were beaten by a last-minute goal. I can remember winning once on that ground, that's all, and our best results were away from home. It was so bad that we were mentally beaten before we kicked off.

I tried to do my best for Tommy Craig. He would go in the next day and report to Gullit, telling him who had played well. Gullit would respond, 'I saw your team last night – they were shit!' It was depressing for Tommy and I wanted to do well for him so that he could go into Gullit with his head held up. I could see in his eyes how much it hurt. Ruud would turn up occasionally and watch half a game and then get up and go for a pizza or whatever he did away from the ground. He said that he wasn't interested in the reserves or the youth policy and he wasn't. If anyone came through then fine but he wasn't going to bust a gut to look for the talent when he had the money to go and buy foreign players.

I sat in many a time when Tommy had a team meeting with the youngsters. It was soul destroying to listen to those kids saying that the manager didn't even know their names, that it didn't matter how well they played they were not going to be considered because they believed that the man who picked the first team didn't know who they were. What incentive is that for a 17-year-old? The youngsters thought that Gullit belittled Tom and them. I felt for them. I knew the situation Tom was in and knew that there was no way out until Gullit left the club.

I was desperate for Tommy to do well and, in the end, we won the League, mainly because we won the first dozen games and no one could catch us. There were old pros like John Barnes and myself in the team; John tried his best, too. There were others who didn't want to know at all. George Georgiadis, a Greek signed from Panathinaikos, was a shambles. He didn't want to be there and let everyone know it. He was regularly the worst player on the pitch. The kids would work their socks off to carry the passenger and then look in despair when he was put back in the first-team squad the following Saturday. He would play so badly that Tommy would substitute him and by the time we returned to the dressing-room he would have showered, changed and gone. He was a standing joke among the reserves.

I found it all quite sad and I kept telling the lads to keep working at their game and if it didn't work out for them at Newcastle they would have a chance somewhere else. Tommy would point at me and tell them how I hadn't broken through until I was 21.

He would also dig me up during a game if I played badly. In the dressing-room I could see he was unsure but he would have a go at me and he was right. One time I had arrived with the hump and it showed. He thought that if he dug the big fellow out and I didn't have a go back, he could handle the others more easily. I realised his position and told him, 'You're right, Tom. I have been an absolute joke.' I went out for the second half and played a lot better and enjoyed it much more. No matter who you are or how much you try to keep up your own standards, sometimes it is good for someone to have a go at you and tell you that you can do better.

The next morning he came up to me at breakfast and thanked me for not having a go back. I told him I wouldn't have dreamed of it. It is not my natural reaction to have a go back; that's normally the reaction of someone who doesn't look at themselves truthfully. They tend to cover their own backsides. If I'd thought that he was wrong to have a go at me, I would have pulled him later on his own and not undermined him. I had also gone out of my way not to undermine Frank Clark at Nottingham Forest.

It was so depressing that many times driving home on the A1 after a reserve game I would begin to doubt my own ability and think seriously of packing it all in. I realised then that it is a hell of a lot harder the lower you go. You can scratch around in the third division and make no impression, whereas you can go up into the Premier Division and with a little know-how you have half a chance. That's another lesson I learned. A manager can go and watch the reserves and think that a player is not good enough but when he is given a chance in the first team he suddenly lifts his game several levels.

The reserves used to play a lot of their games on a Monday night. Tommy used to let me go home at the weekend, telling me just to have a run out in a local park. I took a ball home with me and some kit, as I often used to do, rather than not train at all over the weekend. I did my running and kicked the ball against a convenient wall. One day, a couple of youngsters were playing football nearby and they recognised me and came over to ask for an autograph. The ironic thing was that it was just about three o'clock on a Saturday afternoon and for sixteen and a half years I had been otherwise engaged at that particular time. There I was, pushing 37, having a kickabout with two ten-year-olds. I went over to my car and found a couple of brochures from my testimonial, which I signed, and I gave them the Newcastle United ball I had taken home with me.

All in all, it was a desperately unhappy club. When I left the dining room on a Friday afternoon, everyone was in there and yet it was as quiet as a morgue. We had every-thing there – the organisation, the diet and the quality of players – but there was no atmosphere, no buzz about the place and this was just a few days before the season began. No wonder they started with only one point from their first seven games before Ruud Gullit finally packed his bags and left for Holland.

It was too easy for me to say what was wrong at the club

at the time but it would have been seen as sour grapes so I kept my mouth shut. But the club and especially the supporters deserved more than that. I wasn't making a statement by not selling my story to the papers; that's just how I am. Let people look at it and make up their own minds is my philosophy, as it was with Irving Scholar when I left Nottingham.

I swear I was the only one who walked out with a smile on my face, not only on the day when I finally left for good, but on all those Fridays when I would wave and tell them I would see them on Monday as I was off home for the weekend.

Gullit could have treated me a lot worse. There was no dialogue but no problem. He could have worked me day and night and had me turn up for everything without playing me. But he didn't; he allowed me to do very much as I wanted and I respect him for that.

I am not sure how much dialogue he had with anyone. I know there were team meetings but I wasn't invited and I don't know what was said. I can't imagine that much was discussed because English players are different from their Dutch counterparts. After a bad game an English player will hold up his hands and take the blame, but a Dutch player will look for someone else to blame. This was evident at a succession of World Cups and European Championships. They are very opinionated. When England played against Holland in Euro 96 at Wembley I was marking Jordi Cruyff and when we went three up he turned to me and said, 'I cannot believe this is happening. I do not believe it.' I said, 'You better fucking believe it,' but thought to myself then that he seemed to be abdicating himself from all responsibility and perhaps blaming others for the fact that they were getting thrashed.

I also had an experience with a Dutch player when I was briefly manager at Forest. Bryan Roy wrote in the local newspaper that he and I had different ideas on how football should be played when I left him out. My idea was that when I picked him he had to try to play reasonably well. If he didn't he would be out of the team because we didn't need a passenger when we had our backs against the wall. If his criteria is different from that then fine. When you're away from home scrapping for a result and someone is standing out on the wing, screaming, 'Give me the ball, give me the ball,' maybe we did have different ideas. The best players in the world also tend to be the hardest working.

It was certainly a happy day for me when I departed the club on that Friday. By the Monday I was at West Ham for the team photocall. I hadn't even completed my medical at that stage. Later they told me they stuck me on the end of a row so that they could cut me off if the deal fell through. I trust that was a joke, at least I hope it was!

On the Saturday I made my return to Premiership football. We played Spurs and won 1–0. What a start. What a dramatic turn of events.

the broken hammer

It would have been easy for Harry Redknapp to ignore me when the opportunity arose for him to sign me the second time around. Fortunately for me, he is an honest man who bears no grudges. I was not the only one who had been nipped away from him by Newcastle. John Barnes, according to Harry, had even agreed terms on the deal before he signed for Newcastle. But Harry was brilliant then and from that moment on. He lived up to everything I'd thought and heard about him.

I knew my time was limited at Newcastle. I was like a lost soul in limbo, still living in Nottingham and moving around the north east like some homeless person, trying to find somewhere to rest my head. I was constantly on the move, sometimes staying with physiotherapist Derek Wright, who would leave me the key to his front door, or with goalkeeper Steve Harper. Invariably if I stayed for a game of golf in the afternoon I would be on the mobile afterwards trying to find somewhere to lay my head that night.

There was a time in Durham when we didn't finish golf until 9.30 p.m. I telephoned Liz to tell her I was looking for somewhere to stay for the night. I told her that if I struggled to find Steve Harper I might even stay at the golf club, hide in the toilets until they locked up and then sleep in the nice reclining leather chair in the lounge and use the beautiful showers in the morning.

With no club coming in for me and the clock running on my own deadline, I had made up my mind that on the first day of the season I would commit myself to the academy, get out of Ruud Gullit's dreadlocks and try to make that last year of my contract as comfortable as possible. I could come and go as I pleased and would give up football, stopping training. There seemed no hope with either a total lack of response or 'no' votes from Nottingham Forest, Coventry, Southampton, Watford, Aston Villa and West Ham. I could have rung Manchester United all day, every day but I went in at what I thought was a realistic level.

Because of West Ham's interest in me the first time around, Kevin Mason was pestering Harry to sign me. He was ringing him morning, noon and night and it became so bad that even Liz chipped in and said that surely 'no' meant 'no'. Kevin had told me that Harry wanted to sign me but was trying to get his chairman to release the necessary money to pay my wages. The wages were very much the same as Newcastle but had they asked me to take a drop I would have done so to extend my football career. This had gone on for a couple of weeks and I had more or less given up and told Kevin to leave Harry alone. That was when I took the call on the mobile on the golf course and Kevin told me it was on.

I couldn't believe I was playing against Tottenham in a week's time. Harry was quite nonchalant about it all and asked if I wanted a reserve game first but didn't try to press me despite my lack of match practice over such a long period.

I trained with Newcastle on Saturday, secured my release documents from them and drove down the motorway to London that very day. I had played just the one game between October and August but at least Harry had brought in a fresh player and someone who was bursting a gut to prove someone else wrong. I desperately wanted to do the business for him because he had been so decent. I hoped for a minimum of 20 games for Harry and to do enough to sign for another season – until I was struck down by injuries!

How I enjoyed my move south. West Ham are a fascinating club, a bit of a throwback in football terms, rather like going back to Forest as they were 15 years earlier. I had come from the antiseptic St James' Park where sitting in the offices is like sitting in the dentist's waiting room, a plc probably run by bankers in London. The Happy Hammers are such fun and it's very definitely a family club.

I turned up for training one Sunday while I was recovering from my first broken leg. The kit room was locked so I had to hunt around for a pair of shorts, a sweat top and an odd pair of socks. Fortunately I had my boots with me. They are not the kind of thing that you leave around at Upton Park because they, like everything else, tend to go missing, as mine did once. In the dressing-room in the time I was there we lost three clocks off the wall. People would just come in from the car park and help themselves to a souvenir. Before that someone unscrewed the picture of Julian Dicks off the wall and took that away with them. As for my boots I can only imagine the young kids took them.

You couldn't leave anything. I came in from a workout in the gym, changed out of my trainers and put on my boots to go out for a run around the pitch. By the time I came in my trainers had disappeared. I checked all the players and found Joe Cole was wearing them. 'Joe, those are my trainers,' I said. 'I knew they were someone's – but someone has nicked mine,' he replied.

On another Sunday when I arrived the training room complex was heaving with all the kids and parents of the Under-12s and Under-14s teams. I eventually pulled on jock strap, sweatshirt, socks and boots but could not go running because there were no shorts. I eventually pinched a pair from a youngster who was having treatment and even then he had 'found' them and they turned out to belong to the physio who was treating him!

Shaka Hislop kept what the boys called a goalkeeper's fund which was basically a swear box, topped up regularly during training and used every now and again for the players to go out for a drink or two. He kept the money in his locker and, sure enough, he opened up one day to find it gone and in its place a McDonald's box with a half-eaten burger inside and the words 'Thank you' scrawled over the outside.

That's what it's like there. It can be infuriating but it has a tradition about it; an aura that's unique. It's been the same for years and looks unlikely to change.

They do their little bit on nutrition but it is hardly top of the agenda. Over Christmas we played at Wimbledon on Boxing Day, missed a day and then played Derby County at home the next day. Any dietician will tell you that the most important time to get the nourishment in is immediately after the game or the next day. The team was in training on the middle day and I expected pastas, rice and all the usual stuff to be waiting for us at lunchtime. There was not only nothing brought in for the players but even if there had been there was no one to cook it. There was a packet of biscuits, jaffa cakes and mince pies to show it was Christmas! The dinner ladies were off because it was holiday time. It was against everything that had been learned over recent years and totally alien to my regime.

What a contrast it was after my miserable last few months at Newcastle, a very professional club with much of its heart ripped out. Harry and Frank Lampard had been at Upton Park for years as players and in their managerial and coaching roles and they were happy to maintain the traditions of the club. There was a good team spirit and a nice atmosphere to work in.

I don't know what the foreign players must think of it all. The showers in the training ground are mouldy and grotty, scraped now and again and the odd tile replaced from time to time.

When the kit man went missing for a day, Shirley, who cooks the dinners, loaded up the machines with the muddy shirts and shorts and then went straight to the kitchen to prepare the meals.

The gym was total chaos. While I was recovering from the first broken leg, I was working on one of the bikes. The youngsters were thrashing a ball around when it flew very close to me. I punched it and glared at the young boy who had kicked it my way. His knees wobbled a bit and he looked very miserable. I was cross because I wanted to focus on my recovery. Then, a few days later, I was doing sit-ups when a ball hit me on the head, rolled down my face, down my body and stopped on the other side against the wall. I ignored it and carried on while the boys who had been playing left it. None of them had the courage to come and get it and they eventually left the gym with the ball still lying where it had settled.

It's bedlam but the club has its own identity. It was thoroughly enjoyable to be there despite all the bits and pieces and the ragged edges. The boys just laughed and got on with the job. There was a young lad named Jimmy, who wandered in when the team were training. One day I walked in to see him running round the gym as fast as his legs would carry him before collapsing in a corner exhausted. A player had wound him up. Can you imagine that happening anywhere else in the Premier Division?

When I arrived I was told that training started at 10.30 and in my first week I was, as usual, there on time only to find that I was training on my own with a young Bulgarian trialist. I had just changed with all the boys so I knew they were in and, sure enough, they began wandering out ten or 15 minutes later.

That first game against Tottenham was another experience. It was a big game, far bigger than I had realised from a distance, a real London derby for the fans with a lot of rivalry. I had also enjoyed some stirring battles with Spurs over the years and I always liked to beat them.

It was the usual nice warm opening day of the season. I was wondering whether I was fit enough without my usual pre-season build-up, having had just one full game at St Albans for the reserves on the Monday night and then only after Harry left it up to me whether I played or not. I managed the 90 minutes but it was in an easy game and did not stretch me nor test me nearly enough and I still felt that I needed a bit more. Harry once more left it up to me whether I should play in the reserves at Dover on the Wednesday. I played centre-back for 45 minutes and in both games it was a case of building up my fitness.

Then suddenly I was thrust straight into a London derby in front of a new lot of fans, many of whom must have been wondering whether I was too old and past it. The bigger the name you have, the more you have to keep up your standards. You can have ten good games and then one bad one and immediately everyone is saying that you are too old. The one wish is to get through the game without making a fool of yourself, and I hoped that I was up to the pace after only one outing in ten months. There was added pressure because the team had finished a very respectable fifth the year before, so the expectations were quite high.

I need not have worried. We kept a clean sheet and won that opening game 1–0. I was happy with my personal performance and, in fact, we had a very good start. The only problem was that, in attempting a clearance, I cleared out my own man, Ian Pearce, as I tried to tackle David Ginola. Our knees bumped and I put my fellow defender out for the season in the opening game. We immediately had to reshuffle, playing four at the back instead of three with me as a centre-half. I believed that was now my position, just as Terry Venables had predicted a couple of years earlier. As left-back I don't think I could do as good a job as someone younger, defensively perhaps but not charging up and down the line. For that you have to be an athlete in prime condition.

In the four and a half games I played, we won four and drew away 2–2 to Aston Villa. After the Spurs game, we beat Bradford away 3–0, Leicester at home 2–1, and Watford 1–0 when I was injured. Before the Watford game I had the call from England and everything in the garden looked rosy with Harry saying how well I had played to anyone who wanted to listen. He was good like that; if you do well he sticks up for you and shouts about it on television and radio. It was a pleasure to be playing and a pleasure to be giving something back to Harry. Even though I had cost nothing in terms of a transfer fee, I still like to be seen earning my wages.

Watford was a funny game for me, full of mixed emotions. Watford manager Graham Taylor had made me England captain, and only six weeks earlier he had knocked me back, not wanting to take a gamble on me. I bore him no grudge. Football and its players are subjective.

I was enjoying the game and just before the tackle I hit the bar from a corner. We had a lot of chances but the score was still goalless ten minutes before half-time. There was a stoppage for an injury and, feeling full of the joys, I picked up a water bottle and sprayed it towards Graham Taylor on the Watford bench where he sat with Kenny Jackett, with whom I used to play Sunday football. Some water landed on Graham's foot and he turned to Kenny and asked him who had done it. Kenny pointed at me, a laughing Stuart Pearce. Ten minutes later I was laughing on the other side of my face, being carted off with a broken leg.

It was ironic; here I was trying to prove to Graham Taylor that he had been wrong not to take a gamble on me and at the same time trying to prove to Harry Redknapp that he was right.

Two minutes before half-time I took a throw-in and the ball came back to me leaving me in a 50–50 situation with Micah Hyde. The pair of us slid in and I heard a slap but I thought it was my shin pad. I used to wear very thin shin pads, about the size of a saucer. I was never a lover of the big, thick ones that are in favour nowadays. When I first turned professional, I used those old-fashioned plastic things with strips of cane inserted at intervals. My dad bought them for me and I wore them non-league and also when I turned pro. Eventually I believed they were a good luck omen. In fact, I still have them, along with the pair of boots I wore in that first game for Coventry City. It was only when the old shin pads, stinking with all the liniment that had soaked through, began to fall apart after 12 years or so that I replaced them but kept to the same size.

I was two yards from the touchline when the clash occurred and my leg went numb. The physio came on and my old Forest team-mate Des Lyttle, who was playing right wing-back for Watford, came running up saying, 'Skipper, Skipper, are you all right?' I was trying to put on a brave face and told the physio that my leg had gone numb. He pulled my sock down and manipulated my leg with a jarring movement and asked me how it was. I began to get a little feeling back and the pain was general rather than specific. I thought that maybe I had just hit a nerve.

One of my pet hates is to suffer an injury and be substituted and then five minutes later discover the pain has worn off, leaving me frustrated realising I could have carried on. Over the years, I have done some pretty silly things to stay on. Once I damaged my knee ligaments and cartilage after 20 minutes and played on until half-time; I did the same in a Mercantile final at Wembley and played on for another ten minutes. But one of the worst was when I was caught by David Campbell in a league game playing for Forest against Charlton. His studs went right through my little shin pads and split the muscle sheath. There was a distinct hole and then a little egg-shaped protrusion appeared. Liam O'Kane, who had run on, was nearly ill when he saw it. 'What the fuck is that?' he said. I didn't know so I just told him to spray some painkiller on it to get me through the last 15 minutes.

This time it was close to half-time and Harry solved the problem by saying to come off and he wouldn't substitute me before half-time. Personal pride dictated that I wouldn't go off on a stretcher, so I lifted myself to my feet and the physio helped me off into the dressing-room where the club doctor was waiting to have a look at the leg. He wriggled the shin a bit and repeated exactly what the physio had said – 'I don't think there's anything broken.'

They iced it for ten minutes and Harry came in for a progress report. I was getting some feeling back so I said I would have a little run. There is not a lot of room at West Ham at the best of times, so I made my way to the tunnel to have a little run before going back on to the pitch. But it hurt like hell and I came back in and told Harry it wasn't going to work; there was too much pain to carry on.

West Ham, by a strange coincidence, had just acquired an X-ray machine and I was the first one to test it. The operative took one look at the plate and said, 'I've a bit of bad news for you. You've broken your shin.' I had broken the tibia but it was a very straight break and wasn't displaced in any way. It was good news, bad news.

I went back into the dressing-room, limped into the shower, changed and telephoned Liz to tell her I had broken my leg. I was able to tell her that there was no need for me to attend hospital because the break was so clean. They gave me a plastic boot and sent me home. Two of the groundsmen played the good Samaritans with one driving me home in my car and the other following behind in his to take his mate back. It was a long way, two hours' drive, but they were happy to make the long journey from East London to Wiltshire.

We must have spent a year looking for the right place to live and received the details of properties in five different counties. We probably looked at a dozen before finding the perfect spot just outside Hungerford, deep in the heart of racing country. We had only been in the house for a couple of weeks and we were up in the air. It was a nightmare for Liz; she had the horses, a young baby and me. I was useless and couldn't even baby-sit because I couldn't climb the stairs to change Chelsea. Liz had to take the whole lot on and she coped magnificently.

But however I looked at it, it was a massive blow. We had started so well, we were unbeaten, playing in Europe, and I felt I was genuinely contributing. The timing was so bad. I could have broken both my legs at Newcastle and no one would have noticed or cared; I would have recovered before they even thought about it!

Fortunately, I am not one of those people who sit about and mope. You put the worst moments behind you and try to come out stronger. It doesn't help to sulk. It was a case of accepting what was done, spending a couple of weeks recuperating and then going onwards and upwards. I told myself that I was recovering and not that I was injured.

If you look at it as a long-term thing, at my age it could have finished me there and then. I have to admit that, at 37, if I hadn't just joined the club I would have been tempted to call it a day and hang up my boots, but I felt that I owed something to Harry and to myself to prove the doubters wrong. I decided instantly to carry on. I thought, 'Sod it, I'll stick around and show people I can play.'

There were three roads open to me – I could come back, break down and pack it in; I could come back and not be the player I once was and pack it in; or I could come back, play as well as I had been and go for England and Euro 2000. There was no doubt which route I wanted to take. But the first priority was to get fit, get back into the West Ham side and play as well as I could. As insurance I also enrolled in a two-week residential coaching course with the Football Association. You never know what is round the corner; I certainly never suspected the twists that awaited me or that there would be a fourth road.

I was pleased with my progress, no one tried to hurry me and I took my time making sure that the leg was right before I made my commitment. I worked extremely hard but it was nigh on five months from the time I did it until the time I was back in the first team. I played a couple of reserve games, took some hard bangs and went in for some strong tackles without any adverse effect. The first game for the reserves was an easy, gentle affair and a case of getting through it. There was not a great deal of tackling and my leg felt fine. The second one was more lively with plenty of tackling. Harry Redknapp watched half the game and told me on the Friday that he didn't feel that I was ready for the first-team game on Saturday. I played by Brian Clough's rules that you are fit or you are not fit without any grey area in between. I told Harry that he was the boss and that whenever he wanted me to play I was ready to do so.

On the Saturday at 1.45 he came up to me and asked me how I felt. I told him the same as I had told him 24 hours before: that I was ready when he was. He told me that he was going to play me against Everton. We were thrashed 4–0 but I don't think that it was down to me and, indeed, after the game Harry picked out Richard Gough and me, two 37-year-olds, as the only two who had performed.

I was gutted that we had been beaten 4–0 but, strange for me, I felt some satisfaction that I had played a full 90 minutes and had played as well as I had five months earlier. We had a game away at Watford, the team I broke my leg against, the next Saturday where we won and I once again came through it without any mishaps.

I was as happy as Larry to think that I had returned so quickly and so well. It was on my mind from then on that I had had a nibble with the England team before Christmas and if I could get a good run of form between February and the end of the season, I might still have a shout for Euro 2000, especially in view of the fact that, with the continued absence of the unlucky Graeme Le Saux, Kevin Keegan was struggling for genuine left-sided players. There was a berth there available and it was up to me. Kevin had kept my interest going when he invited me to join the squad in the February against Argentina. I was pleased to be along.

The next game was on 5 March against Southampton and it was an eventful day one way and another. Just as we were getting ready to go out Harry Redknapp changed me from the left side of a back three to left-back of a flat back four ten minutes before the kick-off. As we trotted out Roger Cross told me that I would be up against Marian Pahars and to rough him up a bit early on as he wasn't the bravest of players.

Message was received and understood. In the first five minutes, the ball was played to his feet and John Moncur and I arrived at the same time with the Saints player finishing up in a heap as though a ten-ton truck had hit him. I went over to the player to help him up, lifted him up to his full height only for him to fall to the floor again.

The next challenge I went into was with Kevin Davies. I was to the ball before him as I slid in, kicked the ball against his legs and slid onwards clashing with his knee right on the same spot that I had damaged before. I knew immediately that I had a problem. It was either badly bruised or another break. I got to my feet as the ball went for a goal kick. I was hoping that it was just bruised and that I would be able to run it off but it was evident that was not going to happen and I limped off to meet the physios who were jogging round the pitch. I told them it was in exactly the same spot as before and asked if I could have an X-ray. If it was not broken I would carry on. They looked at me as though I was mad and told me that there wasn't time to do that and leave the team playing with ten men. I asked them to hang on to see if I could get some feeling back into it. But it wasn't right and they helped me off the pitch to the dressing-room where I had an immediate X-ray.

It was the same old routine again. They told me they had some bad news for me as they confirmed that I had broken my left leg in the same place. If I was gutted the time before, this time I was shattered. As far as I was concerned at that moment, my career was over, pack it in. How can a player, 38 in two months' time, hope to come back after two broken legs in the same season? I was almost in tears as I sat in the dressing-room feeling sorry for myself. The physios left me alone to my thoughts.

I had treated Liz and her mother to a day at a health farm and she was on her way when I telephoned her to tell her that I had broken my leg again and couldn't look after Chelsea as I had promised.

I am pretty philosophical and strong about most things. Nevertheless, after five months' hard work I was very depressed, but when I woke up a few days later I was totally comfortable about the whole thing and prepared to accept whatever fate held for me. Harry telephoned and helped me a lot by telling me that if I could get fit, they would love to have me at the club for another year. That was a great confidence booster and gave me a target. Two mornings later, I had a telephone call from Kevin Keegan who was also very encouraging.

At first I accepted that I wouldn't play again but the leg healed much better this time around and after a couple of months there was no pain at all. There are two lines of thought from the medics. The first is that the leg wasn't healed properly or that I was just unlucky to have such a heavy blow on the same point again. I had been in much harder tackles before the break and they were unhappy to work on the luck theory so we have to assume that, despite how good I felt, I came back before it had healed 100 per cent.

I popped into West Ham every now and again but they

let me work on my fitness at Newbury Racecourse in their gymnasium and every two weeks I went to a rehabilitation centre in Manchester for two days where they have a water flume. It is about ten feet long by five or six feet wide and you run against a current of water with the inverted sides allowing you to bound from side to side in the current. I was the first from Upton Park to use it but several of their players with bad injuries have followed me. I was quite happy to be used as a guinea pig.

I was determined to try my damnedest and give it a go while being prepared to call it a day if the leg let me down medically. I really wanted to get fit and give West Ham the season I was unable to give them when they signed me from Newcastle. Harry and the chairman agreed that they wanted to keep me on. I told him that I wasn't concerned about contracts or money at that stage and it was Harry himself who suggested that I sign a month-by-month contract until I had proved my fitness to myself at which time he would offer me a proper contract. I had a doctor's appointment on 12 June when he gave me the all-clear to begin running again and I really felt I was making progress.

One thing I did was throw away my tiny shin pads and replace them with a pair specially made for me at Lilleshall. I was away with the England Under-18 squad and their manager Martin Hunter mentioned that a couple of the youngsters had their shin pads tailor-made for them.

Kevin Keegan kindly invited me to join the squad for the European Championship but once I had decided to try to play again the next season, I felt ethically bound to decline, particularly as the club had already given me permission to do my two-week coaching badge course at Lilleshall in the summer for my A licence.

I will be eternally grateful for the way that Harry and West Ham stood by me when they had no need to, and to Kevin Keegan for his support then and since.

Even after the first break, I had a couple of telephone calls asking me what my plans were, with the clear indication that someone, somewhere was thinking of me for a job in management or coaching. I had a good idea about the identity of one of the clubs but not a clue who the other caller represented.

In an ideal world I would rather play for as long as I can but if I am not doing myself credit or not maintaining the standards I have set myself, I'll stop. I wouldn't like to be taking wages and not be giving something in return. It irritated me that I was not able to do myself justice and earn my wages after joining West Ham.

If I had been offered a two-year contract at the start I would have refused because I needed to prove to myself that I could do it and if I couldn't I would not have enjoyed taking money for not doing the job. Even with broken legs I feel a bit guilty about being paid but then I think that I suffered the injuries in service with the club and they are physical injuries, not an old man's complaint like rheumatoid arthritis.

Throughout, Harry Redknapp maintained contact and gave me unstinting support. I talked to him more than I have any other manager. He involved me at games and talked to me about decisions. Against Aston Villa he came over at half-time and said that Rio Ferdinand thought Paul Merson was getting too much space and hurting us. I couldn't see that; Merse was picking up the ball but as long as we were shutting him down before he could shoot he wasn't damaging us. Harry agreed and told me to go and tell Rio. I enjoyed the experience and it showed that Harry had confidence in me.

Once I was mobile I offered to watch players or clubs if he wanted me to. He took it in the spirit in which it was offered. Harry did an excellent job with so many good young players coming through that the future looks extremely bright at Upton Park. The one they were all talking about when I arrived was the young midfield playmaker Joe Cole. I played a couple of reserve matches with him when I joined and appreciated that he looked good but I wondered whether he influenced the game enough. Harry held him back, held him back and then gave him a run and he looked superb. He has built himself up and is now very strong and can fight his corner with the strongest. How unfortunate he was to break his leg towards the end of April after a dreadful tackle by Derby's Rory Delap. He might not have made the full England squad for the summer but was a certain starter in the Under-21 Championship finals.

I thought a lot of the publicity over young Cole was hype, but it wasn't. He is an outstanding prospect and what is more he is not alone. There are plenty of others at Upton Park who have caught my eye, especially Michael Carrick, another midfielder, but a different sort of player from Joe. Joe has all the circus tricks and silky skills while Carrick is a two-footed passer, tall, comfortable on both feet and in the style of a young Glenn Hoddle.

I have just a small window on a young player's life but

personally I had no doubt that Joe Cole would go on to the full England squad. His natural flair is probably on a par with Paul Gascoigne's, complete with party tricks, and, like Gazza, he is not afraid to put his foot in when it is needed. Skill and forcefulness don't usually mix but with Joe they do. He doesn't, however, have that electric pace that Gazza had before he injured himself against Nottingham Forest, and also I cannot see him scoring as many goals. He is not an out-and-out natural striker.

Joe is making steady progress. People in the game were trying to rush him too quickly; they were talking about him playing for England before he had made his full debut for West Ham. That was ridiculous and unfair. He should have at least 100 club games before that happens.

You have to have a good head on your shoulders to cope with that sort of hype and fortunately he has. Most of all, he wants to learn and do well. He will train and train and train. Even when his knee felt a bit dickey he would go back out again after training to practise shooting. I keep wanting to tell him to take it easy, that there is a long career ahead, to train well but don't do extra. The games will take care of the fitness and on days off I advised him to put his feet up and rest. He is like a young kid; he wants to go and play all the time. But Harry used to keep a careful eye on him, giving him a run and then pulling him out. Joe might not like it but, in the long run, it will help his game and his future.

When you have a Michael Owen or a Joe Cole in your ranks it is very difficult to leave them out. It is easy to forget how young these gems are. You have to look after them and nurture them. The trouble is that the pressure is on managers to achieve results now, so what's the point of holding them back and leaving the benefits for someone else or risking the player moving on at the end of his contract?

It's great to see so many good young English players around. I had no doubts that Joe would make it to the England squad but it is impossible to tell what he is going to achieve. In any youth team, if you can see one or two coming through you have done well but West Ham seem to have a few more than that after their Youth Cup victory in 1999.

Rio Ferdinand is still a young man. When I joined the club, obviously I wanted to play well myself but I also wanted to help those around me, especially Rio. He is a very good player whose raw ability was wonderful. We used to do one-on-ones in training and he was unbeatable. No one can take him on, he's that good. But where he falls down is that he suffers the occasional lapse of concentration. When you are as good as he is, you can switch off because you have confidence that your pace and skill will get you out of trouble. But, at the top level, that's the very moment when you become vulnerable yourself. Harry said to me straight-away that he thought I could help Rio, simply by keeping at him all the time and making him concentrate, not bullying him exactly but shaking the fist in encouragement when backs are against the wall.

Rio has all the attributes and if he adds concentration to his natural ability he will be a phenomenal player. With his talent he should be a regular with England but he won't be until he is complete across the spectrum and able to apply himself for the full 90 minutes. The higher he goes the more important it is, as I found out to my cost against Brazil.

West Ham are a very quiet team with not too many natural leaders, something many top teams in the country are missing at the moment. There are very few Tony Adams around and every manager wants one.

Harry told me when I arrived that he felt he had the best squad he has ever had and I was impressed. If I were a manager, I would sign Trevor Sinclair tomorrow because he has skills as a winger and will battle back for you. What more can you want from a player? Paolo di Canio will flit in and out of games but he has the talent to turn or win a match. Joe Cole can only improve with age while Shaka Hislop, another broken-leg victim, was playing as well as any goalkeeper in the country before he was injured. It is an exciting team for anyone to be involved with.

When I finally stop playing, I don't want to look back and just be an old footballer; I want to look forward as a young coach or manager.

CHAPTER 11

that's entertainment

One of my biggest problems has always been to interest
other players in punk music, to the point of joining me at
concerts or listening to my music in the dressing-room
before a game. Fortunately, being the club captain for so
long gave me that little bit of authority that, on occasions, I
was not afraid to use. Eventually at Forest, I succeeded
with a handful of people although I suspect that the crates
of lager I brought along were a bigger attraction than some
of the bands. We used to load the lager on the borrowed
team bus and pay the groundsman to drive us to and from
the designated venue.

We would not have gone at all unless I organised everything. I used to buy the music papers to see who was on and
if I spotted a band such as Spear of Destiny performing
locally I knew that a few would come, most of them for the
beer. It certainly wasn't for the girls. Punks used to come up
and say it was good to see us there and that I was one of
them. I didn't argue. I just liked the music and as far as I
was concerned it was 'our' music not 'their' music.

There must have been around eight of us who went to see
the Stranglers at Leicester University, taking advantage of
an invitation to go backstage after the concert. We enjoyed

a few drinks with the band and everyone was quite relaxed, so relaxed in fact that one of the band was on the old wacky baccy and demonstrating the best way to gain full benefit from smoking it to one of the young players. Fortunately, none of the Forest lads followed his advice or example.

Eventually the band excused themselves to load up their gear on the gig bus ready to move on to the next venue. Some of our lads were a bit disappointed because it was all so tame and they had expected action after hearing how these wild groups smashed up their dressing-rooms after a gig. So I said, tongue in cheek, 'Do you mind if we trash the room?'

'No,' one of them replied. 'Trash away, boys, trash away. Have this one on us.'

To be honest, you would do well to trash Leicester University dressing-rooms when they have had bands on. It could only be an improvement.

The first music I was into as a youngster was David Bowie's but it was not long before the punk thing happened in 1976–77 and that was when I really fell in love with music. I wouldn't say I threw myself into the punk culture body and soul – I drew the line at the spiky hair and the other outrageous symbols – but I lived and breathed the music and never missed an opportunity to go to listen to the bands. I suppose I was a bit of a closet punk.

It was a great release and alternative entertainment. It happened at the right time for me. I used to go to concerts straight from school, catching the number 52 bus to the West End for the Marquee Club or the Music Machine (now called the Camden Palace) and then ducking home early because of school next day. Three or four of us would go together to the gigs. It was the times as well as the music. Some of the bands have stood the test of time but a lot fell by the wayside. The times have changed and music with it.

One of the first times I went to see Stiff Little Fingers, a top punk band from Belfast and one of my favourites, was at Acklam Hall in Ladbroke Grove, a small room under the flyover. The stage was only a few inches high and at the end of the concert I asked the drummer if I could have one of his drumsticks. As a young kid, I was made up when he gave one to me and I have to confess that I still have that drumstick now.

Another concert I went to was the Damned at the Rainbow. They didn't come on stage until nearly midnight and by then a sea of punks were breaking up chairs and throwing them on the stage. The band arrived without the lead singer and the audience blew up. It was mayhem but, strangely, there was never any violence directed against each other. The singer came on and started picking up all the bits of chairs and lobbing them back into the crowd. The atmosphere was electric – you just had to avoid the flying chair legs.

I still go to see the same bands all these years later but the difference is that now I know most of them as friends. I have been to see the Stranglers pushing 40 times – they even named a record label after me, Psycho Records – and a hell of a lot of other bands as well. I have travelled all over the country to see concerts, just jumping in my car and going. I always telephone the venue to ask what time the main band are on and arrive five minutes before they start and stand at the back. No one fusses you and I am away as soon as it finishes.

We all seem to have grown up together; the bands and fans are the same age as me, pushing 40 or more, and still enjoying the music even if they aren't breaking up the furniture any more.

Jake Burns, the lead singer with Stiff Little Fingers, is a Newcastle United season-ticket holder. When I signed for Newcastle he was delighted and we met up regularly after matches when I was at St James' Park. Nowadays all of these angry young men have gone through the rebellious stage when they shocked people and are normal members of society; after all, the drummer of the Stranglers is over 60! I appeared on *TFI Friday* a few years ago and a guy came up and introduced himself as Manic Esso, the drummer from the Lurkers. We chatted and I discovered that he was doing a lot of work for kids and the disabled.

Every Christmas, all the old school friends and their wives and girlfriends have a get-together. One year we decided on Bath as a venue. A big punk festival was being held at Bath Pavilion, and Stiff Little Fingers were staying at the same hotel as us. I told Liz that we were meeting Jake and she was expecting some giant with a Mohican haircut and a nappy pin through his nose. She was stunned when he appeared sporting a little shaggy perm and wearing a flowery shirt and glasses.

Music remains a terrific release from what I do. I enjoy indie music, I still like Bowie, but it's mainly punk that stirs the blood.

I also went (and still go) to see some of the new up-and-coming bands, including Oasis when they first started off and another band called Green Day. They were excellent. The atmosphere was vibrant; they were all so much younger. It was the same sort of feeling I had when punk emerged on the scene. It was also good to go to a concert that was packed because, to be honest, the punk concerts aren't that crowded these days. I stood there giggling because all I could see were Doc Martens boots going overhead as they passed people down to the front and with the students jumping around like idiots and diving off the stage it took me back to my early days at concerts. There are pictures to prove it – I feature on an album cover of the Lurkers, standing in the audience.

I was on the young end of punk music so I didn't get involved in the drugs or booze. The high for us at our age was going to the concert and getting home in one piece. The biggest danger was not so much avoiding the drug culture but the teddy boys and the football hooligans who were looking for sport at our expense. There was violence between the punks and rockers but rarely at the concert venues.

Once I wore my Lurkers jean jacket to a Lurkers/Adam Ant concert, totally unaware of the friction between the two groups of fans until I was hit over the head with a lump of wood. I turned round and there was a group of skinheads leering at me. I immediately apologised for putting my head in the way of their piece of wood, hoped I hadn't damaged it and made a hasty exit. That was the only violence I have ever personally experienced. In the main it was a good-natured fun.

Punks were mostly white males with very few women other than the out-and-out punks, but there were also a lot like me who were just there to listen to the music.

Although I didn't look for a punk barber or stick bits of

metal through my nose and ears, I tried to dress the part. Johnny Fingers, the keyboard player of the Boom Town Rats, always wore pyjamas on stage so I took my pyjama top to have Johnny Fingers and the Vibrators screenprinted on the back. God knows what my father thought about me going out to a concert wearing my pyjamas.

I used to have things like bath plugs or toilet chains pinned to my gear or wrapped around my neck. My little mate would sidle up to me and whisper in my ear, 'My snout in the punk world says that bath plugs are in.' In fact, his snout seemed to think everything I wore was 'in'. I also sewed zips into my white Dunlop plimsolls.

The Stranglers had an air of menace about them that made them even more appealing. I recently took my brother Dennis to the Shepherds Bush Empire to watch them. He had never seen them before but knew their records. As they played each song, my mate and I would tell him the background to the track, like it being made after the nuclear tests in Australia ('Nuclear Device') or after they were arrested in France ('Nice in Nice'). He was amazed at how much I knew about them. They still have a close-knit, cult following.

I found them an even more fascinating group of guys when I got to know them. Bass player JJ, for instance, has a black-belt in karate and fights around the world, while the keyboard player Dave Greenfield is into the occult and black magic. Jet Black, the drummer, founded the group, touring in his ice-cream van. He is mean and moody and if you stand in the way of him and his food he is likely to bite your leg off.

The early eighties were a barren spell for me in terms of

music so I didn't go to a lot of concerts, but in the late eighties punk made a comeback along with groups such as Carter and one or two others. They rekindled my spirit. Of the modern bands, I enjoy Oasis and those with a cutting edge such as the Levellers. Liz is not into my sort of music. In fact, she's hard work to take to listen to punk music.

When I first joined Forest, I wrote an article about my likes and dislikes and one of the things I mentioned was my love of punk music. It prompted a guy named Kieron Egan to write to me and send me an album of his band called Resistance 77. He lived in Derbyshire and was a Forest season-ticket holder. I listened and while the music was a bit raw it wasn't at all bad. I even went to see his band in a miners' welfare club in Derbyshire. As a result we got to know each other. I went to watch his band several times and he came with me to listen to other groups, which was good because it was becoming increasingly difficult to find someone who enjoyed the same music as me.

As I have matured my tastes have broadened. I am ashamed to admit that I never read a book until my thirties. That is both sad and a crime. I was never a good reader and when it takes you months to plough through a book it takes some of the shine off it. Now I go from one book to another. I enjoy thrillers with a twist, *Silence of the Lambs* is one, and Sherlock Holmes stories. From there, I went to Oscar Wilde's *Picture of Dorien Gray*. I really enjoyed it and it encouraged me to experiment. I've tried such diverse authors as Patricia Cornwell and Tolstoy. It still takes me a long time to read a book. I might read ten pages on the train or in bed and then put it down for a week, but I'm enjoying it.

I have also fallen in love with the theatre, often going on my own. I have thrown myself into Shakespeare; I couldn't believe how good it was on stage. The Royal Shakespeare Company has a sell-out season in Newcastle every year and that was where I discovered the Bard's work. I used to telephone Neil Webb's wife Shelley, quite a learned and well-read girl, and she used to advise me on what to go and see. I loved it. I couldn't believe how good it all was. I really enjoyed Leslie Phillips in the *Merry Wives of Windsor*. I started with the lighter stuff first and graduated to the history plays.

One wet Wednesday afternoon, I had the choice of sitting in my flat on my own or going to the theatre so I went to see *South Pacific*. What I hadn't realised was that I would be the youngest there by about 50 years. It was half price for pensioners and it was more like the Derby and Joan club and almost totally sold out.

The theatre manager found me a ticket that he had been keeping back, one of seven near the front of the dress circle. The auditorium was full except for the six empty seats next to me and I stood out like a sore thumb.

I wanted to keep my head down and I was grateful when the lights eventually went down and the production started. All went well for about half an hour when one of the old dears suddenly stood up and started to move down her row. I thought what a time to go to the toilet. She climbed two steps and then collapsed at my feet. I had been uncharitable. She had been feeling faint and had struggled up to get some air.

Immediately all eyes turned in our direction. I didn't know what to do. I froze. Here I was wanting a quiet afternoon and there was this woman lying at my feet. Even the players on the stage were aware something had happened although, like good troopers, they carried on. Then a man ran down the stairs saying he was a doctor while others came to her aid. All of this was going on right around me. The usherette came down the aisle and said that we would have to move her, as she was a hazard. Three men picked up a limb each while a woman tried to lift the other leg. She was struggling.

I was sitting there saying to myself, 'Do something. Get up you effing idiot and help.' Eventually, I jumped up and relieved the struggling lady and between the four of us we carried this old dear up the aisle with the entire theatre watching the wrong performance. We took her outside into the foyer and I returned to my seat feeling more conspicuous than ever. I checked up with the manager later to make sure she was all right. It transpired she had suffered a heart murmur and had to be taken off to hospital but, thankfully, she was comfortable and on the road to a full recovery.

She was certainly in better shape than the theatre manager who had had a really bad day, having thrown out a drunk earlier who then came back and hit an usherette. I couldn't believe it – a matinee and all that excitement.

If I have a choice of doing something or slobbing about, I would rather be active. I remember going to Australia, New Zealand and Malaysia with an England team under Graham Taylor. When we were in Auckland we noticed that *Les Misérables* was showing at the theatre literally over the road from our hotel. We had a night off and Graham asked if any of us wanted to attend. I was one of only four players to respond. Nigel Clough, goalkeeper Tony Coton, defender

Keith Curle and I made our way over the road but within five minutes Curle was up and off followed five minutes later by TC who announced to the rest of the audience that he was going for a beer. Nigel and I stayed and really enjoyed the show; in fact, it was so good that I'll remember it for the rest of my life. But the rest of the squad are not going to remember going to a wine bar in Auckland.

I would rather go to a theatre or a concert than to a bar. For a start, it's better for you to sit and relax rather than stand in a smoky wine bar when you are on tour or away for a match. That may sound hypocritical but even when I was playing non-league football and all my mates were down the local on Friday, Saturday and Sunday nights, latterly I would have a couple of orange juices to keep them company on Friday and then go home to rest. The alternative was to go to Wembley dogs either on my own or with a pal to break the monotony.

Football came first and because of my attitude I had my chance as a professional. There were so many players in the teams I played for on my way up who were better than me but they didn't go on to make it. A large dose of professionalism and, of course, a little bit of luck like being spotted when you are playing well, always help!

the nearly man

Liz calls me the nearly man and if I browse through just my England career, never mind lost semi-finals and finals at club level, I can see exactly what she means.

- I was injured playing for England when earning my fifth cap against Hungary. As a result I missed the European Championship in Germany in the summer of 1988. It was all very innocuous. I went to push off on my back foot and immediately felt a very bad pain in my knee. I carried on playing and every time I struck the ball normally there was no problem but when I sidefooted it I suffered a severe reaction. At half-time I told the doctor what was happening and it was discovered that I had pulled my cartilage away from the bone and damaged my ligaments.
- I missed the crucial penalty against Germany in the World Cup semi-finals when we were on the brink of winning the biggest trophy of them all.
- For the next European Championship in 1992 we were half a game away from qualifying.
- Having reached the semi-finals of the World Cup four years earlier, we failed to reach even the finals in 1994.

What made it worse was that I was captain and missed five months of that campaign through a groin injury, including the games against Norway and Holland home and away and San Marino at home. We had started that campaign really well but when I came back I didn't recognise the squad after a trip to America had drained the confidence. To add a touch of farce, the nearly man gave away a ten-second goal against San Marino in Bologna in the last game.

- We went on to the 1996 European Championship when the Germans turned us over again on penalties when we were just beginning to fancy ourselves to win the title at home.

- I missed out on the 1998 World Cup squad for France when Glenn Hoddle rang me up after I had been out with a hamstring injury to tell me that I was too old, even though I was the same age as Ian Wright who had also missed a chunk of the season with an injury. The only difference was that I had played five months' solid football leading up to it and he hadn't!

- After being brought back by Kevin Keegan for the Euro 2000 campaign, I broke my leg not once but twice.

That's how nearly I am. There seems to be an awful lot of pitfalls scattered through my 78-cap international career interspersed with a few highs. But back to the beginning.

I remember my name being projected for my first England cap back in the spring of 1987 when the regular left-back Kenny Sansom was scheduled to have an operation that summer. I had long lined up behind Kenny who, previously, had appeared to be impervious to injury. Throughout the eighties I couldn't remember him missing a single squad get-together. But now he had a problem and I was being seen as a possible successor, even though I had not been in a squad at that stage. Being the person I was, I totally ignored the rumours and speculation.

The call-up finally came for a competition called the Rous Cup, named after the famous English administrator Sir Stanley Rous. The games were against Brazil and Scotland, a mouth-watering prospect against the best side in the world and England's oldest enemy.

I first heard about it when I was away with Forest on a close-season tour in Bulgaria. We were sitting around a swimming pool when a couple of the local Nottingham journalists who were with us came over and told me I was in the squad. The other players heard and came over to congratulate me. All I wanted was a bit of privacy with Liz. I just wanted to scream and shout because I was so thrilled, but I couldn't in front of the other players and their wives. I just had to sit there and pretend it was water off a duck's back, which I did until I reached the privacy of my room.

The nearest I had come before that was to play for the Under 21s as a permitted average player – I was 25 – against Yugoslavia the previous November. Bobby Robson picked me but Dave Sexton was in charge of the game, which was played at Peterborough. It was home from home; Des Walker, Nigel Clough and Franz Carr were also in the squad. I had a decent run out. It was obviously enough to keep my name in front of the manager.

I was thrilled to be picked for the Under 21s and went looking for Liz in a restaurant where she was working to tell her about it. She looked doubtful.

'But you're over 21,' she said.

'I know, I know,' I responded. 'That's just a technicality. The important thing is that I'm going to play for an England side.' She still seemed highly doubtful.

I was even more excited about being picked for the full squad. Think about it. We are talking about a boy who, five years earlier, was an electrician with Brent Council watching players like Glenn Hoddle, Bryan Robson and Peter Shilton – my boyhood heroes, the demigods of English football. All right I was playing against them week in and week out by then but when I sat down for dinner with them the first time I looked on them with different eyes.

I once walked behind Bryan Robson at an airport coming back from Hungary and was in awe of his stature and presence. Whether that was just in my own mind or whether he has that aura I don't know, but he was the only player who was consistent in the eighties and one of the few who came back from the disastrous European Championship in 1988 with his reputation still intact.

I had so much respect for the England captain at that time. He was Manchester United's and England's best player and headlines game after game talked about 'Captain Marvel'. He scored goals at one end and cleared them off his own line at the other. When you played in the same team as him and he shouted at you to get tight on your man, you would want to do it for him because you didn't want to let him down. That's a mark of a good captain. You upped your standards because he demanded it of you. He talked sparingly on the pitch but led massively by example. Sometimes you can just look at someone and respect them, him more than most.

I also came to respect Terry Butcher and Tony Adams. I remember Big Butch facing a nippy little forward, not the sort a big man wants to mark, but he wouldn't hear of anyone else taking the job on, snapping, 'I've got him – just make sure you've got your man.' That's the sort of defender you want to work alongside, someone who will never hide or shirk. Those are the players I want in my side, big personalities who play for years and years to the highest standard.

Butch was a great motivator and he would start to wind it up in the tunnel when we were standing next to the opposition. He would be shouting things like, 'Come on, come on, we're England,' and 'Remember the three lions.' He wore it on his sleeve. Fans will never forget when he split his head against Sweden in Stockholm and played on with 16 stitches, a blood-soaked bandage wrapped round his head like a turban. Wild horses wouldn't have dragged him off. He was a strong man and a strong captain, like Bryan Robson.

Peter Shilton was another strong character in his own way. He had a one-track mind on the pitch and that was not to concede a goal. He was obsessed with keeping clean sheets. He was so protective of his goal that he would set up walls if someone were trying to shoot from 100 yards! Peter is a complex man but look at his record and see how many clean sheets he kept for England.

I suppose I was a little awestruck and wondering whether I was good enough to be in this exalted company. That was when Brian Clough called me into his office and told me he didn't think I was good enough to play for my country. It was a good job I wasn't the nervous type or I might have jacked it in there and then. I suppose every player harbours doubts over his ability to make that giant stride from club to international football and I was no different. I had no idea whether I could or not. But as far as I was concerned, if I was going to make my debut what better match than against Brazil in front of a full house of 92,000 at Wembley.

In those days, players could afford to be a touch reckless in their tackling. Nowadays, of course, you cannot get away with it and Bobby Robson showed great faith in me when many of the critics were casting doubts on my temperament and ability to stay on the field for 90 minutes in an international without being shown the red card. In a normal league game against someone of the quality of Pat Nevin, I would rattle him as quickly as I could. Within the first five minutes I would get as close to him as I could, upend him and leave a bit on him in the hope that it would quieten him down for the remaining 85 minutes. More often than not, I would have a lecture and warning from the referee but I would carry on being robust as it was part of my game, only calming it down if I received a yellow card. I would deal with it on its own merits. My record of three sendings off in 17 years of professional football is testament to the fact that I do have some brains and it's not all brawn. I was prepared to rough my opponent up until I received a caution and then it would change. It was no good for the team or for me if I spent part of the match watching from the tunnel because I'd been sent off.

I was sent off for two bad tackles against Leicester in a League Cup game in 1989, for accidentally elbowing Trevor Sinclair when I was playing for Newcastle against West

Ham, which didn't deserve a red card, and the third time was for swearing. Paul Stewart of Spurs had upended Roy Keane with 90 minutes gone. Young Keane, who had taken a battering, was lying on the ground and the referee delivered a mild rebuke. I was incensed and let him know in no uncertain terms. He sent me straight off.

The consequence of my aggressive play was the speculation about whether I would let down my country if I were to be picked. Some people were quite strongly against the manager selecting me at all. Mike Langley at the *People* led a vociferous campaign against my selection. I went on to make 78 caps and, in my humble opinion, I do not believe I ever let England down either on or off the pitch. Sometimes it's better to give someone a chance to prove themselves rather than trying to stifle their international career before it has started. Incidentally, no one has ever written that they were wrong about me!

Bobby Robson ignored the entire clamour and picked me. It was a nice, warm May day for my debut as the 999th player to be picked for England and I quickly learned a bitter and valuable lesson in that first game. We had gone a goal up and I had played an early part in it by winning a defensive header. Tony Adams came over to me and congratulated me for my small part but about three minutes later, when I was feeling quite pleased with myself, the winger Muller drifted across me, spun inside, received the ball and crossed for Mirandinha to score. I remember Bobby pulling me aside at half-time and telling me to concentrate at all times. He said that I had missed my man and he was right. The lesson was the higher you go, the harder you must concentrate. I was thinking I had Muller but he made the run before that ball was on its way and by the time I realised he had reached the by-line and made his cross.

We drew 1–1 against a good Brazilian side and didn't play too badly. I was happy to come through it with only the one black mark against me. My philosophy from that game onwards was that if I played well it would be worth two caps, one for the game I played in and the next because I would keep my place. I roomed with Des Walker for many of my England games and we would always say to each other before the games, 'Come on, good game today. Two more caps.'

I kept my place against Scotland and we drew 0–0. Two games, two caps, two draws and when I think back it couldn't have been a tougher baptism. They don't come much bigger than those two.

England versus Scotland is a massive game at any time. I was gutted not to be involved when we played them twice in the Euro 2000, qualifier.

I must have impressed Bobby Robson in those first two games because I was in the squad after that, albeit as Kenny Sansom's understudy. I learned a lot from Kenny even though we were such contrasting players in the same position. I often wondered whether Kenny remembered the time when my manager at Wealdstone embarrassed me at the PFA dinner by telling him I would take his place. He was a better player than me, cultured, stayed on his feet, and passed the ball well. He was the neatest winner of tackles I have ever seen. He did all the things well that Clough told me I couldn't do.

Basically, I stayed in the squad from 1987, picking up the odd cap when Kenny was out, and I learned my international trade.

My next appearance was early the next season, this time as a substitute against West Germany! All the big ones first. Talk about a baptism of fire.

The game was in Dusseldorf. We were losing with about ten minutes to go when Bobby Robson, who was known to get the odd name wrong in his time, started shouting down the bench, 'Gary, Gary, get warmed up.' I knew he was talking to me but I thought no, I'm not going to look at him, I'm going to wait until he gets my name right. Then I thought if I don't look up in a minute I'm not going to get on at all. My philosophy thereafter was no matter what name he shouted I would jump up and start warming up, even if he shouted Glenn.

That game passed me by. When I looked for a pass or looked down to play the ball, by the time I looked up again a German had moved from there to there and intercepted it. It was all that much quicker – not just speed of foot but speed of thought. You start to think that the quality and the speed are beyond you, but it's a case of getting used to it. Bobby Robson's yardstick was that after a dozen international games a player should be playing to his standard. I thought that was about right.

Bobby had been around for a while and was comfortable in the job despite an immense amount of pressure from the media. He had his old England team-mate Don Howe working on the defence. Don was an out-and-out defender; he loved a clean sheet every bit as much as Shilton. He would take the defenders away from the others and there would be a few moans and groans and we watched the rest go off for a five-a-side or crossing and shooting. We would be in the penalty area with Don. 'Swivel your head,' he'd shout, 'Get your head round,' 'Get your head on it,' 'Go and win it.' Rodders (Tony Adams), Big Butch (Terry Butcher), me and the other central defenders would come off with headaches while the others had been enjoying a jolly-up.

But, when all was said and done, Don drummed it into every defender what it meant at this level. That was where I really started learning my trade, going from being a club player with potential to having Nottingham Forest and England after my name.

I managed to fit in two more games after West Germany, playing against Israel and Hungary and it was in Budapest that I damaged my knee. Silly really, just pushing off to run and slipping on the grass after 15 minutes. The doctor pulled me off at half-time, strapped me up and I went straight back home to have an operation.

That was me finished for a while. I missed the disastrous 1988 European Championship in Germany. I would have gone as understudy to Kenny but would almost certainly have had a game against Russia when we were already out and Bobby Robson made a number of changes. It was a massive disappointment. Even if I hadn't been playing I would have willingly gone and sat on the bench for every match because there are only 22 people selected out of the entire country. I was just proud to be in the squad.

I watched the tournament on television and, like all England supporters, I was disappointed that we did not play to our potential because of injuries and illness. It proved to be something of a watershed. Kenny and a few others retired from the scene, giving players like me the chance to establish ourselves in the side.

We had qualified well for 1988, building up high hopes.

We qualified quite well, too, for the next World Cup two years later. In fact, in the eight years that Bobby was in charge, he lost only one qualifying match in both competitions and none while I was in the squad.

Paul Gascoigne was breaking into the squad and there were some good established players. Gary Lineker was scoring a phenomenal number of goals. Peter Beardsley was there and Clive Allen, Mark Hateley, Chris Waddle, John Barnes, Shilton, who had been around for a million years, and Big Butch at the back. Captain Marvel Robson was still in midfield along with Ray Wilkins, another of my heroes whom I had watched and admired when I was a non-league player. The closest I had come to him before was playing with his brother Dean in the district side when I was at school.

It was a big, big tournament but I had more than a dozen caps under my belt by then and was one of the seasoned players. In fact, by the time of the 1990 World Cup I had a couple of dozen and had not missed a match since I became a regular in Bobby Robson's team. Tony Dorigo was coming along, pushing me. He was an outstanding player and he deserved more caps than he won. I was glad he didn't get them because they would have been at my expense. That big, strong player Mitchell Thomas was coming through too, so there was plenty of pressure and I was always looking over my shoulder. My personal adage of playing for two caps at a time was never more appropriate.

Leading up to the World Cup, some journalists were still saying that I was too fiery and too aggressive for a competition of this nature and intensity. They were sure that I would land myself in trouble and cost England. It reached something of a crescendo after we had played a friendly against Yugoslavia at Wembley in December 1989. They had quite a talented young midfield player who was playing really well and I felt that I had to sort him out a bit. I caught him just in front of the trainer's bench on the halfway line. It was a ridiculously late challenge and I did clear him out totally but I didn't do it just for the sake of kicking him. He was dictating the game and I wanted to give him a jolt and upset his rhythm. There are those who will say it was a disgraceful thing to do, but there was method in my madness because he was threatening to tear England apart. I was booked and later substituted by Dorigo. After the game, I took a lot of criticism from the media. But, as at club level, I stepped up to a certain mark and tried not to step over it. Once I had been booked, I settled down. There were, and still are, others who didn't; they continued to play at the same intensity and paid the penalty.

There seemed to be a glut of fairly wild left-backs around at the time – the big Scot Doug Rougvie, Pat Van Den Hauwe, Julian Dicks, Mark Dennis – and I was slung into that category. They were players who liked to leave their mark. I admit that I pressed it to a certain level to make my job easier. If opponents were scared of me so much the better. I would do it coldly and deliberately; emotion didn't come into it. Others maybe didn't have that strategy.

I learned from an early stage and being sent off at Leicester probably did me a lot of good. Clough made it clear that I had let down both the team and myself. You either learn your lessons quickly and move on or you end up sinking. I have never had any manager tell me to kick anyone directly but when I first started off it was a known thing that you went as tight as you could and made life as unpleasant for your forward opponent as you could.

In my first season at Coventry City, Bobby Gould asked Terry Gibson before a game against Spurs whom he would rather play against, Graham Roberts or Paul Miller. When Gibson told him Miller, Gould asked why and he told him because Roberts would give him a bigger kicking. I rest my case. If someone doesn't like it, do it some more. If they enjoy it, you have to change your game plan and do something else.

Football revolves around little battles. You know you can scare the life out of some and others aren't troubled and you have to handle them differently. Some you let have the ball to their feet because you know they are not good enough to go past you; others you have to stand up tight on tight. That's when you say to Des Walker or whoever's playing that you can't cover him today because your man is a threat not only to you but also to the team.

The game has changed and the philosophy has changed but I haven't. It might seem cold-hearted but as long as I can look in the mirror at the end of the game and say that I have played well and done my best for my team then I'm happy.

Bobby had a word with me after the tackle in the Yugoslavia game and told me to calm down on the tackling and to use my head. He had seen an awful tackle from his left-back 20 yards in front of him and he didn't know what was going through my mind or how well in control I really was. He obviously thought I went too far because he took me off in that game and that meant that I had lost out.

Looking back now, I wish I had thought about the game

a lot more then than I did, but that is all part of growing up. You have to learn and learn quickly and the higher up the ladder you go the quicker you have to learn. In some ways I have been lucky because if I were graphing my career it would show that I have gone up very gradually. I would have found it difficult if I had gone in as quickly as Michael Owen, for instance. He almost certainly has a wiser head on his shoulders than I ever had; at his age I was being arrested for bad behaviour.

The game has changed and the tolerance has changed. Managers are sacked after a couple of bad weeks and that was unheard of then. You have to be cute and change along with it. When the rules changed about a booking without a warning for instance, I changed straightaway and that's why I'm still knocking around. These days, you can go off for one tackle that less than ten years ago would have resulted in a finger-wagging admonishment from the referee. In all, I was booked five times for England and was never sent off. I consider that a fair return for an aggressive defender playing so many internationals, many of them of an extremely competitive nature.

A cheap booking is for swearing at a referee. I did it once and learned my lesson. I would never swear at a referee now. I don't even bother talking to them. I would rather get booked for kicking someone, which could help my game, rather than calling a referee a twat, which helps nobody.

I was lucky that once I left non-league I didn't really come across anyone who set out deliberately to kick me. They were queuing up when I was at Wealdstone and perhaps those five tough years moulded me and the non-league mentality I had served me as a good apprenticeship.

I took that with me into the professional game. It was a case of stand up and be counted or you were out of it. There were a lot of nasty sods about 20 years ago.

At international level they can be a bit slyer, certainly a bit quicker, but there has never been an opponent who has physically intimidated me. There has been more than one who has been prepared to have a go at me. When I was playing in Europe with Forest against Bordeaux, I went up with the French international Yannick Stopyra and we clashed. I won the header but he thought I had elbowed him. The ball was quickly transferred to the other end and with everyone's attention elsewhere he promptly chinned me. I lost my rag but stayed in control. I waited for the next tackle because if I had punched him back it would have been me who would have gone off.

I have been able to keep a lid on it with everything except spitting. That's a habit I despise. The closest anyone has come was Savo Milosevic at Aston Villa. I tackled him, he looked at me, went to spit, and then changed his mind and spat at the floor. If it had hit me I would have done nothing then but I would certainly have gone looking for him in the dressing-room after the game and sorted it out. I'm usually able to deal with a situation later, when I won't be sent off.

If you live by the sword you have to be prepared to die by it. Opponents know they can try it on with me because I won't be running to the referee. John Fashanu was close to breaking my leg when he stamped on me. I won't stand up and shout my mouth off to the referee or to the press because I have given as much as I've taken. My career means too much for me to let someone walk over me. I have never broken anyone's leg, I have never been malicious and I have never deliberately gone over the ball when I've been face-to-face with an opponent. Somewhere among all of the clippings there are sure to be one or two to prove me wrong but they will be few and far between and they have never been on purpose.

I was lucky that in my international career, particularly in the early days, we played mainly 4-4-2 against sides who were playing wing-backs. It meant that I didn't have to face players who would take me on in a one-to-one situation like I did at home with genuine wingers like John Barnes, Chris Waddle or Pat Nevin who could dribble past you. I was never that exposed. It was more often the subtle things that showed me up, like the Brazilian winger Muller's move when my error cost us a goal and a win.

I've had my bad, indifferent and good games for England, as most have, but I have never gone away thinking that a player has destroyed me. For the two games we played against Holland in the 1994 World Cup qualifiers, when I would have been up against Marc Overmars, I was out injured and Tony Dorigo had to cope with him. Now Overmars is the sort of player who can hurt you.

Qualifying for the 1990 World Cup was never easy but we went to Poland for the last game undefeated, wanting a point to be sure. In the last minute, a lad named Tarasiewicz fired in a shot that hit the bar so hard it rebounded to the halfway line. Peter Shilton said he had it covered all the way, of course! It's amazing how often Poland cropped up during my international career. I swear I have more Polish shirts in my cupboard at home than any other country in the world. In fact, if you took away Poland and Brazil I would be down to my last 60 caps. Funnily enough, while everyone wants that famous Brazilian shirt, the first time I played against them in my debut I wouldn't give my shirt to anyone. It was a proud moment and I wanted to keep it. The England shirt was a much more prized possession to me than any Brazilian shirt. I wasn't cute enough at the time to tell a Brazilian to come to the dressing-room afterwards so I could have given him my spare shirt. I wanted the one I had worn.

The 1990 World Cup finals was the next step up. Playing for your club is one thing, stepping up to international level is another, but going to a major tournament, and they do not come any bigger than the World Cup, is different altogether. You cannot go any further in football; it is the pinnacle of what you can achieve.

There was quite a lengthy build-up to the finals, so much so that we were able to invite our wives over for one of the weeks we were on the holiday island of Sardinia. Without being mean to Liz I told her that I would have preferred to be on my own. I explained it was a football environment and that I would rather have been there focusing on the job in front of me. All I was thinking about was the World Cup two weeks away and it didn't feel right lying on the beach sunbathing with Liz and the other players' wives. Probably further down the line I would have been more relaxed about it but not then. I am not complaining about the organisation, which was perfect, right down to moving hotels once the girls had gone. We left the quiet luxury of the Is Morus hotel, on the beach, for the more spartan and workmanlike Is Molas Golf hotel, further inland and, as its name suggests, on a golf course. For a lot of players it was perfect. We had the odd meal out and we were still training, of course, but as I said to both Liz and Des Walker, I would rather be in a football-only environment.

The friendlies and bits and pieces were eventually out of the way and we played the Republic of Ireland, Holland and Egypt in our qualifying group. Not so long ago I watched those three games again as part of my coaching badge course. It was my choice. I thought they would be ideal because they were part of a tournament. Three worse games you probably wouldn't see. The Irish game, played on a bitterly cold, windy, wet night, was typically dour with Jack Charlton's team launching the ball up the middle. We took the lead, inevitably through Gary Lineker, but finished up drawing 1–1. The nerves struck us. I remember Bobby having a little go at me and asking what was the matter. I said it must be nerves and he responded that the reason he had given me more than 20 caps was that I didn't get nervous. It was spot on by him, but this was another big step.

We lost Bryan Robson early on in the second game against Holland and he had to go home injured. He had problems with his Achilles, then suffered a further injury to his toe in an incident in the team hotel. There was bad feeling over this with the press complaining that they had been misled and lied to. The result was that some of the players decided they weren't going to talk to the press anymore. It made no difference to me because I had used the old Brian Clough escape clause.

It became even worse later on when the *Sun* ran a story that some of the team had been out disco dancing with one of the World Cup hostesses and that three of the team had gone to bed with her. Bobby Robson called a meeting the night before and told us that he had been warned that they were carrying this story and that it named three players – Peter Beardsley, John Barnes and me. Everyone immediately burst out laughing. Barnes may have had a bit of a reputation, but Peter and me? They had to be joking!

I went back to my room with the right hump and telephoned Liz. I told her that I had been with England for six weeks going from my room to the restaurant to the video room to the swimming pool, to training, to matches. I had not even had a drink, out of choice. I was there to work. I told her about the story in the paper but she was not worried because she knew what I was like where my country was concerned.

I found it more than a little bit irritating that I was there representing my country and that family and relatives of Liz had to read this garbage. She laughed it off, as did Bobby Robson, but from then on my attitude hardened. If a youngster asks me what it's like to play in a big tournament I tell them that there's a cycle. The football season in England ends and until then everyone is concentrating on the championship and the Cup. Then for a couple of weeks not much is happening and the papers look for stories about players. When the first ball is kicked, that's all forgotten and everyone is concerned about the football again. You don't notice the pattern when you're at home watching on television but when you're away you realise that's how it works. I learned to keep my head down.

Invariably it forges a siege mentality. Even before the World Cup the press had been hammering Bobby Robson. On arrival they turned their attention to what we were up to, trying to find out what and how much we had been drinking. Then came the accusations about the hostess. Everyone in the squad turned inwards. As a bonding exercise it worked quite well, although I'm sure that's not what the papers had in mind.

We played seven games in that World Cup and it was only in the later ones that we really did ourselves justice. When we came home to a heroes' welcome, the early matches were glossed over. No one seemed to remember the stick we took in the papers over the way we failed to perform, preferring to recall only the semi-final when we were unlucky not to go through.

We had fun and games at the hotel, a big video, horse racing games, all sorts of things designed to kill time but at the same time to conserve energy. We were advised not to sit in the sun day in and day out, although some did. Gary Lineker could have swapped passports with John Barnes after a couple of weeks.

The biggest source of entertainment was Paul Gascoigne. He couldn't sit still for two minutes; he'd be up and down, here and there. We were relaxing by the swimming pool one day when he disappeared yet again only to reappear minutes later having covered himself from head to foot in toilet paper. He dived off the board into the pool. Only he knows why.

On another day, sponsors Wilson arranged a golf day for us on the course adjacent to the hotel. In England clubs are a bit picky about what you must wear on their courses. They are more relaxed about it in Sardinia but not so much as Gazza thought. He tried to play his round in shorts and flipflops. He also upset a few by driving his buggy through the bunkers and parking it on the putting green.

Bobby Robson had his big day out when the RAF took him up in a jet fighter while we were there. He came back that night late for dinner and he was absolutely made up, with that same look on his face that he had when he took over at Newcastle United. He couldn't stop talking about it until he looked over at Terry Butcher, Gary Stevens and Chris Waddle. They had persuaded the wine waiter to fill a load of empty wine bottles with water and they were sat at a table for four wearing everything back to front or inside out, with their hair greased back. They were there when everyone arrived and we watched in amazement as they ate their meal backwards, starting with coffee, dessert, main course and soup while quaffing bottle after bottle of 'wine'.

When Bobby spotted them he stopped mid-eulogy and stared at his former Ipswich captain Terry Butcher sitting there with a full glass, surrounded by empty bottles and wearing a baseball cap inside out and the wrong way round. It was like a red rag to a bull. He thought they were drinking wine and muttered idiot, idiot until he twigged that he was being wound up. It was brilliant because no one knew that they were going to do it. At the end of their meal they stood up and said, 'Thank you, gentlemen, and goodnight.' As they emerged from the shelter of the long tablecloths, we could see that they had nothing on, apart from G-strings, from the waist downwards. They were applauded out of the room.

Little things like that get you through the long weeks. Another diversion much appreciated by everyone was a race night with Gary Lineker and Peter Shilton nominated as the bookmakers. The rest of the boys persuaded the physiotherapist Fred Street to have a peek at the penultimate race in advance and then pass the winner on to the lads. We received the nod for number seven and we all piled our money on, some putting on as much as £2,000. Everyone was on number seven. Halfway round, number seven was nowhere to be seen and we were all beginning to wonder if this was a double bluff to match *The Sting*. Fred was trying to reassure everyone but by the three-quarters stage number seven was still not in the frame. Shilton, a man who likes a gamble, was rubbing his hands in expectation. Then suddenly number seven appeared from nowhere and stormed past everything with the entire room going up and Shilts totally devastated. Gazza was doing forward rolls and everyone was giving it the high fives. You would have thought that we had just won the World Cup. Shilts honestly believed that he had been wiped out. His losses came to thousands of pounds and he looked ready to do something silly until we took pity on him and admitted it had been a wind-up.

We had the English newspapers delivered every morning. I used to take the *Daily Express* at the time but one day when I came down for breakfast all of the papers had gone. Steve Hodge and Paul Parker had taken them all to their room. I knocked on their door and Hodgey opened it half an inch and asked what I wanted. When I told him I would like to look at a newspaper he asked which one I wanted. I told him the *Express*. He wanted to know what I wanted it for. I told him that I wanted to do the crossword. The door closed and reopened minutes later and he handed me the crossword, neatly cut out of the paper but with no clues. It wasn't until late afternoon that they returned the papers. Goodness knows what they did with them.

Bobby Robson changed the team for the Holland game, bringing in Mark Wright as a sweeper and replacing Gary Stevens with Paul Parker. The word was that the deep-thinking Chris Waddle had influenced the choice. He was a senior player and strongly in favour of playing three at the back. It was revealed later that Bobby had made the decision a long time before, having been turned over by the Dutch in a European Championship game when Marco Van Basten scored a hat-trick. The way I remember it, Chrissie was pivotal in the decision. Whoever made it, the plan worked and we were all very comfortable with the system. Paul Parker and myself were both pretty athletic up and down the wings, Des Walker, Terry Butcher and Mark Wright gelled while Gazza and Chris Waddle worked the midfield.

As a 4-4-2 line-up we hadn't really fired. We had been a bit predictable and I think even now that we play better with the sweeper system; it gives us a lot more flexibility. Although we drew 0–0 I 'scored' from a free kick with ten minutes to go from just outside the box. It was an indirect free kick but I thought I would hammer it goalwards believing that it would be a brave goalkeeper who would just let it go straight into the net. Hans Van Breukelen, the Dutch goalkeeper, dived but it went past him and in. I knew all along that it was indirect but it was as good an option as any. Van Breukelen told me that he knew it was indirect and deliberately let it in. I thought if that was true he made a bloody good effort to save it.

The Dutch team had all their stars playing, including Ruud Gullit, Marco Van Basten, Wim Kieft, Frank Rijkaard, Ronald Koeman and the rest, but when I returned to the dressing-room it was to hear Shilton ranting and raving at Des Walker, calling him a cheat because Van Basten had beaten him once in the game and got in a shot from 30 yards. I bristled on behalf of my mate and had a go back at Shilton. Des had nigh on marked Van Basten out of the game. One thing Des is not is a cheat. A more honest player you would never come across. We had the right hump with our goalkeeper but that was nothing new. He used to go through black moods and was often at logger-heads with several of the players.

We now had to beat Egypt in our final game to qualify. We would have settled for that at the start of the tournament. We didn't play well but we won with a Mark Wright header and we were into the next round against Belgium in Bologna.

We went into the game thinking we had a decent draw but they shook us. Enzo Scifo played brilliantly in midfield and almost put Belgium in front when he struck a post. There was little in it and as extra time ticked by penalties appeared to be a racing certainty. I believe that's where the Belgians slipped up. They thought the same deadlock was not going to be broken and they lost concentration. With a minute remaining, Gascoigne took a free kick near the halfway line and David Platt, who had come on as a substitute for Bryan Robson's replacement Steve McMahon, took the ball over his shoulder and volleyed a spectacular goal.

The pressure is on when you are in the knock-out stages, especially with England. Whatever the tournament, if you go out in the league stages that is considered abject failure. Once you are in the knock-out stages, you start to get a bit of momentum, dropping the nerves and beginning to feel that you are there by right. The more we progressed the greater was the confidence, especially when we heard that we were to play the surprise quarter-finalists Cameroon. Without any disrespect, we would have settled for that any day of the week and Howard Wilkinson, who had spied on them for Bobby, reported that we had as good as a bye. It turned out to be the hardest bye we had ever played and for a long time it looked as though we were going out.

We might have settled for the quarter-finals, having got that far four years earlier in Mexico, but when we drew the African outsiders we were expected to get through to the last four and we believed we could do it.

It was a long walk from the dressing-rooms in Naples. You go from the centre of the pitch at one side, behind one of the goals and up the other side. We walked out together and the African side were singing tribal songs. Some of our lads found it amusing; I didn't think that it was at all funny. After all they might just turn us over in a few minutes. I tried to stay focused.

Everything went to plan and we were very confident when, after 25 minutes, Terry Butcher sent me off down the right and I crossed for David Platt to score the sort of goal he was scoring regularly for Aston Villa. Usually when you score that first goal you are home and dry, particularly against the still-emerging African nations. Cameroon did not have the best of disciplinary records and had players sent off for fun in the early rounds. In fact, four of their best players were suspended.

Nevertheless, this was a team of giants. A very physical side, they came back at us instead of letting their heads drop. When Gascoigne brought down the veteran substitute

Roger Milla in the penalty area, Kunde beat Shilton from the spot to equalise and then another substitute, Ekeke, scored from a pass from Milla. I tackled someone and received one of my few international bookings, which as it turned out sent me into the semi-final against West Germany, along with Gazza, on a knife-edge. When you are 2–1 down you tend to become a bit more robust because you think you may be going out anyway. It looked as though that's just what would happen but suddenly Gazza and Peter Beardsley began to play and slowly we forced our way back into the game. Even then it took two penalties to see us through and both times it was Gary Lineker who was brought down, the first eight minutes from time and the second 14 minutes into extra time. Each time he picked himself up and scored.

I remember just into extra time I left a back pass short and let Roger Milla in. It took a fantastic save from Peter Shilton to stop us going behind again and Shilton gave me an almighty rollicking. It did me the world of good, a real kick up the arse.

No England team had ever been to a semi-final in a World Cup away from England and the momentum was growing. We were beginning to think we were a team capable of doing something. The draw for the semi-final threw us up against our old rivals West Germany in Turin. We weren't afraid although we would have much preferred to play either Italy or Argentina at that stage. In a strange way the pressure was off us because we had reached further than anyone back home had expected at the start of the tournament. Cameroon had shaken us but we were through and began to fancy ourselves, with some justification.

We played as well against the Germans as we had done not only in the tournament but for the previous couple of years or so. Early on in the game I was man to man with their wing-back Thomas Hassler and when I brought him down I feared the worst. The Brazilian referee Jose Ramirez Wright just awarded the free kick and I breathed a huge sigh of relief.

I felt they were fortunate to be in front with a freak Brehme goal that spun over Shilton from a massive deflection off Paul Parker after an hour. We fully deserved our equaliser, an outstanding effort from Gary Lineker ten minutes from time.

So for the third game in succession we were taken to extra time, very draining in the heat of the Italian summer. Eight minutes into the extra period Gazza mistimed a tackle on Berthold and was booked. I thought the referee was influenced by the reaction of the German bench who were close to where the foul took place. Even then we might have won it. Waddle hit the inside of a post. Normally from that angle the ball will deflect into the net but this one came straight back out and we were heading for penalties and my historic miss.

Chrissie managed to exorcise some of his personal ghosts in the third place play-off game against Italy when he replaced Steve McMahon. Neil Webb took over from Mark Wright when we were chasing the game. We'd gone down to a Roberto Baggio goal a minute earlier after a Shilton mistake. David Platt equalised but Schillaci dived over Paul Parker's outstretched leg to win an undeserved penalty and with it the game.

I had the utmost respect for Bobby Robson who was,

even then, an elder statesman of football. I could never see anyone fronting Bobby in the dressing-room in an aggressive manner. Everyone respected him. His decision not to play me in that final game did not cloud my judgement of him at all. He made decisions that were right for England; all I had been thinking about was Stuart Pearce.

That was his last game in charge of England and I could see how sad he was having had such a hell of a tilt at the title. World Cup quarter-finals and semi-finals, both away from home, and the loss of just one qualifying match in eight years – that's a tremendous record. We were disappointed not to win for him but were also disappointed for ourselves. Winning the Fair Play Trophy was hardly compensation – in fact for me it was a positive insult!

Just before Bryan Robson left we were sitting by the swimming pool and he was putting on a brave face, saying that he would be able to attend his brother's wedding after all, but it was clear he was devastated. He had been to both the 1982 and 1986 World Cups and this was going to be his last. He was gutted. He had tasted two World Cups and he was looking for more. He would have given anything to be on that open-topped bus going through the streets of Luton. I didn't realise how important the World Cup was for so many people until we came home.

We came back with so much more stature than when we went. We didn't know what we were capable of when we went but coming back we knew what we could have done – we could have won it. Had we drawn anyone else, either Italy or Argentina, in that semi-final we would probably have won because we were getting better with every match.

I am often asked who is the most difficult player I have faced over the years and people are usually surprised when I reply Mark Ward; some even say Mark who? Even West Ham supporters seem surprised that I have picked out one of their less lauded Hammers rather than Marco Van Basten, for instance.

Mark Ward was a direct little player who liked to run at you with the ball at his feet. It is probably through him that I have had more bad games at Upton Park than at most other places. I was up against him when I was substituted for one of the three times in my Forest career.

Pat Nevin was another difficult player. When he was on fire, he was tricky and direct with a few skills. He was probably on the receiving end of some of the worst tackles that I have ever dished out. He agreed with that when I discussed it with him but he bears no malice.

Every player throws up a different challenge and if you are not up to it you will be slaughtered whoever it is. The odds, though, weigh heavily in favour of the defender. The more often I play against a forward the better I feel against him. You get to know their tricks and style but if you are weak in character and you have a bad time against an opponent, the next time you will not fancy it.

How often do you see a player come into the League, a foreign player or a youngster, and he does really well in that first season? Gianfranco Zola is a classic example. He was outstanding in his first season for Chelsea and was named Player of the Year but, in his second season, teams were playing man-for-man against him. Defenders knew what was coming and he was not quite as lethal. But it's hard to be a surprise package in the Premier Division these days.

To do my homework, all I have to do is switch on the television two or three times a week and there they are in front of me.

At international level, for the majority of matches we would watch our opponents on video. It would have been naïve not to. As a defender you don't want to be surprised.

Aggressive opponents have never bothered me. What I fear most, along with every other defender, is sheer, raw pace. It doesn't matter how quick you are, there is always someone quicker. Michael Owen is a case in point. On skill alone you fancy your chances but his pace is frightening and puts you on the back foot. His finishing is a bonus. If an opponent is tricky but not too fast, that's not such a problem because you simply get close to him. But if he's tricky and fast, you have to give him a few yards in case the ball is played over the top. If you are not tight he can get the ball to feet, turn and take you on. In the old days you could try to intimidate them but that is not the case anymore. You have to be a lot more artful.

Des Walker used to say that top international players always have one characteristic that lifts them above the others. With Gary Lineker and Alan Shearer it's their finishing, with Michael Owen and Andrei Kanchelskis it's their blinding pace and Les Ferdinand and Duncan Ferguson are the best headers of the ball in Britain. The first choice on my list of defenders was also the first choice of Bobby Robson's England team list for many years. Who else but my old friend and playing partner Des Walker? He was magnificent in terms of consistency for Forest and was one of the reasons why we achieved what we did and why I was able to go forward so often to join attacks.

In the modern game I love Jaap Stam of Manchester United. He defends strongly and well. He is a terrific player with good pace. In one Champions League game, a forward backed up towards the penalty area while waiting for a free kick from the halfway line. Stam just stood there and let the player bump off him as if to say to his opponent that he was going no further. It showed that he has something about him. I read that he loves his football, isn't too bothered about having a big flash car and is as happy going to the supermarket shopping with his wife as to a celebrity function. He seems to be an ordinary bloke and I like to think that he and I are a little alike. I reckon he was cheap at the price of £12 million that Alex Ferguson paid for him.

Tony Adams is another who stands up to be counted. In a rich vein of form he is a world-class defender. He always stands tall, shouting the orders and taking responsibility. When things aren't going right he can be exposed but ten times out of ten I would want him in my team.

As far as left-backs are concerned I favour those who offer something a little bit different. Tony Dorigo, who had electric pace and was neater than I was on the ball, pushed me for years. I admire the skills that he has and I haven't. He has been unlucky not to win more caps than he did, a bit like West Bromwich Albion's Derek Statham who had to follow Kenny Sansom around for so many years.

In international terms, in my spot I would pick Roberto Carlos of Brazil. He has stunning pace but people say that he can't defend. Sometimes when you can run as fast as he can, you can get yourself into the right positions, but I am not so sure that he can't defend. I certainly haven't seen too many forwards take liberties with him! For me the man can attack, defend, score goals and has that pace.

Kenny was another who had something I didn't. He was neat and such a clean tackler he never gave away free kicks. Forwards would run at him but he would stand up and just take the ball off them whereas I would back off and jockey, wishing I could do it like Kenny. When he won the ball he used it so well. I had aggression and was better in the air so I scored a lot more goals than he did – in fact, more than most defenders, with 87 in my career. But I happily acknowledge that Kenny kept me out of the England team by right because he was a hell of a better player than I was at the time.

It is odd that currently we have such a dearth of left-backs. It is nothing to do with the way the game has developed but simply cyclical. When I was in the side with Tony Dorigo breathing down my neck, he had Julian Dicks breathing down his. Julian was a player something like me – combative, a goalscorer. When he was playing well we were carbon copies. But it didn't end there; Mark Dennis was also a strong, powerful left-back and Arsenal's Nigel Winterburn earned an England cap while I was around. The only other time our paths crossed was when Dave Bassett tried to sign me for Wimbledon from Wealdstone, couldn't get me and signed Winterburn instead. It turned out to be one of his best signings. Nigel did well not only for the Dons but went on to win just about every honour for Arsenal, playing in what became a legendary back four with Lee Dixon, Tony Adams and Martin Keown or Steve Bould.

How strange it is that left-backs through the years have tended to be so much more aggressive than right-backs. Apart from those mentioned, Pat Van Den Hauwe and Doug Rougvie, name me a right-back in that same style. It is not easy.

from bad to worse

Bobby Robson was the man who gave me my international chance and helped me to play in a massive tournament, falling short just one step from the final. He was succeeded by Graham Taylor and, while I am grateful to Robson for giving me my start, I am equally thankful to Taylor for making me captain of my country, a great honour.

Over my time England have ridden a roller coaster. We did badly in 1988 in the European Championships in Germany and then did well in the 1990 World Cup finals. We reached the European finals in 1992, where we were disappointing, and did even worse when we could not reach the 1994 World Cup finals, but then we excelled in the 1996 European Championships in England, before we failed to fulfil our potential in 1998 in the World Cup in France.

As a nation, we have too many troughs and not enough peaks, never having that remarkable consistency of the Germans who can turn it on tournament after tournament, which was why their dismal showing in Euro 2000 was such a surprise to so many, even though it was clear they were not the force they once were.

In this respect I felt sorry for Graham Taylor when he took over. In many ways it was like following Brian Clough at Nottingham Forest, because Bobby Robson had gone out on a high and come back to England a hero.

I thought Taylor was the right choice for England manager at the time. In fact, I will go further and say that every time an England manager has been chosen he has been the right one at the time. I have been involved for 12 years and I am sure the clever beggars will look back in hindsight and say they knew that the FA had picked the wrong one. But for me there is no doubt: Robson was the right choice; Taylor was the best at the time; Terry Venables was the right choice and so was Glenn Hoddle. Then few would argue with the selection of Kevin Keegan, although it might be argued that they could have brought back Terry Venables who was available.

It was unfortunate for Graham in that we hit such an all-time high in Italy and the only way to go was down. Bryan Robson played only three more times for England, while we also lost Terry Butcher and Peter Shilton, experienced cornerstones of the team.

I was in the frame to replace Captain Marvel as skipper, along with Gary Lineker plus two or three other outsiders. I have never talked to Graham about it but I am sure that in hindsight he would have gone for me as captain rather than Gary. In some ways I am more of a Graham Taylor player than Gary was. We are different people; he was good with the press, a model professional, and a good goal scorer without being blessed with a great deal of talent outside the box. Whereas I could hardly be described as being good with the press, although I would do it if I had to, and I had a bit of nastiness about me whereas Gary had never been booked. Public perception would have probably given it to him, but I was more of a captain on the pitch than he would ever be.

It wasn't until the end of 1992 that Graham Taylor finally came to me and offered me the captaincy. That was an unbelievably prestigious thing to have thrust upon you. There are few players who have the good fortune to be selected for England and even fewer who are able to say they captained England.

Graham, like so many managers, plays the odd mind game and, in summer 1991 when we went on tour to Australia, New Zealand twice and Malaysia, Gary was made captain for the trip. Taylor saw us beaten only once between Italia 90 and the European Championships in 1992. While we were there, Gary had to pop over to Japan for some publicity event and that was when I first captained my country against New Zealand, and I celebrated with a goal.

The first time I captained England at Wembley was in February 1992 against France. It was another proud moment, and Liz was due to come and watch. Sadly she had a strange problem to contend with and didn't see me lead the team out that night.

When we bought our house there were chickens and the previous owners asked us did we want them to put them down or did we want to keep them. Put like that there was only one choice and we kept them. I had to ask how to look after them and was told it was just a question of throwing a handful of corn down every day. I thought even I could handle that little chore.

But on the day of the game one of our horses, a thoroughbred named Archie, found it amusing to boot them when they came near him. All of these chickens were named after meals and Archie took it on himself to go over the top on poor Chicken Kiev, putting a big hole in his side. So Liz couldn't come to the game because she had to take the injured chicken to the vet's. While I was captaining England, Liz sat waiting her turn at the vet's with Chicken Kiev in a box and missed my biggest day. Not only that but she was also embarrassed when she had to answer the receptionist's questions. Imagine it: 'What sort of pet is it?'

'A chicken.'

'What's its name?'

'Chicken Kiev.'

'How do you spell that?'

'K-I-E-V.'

'What sex is it?'

'It's a chicken, so it must be female!'

At least Archie only kicked him once and then backed off. He had learned well and wasn't shown the red card.

Two years down the line, when Gary had retired after being pulled off in his last game in the European Championship, Graham telephoned me to ask if he could come to my house in Nottingham. In the back of my mind I thought that I was either going to be offered the captaincy or I was in for the chop.

He was very proud and passionate to be the England manager and I don't think the public realised just what it meant to him, because he didn't wear it on his sleeve all of the time. I knew because I was in the dressing-room all the time with him and I could see in his eyes how important it was.

I believe that, probably because of his background as

manager of Watford, he was more comfortable with players like me around him than he was with the superstars who were always in the media spotlight. I wanted to work and would rather not see my face splattered across the papers. That made me Graham Taylor's sort of player. When he asked me to be his captain, it was phenomenal. I couldn't have been prouder.

But perhaps Graham overdid it with his selection of honest, hard-working players. When I look back over that period at some of those he introduced to international football I wonder where they are now. Players like Andy Sinton, Tony Daley, Carlton Palmer, Geoff Thomas, Keith Curle and others appeared under Graham and then vanished. When other managers picked players regularly, they generally stayed around a lot longer when a new coach came in.

Bobby certainly had more international class players, in some case world-class players available to him. For, in the main, England players – with a few exceptions on the periphery – pick themselves. It might be argued that Graham was not blessed with a good crop of players at the time, having hit a downward spiral after the semi-finals.

I must say, however, that I enjoyed my time working with him. It didn't go too badly as we qualified for the 1992 European Championship in Sweden and a good many fancied us to win it. Graham, in fact, had a long honeymoon period before it went pear-shaped. In club terms, we would have won several championships as far as I was concerned, for in my 78 games, disregarding penalty shoot-outs, I can only remember being on the losing side half a dozen times, including a couple at Wembley against Uruguay and Brazil.

So the spirit in the camp was good when we went to Sweden and we quite fancied our chances. We opened with a 0–0 draw with Denmark and were then held 1–1 by France. It was similar to the 1990 World Cup when all the pressure was on the team in the group stage to do ourselves justice, live up to the nation's expectations and qualify. It is as simple as that.

In fact, Denmark hadn't even qualified for the tournament and their players were sitting on benches around the world when they were called into the finals after Yugoslavia had been thrown out because of the political situation there. That was the game we should have won, catching the Danes cold before they settled in but it was a pretty nondescript, poorish game.

England against France, like Scotland or Germany, is a grudge game and it was one we all looked forward to with great anticipation, but it was a big let-down and the nearest we came to winning was a 25-yard free kick of mine which rattled Bruno Martini's crossbar. The nearly man rears his head again! But it wasn't that incident for which I will be remembered from that game, because shortly before that moment I was head-butted by Basil Boli.

I was attacked because I left a little bit on their winger Jocelyn Angloma, who had come on at half-time. I had sorted him out on one or two occasions and Boli had spotted it and when the ball was tossed into the box he took retribution and did it well, I have to say. It was a bit like the old wrestler Johnny Quango as he butted me on the run and I went down, not because he'd knocked me down with it, but because I thought that the referee would see it and send him off. If someone puts the head on you are entitled to go down.

When I realised that the referee had not seen it I was extremely annoyed, but I kept it to myself, waiting for the right moment to gain a little of my own back if I could. The last thing I wanted to do was to chase an opponent, throw a punch and get sent off. Instead, I turned on the unsuspecting Angloma and said: 'That was you, you little bastard. I'm going to kill you.'

He was shaken to his boots and pleaded: 'Not me, not me.'

By this time he was frightened to death, thus making my job a lot easier.

A few minutes later we had a free kick on the edge of the box, perfect for the left-footer. It was mine, but the only problem was that the Hungarian referee Sandor Puhl had ordered me off because I still had blood streaming down my face from the cut on my cheekbone caused by Boli's head butt. I said to Lineker, who was standing over the ball: 'Don't you dare take that free kick. Wait for me.'

I ran over to the touchline, had the cut cleared up and vaselined and then raced back to take the free kick. By then I was steaming mad and Lineker said: 'Just smash it.' I did. It rammed against the underside of the crossbar, bounced on the line and out of the area. Where was the Russian linesman when you needed him?

It was late in the game and had that gone in we would have been through to the semi-finals. I can't remember hitting a ball as hard as that before or since. The whistle went soon afterwards and, as I left the pitch, with the blood still pouring down my face, I was stopped by the television people. I was the natural target mainly because the only two things that had happened of any note in the entire 90 minutes were Boli putting the head on me and then me hitting the crossbar.

As I was waiting for the interview to start Boli walked past me, but as I had cooled down by then and taken it as part of the game, I ignored him. Graham Taylor saw what was happening and sensibly dragged me away to the dressing-room to have my face cleaned up and gave me a little more time to cool down.

Those cuts always look worse on the face than they really are and all it needed was four or five stitches. I then told the manager that I didn't mind seeing the press as they had asked for me. I knew what they wanted and thought to myself if I had launched into Boli and said it was a disgrace and he should have been sent off, the tables would be turned on me and the cry would have gone up about my tackling Angloma. So I sat down at the press conference and told them that it was an innocent clash of heads. If I had told them I thought it was deliberate, I am sure that Boli would have been in a lot of trouble. But what was the percentage? We hadn't got to play them again and it was time I lived up to my adage of living by the sword. Had the incident happened now, I have no doubt that video evidence alone would have been enough to hang him and see him out of the remainder of the tournament.

Equally, if I had caught up with him and had the chance of gaining my revenge during what was left of the match I would have done so. But it was now all water under the bridge. I told them that I was more concerned with the free kick not going in and thought no more about it as we went back to our hotel.

Trevor Steven, who played with Boli at Marseille, later presented me with a fax that had come through to the hotel offices. It was from Boli, written in pidgin English, thanking me for my sportsmanship and wishing me well for the future. The press were desperate for the story but I had played it down and he appreciated it. I could understand his mentality. He had seen me whacking one of his weaker players and had come to look after him. I would have done the same thing, but I would not have resorted to head butting. That, like spitting, is for the thugs in the back street. Having something like that winds me up and gets the adrenalin flowing so that I play better. Certainly I wouldn't have hit that free kick as hard as I did without the Boli incident.

Having played those opening two games in Malmo, we then moved on to Stockholm to play the hosts, still needing a win to go through. We were nice and relaxed and had been to watch Bruce Springsteen in concert, along with most of the Swedish players, and I still quite fancied our chances.

I fancied them even more when David Platt scored from a Lineker centre after only four minutes and everything looked sweet. They made a couple of changes at the break and it made a difference. Central defender Eriksson scored with a header and Brolin scored the winner in the 82nd minute. But the big talking point afterwards was Graham Taylor's decision to substitute his captain Gary Lineker in the 64th minute of what turned out to be his last game for

England, replacing him with Arsenal striker Alan Smith. I don't know whether there were any politics behind that decision – only Graham and Gary would know that – but I am sure that Graham would not have pulled Gary off unless he thought that he could win the match by doing it and England must always come before the individual.

Gary was clearly annoyed and made it look bad by taking off his armband and throwing it on to the floor, in my direction, as I was taking over the captaincy. There was no doubt at that stage the way the game was going that we were never going to score a goal and it needed a change. But everyone was asking: why take off the player who had scored 48 goals for his country and had pulled us out of the fire more than once? I didn't think that at the time; I just thought we needed a substitute, anyone. We were going route one at the time, so Alan Smith seemed to be the logical choice.

It was really weird going back to the hotel that night. On the way to the match we had been thinking of a semi-final in Stockholm against Germany, but instead we were going back to pack our bags and go home the next day. It was so different from the World Cup two years earlier when we had come within the width of a post of reaching the World Cup final. It was a total anticlimax.

I have never known a feeling like it. The dinner was quiet because we knew we were finished and out of there that next morning. I wasn't ready to leave; it was too early. But, in truth, we were a few players short of being a good team and we didn't play well in the tournament. There was certainly something missing.

I felt before we set out for Scandinavia that Paul Merson

was going to make a name for himself in the competition. He hit a post in the first game against the eventual winners Denmark and had that gone in everything might have changed for him and the team. It didn't happen for Merson and it didn't happen for England. You create your own bit of luck, and had it gone our way in that first game, who knows? It wasn't a great tournament with few decent games and even the final, when Denmark beat the favourites Germany 2–0, was only exciting because of the triumph of the underdogs over the favourites.

Despite our lack of success in those finals, it was still a good squad to be around. We did everything together and there was a good spirit. One night we went to see the West End show *Buddy*, based on the life of Buddy Holly, and afterwards we were given the use of a private room in a hotel where we had a nice meal and then a karaoke afterwards. I have memories, or is it nightmares, of Graham Taylor, with his shirt open to the waist, singing a duet with Paul Gascoigne of 'Singing in the Rain' with some of the players pouring water over their heads.

We also had Steve Harrison in the squad for his banter as well as his coaching, a bit like Terry McDermott with Kevin Keegan and Kenny Dalglish at Newcastle. The boys loved him. The stunts he would pull were fantastic. One morning we were leaving the hotel for training when we heard someone shouting: 'The bells, the bells,' and throwing gravel at us. We looked up and there was Steve on the hotel roof playing Quasimodo. On another occasion, he sat with John Barnes on the team bus. Digger knew him from old and knew he was up to something when he sat there saying nothing, just smiling. He had been round the hotel garden in the morning collecting worms and it was only after about 15 minutes he opened his mouth and let one of the worms crawl out, followed by the others. It was thoroughly revolting but memorable. Hence the saying 'soppy as a bag of worms'.

There was nothing he wouldn't do to make the troops laugh. He would come into the dining hall and say how thirsty he was, pick up the pitcher and pour the water all over himself. He would sit there soaking wet eating his dinner as if nothing had happened. The lads loved him and he certainly eased the tension with his antics. Graham had him in the squad, I am sure, to take the pressure off and loosen people up a bit, especially the new boys. He broke the ice with a lot of players. I am sure it helped having him acting the fool. He eventually carried it too far, but none of the lads would have a word said against him.

The other regular face about the squad was Lawrie McMenemy, who was quickly nicknamed the Big Bopper after we had been to see the Buddy Holly story. I have heard since that there was animosity between Lawrie and Graham, but I can honestly say that we were not aware of it at the time. That can happen; you have your head down and sometimes you don't see what is going on around you because you are totally focused on the football and nothing else.

Although we were slaughtered for not qualifying for the semi-finals, our overall results were still not bad and while we had been overwhelmed in 1988, at least we had taken a couple of points this time and lost only once by the odd goal. From there it was straight into World Cup qualifying after that, with me as captain, but it was a short campaign for me. I picked up a groin injury playing for Forest, which didn't seem bad at the time, but twice I tried to come back and twice I suffered a reaction.

It happened when I went running on the track at Forest in late January 1983. I went back into the physio's room and he had me doing the splits to see how far I could stretch. As I was spread, Liam O'Kane came in and pretended to kick one of my feet away, I jumped, my foot slipped and I have never suffered pain like it, not even with the broken leg. It transpired that I had ripped the groin muscle away from the bone. I was in agony; I could put my finger deep into the hole and I couldn't get up off the floor. That was me finished, club and country, for the remainder of the season.

Typical of the nearly man again, I was made captain in September and then missed five qualifying games and a disastrous tour to America. It was one to miss as they say. We lost to the hosts 2–0 in Foxboro, Boston; drew 1–1 with Brazil in Washington and then lost 2–1 to Germany in the Silverdome in Detroit. Prior to that we had drawn 1–1 with Norway at Wembley and beaten Turkey 4–0. I was injured doing forward rolls in training at Wembley before the game against San Marino that I missed but we won 6–0. It was not the sort of game where a left-back is missed.

It still went quite well after that with a 2–0 win over Turkey in the intimidating atmosphere of Izmir and a 2–2 draw with Holland after leading 2–0. Des Walker gave away a late penalty and that draw was to have serious consequences. There was another draw in Poland, when Ian Wright at last scored his first England goal, and we then ended the season disastrously with an awful defeat in

Norway when Graham Taylor got our tactics all wrong.

When I left the squad, there was a good spirit and things weren't going badly. When I came back into the squad in September the atmosphere was totally different. The confidence and the self-belief had gone, not only in the players themselves but also in the manager. Suddenly, Des Walker was being vilified, after being the mainstay for the side over five years. He was no big favourite with the press because he wouldn't talk to them and so they jumped on him when he had a couple of poor games. He lost his place, something that was unthinkable two years earlier.

We had a decent result when we beat Poland 3–0 at Wembley that restored a little heart and a faint hope for qualification leading up to our crucial match against the Dutch in Rotterdam. I was again injured in the build-up, but I was told by the manager that whether or not I trained I would be playing in the game.

We lost 2–0 and were rocked by a decision by the German referee Assenmacher when Ronald Koeman committed the 'perfect' professional foul as he pulled down David Platt when he had only goalkeeper Ed de Goey to beat. Not only were we not awarded the penalty, Koeman was inexplicably allowed to remain on the pitch. To rub salt in the wound we couldn't take advantage of the free kick that was given on the edge of the box. Koeman then took massive advantage of his reprieve to score at the second attempt from an identical free kick at the other end of the pitch. Dennis Bergkamp finished us off with a second goal after a blatant handball. It summed up everything that was going wrong with us at the time.

The dressing-room was like a morgue, but totally different from Germany after the shoot-out. Then we felt we were unlucky. We had confidence in the manager and among ourselves, but I think after this one the players had lost a little confidence in the manager and he had lost a little confidence in himself.

Looking back on it, I have to say that Graham Taylor was an unlucky manager and sometimes it is better to be lucky than good. Nothing went for us in that qualifying campaign, including my injury as captain which meant I missed two-thirds of the games.

I am sure that Graham would rather have come in when we were at rock bottom – but he didn't. He was proud, passionate and honest . . . And unlucky. I don't think he deserved the criticism he received. I liked the man and that has nothing to do with him having made me captain. Some of the criticism he fielded was personal. Being called a turnip was naughty and unnecessary. It simply wasn't funny. People should make their criticisms at a professional level and not at a tacky level like that. It affected his ability to do the job, and so harmed England's prospects.

The major accusation about him was that he had never played at international level, but I don't think that is why we didn't succeed under him. He had players he liked and he picked them but they were of a certain standard and maybe they weren't good enough. I wish he had succeeded for England's sake and for my own sake. But we didn't and after the helter-skelter of Italia 90 we were faced with watching the 1994 World Cup in America on television. It was a bitter pill.

We finished off against San Marino in Bologna and to

qualify we needed Holland to lose against Poland and us to win by seven clear goals. The nearly man struck again. They took the kick-off and with only seven seconds gone I gave away the ball and they scored an embarrassing goal. I saw the run by the right-winger and did everything right until I took my eye off the ball. It is the same old things at the highest level, even against a substandard side like San Marino. Lose your concentration for a fraction of a second and you are punished.

Thank God Holland won because we went on to win 7–1! But that wasn't the point. We were out and when I arrived home it was to be met by Liz and the first thing she said was: 'It had to be you again.'

But imagine if that mistake had been the difference between whether we went to the USA or not. Coupled with the penalty miss four years earlier it would have about finished my international career. It doesn't bear thinking about.

Graham Taylor knew that he would have to go after the San Marino game. I believe that the confidence was shaken out of him by not qualifying and that it took him a long while to regain it, probably not until he was back in the familiar surroundings of Watford at Vicarage Road. But one of the biggest mistakes he made was to make that notorious fly-on-the-wall film, with Phil Neal repeating every word he spoke and the bad language that was totally against the grain.

There were a number of people Graham had introduced during his time in charge. He brought in a psychologist, World Cup winner Alan Ball, a politician who acted as a buffer between him and the press, all sorts of people. But in the end none of it worked. England were out of the World Cup and Graham Taylor was out of a job. As for the nearly man, I had to wait and see who was going to be appointed and whether he would send me the same way.

euro 96

Terry Venables didn't want me as his captain or his left-back. He told me as much in a telephone conversation when he opened the door for my international retirement. He was very honest about it. He told me that he doubted that I would be his first choice. I had the firm impression that he was telephoning me out of courtesy because I was the captain and perhaps he felt he owed me that at least. He asked me how I felt about it and I guessed that he was waiting for me to say, 'Thanks but no thanks. I'm quitting.'

Terry did not know me well. I told him that if I was good enough to be part of his squad I would like to be along. He was a bit taken aback. He was offering me the opportunity to tell the world via the media that I was retiring from the international game rather than being reduced from captain to an also-ran. I didn't relish the prospect of sitting in the stand watching the games but it was better than sitting at home and watching it on the television! I felt I was man enough to sit there and wait my turn. There was no question of my ego needing to be satisfied.

I was obviously disappointed. I had hoped the telephone call was to say that he was keeping me as his captain. But a new man has his own ideas. He brought in Graeme Le Saux as left-back and named David Platt as captain. I spent a year sitting in the stands but every time I was called up for the squad I responded.

It was tough and it was never tougher than when we went to Dublin to play the Republic of Ireland on 15 February 1995. The game was abandoned after 27 minutes and as I sat in the stands I was genuinely disgusted to be English. I thought that the hooligan problems were, if not resolved, at least under control. I am probably the face of English football – passionate, bulldog spirit and all the rest of it – but I also have a streak in me that respects other nations. For example, I hate it when our fans jeer other teams' national anthems. When we play away, apart from our closest neighbours, foreign supporters tend to respect our anthem. It irritates the English players and every England manager I have played under when our fans do not do the same. If there were one thing all six of them wish they could change it would be that lack of respect for the opponent's anthem.

There are very few people prouder than I am of being English but part of that pride is to respect others. Much of that has come about because of the travelling I have done. That night in Dublin disappointed me. I know Ireland and I like the Irish. There is plenty of good banter but that day it was all rubbish. I met a Forest fan who was almost killed when someone hit him on the head with an iron bar. It has nothing to do with football and everything to do with criminal behaviour. I was sitting not far away from the troublemakers but there was little I could do.

I was with the other non-playing members of the squad and some of the FA staff and I was concerned for them, particularly the women, because if the police had charged in indiscriminately they could have caused a stampede and in that old stand at Lansdowne Road there could have been hundreds killed in the crush. Sometimes we shoot ourselves in the foot with that slob culture and that was what happened that night. Football, and English football in particular, lost heavily.

But I was not going to walk away from something that had become part of my life. I turned up whenever invited, trained hard and settled for being number two left-back to Graeme Le Saux. I was still involved with England and my reward came a year later when Graeme suffered an injury. I was called in for Euro 96 and it turned out to be the best tournament I have ever played in. In contrast to that day in Ireland, this had everything that was good about English football.

My instant decision to stick around was totally justified. I was sorry for Graeme and would much rather have beaten him for the place in a face-to-face confrontation but the chance had come and I wasn't going to throw it away. That happens in football and it was why I hadn't let go.

There has never been a time before or since when I was so emotionally involved. I have never played in such a cauldron as Wembley in that tournament after freezing my arse off for a year. It was the best England team I have ever played in and that includes the 1990 World Cup team.

We played some superb football, particularly against Holland and Germany. Our victory over Scotland wasn't the best performance but it was an important result and produced a spark of pure magic from Paul Gascoigne.

I have never experienced anything like it. I thought that

Skinner and Baddiel's 'Three Lions' song encapsulated everything. I remember the two comedians coming to the hotel and telling us that this was going to be our song. They played it and we all laughed and shouted 'rubbish, rubbish' but a couple of weeks later we were all singing it along with the rest of the nation. God only knows what it would have been like at Wembley, in London and around the country had we gone on and won that trophy. It was an incredible way to play football. In Italy and Sweden we were remote from the public reaction; here we were right in the middle of it all. Our families felt as much a part of the growing hysteria as we did. But to reach that euphoric state we had to go through that old familiar pattern in the build-up.

The season had ended and everything was quiet with no games, other than the odd friendly. As usual, the media were scratching round for something to write about, having a knock here and a dig there, picking up stories on individuals and, once again, succeeding in pulling the squad together.

Then came the ill-fated trip to China and Hong Kong. The Football Association were worried about going to Europe on a pre-tournament tour because of the potential for crowd trouble so we ended up travelling to the Far East. China was fascinating and a great adventure for me, visiting Tiananmen Square and the Great Wall. I didn't play in the game but I wouldn't have missed the trip for the world.

The fun and games began long before those extravagant stories of happenings in Hong Kong and on the flight back home. The day before we left, Rangers had clinched the Scottish double of League and Cup and Paul Gascoigne had celebrated in true Gazza fashion. He hates flying and so he topped up on the night before's intake before boarding. We were not even off the tarmac at Heathrow when he was asking for a Budweiser. The steward, preparing for take-off, was quite patient with him, finding him a beer, but when Gazza wanted another one he began to get a bit irritated and asked him to hold on. He was standing just ahead of Gazza at the time, looking after the row in front, so Gazza reached forward and to attract his attention patted him on the bum. The steward turned round and punched him straight in the face! He caught him a classic right in the side of the head. I was sitting close by with Steve Stone and we just fell about laughing. If you can remember that look Gazza had on his face in the World Cup when he was booked against Germany and for the second time in the tournament, that crumpled face and quivering lower lip. He looked exactly the same.

The steward strode off, leaving Gazza wondering what the hell had happened. A couple of the players sitting directly behind him started winding him up.

'You're not going to take that from him, are you?' they said.

'If Jim [five bellies] and my dad were here . . .' Gazza said, nearly in tears.

That just made it worse and the two boys behind dug the knife in deeper, trying to goad him into having a go back. We had a stopover in Copenhagen and we calmed it down with the help of FA official Jack Wiseman. The captain was threatening to throw Gascoigne off the aircraft. It was a public warning and it wound Gazza up even further, especially when the captain again threatened to put him off, this time in Russia. That made the poor boy even worse and both lips started quivering. He was whimpering. 'They're going to put me off at Moscow.' Watching the entire episode unfold was hilarious and far better than any in-flight movie.

For once Paul escaped the media spotlight because all of the journalists had flown at different times and with different airlines. Imagine the headlines that story would have made.

I played in the second game in Hong Kong. We won 1–0 but we played very badly. At the time I was rooming with Steve Stone, who was my team-mate at Nottingham Forest. Stoney was the typical Geordie boy, always up for a beer and a good time. The two of us sat with Gareth Southgate at dinner and I warned them that the night ahead was fraught with danger. I had seen it all before. There would be journalists looking for stories and it would be a good idea not to get involved. Gareth, a good professional who would have drunk no more than an orange juice in any case, agreed with me and we decided to stay at the hotel. Steve knew better, finished his dinner and went off into the night. We heard all about it when the boys came lurching back to the hotel – just another typical night out, getting smashed, ripping each other's clothes off and sitting in a dentist's chair while having neat spirits poured down their throats.

Over the next couple of days the pictures were plastered over every newspaper and Gareth was thanking me for the best piece of advice he said he had ever had. The boys had harmed nobody but themselves and they had just had a good time, but this was before a big tournament and we had just played very badly.

I had even predicted what would happen when I telephoned Liz after the game. If you go out as a group, especially a group of England players, you are immediately the centre of attention whatever you do. That's not my cup of tea at any time never mind before a European Championship. Teddy Sheringham came out of the incident looking more like Ollie Reed than an international footballer!

As for my room-mate, Steve had gone out and joined in the fun but in the picture of the boys all standing together with their T-shirts ripped he was right on the end of the line and the picture was cropped, leaving him off. He was lucky. He had the night out and took no flak.

It was very naïve; the lads should have known better. It is not a lot to ask to keep your heads down for two weeks. After the tournament is the time to go berserk and have a drink and celebrate.

Even then the lesson wasn't learned. On the flight back I was sitting up the front reading and sleeping when there was a commotion from behind where the inevitable card school was taking place. It turned out that one or two of the personal televisions had been broken. There was no hiding that one because the airline, Cathay Pacific, were claiming damages from the Football Association.

When we returned to our base, Terry Venables called a meeting and told us that he could find out who the culprit was but did not plan to. He said that as we were a squad we were all in it together and every player would have to chip in £5,000 to pay the damages out of the bonus we had already accrued. I had a good idea of who had caused the damage because I knew who was sitting there. I didn't think the solution was fair but for the sake of squad harmony I kept my lip buttoned and put my hand in my pocket. Liz didn't agree when I told her but this was a team thing and sometimes you have to go against your natural instincts for the good of the whole.

We had arrived back under a real cloud after the drinking episode in Hong Kong and the damage on the flight back. It was incredible that the Gascoigne incident on the outward journey had never come to light. As so often happens, the siege mentality took over and we became a closer, tighter knit and better squad because of it, culminating in the cameo when Gascoigne scored his magical goal against the Scots and mimicked the dentist's chair.

Gazza was fortunate to have the ideal manager in Terry Venables. After the trouble going out, in Hong Kong and then his involvement in the nonsense coming back, he could easily have found himself out of the squad. Terry liked Gazza and Gazza respected him as a manager. They were able to extract the best out of each other. Terry was very shrewd; he knew that he could not squeeze the best out of his enigmatic player if he put constraints on him. He let him have his head and then reined him in with a few well-chosen words. He was right because despite all the daft things Gazza does, he means well and he was an outstanding, gifted player. At times you just had to stand back and laugh at his antics and at others you appreciated his God-given talents.

Gazza also has a heart of gold. Ask him for anything and if it was in his power he would do it. I asked him for a signed Lazio shirt when I had my testimonial and he said no problem. I thought, unfairly as it turned out, that the request would go in one ear and straight out the other, especially when I heard nothing from him for a couple of months. But, sure enough, he turned up for the England squad one day with the signed shirt.

On another occasion a group of us had taken the minibus from Nottingham to White Hart Lane to watch the Michael Watson–Chris Eubank world title fight which ended so tragically. We had played at Villa that day and the groundsman had driven us to London with a few beers on board. In the foyer I bumped into my England team-mate Gary Mabbutt. I asked him if there was anywhere we could have a quiet beer away from the public gaze. Basically, he said no, he couldn't think of anywhere. I was just about to go and break the news to the boys that we would have to find a local pub if they wanted a drink when Gazza appeared and asked us what we were doing. I told him we were looking for a beer and immediately he invited us to go with him. He took us to a nice big bar in a hospitality box overlooking the ring. By coincidence, our seats were just in front of where we had a drink. As we left for our seats I saw Gary Mabbutt and his mates having a drink at the same bar. I wasn't impressed with that sort of attitude. Certainly if fellow professionals had come to Nottingham, I would have put myself out for them. There was the difference between the two. Gazza was kind-hearted and always wanted to please. That's why he does stupid things, to make people laugh.

I was able to return one of his favours when he asked me if I would play in a testimonial for Steve McClaren. Playing at Ibrox in front of a full house was a real pleasure, especially to return one of his number of kindnesses to me.

I would do a lot for him although I would rather be alongside him laughing than at the end of one of his madcap stunts. He came close to discovering the less kind side of my nature one day when he came into my hotel room wearing an old man's mask. I was looking out of the window with my back to the door when he crept up behind me. Startled I turned and was just about to let one fly because I thought I was about to be mugged in my own room when he shouted for me not to hit him. I wasn't on the end of any of his japes after that.

A football squad needs a Gascoigne or a Steve Harrison because if everyone were totally professional for every moment of every day it would get pretty boring and add to the tension and the pressure. They are like safety valves. All the time I was in the squad, it was Gazza who provided the light relief. He was also the best footballer, a genuine match winner. When he was flying, he was world class.

I worry about his future. I count myself fortunate in the influences around me. With my wife and parents and others, I have a very stable life. In the north east it can be different; the mentality there is different. Things that are the norm in Newcastle aren't the norm in London or Nottingham or the West Country. I can't imagine Liz's grandmother or my grandmother, for instance, sitting down in a bar and drinking a pint of lager but Steve Stone's grandmother does. Gazza was brought up there and, from my experience, the attitude to life and the drinking culture are different.

When football is finished, he says he would like to coach but I can only see a club taking him on for the publicity or to stir up spectator and media interest. He is going to have to prove himself first. Steve Harrison is a good coach because he can switch off the tomfoolery in an instant. If Gazza can do that he can succeed, but Gazza never seems to switch off. Even on the pitch he pulls faces at opponents and jokes with the officials in the middle of a crucial match. But who knows what makes a good manager? I listen to the so-called experts talking about what constitutes a great coach and wonder why, if they know so much, they aren't top managers themselves.

Gascoigne gave a good hour in all of those games in Euro 96. He was not the player he was before his injury but he was still the one player who could turn a game for us. He enjoyed a renaissance under Terry's gentle but firm guidance. The relationship hadn't gone too well under Graham Taylor probably because Graham tried to get on top of him and change his way of life.

I had made up my mind before the tournament started that after it I was finally going to retire from international football no matter what happened. My reasoning was that I was coming up to 34, I was on borrowed time anyway and only playing until Graeme Le Saux was fit again. I hadn't at that stage realised how well the competition would go for the team and for me in particular.

There was no real indication of what was to come in the first game against Switzerland with that old nervous nonsense again. We were expected to win and we should have done so after Alan Shearer had given us the lead. But I gave away a penalty seven minutes from time and Turkyilmaz scored to level it up. I thought to myself, 'Hello, nearly man is here again.' The ball was kicked at me and I couldn't get out of the way. Referee Diaz Vega of Spain shattered me when he pointed to the spot.

Seven days later we took on the old enemy and by half-time it wasn't going the way we wanted it. We had cancelled each other out. Terry gambled by taking me off and putting on midfielder Jamie Redknapp. It changed the game.

I sat on the bench watching as Alan Shearer scored and just when I was thinking we were on our way we conceded another penalty. David Seaman made a magnificent save to keep out Gary McAllister's spot-kick. Gascoigne rubbed salt in the wound with his spectacular solo goal and suddenly we were on our way again. There was a touch of déjà vu about it all, reminding me of Italia 90.

I was delighted. We were through to the next phase of the competition but I didn't know where that left me. I had conceded a penalty in the first game and was taken off in the second. Jamie Redknapp had come on and influenced the game, laying foundations for Terry and England to build upon. Terry had played me as one of three central defenders and he told me at the time that it could extend my career by a few years. How right he was. I was not a good left-back anymore because part of that job was banging up and down the line for an hour and a half, but I felt I could do a good job at the back, especially as part of a three with two wing-backs. I don't know whether Kenny Dalglish would have taken a gamble on me without that, or even Harry Redknapp at West Ham. Making the switch was no problem because I had played at centre-back in my early days.

Terry decided to change the formation for the next game against Holland. He went with four at the back to counter their two wide players and one central striker. He is one of the most tactically aware coaches I have ever played for. His decision brought me back in and I had the pleasure of playing in what turned out to be the best performance of any England side in my 12 years' involvement. We didn't just beat the Dutch – we whacked them, a big footballing nation, 4–1. We played them out of sight. Teddy Sheringham and Alan Shearer scored two each. A fair result would have been five or six nil and I was aggrieved that we gave them a consolation goal.

It can be imagined what that result did for our confidence and for the supporters. They were delirious and so were we. The atmosphere at Wembley was like nothing I had ever known before and to be involved was very special.

David Seaman was outstanding, absolutely brilliant throughout the tournament, while Alan Shearer, after a quiet build-up, was on fire and Terry was getting the very best out of two of his old Spurs players, Teddy Sheringham and Paul Gascoigne.

We were now out of the league stage and into the knock-out section of the competition, drawn against Spain. I tried to convince myself that my old adage of playing for two caps would work, even if Terry changed the formation to fit the occasion and the opposition. But I was relieved when I found myself in the side for the quarter-final on the following Saturday.

Now Terry had a team bubbling with confidence and a crowd who were totally behind us. I told myself that as I had only ever lost twice at Wembley with England, the percentages were in our favour. I was certain that we could reach another major semi-final.

Spain played well against all the odds. They deserved

more out of the game than they achieved and I have to admit that they were unlucky to have what looked to me like a good goal ruled out for offside. We dug in well, particularly the defence and Tony Adams in particular. It was a tough game, culminating in that penalty shoot-out. That emotional explosion after converting my penalty, came up from my boots somewhere; everything that had been generated throughout the entire tournament bubbled up. It was like an internal earthquake, a moment of release.

When David Seaman saved Miguel Angel Nadal's penalty, every member of our team mobbed the brilliant Arsenal goalkeeper, except me. I remembered how I had felt six years earlier and so I went over to commiserate with Nadal. I didn't have it in me to join in the celebrations at his expense; it could wait until I reached the dressing-room.

I did the same with Teddy Sheringham a few months earlier when Nottingham Forest beat Spurs in the FA Cup on a penalty shoot-out. Mark Crossley made a good save from Teddy and took off towards our fans at the other end of the Spurs ground, followed by the rest of our players. I stayed back to shake hands with Teddy because I remembered how good the Germans were to me.

I cannot imagine enjoying a euphoric experience quite like that again. After the game, David Seaman and I were interviewed on television, me having scored that penalty and Dave having saved one. The interview was a long way from the crowd but we could still hear them singing 'Three Lions'. No one would go home. It sent tingles racing up and down my spine.

Terry gave everyone the day off after that game, to do whatever we wanted. I went to see the Sex Pistols at

Finsbury Park. I dragged along Gareth Southgate and a couple of people from the FA. It was a blinding weekend for me, beating Spain, that great atmosphere and seeing a concert I thought I was sure to miss. We didn't trash the dressing-room afterwards – we were representing England. It was orange juices only!

Six years on and it's Germany all over again, but this time the thinking was totally positive. We are at home, on a roll and they were supposedly on that downward spiral after years on top. To add to the tension not only was there the threat of penalties but also the golden goal scenario where the scorer of the first goal in extra time won the match.

We played extremely well, not as well as against the Dutch but better than against Spain. Alan Shearer scored again, this time after only two minutes, meeting a little flick-on header from Rodders at a Gascoigne corner and we had our noses in front.

Then I thought we had half a chance of making our first final for 30 years. If I'm to be honest I have to hold up my hands and take the blame for the equaliser. It was just ten minutes or so after our goal and I allowed Kuntz to run across me, nip on and score. It was concentration again; if you don't concentrate for every second at this level you are punished. I saw him, thought 'I've got him, I've got him, I've got him,' watched the ball and he was in for a goal.

Golden goal is big pressure. For every corner, every free kick and every attack, you are on tenterhooks. If people tell me what a bad way penalties are to decide a game I would argue with them because no one ever turns it off on television. As for the golden goal, as a player there can be no better feeling than to score, knowing that the opposition

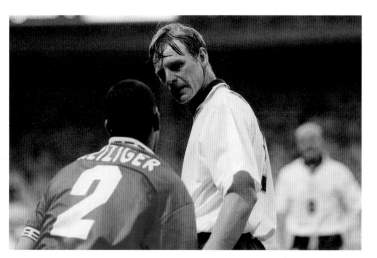

Watch it! I tell Dutch defender Michael Reiziger exactly what I think of his attempted tackle during our 4–1 Euro 96 win over Holland. (*Popperfoto*)

Commitment: making sure I'm first to the ball whatever the cost in a tussle with Alfonso during the Euro 96 quarter-final against Spain.

Exorcising the ghosts: scoring our third penalty in the shoot-out against Spain and appreciating the positive side of spot kicks. (*Colorsport*)

Take three: Chris Waddle, Gareth Southgate and me in the Pizza Hut television advert which made light of our penalty misses. (*Pizza Hut/AMV.BBDO Ltd*)

Good evening, ma'am: I have the privilege of being introduced to Her Majesty the Queen as rower Matthew Pinsent and heavyweight boxer Lennox Lewis look on.

Treasure trove: a life's work and reward spread in front of me.

Late kick-off: marrying Liz in Nottingham in 1993 after a nine-year courtship.

A golden couple: my parents celebrate 50 years of marriage.

A special medal: enjoying my investiture as a Member of the British Empire at Buckingham Palace with my wife Liz and daughter Chelsea in March 1999. (*Charles Green*)

How it might have been: memories of my interview with the Army as I pay a social visit to the Sherwood TA in Nottingham.

Growing old gracefully: two ageing punk rockers, with myself on guitar and Stiff Little Fingers lead singer and Newcastle United season-ticket holder Jake Burns, backstage after a gig.

What a load of rubbish: how did I walk out of this? The garbage truck writes off my sponsored Rover as I crawl out of the passenger side unscathed.

Horsing around: Liz and me with mare Goose Green, yearling Key Witness and two-year-old Crystalline.

Sport of Kings: Man of the Match ridden by Rodney Farrant at Uttoxeter, finishing third, trained by Jenny Pitman. (*Colin Turner*)

Taken for a ride: Chelsea still relies on mum and dad to give her a push. (*John Davies*)

Teaching Chelsea: helping my daughter with her books – she isn't yet quite ready to help me with mine! (*John Davies*)

This was one of my best games of the 2000–01 season, when I was pitted against Newcastle's Alan Shearer. (*Colorsport*)

Our quarter-final tie against Spurs in the FA Cup was a typical blood-and-guts derby. This tackle stopped Les Ferdinand scoring when he was clear on goal. (*Colorsport*)

can't come back. You can run round like a lunatic knowing that there is no more football to be played. But for the losers, there is nothing worse, knowing that there is no way back.

Darren Anderton hit a post and Gazza missed converting a cross almost on the goalline itself by a matter of inches. If either of those had gone in, the celebrations that day would have been something to behold.

We thought we deserved to win, especially with those two late chances, but suddenly it was penalties again.

As a coach, Terry Venables was one of the best. He was good at man management, too, in the way he handled Gascoigne and others. He had more than a few problems along the way. The business in Hong Kong and the broken television sets were not easy things to deal with. We had shot ourselves in the foot as a squad but he handled it well and all the players believed that he was on their side. We never felt as though he was double dealing, even though he has the reputation of being a bit fly. He was an ideal England coach in my opinion.

Terry came in straight after Graham Taylor who, in some ways, was too honest for his own good. Graham would become involved in a press conference, start talking and not stop. That's clever journalism and bad management. Sometimes you have to be like a politician – give so much and know when to call a halt. Too often Graham was led down a road for which he was unprepared. Terry was a different animal, very streetwise. He could play the journalists at their own game. He has had his fair share of nonsense but he has all the credentials and he could stand and fight his own corner.

Tactically, he was as good a coach as England has had, very astute. I was disappointed when he left. I had no axe to grind because as far as I was concerned I would have quit international football whether he had stayed on or not. If my dad had taken over at that point I would still have quit.

England and club football should be getting more mileage out of Terry Venables. He has been allowed to sit on his backside for far too long. He has such a wealth of knowledge that it is a waste for him to be working for some radio station. He knows the game inside out and is one of the best coaches in the country. He should always be in there working at the sharp end of the game and, if he's not, the Football Association should utilise his skills with the youngsters until he is back in full-time work.

Straight after the semi-final Liz and I packed our bags and went on holiday. I have a personal rule that if I'm playing in a tournament we book a holiday for two days after the final.

I did the same thing after Italia 90. It was straight back home, pack and off to Mauritius where we were booked into the fabulous Le Toueserok. In the reception when we checked in, Gianluca Vialli, Pietro Vierchowod and Roberto Mancini and their wives were doing the same thing, a couple of days after England had played against them in the World Cup play-off. I thought then what a small world it was but the same thing happened two days after Euro 96. At Heathrow Airport on our way to Zimbabwe, the entire German squad filed past carrying the European Championship trophy. We were too far from them to make contact. If they had been walking closer I would have shaken hands with them because I have so much respect for them as a football nation.

Funnily enough, I became known as 'The German' at Nottingham Forest that next season. It started when the opposing fans chanted 'Pearce is a German, Pearce is a German.' Ian Woan picked it up and started calling me Hermann the German and that was eventually shortened to the German.

At the Christmas party we had this little routine that we pinched from Derby County. Everyone would draw a name out of a hat and they would have to buy that person a suitable Christmas present. After Italia 90 I was bought German shirts, Nazi helmets and Freddie Starr-style German shorts with a swastika emblazoned on the leg. Whatever you were given you had to wear it all day at the Christmas party until the early hours of the morning.

I wasn't the only one to suffer. Steve Chettle had the reputation of being under the thumb at home so he was given a collar and lead. Kingsley Black pulled out Bryan Roy and gave him a little puppet with a pea as a heart because Bryan wasn't the bravest of players.

Fortunately, they eventually tired of the German gear and as I got older it was walking sticks and zimmer frames.

I took the idea with me to Newcastle, along with my music, and the first Christmas it worked like a dream. I pulled Warren Barton out of the hat and I bought him a hairdryer, nabbed a pot of cream out of the physio's room on which I stuck my own label which read 'Dwarf growing cream' and finished off the collection with a pair of trousers cut down to a pair of shorts with turn-ups.

The first present was because I had written in my column

in a local paper that I had tackled him in training and knocked the hairdryer out of his hand. He didn't like that, nor the fact that the boys called him the Umpa Lumpa man because he had a long body and short legs, hence the other two gifts.

Goalkeeper Shay Given pulled out the Italian defender Alessandro Pistone and bought him a sheep's heart from the butcher. Duncan Ferguson drew Nol Solano and went round the north east of England trying to buy a llama. Honestly! As luck had it, there were no spare llamas around Newcastle. Andreas Andersson was brave. He made up a prisoner's suit with arrows for big Dunc while Alan Shearer was given a lovely Mary Poppins doll by Solano. The foreign boys really made an effort and it worked very well.

Rob Lee, not that much younger than me, drew me and it was back to the hearing aids, slippers and other senior-citizen accoutrements. It went with my retirement from the international stage.

CHAPTER 15

more comebacks than sinatra

After Euro 96, Nottingham Forest were playing a pre-season tournament at the City Ground when manager Frank Clark asked me if I would have a word with the new England coach Glenn Hoddle. I had the idea in the back of my mind that he might ask me to carry on playing at international level. Why else would the England manager ask to see me? When we met up, the first thing he said was, 'Can I ask you why you're not playing for England anymore?'

'I'm 35 years old, a new manager has come in and I thought it was the right time to retire.'

'For no other reason? No personal reasons? To spend more time with your wife and family?'

'No. Sometimes it's a wrench but the passion of playing for England and a short career outweigh the time it cost me with my wife and we have no children.'

'Would you consider coming back?'

'I'll think about it.'

'I'll need to know fairly quickly. Can you let me know soon?'

As soon as he said it I knew I was hooked again but I told him that I would ring him and let him know the next day.

'To be honest,' he said, 'I'm looking at playing three centre-halves and you're as good as any left-sided centre-back I've got. There's no one as good as you playing in that position. I can't guarantee you a game, but I would like you available.'

I telephoned him the next day and told him that I would come out of retirement. Basically, he picked his squad for Moldova, I was in it and what's more I played. I was also in the next squad against Poland at Wembley, which we won thanks to a couple of goals from Alan Shearer. The team didn't play particularly well but I didn't have a bad game. Then we played Italy at Wembley and lost to a goal for which I was to blame. Zola spun off me. Sol Campbell took some of the flak in the press but largely it was down to me. We were reasonably flat as a back three. Sol couldn't get near me and subsequently couldn't reach Zola quickly enough. After that I was left out of the side and they started to play very well.

I learned a lot from that game about playing in a back three. Glenn had a camera positioned above the stadium and he showed the defence, and the team, how the Italians defended as a back three with the markers so tight on Shearer that he couldn't move and the spare man 15 yards behind. They played the system really well while we were flat and not tight enough on certain individuals. It showed how we went to sleep when the ball was at the other end while the Italians were always alert.

I found Glenn very good tactically. I thought he was a good coach. He really understood that system and was able to pass on the relevant information. I also learned about improving my diet. You are never too old to learn about these things. He was obviously from the Wenger school of proper eating, having studied under him at Monaco.

He changed the side after that defeat and we won away against Poland and Georgia, both 2–0. They were among the best away performances I have seen from England. David Batty was outstanding in both games, sitting in front of the back four, mopping up everything and ratting around. The only away game I can remember that was better was a European qualifying game in 1987. I sat on the bench as a non-playing substitute when England beat Yugoslavia 4–1 in Belgade.

Hoddle had the team playing really well which didn't bode well for me. Apart from nicking the odd appearance as a substitute, I found myself back up in the stand again. There were no cast-iron promises and I had been around the game long enough not to expect anything.

Graeme Le Saux had come back from his injury and was playing at the back with Tony Adams and Gareth Southgate. It was a disappointing time for me but I was pleased to be around the squad and determined to see it through to the end of the 1998 campaign whether I was in the squad for France or not. I made myself available as promised and spent most of my time in the stand watching the side playing very well, culminating in that away game in Italy when the goalless draw clinched the place in the World Cup and forced the Italians into a play-off.

In the summer of 1997 we played in Le Tournoi and, surprisingly, I found myself back in the team against Italy for the first game, which we won 2–0. It was one of my best performances and my 76th cap. The next morning, I attended a press conference with Terry Butcher who was working for BBC Radio 5 Live. I was pleased with myself and Terry told me that I was getting better with age. I thought my old practice of playing for two caps had worked again and I was looking forward to the next game.

'You never know, Tel. That could have been my last game for England,' I joked.

'No chance,' he laughed.

The next game was against France and Glenn left me out. We finished up against Brazil and I was on the outside looking in again. Martin Keown played and injured his shoulder early on. I thought I was going on but rather than send me on in a straight swap, Glenn changed the side around and used Gary Neville instead. I felt it would have been a more balanced side with me there, being a left-footer. My joking prediction to Terry was right. It was my last game for Glenn and I was more than a little annoyed because I had played so well against Italy and was still dropped.

By the start of the next season, I had moved on to Newcastle and after starting pretty well picked up a hamstring injury that kept me out for three months. I wasn't available for three England squads, including the visit to Rome. I worked hard to get fit for my club and played quite well in the Champions League game against Barcelona in November when I came on as substitute. I stayed in the side for the rest of the season so had been playing regularly when what amounted to the England World Cup squad was due to be picked in February.

Glenn rang me and told me he was picking the squad the next day and he was leaving me out because he was concerned about my fitness when it came to playing games every three days. That was bullshit. He should have told me the truth, either that he thought I wasn't good enough anymore or that my legs had gone or whatever the real reason was for axing me. I would have appreciated that a hell of a lot more. I was old enough to see through his nonsense but I made it easy.

'Fine,' I said. 'I'm always available if you need me. I said that I'd keep myself ready until the World Cup if wanted and I will.'

I played from the end of November until May and missed no more than a couple of matches. There was no doubt about my fitness. By contrast Ian Wright, about the same age as me, had missed most of the last three months of the season but Glenn kept the door open for him. That rather destroyed Glenn's flimsy excuse. How much better if he had told me that I was out of the running and he would need me only if he had a lot of injuries.

In fact, the squad for February and March did suffer a lot of injuries and he called me back in for the game against Portugal. I turned up, trained but wasn't used in the side or on the bench. I lived in hope. It had worked for me in 1996 and I could always hope that it would work again.

It rankled me when he said that I couldn't play two games a week – I had been playing two games a week since I was six. I also couldn't understand why he would decide in February that I wasn't fit for a tournament that wasn't taking place until June.

I prefer straight talking but Glenn seemed to have a problem in that direction in this instance. Having been involved for the last ten years, there was an empty feeling when the World Cup came around. I went away on holiday.

I wasn't really watching England as a supporter and felt very detached from it all. If there was a television nearby, I would make the effort but I'd been at the cutting edge for so long it was galling to miss out this time, especially as I thought I was so close to going at one stage. Only a month or so before, I had still been in the squad and clinging to the hope that I would go to France. It would have been a great way to finish my international career. I had been involved at the top level for so long, it was disappointing to have been to just one World Cup finals.

When we came back from holiday, we flew out to the horse sales in Ireland. Our flight was delayed and it meant I was able to watch the England v. Argentina game on a television in the airport lounge. Most people who came in were desperate to watch the football and were saying how glad I must be that the flight was delayed. I had to say yes but I wasn't. Of course I wanted England to do well because a lot of the players are my mates and I always want my country to do well. But I didn't feel any part of it. To go from those massive highs to fading out of it was hard to stomach. It wasn't the way I wanted to go. In fact, that was why I made my original decision to quit at the end of 1996.

I still feel that I was right to agree to play; after all I won an extra six caps for my country by doing so. What would I have done if I hadn't won those extra caps? I would have stayed at home and been bored stiff.

I don't bear Glenn any grudge other than wishing he had been a bit more honest with me. I met him at a dinner afterwards and we had a chat but I never did ask him why he hadn't told me the truth. I appreciate that a manager's job is hard work enough without players making it harder for him. I had never spent a lot of time with Glenn so he didn't know my character or my nature.

I watched in the lounge at Dublin airport and saw Graeme Le Saux come off injured and then the game go to penalties. It was a back-to-the-wall situation after David Beckham had been sent off and if I could ever have done England a service it was then. If he had taken me he could have slung me on when Le Saux came off and I would have rolled up my sleeves and taken a penalty for him.

I turned to Liz and said bitterly, 'Why the hell didn't he just take me?'

My place in the squad probably went to Rio Ferdinand and while it was great for Rio was it the right thing for England? Rio hadn't won a cap so it would have been hard to toss him on in that explosive situation. By contrast, I had been there, seen it, done it. In one or two quarters in the game, I was asked why I hadn't been taken when a game like that was so much up my street. I am not naïve enough to think I can change a game or win a game, but I certainly won't buckle no matter how much the odds are stacked against and I won't be intimidated.

Tony Adams is that sort of player and I really did become anxious when, in extra time, the old warhorse played a one-two and went charging up the line. I was on my feet shouting at him, 'Tone, don't do it, get back, get back, we're down to ten men.' It was the only emotion I showed throughout the entire match. When David Beckham was sent off, that didn't mean a lot to me and I just thought that we were down to ten and that we had blown it. But the boys battled brilliantly and I was proud of them.

I didn't get involved in the controversy that surrounded Glenn Hoddle. Certainly I never came across Eileen Drewery when I was with England, nor was I asked if I wanted to pop in to see her. I suppose most people would look at my public persona and think that there is no way I would become involved with that sort of nonsense and, while that may be true, as a professional I can see that if there is an option and it will help just one member of the squad to be a better player and contribute more it is a good thing. It's easy to pick up on bits and pieces and criticise, and I must admit that Glenn rather left himself open because he has such strong views about religion and other related matters and was prepared to air them in public. But if they are your beliefs you have to stick with them and he would have looked even worse if he had shelved them just because he had been slated in the press. In many ways he was pig stubborn but you can't reach the top in his profession without being a bit that way.

Whenever something new is introduced it is open to criticism. Look at food and alcohol and how the perception in professional football has altered in recent years. Clubs are much more aware of the importance of diet allied with fitness and those players who take it on board tend to last a lot longer than those who abuse their bodies. I like to think that I have stuck around longer than most partly because I didn't go out and get blasted every Sunday lunchtime.

Hoddle took a lot of stick over the Eileen situation but I honestly believe that if one player was helped 5 per cent going with the team was justified. If an England manager rejected that opportunity he would not be doing his job.

That can be the difference between winning and losing a game. Those percentages are becoming finer and finer as footballers become more and more athletic. Glenn was probably unfairly vilified but if people are seen to be different they tend to be pilloried.

It wouldn't have been the case had England been winning all of their games; none of that would have mattered. All those chinks in your armour are overlooked when you are successful but once you start losing they all come to the fore, especially if you have taken on the journalists. It is a fact of life that, if you treat people reasonably, when it hits the fan they will be more sympathetic than if you have taken them on as Glenn did. I felt he was a touch hounded, but if you are going to be sacked you might as well go knowing that you did everything your own way and Glenn certainly did that.

Like Terry Venables, Glenn has more to offer the England game at international level and should not be overlooked. I learned a hell of a lot from both of them, probably as much from Glenn as anyone else. I have been away with the England Under-18s and I know how much those boys would have loved to have someone along like Glenn Hoddle or Terry Venables, and how much they could have learned without it being detrimental to the full-time FA coaching staff.

Glenn is close to my age and you have to worry that the opportunity may have come and gone when the best years of his coaching and managerial career should still be ahead of him. It would be short-sighted if both he and Terry were ruled out when, perhaps in five years' time, either of them could be the right man for the job. But with the FA hierarchy you cannot see it happening. They would be too frightened to do it.

To stay in management in England for any length of time is an achievement on its own. As soon as results start going wrong, the chairman, the press and the supporters are down on you like a ton of bricks with all sorts of 'experts' from radio pundits to politicians demanding your head. Look how close Sir Alex Ferguson came to getting the push at Old Trafford. Results picked up and he is now lauded as the best manager there has ever been in the British Isles. Howard Kendall at Everton was one game from the sack and then went on to win cups and titles at home and abroad.

It's criminal to dispense with knowledge too early. With ten more years' experience, who knows where Glenn will be. Maybe he wouldn't want to be involved again after the way he was treated. Considering it is the best job in English football, it is sad that so many England managers are relieved when they leave.

Kevin Keegan was out of the game for too long, but at least that was his own choice. I can't say I had had too many dealings with Kevin in the past, other than when he was brilliant over bringing Newcastle United to my testimonial at Forest. He was so straight down the line with me it was frightening. He said yes down the telephone and turned up six months later with a full team without needing to have any further dialogue. That, needless to say, impressed me.

When he was given the England job to succeed Glenn, he was the obvious choice. As far as I could see, only Terry Venables was in contention. At the time, I was wondering where my next game was coming from at club level with never a thought about international football. I was lucky to get back into Premier Division action with West Ham United and was concentrating on trying to keep my place with them when I took a call on my mobile telephone while travelling on the M25. I pulled over and was surprised to find that it was Kevin. My first reaction was that it was something to do with the Under-18 side with whom I had become involved or that maybe he wanted to have a chat about Joe Cole, Rio Ferdinand or a couple of the other boys at West Ham whom he might see as potential full caps.

'If I called you into the next squad, would you turn up?' he asked.

'Do what? You do know I have retired twice?'

'Yes, I know all that. I'm not bothered. I saw you at Villa and you're playing as well as any left-sided player in the country. If I called you, will you turn up?' I was flabbergasted.

'I'm just on the motorway on my way home. Do you mind if I get back and have a word with my wife and call you back?'

'No problem, but you do realise that you can't sit on this for days.'

I promised to ring him back that very night; not that I really needed the time. It was exactly the same as when Glenn asked me to come out of retirement. As soon as the words came out of his mouth, I didn't really have to think about it. This time, though, I had just spent more than six months playing for Newcastle reserves wondering whether I was still good enough to play at club level never mind international level.

I had been out of the international squad for two and a half years and played only three games for West Ham at the time of the call and I was still in the clouds when I got home and told Liz the unbelievable news. She told me that I had nothing to lose and I telephoned Kevin straight back and told him that I would be honoured if he thought I was good enough. He said that it would be great to have me along but, of course, could give no promises that I would be picked. On the other hand, you don't pick a 37-year-old to sit on the bench or in the stand. He realised that there would be some criticism but he was strong enough to stand for his own beliefs. There were important games coming up, not so much Luxembourg at home but those old enemies Poland away. I had certainly been there and had not been fazed by it.

When we first met up he didn't try to build up my hopes and I told him that I was happy to be along, play or not. But I did play in the first game and became the fifth-oldest player ever to play for England. It couldn't have gone better. We scored six and didn't concede one against the amateurs from Luxembourg. I had a goal disallowed, so the nearly man struck again. There always seems to be someone out there pulling the reins and making sure that I keep my feet on the ground.

I joined up with the squad, tried to get as fit as I could and went into the game with exactly the same attitude as when I played my first international – play well in this one and the next cap will follow. I had to show that I was physically fit and able to do my job.

Kevin Keegan can do me no wrong. I had nothing to prove and he couldn't upset me. He could have picked me for one game and then bombed me and it wouldn't have hurt. As long as I could help him out for one game for a payback, that was good enough by me. He had done me a big favour with my testimonial and then another by bringing me back to the squad. I was going to give him everything for as many games as he wanted me and then if he found a kid to take my place that was fine. There was no contract; nothing written in blood.

I was like a little kid. It wasn't like my first cap because this time I had nothing to lose. This was a bonus because these were caps I never dreamed I would win. It was a great honour and a bit like a testimonial, going back to an old club for someone's benefit match.

The games couldn't have worked better for me, starting at Wembley where I received a very emotional welcome from the fans. My first England manager Bobby Robson was the guest of honour. And the result was right. Then it was off to Poland and a make-or-break game that let us in through the back door for the Euro 2000 Championship. From a defensive point of view, we couldn't do more than keep another clean sheet in Poland and that we did. It was another of those backs-against-the-wall jobs that couldn't have suited me better.

Everyone will admit that it doesn't matter how you get there, but you like to do it with a bit of style. English football had stuttered since 1998 and it spluttered right up until that very last day. Let's hope we learned a few lessons from that bad 18 months.

The squad had changed a lot, not so much in personnel as in the way it was run and its professionalism. The media side had been improved; they had tweaked it a lot since I was on the players' committee in 1990. The changes were all for the better, the relationship was better with the press, it was much better organised and there was a good atmosphere within the camp, more like club football.

Kevin likes his training to be enjoyable and fun, and he likes to join in himself when he can. The players had a lot of respect for him; he is likeable man and a good motivator. Kevin is not one of the more technical coaches I have worked for, so he had Derek Fazackerley and Les Reid to do the coaching.

I chatted with Kevin and Gareth Southgate on the way back from Poland and at the airport I just said, 'Thanks. It was a pleasure to be along.'

When I broke my leg, both Kevin and Arthur Cox telephoned me shortly afterwards. 'Funny old game, isn't it?' Kevin said. He wasn't wrong. Arthur Cox checked with my progress and who knows what my status would have been when Graeme Le Saux was eventually ruled out for the season.

Missing the two play-off games against Scotland really gutted me. I thought I had done well enough in the two games I had played in to be involved in any play-offs in some capacity or other. When we drew Scotland out of the hat, I would have busted a gut to play.

Kevin did not discard me. He invited me to be part of the squad even though I was far from being fit and unable to join in any training. When they trained at Bisham Abbey, I trained on my own in the gym and then joined the card school. I felt part of it until the day of the game when I found myself creeping around, knowing that the players needed their sleep.

I was allowed to come and go as I pleased, even to the extent of being able to pop home to Wiltshire to sleep in my own bed and then join the squad the next morning.

To be honest, it gets no better than being with England. I recall Bobby Robson saying to me when I joined up, 'This is the best team you will ever play for.' He was right. Playing for your national side when you are English is something special. It was still a big honour to be around, after all my caps.

I attended all the team meetings and joined in everything I could. It became a bit of a joke with Alan Shearer and Gareth Southgate because they didn't know whether I was there as a coach or a player. One day I would appear in a players' training kit and that night I would turn up for dinner in a coaching top, only because that was what had been left outside my bedroom door. The players would give me an old-fashioned look and ask me what role I was playing now! I admitted to them that I didn't know what I was there for other than to enjoy myself and have a game of cards.

I travelled up to Hampden Park for the first match and I was proud of the result in what was as very, very big game. We rode our luck but we got everything right and to achieve a 2–0 result was tremendous.

Then came the Wembley game. I have never felt like that after an England match. I didn't think we played and, worse, I didn't think we played with any spirit at all. I was given a seat in the stand. The Scottish substitutes who weren't involved sat behind me and they were the ones who were cock-a-hoop as the Scots outfought and, at times, outplayed us. I was boiling up inside because we were playing so badly. I felt like shouting didn't they realise that this was Scotland we were playing against. I wanted us to win this game 4–0 regardless of the first-leg result.

It was the Scots fans who went home happy, not us. I went into the dressing-room after the game and it was a very strange atmosphere. We had achieved our goal in reaching the finals but we had lost. Even Kevin was quiet. It was as though we had found a pound and lost a fiver. How much better it would have been to have reversed the result. We should have settled for a 1–0 defeat at Hampden and a 2–0 win at home. For me what mattered was that we had lost to the Jocks and I have never gone home from Wembley in such a bad mood. I was furious. I couldn't imagine players such as Terry Butcher and Bryan Robson allowing a performance like that one. Sometimes you cannot help losing matches but I felt as though we went out that day feeling that the job was done. We didn't start and didn't finish. It was the Scots who came away with all the credit.

Talk is cheap and too many players pay lip service to playing for their country. To succeed, we need the commitment of players such as Tony Adams and Alan Shearer and, even more, Viv Anderson, Tony Dorigo and any number of goalkeepers who keep turning up for the English cause in the knowledge that much of their time will be spent in the stands or on the bench. It's easy to win 30 caps, be dropped and then feign injury or announce your retirement, and even easier to suffer a little injury which keeps you out of an unappetising friendly with nothing on it. I treasure every one of my caps and will never forget that lesson of Saudi Arabia when all my Forest team-mates pulled out and Brian

Clough offered to make the excuse of an injury if I wanted to withdraw.

Tony Adams, to me, epitomises the dedication and commitment all players should show when picked for their country. When I first met Tony he was the one being built up as the next England captain. He was young, he was loud and he knew he was good at his job. None of Clough's players were like that; they tended to be quiet. They turned up, did the job and went home. Tony would be in the dressing-room, shouting and hollering with plenty to say for himself. I was 25 at the time. He was some five years younger and, I thought, a bit full of himself and a bit noisy. He was already pushing for the Arsenal captaincy. But Tony, I learned, didn't shout for show. It was how he was. Now he is more thoughtful and concerned. He has been through lean times and has pulled himself together in spectacular style.

Tony is a one-club man and there are very few players who have that loyalty these days. I felt the same about Forest. It was only through force of circumstance that I left. Tony broke through at an early age and hasn't had it all easy. The drinking, according to him, became heavy when he was injured or, perversely, when the team were winning, so it wasn't true adversity that forced him into the bars and the clubs. Whenever he played the big games for England he was there to be counted, just like Terry Butcher before him. He could never be described as the most talented player in the England squad but when the chips are down, he is the one you would want on your side. The arrival at Arsenal of Arsene Wenger has given him a new lease of life and added years to his career.

I give him total credit for the way he has changed. Could you believe Psycho and Rodders sitting down sans alcohol to discuss the merits of Oscar Wilde or books of poetry? That's what happened. Tony suddenly stopped and said, 'Can you imagine this conversation between the two of us a few years ago?' I couldn't. I only had to think back to one of the gatherings in Manchester before an England game. The Arsenal boys had arrived in a hired stretch limousine and had enjoyed a good drink on the way. They were in the bar when I got there and by that time they were steaming. Tony was really bad-mouthing a barman who must have been well in excess of his 50th birthday. I felt embarrassed to be there, had an orange juice and went to my room.

Tony looks back on all that and cringes. I didn't read his book, not even the extracts in the newspapers, but I am amazed at some of the things he is supposed to have revealed about himself. All I can say is that, apart from the drinking, he hid it pretty well from me.

I am equally staggered that he can call himself an alcoholic. No professional sportsman playing at the level and consistency of Tony Adams could possibly be a full-blown alcoholic in the sense of being a constant drinker. It is physically impossible. Can a footballer playing in the Premier Division be an alcoholic in this day and age? My answer has to be no. Certainly Tony drank a lot, too much, but I know how I feel after a heavy night out. There is no way I could play football the next day.

I would define an alcoholic as someone who cannot do without a drink. Certainly, I never saw Tony drinking on the mornings of an international match. If he did, he was very cunning and not only hid the booze but hid the effects remarkably well. There were times with England when I looked at players and wondered how they managed to get that drunk. I've walked down the corridor on a Sunday morning and seen Tony's hotel door hanging off its hinges.

I don't have much sympathy with the drinking stakes. I believe that if you are involved in professional football, or any professional sport come to that, the least you can do is lead a reasonable life which gives you half a chance and doesn't lead down the road of drugs, drink or excessive living of any kind. The rewards are so high, the price you pay is slim and for such a short time as to be negligible.

It was the same whenever we went away for a tournament. I could never understand why players needed to go for a drink during that period. In six weeks' time they could drink themselves silly and no one, not the manager, the press or the supporters, would care or think any the less of them. I can count on the fingers of one hand the number of times I have had a drink when I have been away with England, and even then it's been just a few lagers. Mainly I stuck to orange juice because I saw how the players could become uncontrollable and let themselves and their country down.

Des Walker likes a drink but he would go on his own or to a wine bar in Nottingham rather than a flash club in London. He would rather have a drink at a students' club. He always doubted the wisdom of deliberately going for a drink where you could be seen. When I go out, I prefer somewhere quiet, too, away from that goldfish bowl. Paul Gascoigne, on the other hand, would go for a drink in his

England tracksuit. He might as well have waved a banner to make sure everyone knew he was there. But Paul likes being in the limelight; I don't. I can understand other footballers saying they couldn't live the life I live. That's fine. You have to be comfortable with yourself, sleep soundly and be able to look yourself in the eye in the mirror the next day.

For near enough every game in my professional career I have been at the height of my fitness, allowing for things like flu or niggling little injuries. There is a tiny percentage of matches after which I had to admit to myself that I hadn't given my best because I'd had a few drinks too many over dinner on a Wednesday or Thursday evening. If I have a bad game, I want it to be because I have simply not played well and not because I have stayed out late drinking beforehand. If I've slept well, eaten well and trained well, at least I can look my manager in the eye and say I have done everything I can.

I see more relevance and parallels to myself with Tony Adams than I do with most others and if I were a manager the first player I would sign would be a carbon copy of the Arsenal captain. I would bring him in, make him captain and build the team around him. That is how highly I think of him.

All his problems are self-induced, as are those that have afflicted his former Highbury team-mate Paul Merson. But with Merse, despite following his story through the media and hearing from other professionals, I still don't know where the real problems lay: with gambling, drinking, drugs or a combination of all three. I haven't read either of his books. Of course, I know he likes a drink and a bet and he claims he has done drugs. If he's up against all those things, I salute him for having sorted them out and getting on with his career.

I believe we are all accountable for our own actions, on and off the pitch. I don't have a great deal of sympathy for players who have abused their profession and therefore I don't have a great deal of sympathy for Merson. I hope he has sorted himself out because I like him as a person and have always had a reasonable relationship with him. But liking someone and respecting them professionally is a different thing. It is not in my heart to forgive and forget, especially when we were in the same England side. While I have pushed the ability I've been given to the limit, Paul Merson has nowhere near the number of England caps he should have had with his talent.

In football, the performers carry a lot of hopes and expectations on their shoulders and as more money comes into the game, the higher those expectations will be. I have a number of friends who are staunch Arsenal fans who loved Merson when they saw him in the local pubs drinking pints with the fans, but when all his bad habits became public knowledge they were the first to criticise him when his form wavered or when Arsenal had a bad patch. I told them they were hypocrites. The time to have a go at him was when he was drinking in the Holloway Road when he and the team were doing well.

The majority of professionals I know are good, honest pros. It's usually only the ones who stray from the straight and narrow whom we hear and read about. The arrival of foreign players, particularly from Italy, has brought in good habits and they have helped to educate English players. Certainly the booze culture is alien to them and attitudes generally are changing.

When I was at Forest as manager there was booze everywhere and I told them I didn't want it. It had no more place in my office than it had in the dressing-room. I am a sportsman, not a rock star. I didn't even want it on the bus on the way home from games. The players can let down their hair together come the summer or club breaks and I believe that can play an important part in building team spirit. The pressures are so high that players need to rest and relax and maybe have a few drinks – but always at the right time.

When I started playing for England, we would always meet in the bar on the Sunday but that's not done anymore. It affected training on a Monday morning and the professionals have taken that out of the games. Twelve years ago I didn't know that drinking makes you dehydrated and more susceptible to injuries. We all have that information at our fingertips now.

I have watched Paolo di Canio at close hand and I am impressed with how he prepared himself at the ground. He stretches well, trains well, even if he doesn't like being kicked in a practice match. He is just as likely to walk off if that happens. I look at him and can see that the game means something to him.

Ray Wilkins and David Platt were model professionals and took their game to its achievable limits. Platt likes to say the right thing and be seen to do the right thing, which is very good public relations for football. But at the same time he has learned about the game and he has looked after himself. There are other old pros who have been knocking around since the seventies and their views of the game have remained unaltered since the day they hung up their boots. They are in a time warp. They're like a stick of rock – break them open and they're the same right the way through. Platt has been prepared to look at what is going on and change with the game.

As for Ray Wilkins, I can listen to him all night when he is talking about football. He talks such common sense.

When I was away with England, I asked Gary Lewin, the Arsenal physio, if it would be possible to go and watch Arsene Wenger taking training for a couple of weeks. I know it sounds ridiculous that as a West Ham player I should have wanted to go across London to watch another club train, but I like what I have heard about the Frenchman and the things he does. More than that, I have seen the results in what he has done with Martin Keown and Tony Adams and others. It is easy when you have been around for a while to think you know how the game is played and that you know best. That attitude can be dangerous. Unfortunately, I think Glenn Hoddle has that problem. He comes across to many as one who knows best and is inflexible with it.

Ideally, in the next few years I would like to watch Wenger, talk to him and to other top managers in the game to see what they are doing. Even if you come away from the experience rejecting everything you have seen, at least you have opened your mind and given it a chance. David Platt said that when he packed in playing he would tour around Europe watching the top coaches in action. It was good public relations again, but the concept was right.

Gareth Southgate is another good professional who

pushes himself. When he played in midfield for Crystal Palace he was steady and would never have won an international place, but he earned himself a move by working extremely hard at his game. He has an old head on young shoulders, trains hard and wants to learn and succeed. I can see him going on into coaching and management. I would be very surprised if he didn't and if he wasn't successful.

what now?

When I was younger and not in the public gaze, I enjoyed the company of my mates, being the centre of attention and playing the fool. That's the real me and not the image I have portrayed during my professional life. Even now when the old crowd meet up and we let our hair down, I will be as stupid as the next one.

With strangers, it's different. That's not because I'm miserable but because I don't want to be a celebrity. If I'm at work, I'll sign autographs and do anything necessary but away from it I value my anonymity. I didn't mind so much when I was known solely in Nottingham but since the 1990 World Cup I've become more easily recognised.

Both Liz and I are private people and we enjoy our life away from the game. Also football is such a high-profile profession, and generates such a lot of pressure these days, that I need time to myself all the more.

I'm not complaining. Football has brought me many things I would not have had as an electrician in London – an MBE, for instance. I am a royalist and, consequently, I was deeply honoured and thrilled when I was nominated in the 1999 New Year's honours list. I don't believe our royal family are as appreciated at home as they are abroad, but that's the British.

When the letter arrived, it was a huge surprise. It had not crossed my mind that I could be in line for something like that. It's something that happens to other people. I do a job that I love and I don't see anything special in that. For someone to give me an award for what I have done in football is a massive bonus.

It was announced on New Year's Day and I went to Buckingham Palace in March with Liz and Chelsea to receive it. We had a smashing day. There weren't too many from the world of sport, although I did meet the athlete Denise Lewis, but there were people from most other walks of life – firemen, schoolteachers, nurses, even lollipop ladies – all of them far more deserving of their awards than us so-called celebrities. It was a beautiful sunny day and apart from meeting a cross-section of the working community in Britain, I was also introduced to the Queen.

It was the second time I had enjoyed that privilege. Previously I had gone along to the Palace with a lot of other sportsmen and women, able-bodied and disabled on behalf of the British Sporting Trust, a charity endorsed by Prince Charles. There were around a thousand of us invited and out of those a dozen of us were asked to meet the royal family beforehand. That was quite an honour, too. When I looked around the room, I found myself in the company of some of the biggest names in sport, including Lennox Lewis, Henry Cooper, Prince Naseem, Sally Gunnell, and Steven Redgrave. We were all lined up and I was a couple down from Prince Naseem, listening to what was being said as Prince Philip was introduced to each person in turn.

The Duke of Edinburgh, obviously recognising royalty in

the Sheffield boxer, asked in all innocence, 'And what do you do?'

The Prince looked at him and said, 'I beat people up, man.'

'Oh,' said the Duke, 'you're a boxer.'

'Yeah,' said the Prince, 'I just beat them up.'

It was all I could do not to laugh out loud it was so comical. It certainly broke the ice for the rest of us. It also brought home how difficult it is for the royal family, meeting thousands of people and having to find something to say. What do they talk about to a footballer who plays for a club (Newcastle at the time) they have probably never heard of? But they sounded interested and I thought the entire event was very worthwhile to those of us who were there.

I have done my own little bit with presentations and I know how hard it can be. Multiply that by many times over with the added knowledge that the slightest slip or wrong move and you are all over the front pages the very next day.

Is it worth it? Ask the tourists who flock to the Palace, just as we go to see the Eiffel Tower or the Sydney Opera House. They were all at the gates when we drove into the courtyard to park our cars before the British Sporting Trust event. Palace officials parked everyone, from the canoeists in their Ford Escorts with the canoe strapped to the roof to the four-wheel drives. The only one they parked round the back was Prince Naseem's huge stretch limousine. One way and another, he certainly made an impact.

I enjoyed mixing with the different sportsmen and women, professional and amateur, at the charity event and I enjoyed meeting the other people when I was awarded my medal. I am quite shy when I don't know people, and I spent a great deal of time talking to a fireman from Hereford who had been working in the force for 30 years. My only complaint was that there was nothing to eat! It would have been nice if they had knocked up a few bacon sandwiches at that time of the morning but there was only bottled water.

As well as my visits to the Palace, I also had a couple of visits to Downing Street when John Major was in residence at number 10. The first occasion was immediately after Euro 96 when the entire squad was invited but I was the only one not away on holiday. When the Football Association asked me if I would like to go and take Liz along I jumped at the opportunity of seeing a bit more of British history at first hand. We had a guided tour of number 10 and then enjoyed a garden party outside in glorious weather. I was introduced to John Major and was impressed. He is a very nice man and certainly knows his sport. Whether you agree with his politics or not, you had to admire his apparent honesty and sincerity. He came across as a thoroughly decent bloke. What more can you ask from a politician?

There were a lot of celebrities and the Prime Minister had time for everyone, talking to each of us as we arrived. We must have made a big impression at the European Championship because a number of the showbusiness personalities took the time and trouble to come over and congratulate the team through me.

I was there again a year later when Mr Major invited the England squad back again when they were all available.

We are lucky to have a nice house in the country with a

bit of land, away from the football environment. We used to live outside Nottingham but went into the town for shopping and entertainment. Naturally, having been there for so long, people would stop and exchange pleasantries or ask for autographs. I am never stopped to talk about football in the village where we live now.

As a player, I do tend to take the game home with me but eventually I can unwind and switch off. As a manager, I discovered that the game is with you all the time. You are thinking about training, buying and selling players, next Saturday's team and a million and one other related matters. It will be very important to have that stable home life if I go into management.

In my experience, if a couple get on really well, there's a convergence of opinions and an understanding of what's needed. Liz mirrors my professionalism in football in her work with horses. I admit that I can be a little bit slapdash outside football. But we have found a common interest in horses and I now gain almost as much pleasure out of them as Liz.

We have friends in the horse world who buy and sell foals, known in the trade as pin hooking, that is buying them young and selling them on at the sales for a profit. Liz went to the sales at Doncaster and bought a five-month-old foal whom we named Man of the Match. The idea was to look after him until he was four and then sell him on. It didn't work out that way. Archie, as we call him, became a family friend and when he reached the age of four we decided to keep him for at least another couple of years, put him into training and see what he was made of.

We had looked around Jenny Pitman's yard and liked

what we saw, especially in the care of the horses, so we sent him there when he was six. He had a couple of years at Jenny's, running three times in the first year and being placed third in the last race. In the second year, he ran ten times and was placed several times without ever winning a race. He was a very honest, very reliable jumper but without the pace to go on and win the top prizes. We had a lot of fun with him.

After the two years with the Pitman stables, we had an offer from Jenny Pigeon, based in Towcester, wanting to buy him. We didn't sell but it put the idea in our heads to send him to her point-to-point yard. It was a successful move. In his first year, he ran ten times, had three wins and a couple of places. In the second year, he had only three runs because of the lack of firm ground.

The nerves I suffer watching him are worse than walking out to play at Wembley. You are so scared that something is going to happen to hurt him. The nerves don't settle for the first two or three fences but, fortunately for us, he is such a good jumper that we were more concerned than him or his jockey, Fred Hutsby.

Considering he cost us only £1,500 plus VAT, he has been marvellous value. When he finished at the National Hunt yard we had an offer of £10,000 for him because of his jumping ability. Champion jockey Tony McCoy rode him once and Rodney Farrant was his regular partner.

The betting side didn't interest me at all. The first time he ran I had a tenner on him but it was no more than a gesture. What with being in the stables before the race and then in the ring, there was never time. Anyway, I have seen too many footballers go down that slippery route! A lot of footballers, past and present, own horses these days, but a lot of them are in it because of the betting interest. Betting to me is incidental.

We still have Archie and will keep him. We have added another racehorse, by Be My Native, for the future. As well as these two, we have a mare named Goose Green (because she was born during the Falklands conflict). We bought her for Liz when we were in Nottingham. She was a hunter until an injury prevented her from being ridden. She has foaled three youngsters: Crystalline, Key Witness (whom we sold in 1999) and Cracker. Seeing young foals running around is another special part of breeding horses. Now that we have 28 acres of land we are seriously considering having resting racehorses when they have a couple of months off in May and June.

I enjoy going round the racecourses, especially Cheltenham. Every time we have been there I have had a great time. We usually go with Mark Crossley and his wife and we have also taken Des Walker and Warren Barton and their wives. Everyone who goes enjoys the day, the atmosphere and especially the company of the Irish.

I don't come across too many other football people at the races. Alex Ferguson, Kevin Keegan, Mick Channon and the other big-name owners and trainers are mainly involved in flat racing. For me, jumping offers so much more and the flat holds no interest at all. By the time you sort out your horse, it's all over, whereas in National Hunt racing anything can happen at any time and usually does.

We fly over to Ireland every year for the Fairyhouse sales and take the opportunity to travel round the studs, looking at the stallions. In the evening we go out for a few beers before dinner. It's not solely owning the horses but everything that goes with it which makes it such a good occupation.

Liz has always been involved in horses and they play a large part in her life. She has had horses ever since she was a child. Her father, Maurice, is a retired farmer. Her mother, Mary Cole, used to ride in ladies' races and won the first ladies' race ever staged at Hawthorn Hill. Now she writes about equestrianism. Liz has two brothers, Joey, who is a contract farmer, and Chris, who served an apprenticeship with Richard Hannon before joining Vincent O'Brien in Ireland. He later rode in Australia. I cannot see her existing without horses. That became evident when we first moved to Nottingham. She is a country girl. She could never understand other footballers' wives whose lives consisted of getting up in the morning with no reason to go outside the front door unless it was to go shopping, often just for the sake of it. She says to me that I like football more than I like her but my answer is that she likes horses more than she likes me. It is a happy stalemate.

What makes a good coach or a good manager? It is a relevant question for me to ask because I hope that's where my future lies when I finally hang up my boots.

I really enjoyed my brief time in charge at Forest and relished the responsibility, just as I did as captain of most of the teams I have played for. Even in that first game for West Ham, Steve Lomas was injured and Harry asked me to lead them out. Something like that makes me very proud, as it would to be a manager of a professional club.

Ray Wilkins was a model professional, a genuinely nice

fellow and someone I really like as a person. If ever I listen to a pundit on television I would prefer it to be Ray. He reminds me of Brian Clough in the old days, someone who knows the game inside out, talks well and has no obvious axe to grind as so often happens with some former players. Ray highlights the good things in football and only now and again points out the negatives.

So why hasn't he made his mark as a manager? Maybe it's because a manager needs a nasty streak, something that appears to be alien to Ray. Certainly Brian Clough had it and so do Sir Alex Ferguson, Graeme Souness and George Graham. Players are scared to cross managers like them because they are in awe of them. But this is a quality, if a quality it is, which has to come from within. It can't be manufactured as Trevor Francis, for one, discovered at Queens Park Rangers. He, like Ray, doesn't have that nasty streak in him.

There are enough decent men around who have been successful as managers and if it isn't there you have to manage without it. You are what you are and the reverse applies to the nasty manager who tries to be nice and falls on his backside.

Any manager needs a lot of luck on and off the pitch and particularly in picking up the odd young gem who comes through the ranks. Also, of course, a manager must be shrewd with signings.

It is surely harder now to succeed as a manager than ever it was and the more time goes on so the harder it becomes. The modern manager is governed by financial constraints and the smaller clubs cannot succeed at the very top level anymore. They can nick a cup here and a cup there like

Leicester City have done in recent years. It could even be said that they have been overachieving for their size. Their former manager Martin O'Neill was very shrewd and clever with his signings. He looked in depth at players' backgrounds and took on those who worked hard not only for themselves but for the team. Their attitude is that if you are going to lose then go down fighting. That's Martin O'Neill's legacy to Leicester and his promise to Celtic.

To be a successful manager it seems that you need a bit of everything. No one, no matter how good or great a player he has been, knows enough to take a management job and say he knows the right way immediately. You have to listen to experience and have people around whom you can trust and respect. I don't mean yes men. There are plenty of those around at the moment but they have no value compared with someone who will be brave enough to tell his boss he is wrong and to think along another line. I see some managers with coaches around them who are afraid to offer a different opinion or who will just give another version of the same story.

When I took over at Nottingham Forest, Liam O'Kane helped me a great deal. As player-manager I found it very difficult at half-time to make a speech after running around for 45 minutes. I told him that I felt I had to say something as soon as I walked in instead of getting a cup of tea and relaxing. He took over after a couple of games and I knew it was right because the things I had been thinking as I walked through the dressing-room door at half-time had changed by the time I'd mulled over them. I let Liam chat and then I would stand up and pass my opinions and talk to Liam about what we might do. When you are out there it's difficult to gain a full impression of what's going on all over the pitch. You have a different perspective from the man sitting on the bench or in the stand with an overall view.

If things are going well, like they were for Kenny Dalglish when he was player-manager at Liverpool, fine. More often than not, he would go into the dressing-room at half-time with the team in the lead and little more to say than 'carry on as you are'. It was very much the same after games, and a jolly-up five-a-side in the week keeps things ticking over when you are that good and so far ahead of the rest.

But when you do not have a top club, the results might not have gone for you and you might not have played well yourself, it is far more difficult to come in and point the finger at someone else.

There was the time we played at Blackburn Rovers and I had taken winger Bryan Roy off. He had a go at Liam as he came off the pitch and then he came down the front of the coach to talk to Liam and me to ask why he had been taken off. I told him to go home and watch a video of the game and he would see why. It was because he was doing nothing for the team. When everyone else was defending with their backs to the wall, he was standing on the halfway line waiting for the ball. It was a time when everyone had to knuckle under and graft. The conversation became heated and Liam knew me well enough to calm things down with a little kick under the table. He knew I would eventually lose my temper with Bryan. In the end, I told him to go back down the other end of the bus and ask his team-mates whether they would pick him and to let that be his answer.

I was delighted when the FA called up half a dozen ex- and older professionals to help with the England teams from Under-15 to Under-21. I was assigned to the Under-18s and was thrilled with the appointment because, apart from the involvement with England, it was a big help in my desire to become a qualified coach. I was in the middle of my coaching badge course and it enabled me to gain practical experience. I also felt it was a benefit to the youngsters, who were able to look up to someone who had been there and done it.

Will I be a good manager? I don't know. I am not that conceited to say yes. I could be the worst manager there has ever been. Look at my track record – I was manager at Forest for six months and took them down.

I do not believe that there is a blueprint for a manager. You don't just need a figurehead; you need a good coaching team around you. Rather than ask what would make a good manager, perhaps the question should be what would make a good management team.

I would start with someone who has the respect of the players. They should be a bit wary of him; someone the players wouldn't cross. He would need a good assistant who would be prepared to tell him anything and not be afraid to say when he thought his boss was wrong, although never in public and never in front of the players. There should always be solidarity and if there is a disagreement it should be sorted out behind closed doors.

I also think that technically the manager needs to be on top, especially at fault finding. That was something that Terry Venables was particularly adept at. As an electrician, I would have to find out why a light wouldn't work. As a football manager, you have to do the same thing. You pick a team, plan your strategy and 20 minutes into the game find that it has all gone pear-shaped. All the things you thought could nullify the opposition have gone wrong and you have to change your tactics on the hoof, find out exactly why it hasn't gone to plan. Terry was excellent at that; he would spot a problem in minutes and change it very quickly before any damage could be done.

A manager also needs a good buffer between himself and the players. Kenny Dalglish and Kevin Keegan both used Terry McDermott. He would be in the dressing-room with the players and they felt at ease with him and could talk, giving him a feeling of what was happening. Steve Harrison did a similar job with England. Players don't talk to them thinking they are going to run straight to the manager; the conversation is just normal. It's up to the buffer how he passes on that information without dropping any individual player in the mire. He doesn't have to give names, just pass on the general feeling. If he put a name to every moan and complaint the players would become wary of him and the manager would inevitably finish up fronting anyone who complained too much and too often.

Quite often these days top players go straight into high-profile management without a scrap of coaching expertise behind them. Sometimes it can work but often it doesn't. Peter Shilton always said what a good manager he was going to be because of the depth of his experience but it didn't work for him.

I am not blessed with that self-assured attitude. I simply don't know what will happen. Anyone can bullshit but usually they don't last.

I suppose I have played under some of the great managers but I would never model myself on any one of them. I am sure that some players-turned-managers try to be dominant like Brian Clough. Big mistake. There is only one Brian Clough and it is foolish to try to emulate him. Brian could upset people for the fun of it but it is only the odd person who enjoys being disliked.

I think I would listen to the man on the terraces, not necessarily slavishly following what they say, but taking on board anything that I thought was beneficial. The same applies to anyone who can offer a crumb of intelligence that can be taken on board to help make the team better. That's why I would like to watch Arsene Wenger and talk to him about his philosophies. I quite like the things I hear about him and what he passes on to his players – the vitamins, the diet, timing the training, not over-training the players and other things like that.

With Clough we never trained a great deal, letting the matches take care of the fitness once the season was rolling with two games a week. Having an interest in racehorses I have seen how the top trainers race the best and then rest them. Footballers should be treated the same way.

I believe that training should be looked on more individually than it is. I wouldn't hesitate to have the defenders in one day while the rest went home and relaxed. I would make sure that I had specialist coaches. I would look after the defenders myself but I would have others to take care of the midfield players, the strikers and the goalkeepers.

I noticed when we trained at Forest, if Clough wasn't there there would be some slapdash training, particularly by those who were normally in fear of him. But when he walked through the gates the standard went through the roof. It was match training simply because they were frightened of what he would do or say. It is important to have that little bit of an aura but I also noticed that now and again it didn't hurt if Clough wasn't around and he let someone else take the session. He would always let the players wonder where he was, even allowing them to think that perhaps he was looking at a player in their position. More often than not, he would be away playing squash or relaxing with a drink but he didn't let his players know that.

I believe in coaching and learning more about the game. When I took my UEFA 'B' course, there were players there who thought they knew it all and didn't need it. They were only on the course to get the qualification. That is a bad attitude, very blinkered. I felt that I would go away with some added knowledge and whatever I learned I was better off doing that than sitting on my backside in front of the television. The most important aspect is not so much the certificate but the learning. Again I can use my experience of being an electrician. There are books that tell you how to rewire a house but once you are in that house, it's a totally different ball game. No two houses are the same and no two footballers are the same. Experience and learning from other people will guide you to the best way of doing things and surmounting problems. Football is no different. There is a lot to be learned from other coaches and other managers. No one should ever stop learning whether they are the youngest coach in the League or the oldest manager in the Premiership.

Having experienced being player-manager I accept that the concept is a good one but in practice it is too difficult.

By the very nature of the game you are rarely offered a manager's job when a team is flying. More often than not the new man is taking over because the team are doing badly. Quite often a top player taking the job goes to the club and finds that he is better than anybody else in his position. He might also have a chairman who has made the appointment thinking he is getting two men for one wage. It is very difficult for the new man to say that he is hanging up his boots to concentrate on management.

I found the job difficult at Forest. It was fine when we were winning. We were getting by on the enthusiasm of the players even though we all knew that there were things wrong that needed fixing. It gets hard when you are in trouble and you still have to go out and play. Training, for example, becomes a problem in itself. I wanted to take training but at the same time I needed to train myself and you can't do both properly. Once the game kicked off I couldn't influence things as a manager but at least I could try to do my job on the pitch.

As a player or a manager, no one can afford to have too many distractions. As a player, at three o'clock on a Saturday afternoon, you have to know that you have trained, rested and eaten properly. If you are going out looking at players, attending meetings and doing the hundred and one other jobs a manager has to do, you cannot be fully prepared to play. That's when you have to start delegating and then you are not fulfilling the role you have taken on. Even when you have staff you totally trust, eventually you still have to go to watch the player you want to sign yourself. If it is you signing; you cannot rely on someone else's opinion no matter how much you trust them, anymore than you can rely on the hundreds of videos that are pressed on you. God knows in those six months I was offered at least eight Maradonas and if you watched the carefully edited tapes you could believe them! A player that looks a world-beater on tape can prove to be useless when you have him with a ball in front of him.

Handling the press would be no problem. At Forest I sent up one of the coaches to cover the press conference but that was because my mind was a jumble trying to do two jobs. The pressures of playing and managing meant that the media were bottom of my list of priorities. If I had time, I would do it. I admit it wasn't ideal but I had my hands full and I simply had to delegate and prioritise. Training and getting myself fit were more important than doing a Thursday press call.

I understand the media's demands and if I become a full-time manager I accept and appreciate that they will be very much a part of the job. I will do what I have to do. It's not a problem. I know the faces and I know the ones to avoid and I think I now have a reasonable relationship with the press.

I have also thought about the future without football. I have to because there are no guarantees. My name might land me a job when my playing days are over, with word getting round that I am a decent professional with good standards. Once you have that first job, it is vital to be successful because straightaway if you don't achieve everyone is on your back. David Platt is the classic example. When he stopped playing, everyone was predicting what an excellent manager he would make, the perfect man for almost any job. But not everything went well for him at

Sampdoria in Italy and when he returned to England it was for a battle against relegation with Forest. Suddenly he had gone from being the man everyone thought would succeed to being the object of the shaking of knowing heads. That's happened to managers who have a great track record, never mind newcomers. One bad run and then all the good results are quickly forgotten.

That's the game we are in. Loyalty will mean nothing and we all know it, as sad as it may be. I am under no illusions that I am going to be a great manager but I will give it my very best shot.

If I don't get a job in football, or if I fail, I cannot see myself going back to my job with Brent Council. I doubt whether they would have kept the job open for me after all this time even though they promised they would if my career in football did not work out! I feel quite comfortable doing media work with television but it has to be within the game because football has been my life and my love for so long.

I have looked after my money reasonably well so I won't have to scratch around but I would like to be around football in some shape or form. It is part of me and in my blood. Everyone who plays football is in the sport because they love it and not because they came in thinking that this was a quick way to get rich. It may have changed a little but not that much.

I hope that I will be able to guide young players in football matters, from important issues such as diet down to learning to keep your mouth shut when things are going right because there are always bad times around the corner. I would stress the three criteria of training, resting and eating well. If your ability lets you down, you cannot help that. It is acceptable. What isn't acceptable is when you have the ability but one of those three vital ingredients is neglected.

I would tell them to listen to the experienced people around them. I talk to youngsters and go on coaching courses and I am often asked if I respect a certain coach. Sometimes the answer is no and certainly there are few who measure up to the Terry Venables of this world but whoever they are I will listen to them and argue my point. If you don't listen you don't learn.

Then there are agents. I am fortunate because I work with an agent I rate as honest, good at what he does and not pushy. I wouldn't have an agent I didn't think was honest or whom I didn't respect. I couldn't work with Eric Hall because he is so different from me. I would be embarrassed walking down the street with him. He is a self-publicist on radio and television, waving his big cigar about. I don't think I have ever seen Kevin Mason on television and I don't think I particularly want to. That's why we have a good professional relationship.

Equally if I were an agent, I would rather handle someone like me than a Stan Collymore who you know is going to let you down somewhere along the line. As a manager, I would have no problem whether the agent was Kevin, Eric or Paul Stretford who looks after Stan because I wouldn't be working for them. They would be selling me a product, representing their players. We would get on famously if any of them had a player I wanted in my team.

Working with agents is hard work for managers but then again I use an agent so I can't criticise the system. Kevin gets me better deals than I could myself because he can push my qualities and I would be too embarrassed to do so. He enjoys football and doing what he does and I believe he has enjoyed representing me.

Not all footballers are womanising boozers, not all journalists are disseminators of untruths and not all agents are evil. There is a mix-and-match in every walk of life and they are no different. If they want the best deal possible for their client, I have no problems with that, but if they want the best deal for themselves with their client a secondary consideration then, as a manager, I would have a serious problem. There are agents out there who are unscrupulous and that is bad for the game in general.

If I did go back into management the very first person I would call would be my old Forest team-mate Nigel Clough. I did it last time when I wanted him as a player two hours after I took over as manager but the next time would be for us to work together. He has enjoyed a similar football education to myself; we played together at club and international level. Professionally, I admire him and I respect his knowledge and opinions on the game. He is the sort of man who would not be afraid to turn round and, without criticising, say he thought differently from me.

Nigel has been creating a name for himself with Burton Albion because he wasn't offered anything in the League. He is not too proud to start at a lower level and work his way up and he has a steely attitude about him. He is a quiet person, but he is a very strong character with a strong inner belief, very much like his father. Nigel, however, is a little more flexible than his dad. While Brian has had one or two problems in his later life, I don't think you will see Nigel go down that road. He has too strong a personality.

He had to have to survive in football as his father's son. He, Jamie Redknapp and Frank Lampard are a credit to their fathers and a credit to the game but Nigel undoubtedly had the biggest cross to bear. It must have been the hardest job in the world, especially when things were going badly. When they were trying to usher Brian out at Forest, Nigel behaved impeccably, not being drawn into taking sides or going to his dad with stories. No one could have handled it better; he had respect from the players and his father. The most important thing is that he knows his football and we both believe it should be played in a certain way. If you put us in different rooms and asked us questions on footballing situations, more often than not we would come up with the same answers. He could run a club from top to bottom.

Another thing Brian Clough showed me was the need to take a step back or to take a little time away. That can only be done if you have someone by your side whom you trust. I would know that I could leave everything up to Nigel and come back without having been stabbed in the back.

play it again, sam

I was stunned, to say the least, when I heard that manager Harry Redknapp and his assistant Frank Lampard had parted company with West Ham with one game remaining in the season. It came as a total surprise, so much so that the first I heard of it was when Bob Harris telephoned me. I had no inkling that anything like it was in the wind.

My reaction was not solely due to the shock of Harry going, but because it also left my own future in limbo. I was within days of signing a new contract, which would have kept me at Upton Park for a further season – but I wasn't sure that any new manager would want to take on a 39-year-old full back, especially one who was almost as old as him and who had publicly stated that he would be interested in the job, had it been offered!

My wife Liz was realistic about it all. As I had just been named West Ham Footballer of the Year, she thought it the perfect time for me to go out on top. It was hard to argue with her, as Harry was one of the main reasons for me having decided to give it one more go before retiring and concentrating on coaching. Harry and Frank cut me a lot of slack in terms of having days off to rest and keep myself fresh and ready for the games. They knew me as a good honest professional and were prepared to trust me.

It was not only me, however, who mourned Harry's departure, for he was an institution at the club, having served them on and off for around a quarter of a century. Admittedly the results hadn't been that good since our FA Cup exit, but it was still totally unexpected as we were all looking towards the next season. I am still unclear as to exactly what went on behind the scenes, but then that is usually the case in football, and I have no doubt that the buying and selling of players had a major role in what unfolded. It is typical of how quickly things can change in football.

My point of view, however, was only a small part of it when you look at what Harry achieved over the seven years as manager. Remembering that West Ham were always a team flirting with relegation, he had built a much more stable foundation over the years with great potential for the future, thanks to all the youngsters coming through. The youth policy was outstanding, with three midfield players – Joe Cole, Frank Lampard and Michael Carrick – all developing from the youth team to the full England squad.

Only a couple of weeks before Harry's departure, there was a table published showing how well he had balanced the books, leaving the Hammers as one of only a few clubs to be operating in the black – and that was not even counting the Rio Ferdinand transfer. All things considered, you could say that in the seven years he had only a few months of bad results and, with the purchase of a couple of players to add to the excellent nucleus, things were looking bright for 2001–02. It was certainly a good legacy to leave for any new manager. I am sure the club will miss him.

★ ★ ★

From the club's point of view my comeback season after the two broken legs was absolutely typical West Ham United in that whenever the expectations are high the bubbles burst and when everyone is thinking and expecting the worst we deliver against all of the odds.

Expectations were really high at the start of the 2000–01 campaign with all the young talent available and all the pre-season hype but, in the end, we flirted dangerously with relegation and seriously underachieved. When you look at the squad we should have done so much more. The critics said that once we went out of the FA Cup at home to Spurs our season deflated and ended, but that was not strictly true. We started very badly and although we recovered we could never sustain it.

We did not win a game in our first six, taking just three points out of a possible 18 and from then on we were playing catch-up with the rest. Although we staged a recovery just before Christmas it was never that convincing. Then Rio Ferdinand left us and that proved to be more of a blow than anyone expected. We won at Leeds with him in his final game for the club and then we won at Southampton, beat Middlesbrough at home and drew with both Aston Villa and Everton. At that stage we were up to seventh, everyone was delighted and the loss of Rio was hardly felt.

But the lad is top quality and there was never any doubt that we were going to miss him. When things started to go wrong we came to realise that, in fact, we missed his presence even more than we expected. I hadn't appreciated just how good he was nor the measure of his true potential until I played alongside him and trained with him. In many quarters he was underrated because his occasional cock-up or error was highlighted, but when you play alongside him you begin to realise what he achieves with his pace and power, how many goals are saved and just what Rio Ferdinand does for a side. He is a big lad and, as with many well-built youngsters, you don't realise that he is still a relative beginner. However, with experience and maturity, those little errors are gradually going to be erased.

He is probably one of the best players I have played with and I am certain that he will go on to prove that both at club and international level. He seems to be relishing responsibility at Leeds under David O'Leary and clearly being England's most expensive defender does not trouble him at all. Some players take to the responsibility and some don't, but in my experience it can benefit a good player more often than not. It tends to bring them out of the pack, make them work instead of just ticking along. If they have the ability to cope with the pressure then it can often make them better players. It certainly seems to be doing that with Rio at Elland Road.

It is no coincidence that after his arrival there was a massive Leeds revival and they stormed up the Premier Division and went through the best Europe could throw at them as they outlasted both Manchester United and Arsenal in the Champions League. Everything happened at once when he arrived at Elland Road for his move coincided with a number of their long-term injured players returning to form and fitness and their season simply ignited.

When his move was being talked about he came to me and had a chat. I told him that it would do him no harm to sit tight for a year, but with the money that was being offered I expressed the view that it was almost out of his hands and that West Ham could not reasonably be expected to turn down a fee as big as £18 million.

I liken Rio to Des Walker. In fact in natural ability he has even more than my old Nottingham Forest room-mate but whether he has the same consistency only time will tell. When he gains that maturity he will be something special and I have him in my mind as a future England captain.

As a lad off the pitch I am not one to judge because I am of an age now where they are more likely to come to me for a bit of guidance rather than invite me to join them at a nightclub or ask my advice about girls. They are more likely to turn to others for that! But from my view the West Ham youngsters seem to be a good lot off the pitch as well as on it and I put Rio down with that group.

Joe Cole is still the one who grabs most of the publicity, whether it is of the good or the bad variety. This season I have hardened my view that Michael Carrick may go on to achieve more than Joe. Time will tell whether I am right or wrong, but I believe that Michael will have that vital touch more consistency than the more mercurial and eye-catching Joe Cole.

As a manager or a coach I would have Carrick in my side. Brian Clough would have loved him, especially for his level of consistency, and that he still tries to do the right things when the chips are down. He wants the ball, he wants to play, he has a good range of passing, he will do what he can with regard to tackling and heading, yet he's still only a baby just learning the game. In terms of out-and-out ability Joe has more than any player at West Ham, other than Paolo di Canio. Joe just has to learn the game a little more, learn when to pass and when to dribble, learn what positions to get in.

I have also been hugely impressed with the development of Frank Lampard this season. Considering he is only 22 years old he has remarkable experience and maturity already; he has the head of someone six or seven years older in football terms. He has a good strength about him, and both he and Carrick are mentally strong and no matter how the results were going you knew pretty well exactly what you were going to get from these two.

Sometimes it is nice to see young lads with mental toughness about them. If I were looking as a manager I would go for someone like Lampard. He works hard at his game, trains hard, gives no aggravation to his manager and you know if the kid has a little injury he will do his best to get out on that pitch on a Saturday afternoon whether he is fully fit or not. With the way the game is going now that, sadly, is an increasing rarity. Some players play when they have a slight knock but there are others now who would not entertain it. Football is not black and white and there are times when you need to show your character and get out and help the team when it may not totally suit you.

Some will blame this development on the influx of foreign players, but I am afraid that I see it happening with English players too. It is a problem across the board and I hear the same story from almost every manager I talk to. It is all too easy for a player, when things are not going well, to say he can't make the game. I don't blame the rotation system for it, because only the top three or four teams have the depth of squad to do that and most of us are not good enough to entertain rotation. Even those top teams tend to keep their defences intact as much as they can. Rotation at a club like West Ham comes when a player is injured or suspended – then they are rotated!

One of West Ham's problems was having both Paolo di Canio and Joe Cole in the same team. It was shown that it can work, notably in our Cup wins at Manchester United and Sunderland, but you have to nail it down and Paolo is better at it than Joe when we haven't got the ball. When we have the ball both are fantastic. But they need to be bullied a little, put into position and told what is expected of them defensively. A manager tries to do that to all players to some degree, but some need to be told more forcibly than others.

That is how it worked when we played at Old Trafford in the Cup. Joe and Paolo were asked to do a certain job, leaving Freddie Kanouté up front on his own, with those two sitting off and occupying the full backs more than usual. If one of them was to go walkabout or turn up on the wrong wing, then the top teams like Manchester United would punish you mercilessly.

The tactics worked that day but I'm not sure Joe yet sees the importance of that sort of discipline. He is an out-and-out entertainer who wants the ball, does a few tricks and sees what develops. But as he gets older his role in the team will become more defined to ensure he does not become a player of whom the manager is asking: 'Should we play him or not?' With his talent he should be an automatic choice. As with David Ginola, no one questions what he is capable of doing going forward, or on the ball, but even if you don't expect him to run the length of the pitch to tackle people you do need players like that to drop off in a little hole, stay ten yards off and get the shape of the team right.

That is where the Hammers have slipped up this season. We lacked a proper left-sided player whenever we asked Nigel Winterburn to drop back and play in the back four. Then Joe or Michael have been asked to slot in on the left-hand side, which is not their best place and you can soon be found out if the shape is not right. It did not help, either, losing Trevor Sinclair, our natural right-sided player, for much of the season. Joe has had to drop in there as well. I'd say Joe's best position is probably fitting in behind the front two, but to have the licence to do that you have to give a return of a minimum of ten goals a season or supply the ammunition for the front two to score 30 or more goals between them.

At the moment Joe falls between the two stools. If he plays as an out-and-out midfield player he will give a reasonable performance, but if he plays behind the front two, unfortunately, he does not score enough goals. Hopefully, as he matures and gains the benefit of being coached he will learn how to pick his runs, when to dribble, when to lay off and get in the box on the end of things.

At the end of his first full season you would have to say that, for the number of games he played, Joe Cole did not score enough goals nor damage the opposition as much as he should have. Whereas Frank Lampard is going to get you a return of at least ten goals a season, or more if he has an outstanding season. Joe is not a great striker of the ball and therefore not a natural goalscorer but with all the ability he has he should be peppering the opposition goal a lot more than he has done.

Joe falls into the *wunderkind* category, which means he is

under the microscope every time he plays. That is a difficult environment to cope with for all his faults are scrutinised closely. I feel somewhat harsh in appearing to pick on his faults when he has so many talents. After all, he has progressed into the full England team and clearly he is well respected by Sven-Goran Eriksson and, apparently, Sir Alex Ferguson. On that basis he has had a very successful season. But it is only right and proper to judge a player of his obvious class and talent against the very best.

Hopefully the emergence of Steven Gerrard will take some of the pressure off Joe. I have no doubt from what I have seen of the Liverpool midfield player that he can cope with any sort of pressure. You look at him and know there is a natural mental strength. He is prepared to put his foot in, shoot from anywhere, and is happy to pass the ball around. Steven is phenomenal and I would expect him to go on and really make the grade. All the attention he will attract will be water off a duck's back because this kid seems to take everything in his stride. All he is concerned about is being a footballer and I find that very refreshing and him very exciting. He thrills me like Ryan Giggs did when he first came on to the scene. They are both the sort of player who brings spectators to the edge of their seats. I am delighted that, in this case, he is English.

Up front I thought that Paolo di Canio, like the team, underachieved a little. He missed some important games in the second half of the season when we could have really done with him. By his own high standards, he fell a bit short in terms of goals and performances, and we missed him with his ailments at difficult places like Leeds United, Leicester City, Manchester United, Liverpool, Arsenal and twice away to Walsall in the two cup competitions. We simply did not have the depth of staff to cover for such an influential player's absence.

Davor Suker should have been the answer but he was a big disappointment and failed to put any pressure on Paolo and Freddie, who improved tremendously during the course of the season. He can be sensational, looking a world-beater at the start of the season but then, like the rest of the team, he faded somewhat. He has looked at his best when he has been left on his own up front with five behind him in midfield. He leads the line brilliantly in those circumstances, though I wouldn't say he was a natural finisher but he has great skill and has been a bargain buy at £4 million.

At West Ham we knew as soon as we saw the fixtures that we had a tough start on our hands, but we had hoped for more from our opening half dozen matches. While on my FA coaching course a wing commander told us that a club's season is dictated by how well or badly you do in the first *four* games of the season. In respect of West Ham he was spot on, and for a good few other clubs, too.

We opened up with a 4–2 defeat at Chelsea, lost at home to Leicester, drew at home with Manchester United and drew at Sunderland. We followed that with a defeat at Tottenham and a draw at home to Liverpool and were bottom with just three points. We didn't have our first win until we went to Coventry in September and worked hard to get into that top seven but couldn't hold on to it. Over the whole season we underachieved.

We saved our best performances for the Cup for some reason. In the draws we had there was nothing to lose and it enabled us to play without too much restriction. If we had gone on to the FA Cup final we would certainly have deserved to win it. We started off going to Walsall, who were top of the division, having lost only once in the entire season; we then went away to the favourites Manchester United; there are few places tougher than Sunderland where we went in the next round; and then we drew Spurs at home, a big London derby. Had we won that we would have had to beat Arsenal and then Liverpool to win the competition. That is a tall order for any team in the country. You could not pick a tougher run and something had to give. It was one big team too many, especially when suddenly everyone thought it was our year.

The best I can say about the quarter-final is that it was a typical blood-and-guts derby that Spurs deserved to win. I am afraid one or two thought the hard work had been done at Manchester and Sunderland, and once you take your foot off the gas in English football you are always made to pay for it.

As for my own season, I went into pre-season after the two broken legs prepared to start playing first team football a month into the season. The leg felt much better the second time around, there was not the pain or the soreness after playing and, if anything, it seemed even stronger. But I was still aware that it was only five months again, the gap between the two breaks. The manager Harry Redknapp was brilliant when I reported back for pre-season, telling me to take my time, play when I wanted to but then threw in 'as long as you are ready for the opening game against Chelsea'. That had never even been a consideration for me, as that was a touch short as far as my recovery plans were concerned. I played one and a half games in pre-season, had myself fitted up with a pair of indestructible shin pads and ended up playing at Chelsea.

It was nowhere near as bad as my return after the first break, aided as I was by the pair of shin pads that I put on the very moment I start playing any sort of football involving physical contact. Those shin pads have become as familiar to me as my seat belt in the car. Without it I would feel vulnerable and I am like that with shin pads, so if things turn nasty at home with my wife or daughter, it is on with the shin pads straight away! I was just delighted that, come the first game, I got through without a problem. I finished the 2000–01 season playing as many games as I can remember for a long time. I was physically available for every match of the season, missing fixtures only due to suspension.

Perhaps the only one where I wasn't fit enough to play, but did, was against Spurs in the Cup. In the week leading up to that tie we played Arsenal away and Chelsea at home on the Wednesday before the Sunday fixture. After 15 minutes of the Chelsea game, I went over on my ankle and immediately it ballooned. As soon as I did it I told the physio as he came on: 'By the way, if you are wondering, that big lump is not supposed to be there.' Having tried to play on with a broken leg, I was a bit wiser this time and so was he. He took me straight off with the Cup tie firmly in both of our minds.

I believe that Harry would have been quite prepared to have rested me for the Chelsea game to keep me fresh for the Sunday, but having been brought up under Brian Clough my attitude was to play whenever I was fit. I even told Harry I did not want to be rested as I felt I needed to play as much as possible. I didn't feel as confident when I limped past him on that Wednesday.

I was given no chance of playing right up until the Saturday afternoon when I strapped it up as tight as I could to give it a try. I ran, twisted and turned and thought it was just about acceptable. I told a surprised Harry that I was available for selection. It was one of those gambles. Sol Campbell tried it for Spurs in the next round against Arsenal and he came unstuck, but I survived with hardly a problem. Sometimes you get away with it and sometimes you don't. My gamble succeeded but we still lost as Spurs came, scrapped and deserved their 3–2 victory.

Odd how it turns out. We lost a game we were expected to win, while Spurs went on to sack their manager George Graham despite his having taken them to a semi-final. It is incredible how this game of ours works out.

The puffiness stayed around my ankle for a couple of weeks but I was able to play on. From a personal aspect I wasn't totally satisfied with my performances, but then I have always been self-critical throughout my entire career and there was only the one season – in 1991 – when I was anything like comfortable with my level of consistency and my overall form.

The older I get the more critical I become, because I know that now when I have a bad game it will be put down to my age rather than just a temporary loss of form. It hurts me more to play badly now than it did ten years ago. There were too many games I could have played better and I am acutely aware of my bad games.

I suppose I should be grateful that I have managed to play so many games this last season and that a couple of

West Ham's supporters' clubs thought I played well enough to nominate me as their Footballer of the Year. I was also named Carling Footballer of the Month in February, which is very satisfying when you look around at the quality of the Premier League and its world-class players. Not bad for a veteran!

There have been eight or ten games where I have not been satisfied with the way I have played and, in the main, it has been against the top clubs like Arsenal, Manchester United and Liverpool, who have more of a cutting edge about them, teams who think quicker and move quicker. Those are the games where I have been found wanting, especially against Liverpool at Anfield when I wasn't at the races. I can't just walk away from a game like that, shrug my shoulders and ask where the next game is. I am afraid I take away a bit of luggage, as I did at Arsenal and Manchester United in the League where I was poor in both matches. It is no consolation that others did not play well in less than ordinary team performances. For me they were the worst of the worst.

It tells me straight away that my level of fitness and level of performance is not good enough to rank me alongside the very best of the Premiership these days. I can hold my own with the bottom and mid-range teams and, on a good day, with the top eight, but it is against the cream when they have a good day and are playing to the best of their ability that I am found wanting. They have to have an average game and I have to be at my best in those circumstances to hold my own. That is a fact. It doesn't mean that next time I pull on a shirt at Old Trafford I am automatically going to have a bad game, but I know that I am going to be at full stretch against players who are clever and quick.

If you were to ask which I saw as my best games of the season, they were against Newcastle at home playing against Alan Shearer, when we won 1–0 at Leeds United playing alongside Rio in his last game, and against Charlton Athletic on Boxing Day when we won 5–0. Regardless of the results they were games when I know I played well as I did against Sunderland away in the Cup and Coventry away in the League.

The low spot of the season was being sent off against Everton at Upton Park on the last day of March. It wasn't so much giving away a penalty and being red-carded which got up my nose as being amateurish. I am not one of those to come off the pitch blaming the referee for sending me off or an opposing player for diving. The only person to blame here was me. I had been booked three seconds earlier and, while there are some who would say that a second yellow would have sufficed instead of a straight red, it was a bad tackle – a penalty that cost West Ham the game in a match between two bad teams when the first goal was going to be critical.

I remember the incident well. The young right-winger from Everton hooked the ball over Nigel Winterburn's head into the penalty area. As soon as he did it I set off thinking that I could win a ball that was bouncing up to chest height. He nicked the ball before me and I caught him. There was no doubt that it was a penalty. The referee Andy D'Urso gave me an instant red card for violent and dangerous play. In my defence all that I can say is that his leg was as high as mine, but at the end of the day it was simply bad play on my part. I should have stayed on my feet and read it better than I did.

When I saw it later on television I cringed. There was no doubt it was worthy of a red. I believe that with the amount of stick referees get these days, it is beholden on the players to own up to their own mistakes. On this occasion it was a good decision, a right decision and the referee was spot on. I had to go away and learn from it and be disappointed for what I did.

Managers must also take a share of the responsibility. Whenever there is a controversial moment there is always one manager who has seen it and the other who hasn't. Come on! Let's be honest about it. They always see what happens and should hold up their hands. It can only help the game.

Brian Clough always used to say that we had no trouble with referees. Of course it was kidology but it worked – we didn't badger them, we were polite and we didn't have that much trouble. If I was a referee and I kept hearing managers and players barking at me on radio and television about my decisions, I would hold a grudge against them and relish an opportunity to gain my revenge. From my aspect I cannot see the point of arguing with a referee. They have a tough enough job as it is. I have been into the referees' room and congratulated officials who have been booed off the park for the decisions they have made. I am also honest enough to say well done to a referee when he makes a right decision and I also tell them when they've got it wrong, as a matter of fact.

Referees will always find out when they go home and watch the game on television and in this respect they are more professional than many footballers. While the official will dissect his own game and look where he went wrong, how many players will go and do the same and make such critical judgements on their own performance? Not many, I bet!

I try to be honest with them and, in return, referees have cut me a bit of slack this season. I might have been sent off at Ipswich. I was booked in the first half and Harry Redknapp had told me at half-time to keep out of trouble. Then in the second half I went in thinking I could win a ball, the lad nicked it past me and I took him down. The referee hesitated for an instant and waved play on. The crowd went mad. Had he stopped the game and given the foul he would almost certainly have had to send me off. I was sure I was off and at the end of the game I thanked him because I felt I should have gone off. I am an honest player and, more often than not, I am trying to win the ball and I have been around long enough for referees to know that.

Don't get me wrong, I make sure that I am being physically felt around the field but I believe that I have a good working relationship with referees and their assistants. That was never more evident than in a recent away game when I clashed with a foreign player of whom I am not particularly fond. The linesman had flagged for an offside and rarely do referees take a name or any action for something that happens after they have stopped play, unless you kick the ball away.

I gave this player a little kick and, as he walked back past me, he put his shoulder into me right in front of the linesman who instantly raised his flag and brought over the referee. I thought that we were both going to be cautioned but the referee listened to what his assistant had to say and then showed him the yellow card. Clearly the assistant hadn't seen what I'd done, but my opponent was spitting blood and I could hardly blame him.

At half-time I went to the toilet and who should be next to me but the linesman who turned and smiled and said: 'You must have shit yourself when he pushed you.' I laughed and said: 'Yes. I've just had to change my shorts.'

When the game resumed the linesman was on the same side of the pitch as me again and, right in front of his nose, I made another heavy challenge on the hapless home player who went down in a heap. I looked over at the linesman and he gave me a big wink. I responded with a little thumbs up.

Paolo di Canio has an altogether different sort of relationship with officials after his infamous push, but he managed to surprise them, and everyone else, with his act of sportsmanship when we played Everton at Goodison Park in December. We were scrapping for our football lives, trying desperately to break into the top six, when their goalkeeper went down clearly badly injured. The ball was crossed into the box and Paolo caught it instead of trying to create a shooting opportunity. Personally, I would not have done it myself.

I think that Paolo would have done well to score from the position he was in. His back was to goal, he had two defenders behind him and the ball was chest high. Mind you, if anyone on the pitch could have scored from there it was him with his skill but as I walked off the pitch I was ambivalent about the incident, thinking neither that he should have gone on and scored, nor that it was a great act of selfless sportsmanship. He made that decision, and fair play to him, but would Everton have done the same? I am sure that would have been in the back of Harry Redknapp's mind and most of the others in the dressing-room. If I honestly thought that Everton would have reciprocated then I would have caught it myself.

I am of the opinion that I would prefer for both teams to agree beforehand not to kick the ball out of play because it can cause more problems than it can solve. At least we would all start with a level playing field with the referee able to stop the game when he felt it was right to do so. What we have on face value is brilliant. A player goes down, possibly badly injured, so the ball is kicked out of play immediately and help brought on. As a professional footballer I wouldn't like to be lying on the ground swallowing my tongue as play went on around me. But as manager I would tell my players if they are going to kick the ball out in the first minute, kick it out in the last minute as well. We all know that teams do not do that if they are chasing the game. To me, that is not on. If you are going to do it then do it all of the time or alternatively tell the opposition that you are not going to do it at all and they can do the same.

There can be too many grey areas, such as the Arsenal–Sheffield United Cup tie where someone scored after the ball had been knocked out and asked questions afterwards. If they were going to admit there was an injustice they should have let the opposition walk the ball into the net from the kick-off, saving all the problems that arose after the game.

When I watch Italian football I see them kissing and cuddling before the game, yet 15 minutes later they are kicking lumps out of each other. It begs the question as to why they bothered with the kisses and cuddles in the first place. Cut the crap and let's be honest with each other from start to finish.

For the coming season, 2001–02, if West Ham are to move forward new manager Glenn Roeder will have to bring in some new additions at Upton Park. They will miss Harry Redknapp, who could always wheel and deal and change things around. I grew very fond of the man in my two seasons at the Hammers. Apart from our love of the beautiful game, we both have an interest in horses, albeit that while I am interested in the horses themselves he loves the betting side of it.

I once wandered into training while we were going through a bad patch and one of the ground staff warned me that Harry had the hump big time. I remarked that it was hardly surprising given the recent run of results, but was told that was because he telephoned his trainer who had told him that his horse running at Brighton that day had no chance. It came in at 25–1. I kept out of Harry's way until the next day and then asked him all innocently if his horse had run.

He exploded: 'Run! Did it run? That fucking trainer. I can't believe what he did to me. I asked him if we had a chance and he said we had no chance at all. He won by ten lengths, ten fucking lengths and 25–1. I've had my uncle and all sorts of people ringing me up and there he was telling me not to touch it. Now they think I took the odds and didn't tell anyone on purpose.'

He was as livid as I have ever seen him at a game when we were losing. He is a regular punter and even writes a betting column on the Internet and is a tipster for the *Racing Post*. It became a standing joke at one stage when his tips were so bad that he used to receive hate mail. We would listen to him phoning his tips over from the coach on Friday. He just couldn't get one right for a spell and took terrible stick over it. He was worried he was going to be sacked!

However, I found his column a revelation for another reason – and far more informative than the back pages of the tabloids. He would be discussing who would beat whom and then suddenly he would reveal that he had been after a certain player, not only naming him but also revealing how much he had been asked to pay and how much he was willing to pay.

He is as good a fellow as you are going to get as a manager and a nice bloke with it as well. He has a great sense of humour, and you would see the real Harry in pre-season, when he was refreshed, but like all managers the humour used to wear thinner and thinner as the season progressed and the tension mounted.

But there is always a laugh not far away where Harry is concerned. At West Ham there is a young lad called Gavin Holligan who came to us from Kingstonian, and Harry wanted to send him out on loan. He called the lad in and told him what the position was and that Exeter had been on the telephone and wanted him. Holligan answered: 'To be honest with you, boss, I am not prepared to go up north!'

Harry launched himself across his desk, saying: 'North! Fucking north! Exeter is in the south-west of the country.' That comment has now gone down in West Ham folklore; Harry couldn't get out of his office fast enough to tell everyone. The poor lad will never live it down.

But John Moncur is the real comedian of the club and perfected the 'Arry with the 'Ump impression. Moncs is always up to stunts, like doing the warm-up in front of the Sky cameras in just a pair of boots and socks. At other times you might be doing stretches in the gym and look up to see him doing the same, but stripped naked.

One of my stranger talents is being able to recognise most players in my team by their feet. There is no mistaking Moncur in this respect because none of his toes appears to touch the ground; even his kids point it out to him. His little toes are completely up in the air.

If you look at the shape of him he is a bit like the Elephant Man, with a slight hunchback, and the other players are always asking him if he has the ball up his jersey. He is also a player on the stock market and when Davor Suker arrived he found a kindred spirit. Moncs immediately tapped him up for the best buy and was given the name of a cable and wireless company. He immediately invested in the shares at 99 pence each and two months later they were down to 25 pence, tumbling big time. A couple of weeks later in a practice match he had a ball drilled straight at him. It hit him in the face and he went down poleaxed, with Steve Lomas observing: 'He's gone down quicker than his shares!'

He is a typical East End scrapper and soon gets annoyed if the mickey-taking becomes too heavy. But he is invaluable around the club and in the dressing-room with his noisy sense of humour. This aspect of team bonding is dying due to the influx of foreign players who don't often share the traditional British lavatorial and sarcastic sense of humour. But it will remain strong in West Ham's dressing-room when Moncs is about. If Harry didn't play Moncs, he liked to have him on the bench because he is so good to have around the dressing-room. The supporters like him and when he comes on he livens things up, especially if West Ham have their backs to the wall.

I talked to Harry a great deal over the season and he was, as ever, massively supportive and keen for me to stay on for a final season. I had two job offers near the end of the 2000–01 campaign and both, for one reason and another, fell through and I was left with the choice of signing a new contract with West Ham or going on the dole until something came along.

Then, just when I was thinking of closing the pages on my playing career, a surprise telephone call from my old England boss Kevin Keegan changed my mind. I had always said that I would not drop out of the Premier Division and that I would not combine coaching with playing, but this was too good an opportunity to miss. If I was going to drop out of the top flight it could not have been to a bigger club than Manchester City. It is my sort of club and has my sort of supporters, passionate and knowledgeable about the game.

Kevin Keegan was also a big influence on my decision. He brought me back into the England set-up and even included me in the get-togethers when I was unable to play. He has a great passion for football, and I relish the opportunity to play under him again. My title at Maine Road is player-coach and, while playing is always going to be the priority, I have the chance to put into practice the coaching ideas I have picked up over the summer on my UEFA coaching badge course.

When I'm asked about the appointment of Sven-Goran Eriksson, Kevin's replacement as England manager, I have to say I was pleased. Now I know that will surprise a lot of the football public who see Stuart Pearce as the archetypal Englishman with the flag of St George on his sleeve, but I am no Little Englander where football is concerned and I believe that the Football Association have appointed the right man.

If someone had asked me before the appointment whom I thought it should be, I would have said Terry Venables because he had done the job before, done it well and he was available but once he had been passed by then the choice was thinner. I am not too fussed about Sven's nationality – just whether he is good at his job. His track record suggests that he is, so as far as I am concerned if he is successful he will be the best appointment. Time alone will tell. Sometimes you need an outsider to come in, as an Englishman might not always be able to see the obvious faults, and an outsider brings a fresh viewpoint on players' strengths and weaknesses.

He has the advantage of a couple of coaches from the Premier League to prime him plus his own man in Tord Grip. Add to that the crash course he has taken in watching English football and he has fitted in very quickly and very quietly. He knows English football, has a similar approach, speaks the language well and he also has the advantage of an intimate knowledge of football in other countries. The nonsense spoken about his nationality was an irrelevance and stood in the way of him doing his job. We all have to be behind him and whomever he takes on board.

I don't think it can hurt bringing in English managers like Peter Taylor and Alan Curbishley to work with him; it will help them and help the country, though Taylor decided he couldn't combine this with his job at Leicester. They will learn from working with him and if they show the aptitude one of them could eventually succeed the Swede.

It is also a good thing that he has given the youngsters their head and, if we do qualify for the World Cup in 2002, that will be a bonus. For England needs to qualify. A country our size cannot afford to miss out on any of the major tournaments. Therefore he has to pick his best team but if those also happen to be young players then so much the better.

I believe he could not have taken the job at a better time. England have a great crop of youngsters emerging at present, with players like Steven Gerrard, who could be world class, Sol Campbell, Rio Ferdinand, Wes Brown, Ashley Cole, Gary Neville, Michael Owen, David Beckham, Paul Scholes and Emile Heskey. Sometimes you have got to be lucky when you take over. Graham Taylor was very unlucky when he took over and lost a lot of seniors, but Sven has walked in at a good time and has immediately shown that he is not afraid to pick players who are good enough whatever their age. The only criterion in international football is whether you are good enough, young or old.

As long as the new manager gets the shape right then I am certain that we will qualify through the play-offs. We are good enough to win any play-off. I was surprised at the timing of Kevin Keegan's departure from the England job, but not by the departure itself. I think he had it on his mind to quit when the bad result and bad performance came. After the tournament in the summer I am sure he realised then that he could not take the team any further and that the decision to leave was imminent after the European Championships. It could have been in Paris after the friendly against France, but it turned out to be Germany that was the game too far.

I don't profess to know the man's mind but I am convinced he was ready to resign, because of all the pressure and criticism. I would not say that he let the team down. There is no doubt that his timing could have been better and he left them in the lurch, with another qualifying game only a few days away, but if his reason was that he thought that they would do better without him in Finland then it was the right reason. Kevin was and is a very patriotic man and I do not believe that he would do anything to harm the England football team.

It must have been very hard for someone like him to hold up his hands and admit that he didn't feel up to the job, especially after all that he has achieved in his lifetime. It must have been heartbreaking for him. It would have been perfect to have signed off at Wembley with a win over our old rivals from Germany but it wasn't to be and not only did we lose Kevin we also lost a stadium and struggled to find another.

I find the entire Wembley situation incredible and cannot imagine it happening anywhere else in the world. For our national game, and a very buoyant national game at that, there is no better time to build a fantastic stadium that should be the envy of the world. I don't know the ins and outs of what has gone wrong but as a footballer looking at the game and the brilliant stadiums being built around the country I feel we should have built a stadium immediately and it should be second to none.

The bonus that has come out of the chaos is England playing games around the country. It is a long, long overdue move and surely they could have taken friendlies to places like Manchester, Liverpool and Newcastle before now? I always felt that the big competitive games should be kept at Wembley but the others should be spread around. We are now playing our glamour games out of the country albeit only across the border in Wales.

My coaching has gone really well and I have particularly enjoyed working with the England Under-18s. That is an area of work that interests me as much as club management.

After doing two more weeks towards my UEFA 'A' badge last summer, I went away with the England youngsters to a three-team tournament in Italy and it was while I was with them that the news was broken of Kevin Keegan's dramatic departure.

We had just won our second game on the Saturday. I then went back to the hotel to watch England against Germany on television, and it was after the 1–0 defeat that my wife Liz telephoned asking me to call Howard Wilkinson urgently. By then I had heard that Kevin had stepped down and when I called late that night Howard asked me if I would join Brian Kidd in helping him to prepare the team to play the next World Cup match in Helsinki that following Wednesday.

I must say that when Liz first called me I had half hoped that I was being called up to play in the team, not to help coach it. When I told Wilko he just burst out laughing. That was the player in me coming out, thinking that I could do a job for England. But it was a fantastic experience. Howard involved me in everything and I enjoyed it immensely, especially under the circumstances, with the game being so important and having to try and help lift the players after the awful result at Wembley.

I was probably an ideal buffer between the coaches and the players at the time and hope to play a similar role at Manchester City. I could sit with the players and listen to their problems, the sort of thing that they wouldn't say to the manager's or coach's face. I could then filter through to Howard what he needed to know. I knew what they were going through and could relate to them because I was still playing myself and had been around the England camp a lot under Kevin Keegan even when I was injured.

It was a great experience and when I hand in my log book for my coaching hours the first entry will look very good – coaching the England World Cup team in Finland. It will look somewhat incongruous next to Brent Under-13s, West Ham Academy boys and Newbury AFC Under-15s.

That, however, has always been my life – full of contrasts. From electrician to footballer; from punk rock to Shakespeare; from Brent Under-13s to England Senior. I am happy with that.

stuart pearce

- Born Shepherd's Bush, London, 24 April 1962.
- Transferred from Wealdstone to Coventry City October 1983 for £25,000.
- Transferred to Nottingham Forest May 1985 for £240,000.
- League Cup winner's medal 1989, 1990.
- Simod Cup winner's medal 1989.
- Zenith Data Systems Cup winner's medal 1992.
- Appointed caretaker-manager Nottingham Forest December 1996, resigned May 1997. Was first player-manager to play for England.
- Free transfer to Newcastle United July 1997.
- Awarded MBE December 1998.
- Free transfer to West Ham United August 1999.
- Free transfer to Manchester City June 2001.
- Announces retirement as a player, having played his best game for Manchester City three days short of his 40th birthday. With virtually his best kick, he missed a penalty against 43-year-old Dave Beasant. City are promoted to the Premiership as Champions.

SUMMARY OF APPEARANCES AND GOALS

Season	Team	Lg	G	FA	G	LC	G	EC	G	CW	G	UE	G	OC	G	U-	G	In	G
1983–84	Coventry C	23	-	-	-	-	-	-	-	-	-	-	-	-	-	-	-	-	-
1984–85		28	4	2	-	-	-	-	-	-	-	-	-	-	-	-	-	-	-
1985–86	Nottingham F	30	1	-	-	4	-	-	-	-	-	-	-	-	-	-	-	-	-
1986–87		39	6	-	-	5	2	-	-	-	-	-	-	-	-	1	-	2	-
1987–88		34	5	5	1	3	-	-	-	-	-	-	-	1	-	-	-	3	-
1988–89		36	6	5	-	8	1	-	-	-	-	-	-	5	3	-	-	10	-
1989–90		34	5	1	-	10	2	-	-	-	-	-	-	2	2	-	-	15	1
1990–91		33	11	10	4	4	1	-	-	-	-	-	-	2	-	-	-	11	1
1991–92		30	5	4	2	9	1	-	-	-	-	-	-	5	1	-	-	9	-
1992–93		23	2	3	-	5	-	-	-	-	-	-	-	-	-	-	-	3	1
1993–94		42	6	2	-	6	-	-	-	-	-	-	-	1	-	-	-	3	1
1994–95		36	8	1	-	3	2	-	-	-	-	-	-	-	-	-	-	3	-
1995–96		31	3	4	2	1	1	-	-	-	-	8	-	-	-	-	-	11	1
1996–97		33	5	2	-	2	-	-	-	-	-	-	-	-	-	-	-	6	-
1997–98	Newcastle U	25	-	7	-	-	-	4	-	-	-	-	-	-	-	-	-	-	-
1998–99		12	-	-	-	2	-	-	-	2	-	-	-	-	-	-	-	-	-
1999–2000	West Ham U	8	-	-	-	-	-	-	-	-	-	-	-	-	-	-	-	2	-
2000–2001		34	2	4	1	4	-	-	-	-	-	-	-	-	-	-	-	-	-
2001–2002	Manchester C	38	3	2	-	3	-	-	-	-	-	-	-	-	-	-	-	-	-
	Totals	569	72	52	10	69	10	4	-	2	-	8	-	16	6	1	-	78	5

Headings: League; FA Cup; League Cup; European Cup; Cup Winners' Cup; UEFA Cup

Other cups: 1 Simod Cup 1987–88; 4 Simod Cup (3 goals) 1988–89; 1 Mercantile Credit Trophy 1988–89; 2 Zenith Data Systems Cup (2 goals) 1989–90; 2 Zenith Data Systems Cup 1990–91; 5 Zenith Data Systems Cup (1 goal) 1991–92; 1 Anglo-Italian Cup 1993–94.

Under-21 appearance: v Yugoslavia

G = Goals

Note: All appearances include those as substitute, of which there are only two at club level – v Barcelona, European Cup, 26 November 1997 and v Swindon Town, FA Cup, 5 January 2002.

FULL INTERNATIONALS

Became the 999th player to be selected for the full England team in 1987 and took over the England captaincy from Gary Lineker in 1992.

1986–87	Brazil, Scotland
1987–88	West Germany (sub), Israel, Hungary
1988–89	Denmark, Sweden, Saudi Arabia, Greece, Albania, Albania, Chile, Scotland, Poland, Denmark
1989–90	Sweden, Poland, Italy, Yugoslavia, Brazil, Czechoslovakia (1), Denmark, Uruguay, Tunisia, Republic of Ireland, Holland, Egypt, Belgium, Cameroon, West Germany
1990–91	Hungary, Poland, Republic of Ireland, Republic of Ireland, Cameroon, Turkey, Argentina, Australia, New Zealand (1), **New Zealand**, Malaysia
1991–92	Turkey, Poland, **France**, **Czechoslovakia**, Brazil (sub), Finland, Denmark, France, Sweden
1992–93	**Spain**, **Norway**, **Turkey** (1)
1993–94	**Poland** (1), **San Marino**, Greece (sub)
1994–95	Romania (sub), Japan, Brazil
1995–96	Norway, Switzerland (1), Portugal, **Bulgaria**, Croatia, Hungary, Switzerland, Scotland, Holland, Spain, Germany
1996–97	Moldova, Poland, Italy, Mexico, **South Africa**, Italy
1999–2000	Luxembourg, Poland

Note: **Bold** type indicates games as captain.

index

If you enjoyed this book here is a selection of other bestselling sports titles from Headline

THE AUTOBIOGRAPHY	Gareth Edwards	£7.99	☐
THE AUTOBIOGRAPHY	John Barnes	£6.99	☐
ROPE BURNS	Ian Probert	£7.99	☐
FROM OUTBACK TO OUTFIELD	Justin Langer	£6.99	☐
BARMY ARMY	Dougie Brimson	£6.99	☐
VINNIE	Vinnie Jones	£6.99	☐
FORMULA ONE UNCOVERED	Derick Allsop	£7.99	☐
MANCHESTER UNITED RUINED MY LIFE	Colin Shindler	£5.99	☐
TEAR GAS AND TICKET TOUTS	Eddy Brimson	£6.99	☐
DARK TRADE	Donald McRae	£7.99	☐
A LOT OF HARD YAKKA	Simon Hughes	£6.99	☐
LEFT FOOT FORWARD	Garry Nelson	£6.99	☐

Headline books are available at your local bookshop or newsagent. Alternatively, books can be ordered direct from the publisher. Just tick the titles you want and fill in the form below. Prices and availability subject to change without notice.

Buy four books from the selection above and get free postage and packaging and delivery within 48 hours. Just send a cheque or postal order made payable to Bookpoint Ltd to the value of the total cover price of the four books. Alternatively, if you wish to buy fewer than four books the following postage and packaging applies:

UK and BFPO £4.30 for one book; £6.30 for two books; £8.30 for three books.

Overseas and Eire: £4.80 for one book; £7.10 for 2 or 3 books (surface mail).

Please enclose a cheque or postal order made payable to *Bookpoint Limited*, and send to: Headline Publishing Ltd, 39 Milton Park, Abingdon, OXON OX14 4TD, UK.
Email Address: orders@bookpoint.co.uk

If you would prefer to pay by credit card, our call team would be delighted to take your order by telephone. Our direct line is 01235 400 414 (lines open 9.00 am–6.00 pm Monday to Saturday 24 hour message answering service). Alternatively you can send a fax on 01235 400 454.

Name ....

Address ....

....

....

If you would prefer to pay by credit card, please complete:
Please debit my Visa/Access/Diner's Card/American Express (delete as applicable) card number:

Signature .... Expiry Date...............